43599021

WORKING FOR THE ENEMY

WORKING FOR THE ENEMY

Ford, General Motors, and Forced Labor
in Germany during the Second World War

By

Reinhold Billstein, Karola Fings,
Anita Kugler and Nicholas Levis

Berghahn Books
NEW YORK • OXFORD

Published in 2000 by

Berghahn Books

www.berghahnbooks.com

© 2000 Nicholas Levis
www.history20.com

Library of Congress Cataloging-in-Publication Data

Working for the enemy : Ford, General Motors, and forced labor in Germany
during the Second World War / Reinhold Billstein ... [et al.] ; with the
assistance of NS-Dokumentationszentrum der Stadt Köln ; edited by
Nicholas Levis.
    p.   cm.
    ISBN 1-57181-224-5 (alk. paper)
    1. Forced labor–Germany–History–20th century. 2. World War,
1939–1945–Conscript labor–Germany. 3. World War, 1939–1945–
Prisoners and prisons, German. 4. Ford Motor Company–History.
5. General Motors Coprporation–History. 6. Automobile industry and
trade–Military aspects–Germany–History–20th century.
I. Billstein, Reinhold, 1949– . II. Levis, Nicholas .
III. NS-Dokumentationszentrum (Historisches Archiv der Stadt Köln)
HD4875.G4 W67 2000
331.1'732–dc21   00-026126

British Library Cataloguing in Publication Data

A catalogue record for this book is available from the British Library.

Printed in the United States on acid-free paper.

For those who tell their stories here,
and for those who no longer can.

CONTENTS

LIST OF ILLUSTRATIONS

LIST OF ABBREVIATIONS

ACC	American Chamber of Commerce, Berlin
AG	*Aktiengesellschaft*, stock corporation under German law
AP	Associated Press, New York, wire service
BA	Bundesarchiv (FRG Archives), Koblenz/Berlin
BA-MA	Bundesarchiv-Militärarchiv (FRG Military Archives), Freiburg im Breisgau
BBC	British Broadcasting Corporation, London
BEG	Bundesentschädigungsgesetz, FRG compensations law for victims of Nazi-era crimes
BGH	Bundesgerichtshof (Supreme Court of the FRG), Karlsruhe
BMW	Bayerische Motorenwerke AG, Munich, carmaker
CDU	Christlich-Demokratische Union (Christian Democratic Union), est. 1947
CIC	U.S. military Counter Intelligence Corps
DAF	Deutsche Arbeitsfront (German Labor Front of the NSDAP)
DICEA	Division of Investigation of Cartels and External Assets (1946), OMGUS
DM	Deutschemark, West German currency after 1948
DMV	Deutsche Metallarbeiterverband (German Metal Workers Association), pre-1933 trade union
DNVP	German National Peoples' Party
DP	Displaced Person, official term for foreign nationals in Germany at the end of the war
E1H2	U.S. Army Civil Affairs unit assigned as first Military Government of Cologne from March to June 1945; as a source, its "Daily Reports"
FAZ	*Frankfurter Allgemeine Zeitung*
FRG	Federal Republic of Germany, until 1990 a.k.a. West Germany (Ger.: BRD), est. 1948
GBA	Generalbevollmächtigter für den Arbeitseinsatz, the Nazi plenipotentiary overseeing deployment of civilian foreign forced laborers to the Reich starting Mar. 1942 (Fritz Sauckel)
GDR	German Democratic Republic, a.k.a. East Germany (Ger.: DDR), est. 1949
Gestapo	Geheime Staatspolizei, Nazi secret state police, est. 1933

GmbH	*Gesellschaft mit beschränkter Haftung,* limited company
GUG	Gesellschaft für Unternehmensgeschichte, a present-day research institute in Frankfurt
HAStK	Historisches Archiv der Stadt Köln (Cologne Historical Archives)
HStAD	Hauptstaatsarchiv, Dusseldorf, main state archive of North Rhine-Westphalia
IfZ	Institut für Zeitgeschichte, Munich
IHK	*Industrie- und Handelskammer,* regionally organized chambers of industry and commerce
IMI	Italian Military Internee, i.e., Italian POWs captured by German forces after Aug. 1943
IMT	International Military Tribunal for the prosecution of war crimes, Nuremberg, 1945–1949
JCC	Jewish Claims Conference, est. 1952
JFM	Junckers Flugzeug- und Motorenwerke AG, aircraft manufacturer
KdF	*Kraft durch Freude* (Strength through Joy)
KHD	Klöckner-Humboldt-Deutz AG, Cologne
KJV	Kommunistische Jugendverband (Communist Youth Association of the KPD), pre-1933
KK	*Kölnischer Kurier,* German-language publication of the Cologne MG during the Allied occupation
KPD	Kommunistische Partei Deutschlands (Communist Party of Germany), pre-1933
Kripo	*Kriminalpolizei,* local police detective divisions
KZ	*Konzentrationslager,* concentration camp
MG	Military Government of Allied-occupied Germany or one of its regions
NA/NARA	National Archives and Record Administration, Washington, DC
NKVD	Soviet secret police, predecessor to KGB
NS	National Socialist; Nazi
NSBO	Nationalsozialistische Betriebsorganisation, pre-1933 Nazi shopfloor organization
NSDAP	Nationalsozialistische Deutsche Arbeiterpartei (National Socialist German Workers' Party); Nazi Party
NS-Dok	NS-Dokumentationszentrum der Stadt Köln, Nazi-Era Documents Center of the City of Cologne
NSV	National Socialist People's Welfare
NYT	*New York Times*
OKH	Oberkommando des Heeres (German Army High Command)
OKW	Oberkommando der Wehrmacht (German Armed Forces High Command), est. 1938
OMGUS	Office of Military Government for Germany–United States
pfg	*pfennig* (pennies)
Pg	*Parteigenosse,* "Party Comrade" in the Nazi Party

PWD	U.S. military Psychological Warfare Division
RAF	British Royal Air Force
RAM	Reichsarbeitsministerium (Reich Labor Ministry), Berlin
RDA	Reichsverband der Deutschen Automobilindustrie (Reich Association of the German Automobile Industry), pre-1945
RGO	Revolutionäre Gewerkschafts-Organisation (Revolutionary Union Organization), pre-1933
RM	Reichsmark, German currency until 1948
RMfBuM/	Reich Ministry for Armaments and Munitions (later R.M. for
RMfBuK	Armaments and War Economy), Berlin, after 1942 a.k.a. the "Speer Ministry"
RSHA	Reichssicherheitshauptamt (Main Central Security Agency), est. September 1939, SS-controlled central administration for S.D., Kripo, and Gestapo under Reinhard Heydrich
RüInsp	*Rüstungsinspektionen*, military armaments inspectorates, network of regional mobilization oversight offices
RüKo	*Rüstungskommando*, military armaments commandos, network of regional mobilization management boards
RWM	Reichswirtschaftsministerium (Reich Economics Ministry), Berlin
S.A.	Sturmabteilung, stormtrooper corps of the NSDAP
S.D.	Sicherheitsdienst, internal security service of the SS
SHAEF	Supreme Headquarters–Allied Expeditionary Force, 1941 to 1945, under General Eisenhower
SPD	Sozialdemokratische Partei Deutschlands (Social Democratic Party of Germany)
SS	Schutzstaffel (Protective Echelon), elite military corps of the NSDAP
SS-WVHA	SS-Wirtschafts-Verwaltungshauptamt (Economic and Administrative Agency of the SS), managed SS properties and KZ system
Stalag	*Stammlager*, prisoner-of-war camps administered by the Wehrmacht
Stapo	State Police
StAR	Stadtarchiv Rüsselsheim (Town Archives of Russelsheim)
T&I	U.S. Army Trade & Industry Division
ThHStAW	Thüringisches Hauptstaatsarchiv (Thuringian State Archives), Weimar
USAF	U.S. Air Force
USGCC	United States Group, Control Council, in 1945 provisional authority for U.S.-occupied parts of Germany, reorganized soon after the war as OMGUS
USSBS	United States Strategic Bombing Survey
VW	Volkswagen (car of the people)
WGSVG	FRG Social Insurance Compensations Law
ZStLJ	Zentrale Stelle der Landesjustizverwaltungen, the German state justice departments' coordinating bureau for Nazi crimes, Ludwigsburg

INTRODUCTION

Anyone in Europe or North America who has ever held a steering wheel or a television remote control can name two U.S. carmakers, market leaders on both continents, and their German subsidiaries. General Motors, the largest corporation on earth, is the owner since 1929 of Adam Opel AG, Russelsheim, the maker of Opel cars. Ford Motor Company, founded by Henry Ford in 1903, is currently the world's third largest corporation by revenues. In 1931 Ford Motor built the Ford Werke factory in Cologne, today the headquarters of European Ford.[1]

This book tells the story of what happened at Opel and Ford Werke under the Third Reich, and of the aftermath today.

In the years following the Nazi seizure of power in Germany in January 1933, the two American-owned companies lobbied for military contracts, increased plant investment, and together produced most of the trucks ordered by the German armed forces until the outbreak of war in September 1939. These vehicles provided an indispensable contribution to the German army's unprecedented motorized Blitzkrieg, which nearly conquered the European continent between September 1939 and December 1941. In the first months of the Second World War, Opel also started making warplane parts and engines. German Opel and Ford Werke executives were integrated into the highest levels of the Reich's wartime economic planning. The two companies played leading roles in repairing and maintaining the far-flung vehicle fleets of the Deutsche Wehrmacht.

After 1933 Ford Werke's and Opel's German factory personnel were organized in the same repressive social system imposed by law at German workplaces in general. To cover the wartime labor shortage, starting in the late summer and fall of 1940 hundreds of prisoners of war were held at private labor camps built by Ford Werke and Opel. During the next five years, both companies made use of several thousand foreign civilian detainees and prisoners of war as forced laborers in and around their plants.

An estimated ten million non-German forced laborers were used in the Nazi homefront economy during the six years of the war. More than seven million foreign displaced persons, the vast majority of whom were used as forced laborers, were liberated in Germany by the arrival of Allied troops in late 1944 and early 1945. Very few of the former forced laborers have ever received compensation in any form for their labor or their suffering.

For decades after the war the problem of compensations for Nazi-era forced labor was ignored, kept suspended in German courts and by international treaties, and suppressed from memory. In 1998, many forced laborers went to court in the United States, filing lawsuits against dozens of German companies and Ford and General Motors. In the Ford and GM cases, the plaintiffs argued that the American parent companies were responsible for the actions of their subsidiaries during the war. Since then, the histories of the automotive giants have played a keystone role within the far larger international debates and conflicts over restitution for Nazi-era forced labor. Summing up the questions posed by the media since 1998, a respected German daily asked if Ford Motor and General Motors had served Hitler as "Willing Mechanics?"[2]

Both companies have protested that they had no influence over wartime events in Germany and that the Nazis commandeered their subsidiaries. The first court ruling on Ford, delivered in September 1999, found only that the case was out of the court's jurisdiction. But what are the findings of historical research? What role did Ford and General Motors really play?

As an American writer who has lived in Germany for ten years, I invited three independent, German-speaking researchers—Reinhold Billstein, Karola Fings, and Anita Kugler—to explore that question for English-speaking readers.

The three historians are all specialists in the subjects they cover. Their studies reflect many years of research. Kugler has published a half-dozen previous essays on Opel, while in their work Billstein and Fings have both focused on Ford Werke, forced labor, and Cologne during the war. For this book, each engaged in further months of research and worked with me in writing and translating their new and at times astonishing findings.

For readers who lack specialized knowledge of Nazi Germany, my Prologue introduces enough of the pre-war history, including various matters not directly related to Ford or General Motors, to provide adequate context for the rest of the book. Readers familiar with the literature on Germany in the years 1933 to 1939 can begin at Chapter 1.

In Chapter 1, Anita Kugler explores the paradox of Opel and General Motors in the war years 1939 to 1945, within the larger context of the rise and fall of the Reich War Economy and its forced labor programs. To loyal Nazis, Opel was "enemy property" under an alleged "Jewish influence," a threat requiring containment. To the Reich's military production planners, it was a "Model War Operation," the designation Hitler bestowed officially in 1943. Among its German executives and their state and party contacts, Opel was a labyrinth of petty power struggles. To its German workers, whether they liked it or not, and to its foreign forced laborers, it was a "company community" under the "Führer principle," a miniature regime of terror and force. To General Motors, it was an investment in need of protection. Perhaps the most surprising revelations in Chapter 1 concern the actions of the American GM managers in Germany during the early months of the war, and up to the spring of 1941, when the last of them cleared out of Russelsheim. This was well in advance of the German declaration of war on the United States, on 11 December 1941, but there is strong evidence of subsequent contact between General Motors in the U.S. and Opel in Russelsheim.

In Chapter 2, Reinhold Billstein uses recently revealed U.S. government documents and other sources to reconstruct in detail Ford Motor Company's dealings with Nazi Germany, and Ford Werke's web of operations across Nazi-occupied Europe during the war. That story is viewed through the lens of the American capture of Cologne in March 1945. Billstein evokes the U.S. 1st Army's march to the Rhine and the hundred days of American rule in Cologne, before the city was passed to British control. He describes the Allied efforts to rescue and return millions of liberated forced laborers to their home countries.

During this period, a group of U.S. investigators confiscated hundreds of Ford Werke documents and compelled Ford's German executives to write statements on their wartime activities. These served as exhibits in a secret September 1945 U.S. government "Report on Ford Werke Aktiengesellschaft." The men who evaluated that report were split in the larger, fateful debate over the future of Germany itself, and over the postwar international economic order. Passions ran high. There was universal revulsion at the revelation of Nazi crimes. But in 1945 the American policy makers were also distressed by the immediate problem, with winter coming, of how to handle the ruined German society. Some of the key economic decision makers in the U.S. military government at that time were General Motors executives who had, until 1941, served as directors at Opel. In the end, many conflicting interests were at work in the decision not to publicize or act upon the U.S. government's critical findings on Ford Motor Company and Ford Werke.

Taken together, the first two chapters present the wartime histories of Opel and Ford Werke in the tradition of classical historical scholarship. Although the events on the ground are described in detail, they are viewed largely through the perspectives and choices of leading political and economic decision makers.

We then turn to the same story viewed from the perspective of the forced laborers and other individuals trapped within the Nazi machinery of terror. The second part of this book is an in-depth scholarly and oral history of forced labor at Ford Werke in Cologne. As a transition, Chapter 3 presents a tribute, by the writer and Russelsheim town historian Bernd Heyl, to Walter Rietig, an Opel worker who was executed as a resistance organizer by the Nazis in 1942. Rietig kept up contacts between the German resistance and the French prisoners of war at Opel in Russelsheim.

In Chapter 4, Karola Fings uses interviews and documents to piece together a vivid portrait of life at Ford Werke's wartime labor camps for foreign civilian forced laborers, prisoners of war, and concentration camp prisoners. She examines the company's decisions with regard to forced labor, and the consequences faced (or avoided) after the war by some of the executives responsible for those decisions.

Finally, in Chapter 5, ten people who worked as forced laborers or apprentices at Ford Werke in the years 1942 to 1945 relate, in their own words, their memories of the war and its aftermath. Their stories are a monument to perseverance under conditions that present-day readers of this book may find hard to imagine. (The methodology underlying the interviews and their presentation here is detailed in "Oral Sources on Forced Labor in Cologne," below.)

One of the interviews was held in Cologne in 1995 with Elsa Iwanowa, formerly a Soviet citizen. Today she lives in Belgium. She was the first plaintiff in the March 1998 lawsuit *Iwanowa vs. Ford*, still in appeal as of early June 2000.[3] Filed with the U.S. federal court in Newark, New Jersey, this was the first U.S. class action by a former Nazi-era forced laborer against a company accused of profiting from the practice. As a result, the 1945 U.S. "Report on Ford-Werke Aktiengesellschaft" and its 221 exhibits were finally declassified in November 1998, after fifty-three years.

Iwanowa vs. Ford became the first of many U.S. court cases against dozens of large German industrial corporations. Claims were also raised against Opel and General Motors. At the same time, a renewed wave of labor compensation cases swept through the German courts. In the chain of events that followed, restitutions for Nazi-era forced labor turned into the subject of immensely complex international negotiations between Germany, the United States, Poland, Russia, Ukraine, Belarus, the Czech Republic, various other European countries and Israel, a group of large German corporations and their lawyers, the lawyers of the plaintiffs, victims' associations in the various countries, and Jewish victims' claims groups. I review this ground as best as possible in my concluding article on compensations for forced labor.

For those among our readers who like myself are not historians, I shall now outline, in general facts and statistics, the current consensus among historians concerning the Nazi-era forced labor programs known as "Reichseinsatz." The subject raises inevitable questions about what made such a regime possible in the first place, and about the present-day ramifications of the Second World War.

Reichseinsatz

During the war most adult German working men, about twenty million in all, were recruited or drafted into the armed forces and sent out on campaigns of conquest. As a result, the Reich faced an ever more dire shortage of homefront labor, in agriculture and across all industries. The Nazi authorities and armed forces therefore rounded up millions of non-Germans in the occupied countries for "labor deployment" within the territory of the Reich proper. That meant, for the most part, inside pre-1938 Germany, although the Reich had annexed Austria and the Czech Sudetenland before the war. This practice of forced labor was called *Reichseinsatz*.[4] Different aspects of its history are described in each of the chapters herein.

Reichseinsatz occurred in addition to the use of ghetto, concentration camp, and other prisoners in the occupied countries as worker-slaves, a practice by which many hundreds of thousands of mostly Jewish people were "exterminated through labor." In other words, Reichseinsatz should not be confused with the SS-run concentration camps (KZ) or the Nazi genocide programs, although these systems were linked.

There were three main sources of foreign recruits for Reichseinsatz: prisoners of war, foreign civilians, and KZ prisoners. In Germany, every foreigner received an ethnic label within the Nazis' steep and complicated racist hierarchy. People from the "East" and groups designated "subhuman" were required to wear identifying patches, for example: "P" for Poland, "OST" for Soviet civilians, "J" on a star of David for Jews. The different groups of forced laborers were as a rule kept in separate encampments, and experienced radically different conditions. Conditions also varied from industry to industry and with each employer.

Among German historians, the 1980s and 1990s saw an intense revival of interest in Reichseinsatz. Leading the way has been the work of Ulrich Herbert, who in his twenty years of studies, documentary surveys and statistical treatments derived most of the figures I cite below. Today these represent the broad consensus among scholars of the subject.

After the conquest of Poland in 1939, the Reich drew upon the forced labor of more than 300,000 Polish prisoners of war, most of them at German farms. Already in the first year of the war, Nazi agencies in occupied Poland issued decrees and pursued concerted police actions to detain about one million civilians, the majority female, for work in the Reich, according to Herbert's findings. This was only the beginning. The modern-day association of Polish victims of Nazi crimes estimates that during the six years of the war the Reich used as forced laborers a total of 2.4 million Polish (non-Jewish) civilians, of whom more than 160,000 died or were killed during that time.[5]

After the German victories in the west in 1940, more than a million French POWs were detained for forced labor. Many of them were deployed in industry. Starting in 1940, civilians in the German-occupied countries of western Europe were also recruited for Reichseinsatz. As the war went on this was increasingly accomplished through false promises, threats, and arrests. These "Western workers" were put under a strict working regime, but normally received the "best" treatment among non-German workers. They were usually given holiday privileges. In the early years of the war many went to Germany voluntarily, generally because there was no economic alternative at home. They were often employed and paid under contract, whatever the coercions involved.

The civilian forced laborers from the German-occupied territories of eastern Europe endured generally worse conditions. Their wages, lower by official decree, often went unpaid, or were paid in "camp money," and even then only after a variety of special taxes and, usually, employer surcharges for food and board. Polish and especially Soviet workers were even supposed to receive lower food rations than western workers.

Starting in late 1941, more than 600,000 forced laborers were drawn from the minority of Soviet prisoners of war who survived imprisonment in the Wehrmacht's Stalag camps. About three million Red Army soldiers were captured in the first months after the Reich's June 1941 attack on the Soviet Union. Most were corralled into open-air encampments. Many thousands were shot on the suspicion of being commissars or Jews. With the typhus raging, by the end of 1941 nearly two million of the Soviet POWs had succumbed to starvation and the elements. Historian Christian Streit estimates that about 3.3 million of the 5.7 million Soviet POWs captured by the Wehrmacht in the 1941–1945 "war of destruction in the East" died in captivity.[6] Those among the survivors who were put to work as forced laborers were closely guarded by soldiers and company security forces. Soviet POWs received the worst treatment and the lowest rations of any non-KZ group.

The single largest group of civilian forced laborers in Germany were the close to three million young adults and minors, the majority female, who were rounded up in the occupied territories of the Soviet Union starting in March 1942. They were summoned to occupation authorities, captured in raids, arrested or abducted, and deported en masse to the Reich. "Transports" of laborers were brought in on tightly packed cattle cars. In Germany, the Soviet civilians, called *Ostarbeiter*, were subjected to a harsh and often fatal discipline. Any act might be interpreted as an infraction, and Soviets were more likely to be sent to the Gestapo or KZ camps than other groups. Ostarbeiter often had no access to bomb shelter, and their casualty rates during air raids were accordingly high. As a rule, Soviet civilians were confined in barbed-wire encampments. Many of these were built by private employers and guarded by company security forces, known as *Werkschutz*. A company camp and a company security force were the two main requirements an employer had to fulfill before receiving forced laborers.

In what the Nazi leaders imagined as their "New Order," they would achieve dominance over Europe, "purify" their own people of traitors, eliminate all potential resistance, exterminate the Jews and other "subhuman" groups, and reduce the surviving "Slavic" peoples to a service caste, eternally subordinate to the "Aryan" colonizers of the *Lebensraum*, the new "living space" for Germans in "the East." That was the vision already spelled out in *Mein Kampf.* In practice, the Nazis' effort to realize it caused them instead to populate the German heartland with the very "inferior races" they wished to banish. The idea of millions of Russians in Germany, even as slaves, did not sit well with the more fanatic Nazis. It was put to them as the "pragmatic" consequence of their war of destruction. After the failure of the Blitzkrieg, starting in early 1942 the war economy and its labor policy were mainly orchestrated by the rationalizing, production-oriented logic of the powerful Armaments Ministry under Albert Speer. He was not a propagandist but an architect. The cool-headed scientific industrialism that came to predominate under his aegis does not make the goals and results of the Reich's policies any the less barbaric.

In current scholarship, estimates of the total number of civilians and POWs subjected to forced labor under Reichseinsatz during the war vary from ten to twelve million people. Turnover was high for reasons such as escape, failing health, and death, and it is difficult to ascertain what proportion of the western civilians in the early years were truly forced. Officially, all civilian foreign workers were voluntary recruits. As the war wore on, many of the Polish and western POWs were reclassified as civilian workers—the Soviet POWs were not, however. The high point of Reichseinsatz was reached in August 1944, a few weeks after the Allied invasion of Normandy and the big Soviet offensives of June, after which Nazi Europe began a rapid collapse.

That summer, the Reichseinsatz labor camps deployed more than five million civilian *Fremdarbeiter* (foreign workers, as they were usually called by their masters) and about two million prisoners of war. The latter by then included some 400,000 Italian soldiers, who were detained by the Wehrmacht in northern Italy after the Badoglio government overthrew Mussolini and surrendered to the Allies in September 1943. About 3 percent of the "foreign laborers" were assigned by labor agencies to jobs as servants in well-connected private households. At that point almost none of the foreign laborers in Germany were there voluntarily. They were coerced into working for the enemy at farms and municipalities, in military construction, transport, armaments, mining, vehicle production, and other war-related industries.

Every fourth worker in Germany was a foreigner (see Tables 1 and 2). Keeping this kind of potentially rebellious population under control involved a high proportion of the German people in formal and informal policing functions—even as a large number of Germans, at least according to the accounts of the survivors, practiced the passive resistance of secretly providing forced laborers with strictly forbidden bits of food. Thousands of privately owned workplaces, large and small, maintained and guarded company labor camps. Companies short on labor still lobbied the Reich, SS, and military authorities for more forced recruits, as they had throughout the war.

The above figures do not include KZ labor. The statistics reflect the thoroughness with which the authorities documented Reichseinsatz. Nevertheless, given the scale of these deployments, the loss of documents and confusion of the war, the numbers should not be viewed as exact to the thousand, but as accurate guides to the general situation.

Extermination through Labor

The Nazi genocide of Jews and other groups was carried out in many ways. Jewish town populations in occupied Poland were forced into small and over-crowded ghettos, where a large proportion starved to death and succumbed to disease. Many were shot. Starting in October 1940, all Jews aged 14 to 60 under the Nazi "General Government" of rump Poland were obligated to perform any labor to which they were assigned. War profiteers set up shop

TABLE 1: Foreign Laborers from Selected Countries, August 1944

Country of Origin (Date of occupation)	Classification		Total (% in sector)
	Civilian	POW	
"Protectorate of Bohemia and Moravia" (Mar. 1939)	280,273	–	280,273 (metal 28.7%)
Poland (Sept. 1940/June 1941)	1,659,764	28,316	1,688,080 (agric. 66.7%)
Belgium (May 1940)	203,262	50,386	253,648 (metal 37.8%)
Netherlands (May 1940)	270,304	–	270,304 (metal 32.4%)
France (June 1940)	654,782	599,967	1,254,749 (agric. 32.3%)
Soviet Union (1941–44)	2,126,753[1]	631,559	2,758,312 (metal 29.2%)
Italy (Sept. 1943)	158,099	427,238	585,337 (metal 37.8%)

[1] "Ostarbeiter," the largest single group

Percent figures in parentheses indicate the economic sector to which a plurality of the given group was assigned; 36 percent of all Reichseinsatz laborers in August 1944 were employed in agriculture, 22 percent in the metal processing industries, including motor vehicle production.

Source: *Entschädigung für NS-Zwangsarbeit* (1998), 337.

in the ghettos to take advantage of this. Later all ghetto residents were deported to KZ camps. In 1941, special SS-led forces known as *Einsatzgruppen* moved in to the Soviet Union on the heels of the Wehrmacht and massacred the residents of whole neighborhoods and villages. In reports to Himmler their commanders boasted of killing more than 300,000 people from 1941 to 1942. Anti-partisan actions served as a cause for further massacres. But the greatest number of victims were murdered in the KZ concentration camp system.

By 1939 the SS had already used inmate labor to build the KZ and auxiliaries into an empire, which by then held several hundred thousand prisoners. Anyone could be arrested and detained by SS and Gestapo, without recourse to the law. After 1939 the KZ complex was enlarged through hundreds of new locations in the Reich, Poland, central and southern Europe, and France. The system's various authorities, centered in the SS economic arm, SS-WVHA, and the SS central police agency, RSHA, were dedicated to genocidal goals, but also ran it as a vast (and vastly corrupt) economic enterprise.

TABLE 2: Foreign Labor in Selected Sectors, August 1944

Sector	A Civilian	B POW	A+B as % of all employees in sector
Agriculture	2,061,066	682,172	46.4
Mining	196,782	237,008	33.7
Metals processing (including auto)	1,397,920	293,409	30.0
Chemicals	206,741	45,327	28.4
Construction	349,079	128,978	32.3
Transport	277,579	100,448	26.0
Printing	8,788	880	4.1
Textiles	165,014	18,314	11.1
Commerce and Banking	92,763	21,807	6.0
Administration	39,286	9,799	3.3
Reich economy: 7.65 million	5,721,883	1,930,087	26.5

Source: *Entschädigung für NS-Zwangsarbeit* (1998), 340.

Prisoners received thin, tattered clothing and wooden shoes. They were fed small rations of "water soup" and faced the deadly whim of their overseers. Anything might be punishable by death. The inmates starved and froze to death, there were beatings and shootings, torture and executions, deportations to extermination camps equipped with gas chambers, deaths in medical experiments. A large proportion of the millions thus murdered succumbed to the specific practice of "extermination through labor." They were worked to death.

Countless studies and survivors' accounts have attempted to describe KZ camps and the practice of slave labor there.[7] All of them sooner or later reach a point of desperate speechlessness in the face of the horror.

Karl Brozik is among the minority who survived:

From my sheltered life I was, before I had turned fifteen, deported from Prague to the Lodz ghetto [Poland]. In Lodz there were ninety businesses more or less associated with the war industry. I was assigned to work in a metal plant, making forged nails for the mountain boots used by alpine troops....

You must imagine a large hall with dozens of forges and presses. The work went full steam, from early in the morning until late at night. Who were the workers? Boys of ten to sixteen years, all undernourished, big eyes and scrawny bodies, shaping the product through seven stages at the forge with a hammer.... Handmade nails, no works of art, needing a lot of muscle power. The children, this was thoroughly child labor, they perished like flies....

After I was brought to Auschwitz-Birkenau [Poland], I worked at a scrapping shop. What was that? Aircraft shot down all over "Greater Germany" were brought to a field, and our work was to break up the planes with cleavers and axes, most of these were fighter planes, into metal sheets measuring 2x2 or 2x3 [meters], so that these could be loaded onto wagons and returned to the war industry, to be melted down and used again.... Whom did this work benefit? Again, the war industry. How many private companies were among those to earn money from it can hardly be figured out.

The third station was the most terrible. The main camp in Mauthausen [Austria] kept a group of satellite camps. I was brought to Gusen II, where underground caves and shafts were tunneled out by a commando of 8,000 men. In the other, already finished caves, they were making Messerschmidt 129s, fighter planes for the war. Fuselage sections were carried onto the axles by human power, there was welding and hammering, horrible conditions. There was not enough oxygen ... and very little to eat. The people would collapse in front of their companions and fellow prisoners. They would be brought back to the camp in the evenings on stretchers, dead or almost dead. There we had to wait for an hour for whatever food we got. Before anyone could get into the bunk, there would be an air siren, so that a lack of sleep was one of the reasons that so many died. All this without needing gas chambers....

There were contradictory factors, which I cannot all name here, but which in practice slowed down the presumed overall logic of a will to exterminate. A clever businessman like Hans Biebow in Lodz, who earned well with products made by ghetto prisoners in ninety factories right until August 1944 [when the Soviet army approached]. In Hungary young Jewish women were exploited in the dangerous munitions plants right until the end of the war. In other cases there was a more "humane" treatment because a commander wanted to save his skin, or because he really was against the machinery of killing. But the main direction, the destruction of the Jews through labor ... has been demonstrated beyond doubt in the scholarship.[8]

What must be recalled, Primo Levi once said of Auschwitz, "is the scale of what happened, hundreds of thousands lived like this, possibly without ever being tortured. I was never tortured, and neither were my prison companions. And 95 percent of them died. Without torture, they died of exhaustion, hunger, dysentery, the cold, hypothermia, overwork." Brozik: "In the beginning the only point of forced labor [among Jews in KZ camps] was to humiliate them, by forcing them to perform hard manual tasks that had no practical purpose." "The number of 750,000 Jewish forced laborers in the year 1940 sank to something over 100,000 people by mid-1943, that is, 650,000 Jewish people were murdered in [the first] two and one-half years."[9]

Only gradually was Jewish KZ labor employed in a way that might benefit the war effort. The historian Mark Spoerer writes: "It took years for the SS to understand that economic success cannot be achieved exclusively by way of commands, and that their attempt at this had entirely failed."[10] Starting in 1943, the Reich leadership eased its restrictions on the use of KZ prisoners as laborers in Germany. The rules against this were originally strict. Again, the more fanatic Nazi leaders did not wish to contaminate everyday German life with the presence of "subhumans." But they also did not want to impose labor duties on married German women, fearing the effect on popular morale. With no new territories to plunder, that left KZ inmates as the only available labor reserve.[11] Several hundred thousand KZ prisoners, who had survived up to then, and who were "selected" as "able to work," were assigned to satellite labor camps in Germany. Among the forced laborers in Germany, the KZ prisoners faced the worst conditions by far, for they were guarded by SS officers and often remained subject to extermination through labor.

An additional three-quarters of a million Jews came under Reich authority in March 1944, when Germany occupied Hungary, its renegade Axis ally. Even at this late stage, practical considerations did not prevent the KZ authorities from immediately murdering more than half of these new prisoners in the gas chambers. Only about one hundred thousand of this group were selected for labor.

As of August 1944, a total of 400,000 workplace squad-laborers, from a pool of about 600,000 kept at KZ satellite labor camps within the Reich, were assigned in equal numbers to private concerns, and to state agencies and labor armies such as "Organisation Todt."[12] They mainly worked in large arms operations and at mines, or tunneled underground factories, within which much of the country's industrial plant was ultimately secured from Allied bombing raids.

In contrast to the situation in KZ camps and satellites, the Reich leadership did not "exterminate" the foreign civilian laborers and non-Soviet prisoners of war in Reichseinsatz. They were to be kept (at times barely) alive, and maximally exploited. Relatively few died during the war.

Since the war, companies have occasionally issued statements justifying the practice of forced labor as having in effect saved people from death in the KZ camps. Though this defense may be legitimate in some instances, we may dismiss it generally as disingenuous. Most of the foreign civilian laborers at companies in Germany would not have been taken into KZ camps. They were rounded up in their home countries for Reichseinsatz independently of the KZ system. Companies insistently demanded more workers, encouraging the authorities to step up recruitment.

Did companies profit from the use of KZ labor? That depends on how we define profit. Especially in the last year of the war, when it was obvious Germany would lose and that the reichsmark might soon be worthless, financial results were not relevant. Companies were more interested in saving and expanding their plant for starting over after the war. As the only available labor reserve, KZ prisoners were useful in that regard. Mark Spoerer argues that the relevant normative criterion is whether a company *expected* to profit, i.e. whether the management of a given private firm voluntarily made use of KZ labor. With that question in mind, he undertook the first systematic survey of the scholarly literature on extermination through labor programs during the war.

Spoerer found, first, that in most existing case studies the available documentation is insufficient for a clear answer. However, in sixteen well-documented cases a private company proposed the use of KZ labor on its own initiative, and then met with approval from the relevant Reich and SS authorities. "The literature does not report cases in which firms employed inmates to improve [the inmates'] situation."[13] Only in one of the twenty-four well-documented cases did the state actually coerce a private company's management to employ KZ inmates. In five other cases, state authorities took the initiative in proposing the use of KZ inmates, but were unable to force a firm to comply. Thus it was possible for a company to successfully resist the proposed assignment of a KZ labor squad. Despite what these results suggest about the priorities of management at the vast majority of large private businesses in Nazi Germany,[14] probably the best-known case in the world at the moment, as popularized in the 1993 film, is that of the German businessman Oskar Schindler, who really did hire 1,100 Jewish laborers to save them from the genocide.

Of the two firms treated in this book, it is confirmed that Ford Werke at its Cologne plant made use of a KZ labor squad, numbering about sixty men, all skilled laborers, assigned from KZ Buchenwald (see Chapter 4). It is unknown if the Ford Werke management asked for this assignment, or was compelled to take it. Opel joins the five cases mentioned above by Spoerer. The available evidence leaves little doubt that the Opel management successfully resisted government agency proposals to use KZ labor at its main factories in Russelsheim and Brandenburg, although KZ labor may have been used at Opel's military repair and maintenance locations outside Germany (see Chapter 1).

Oral Sources on Forced Labor in Cologne

In September 1944 an estimated 30,000 inmates were held in 250 Reichseinsatz labor camps and KZ satellites within the city limits of Cologne. Since 1989, the city has sponsored a program of return visits for its former prisoners of war, civilian forced laborers, and KZ prisoners. About two hundred of them, now in their seventies and eighties, have accepted invitations to return to the city, in freedom.

The visitors meet the mayor and the press and speak to gatherings and school groups. Accompanied by guides and interpreters, they visit the locations of their former workplaces and camps. Afterwards, they are interviewed by researchers. The tapes and transcripts, other records of the visit, and materials donated by the subjects (e.g. photos, sketches of the camps, letters written during the war) are kept available to the public at the NS-Dokumentationszentrum der Stadt Köln, a museum and research center.

In the current and past debates over restitutions for Nazi-era forced laborers, the public speakers, whatever their views, are professional mediators: politicians, executives, PR consultants, lawyers, journalists, historians. By contrast, the participants in the Cologne visitors' program represent a cross-section of the "foreign workers" in the city during the war. They tell their stories in their own words.

Ford Werke during the war maintained the largest private Reichseinsatz labor camp in Cologne, numbering about 2,500 inmates at its height. Many of the oral histories now available from the Nazi-era documents center of Cologne are therefore from people who were deployed at Ford Werke in the district of Cologne-Niehl. In recent years their testimonies were the first accounts to convey to the public, from the perspective of survivors, an impression of the Ford labor camp and factory.

A scholarly treatment of these interviews is presented in Chapter 4 by Karola Fings. She has helped organize the Cologne visitors' program since its inception. She and I narrowed down the many transcripts of interviews with former forced laborers at Ford to the accounts by five women and four men presented in Chapter 5. This allows us to follow the course of their lives from childhood up to the 1990s.

During the war, two of the interview subjects were drafted for Reichseinsatz in Poland, five in the Soviet Union, one in Belgium. One was an Italian prisoner of war. Today several of them view Ford Werke as one of the worst experiences they ever endured. For others, it was a relatively tolerable episode within a longer series of life-and-death struggles.

All of the subjects share acute memories of the hunger they suffered, and of the Allied bombings of Cologne. Two spent periods as prisoners of the SS at KZ Buchenwald and its satellite camps. In the final days of the war, Yvon Thibaut survived a death march. One of the KZ prisoners was dispatched to Ford Werke only for a few months. He, Kazimierz Tarnawski, was later imprisoned for ten years in a Soviet Gulag.

A tenth interview is with a German man, Fritz Theilen. He was hired by Ford Werke as a trainee at the age of fifteen, in 1941. Theilen relates how he witnessed the horrors of the forced laborers' sufferings from the other side of the barbed wire—until he, too, was rounded up by the repressive machinery. After the war, Theilen claims he saw defeated Nazis turn into bornagain democrats, and return to executive positions at the factory.[15]

Of course these ten accounts are not simply first-hand. They come to us through a set of filters. As with any oral testimony, the interviewees are relating what they recollect at a later time. This is subject to individual perspective and the workings of memory. No particular detail should be taken as absolutely reliable without independent documentary confirmation.

That the subjects do not speak "objectively" is obvious, but the reader will discover remarkable detail and degrees of distinction in their judgements, for example with regard to Germans as individuals. That the visitors met each other and helped each other recall things is both an advantage and a risk to the research.

The interviews are not run by the rules of a court proceeding. They are held in a supportive atmosphere, with the aim of getting people to talk openly about painful memories. Possible skepticism on the part of the researcher is kept subtle, expressed through careful questioning rather than direct challenges. Internal consistency and agreement between accounts are indicators of reliability. Fifty years on, reports of specific incidents are as a rule more reliable than estimates of numbers of prisoners or other statistics, which in any case would refer to different points in time and different camps.

The discussions were held in the subjects' mother tongues–Russian, French, Polish, Italian, and German. The researchers spoke German, asking questions through interpreters. I translated the resulting German transcripts into English, and cut and arranged them along a rough chronology and by topic. In doing so, I mostly refrained from correcting tenses or clarifying every single confusing detail. Recall always that these are transcripts of spoken testimony.

A few passages were taken from first-person reports or letters written by the subjects. The accounts fit in with what is known about Nazi-era forced labor generally, and are consistent with the available documentation on Ford Werke and other locations. By publishing these accounts, we mean to allow the reader insight into a primary resource of historic scholarship, as used in professional studies such as Karola Fings's in Chapter 4.

Whatever the caveats, these stories are spoken from the heart. Taken as a whole they recreate, not just the experience of forced labor, but of an era of European history.

Unavoidable Questions

The worst crimes committed under Nazi rule began with the war itself, which the Reich prepared, started, and pursued with every means it could muster, invading fourteen European countries and northern Africa, and undertaking the first large-scale strategic bombardments of cities. More than fifty million people died, more than twenty million of them Soviet citizens.

Until the final year of the war the authorities succeeded in keeping a large number of Germans, perhaps even a majority, in the dark, or happily willing to look away, at least about the extent of the organized and spontaneous civilian massacres in occupied territories, and about the organized murder of millions of Jewish, Romany and Sinti people, "Slavs," Soviet POWs, mental patients, the physically infirm, and others considered "subhuman" or politically suspect.

Of course, the fate of the victims could easily be guessed at. The German Jews had all been rounded up in public. But for the willingly naive, there were stories to explain where the Jews had gone. Atrocities were even hidden from many German soldiers on the front. By contrast, the terror, deprivation and injustice experienced by forced laborers in Reichseinsatz was seen by countless Germans in Germany every day, when they went to work.

How was any of this possible, in a country that had been widely admired as one of the most cultured in the world? Was the majority as willing to commit mass murder as the fanatic Nazis themselves? Why was there so little resistance?

Or are those the wrong questions? The oral accounts in Chapter 5 suggest that homefront Germans, as individuals, behaved in many different ways.

In the pre-war years of the Third Reich, the German majority, who had not voted for Hitler in the last democratic elections of 1932, were cowed by murderous crackdowns upon the slightest opposition, even upon *potential* resistance. The first concentration camps held German citizens.

Even as many ordinary Germans howled their approval and participated in the officially sanctioned attacks on Jewish Germans, many other, initially reserved people descended more slowly into accepting barbarism as they watched the Jews endure a progressive legal and social dehumanization.

Once in power, the Nazi movement kept everyone in motion. Most "Aryans" were integrated into the host of Nazi paramilitary, professional, economic, intellectual, labor, hiking, sports, driving, shooting-range, youth and women's organizations, all of which were organized in militaristic hierarchies. An endless procession of rallies and rituals everywhere staged the great German nation and its Leader as a show, one designed to thrill, to stir religious feeling, to brainwash. Almost everyone was required to swear some sort of allegiance to the Führer, as a worker, as a soldier, as a businessman, as a mother of healthy "Aryan" babies, as a child. How many of them meant it? How many of them did it out of fear? And how many of them truly regretted it, when they realized what it meant? There is no way to know, for in the end, after the war, everyone produced their own claim or justification: some true, some not.

After the depression and Weimar era perception of chaos, too many people felt bolstered by Germany's new-found economic and military might, and by its early successes in intimidating and swallowing neighboring countries. Nazi Germany was not the first fascist nation or dictatorship in post-1918 Europe. However, it was the regime with the most pathological and complete application of a total ideology, the most efficient in the organizational sense, and the only one that could, as a result of that combination, harness its people's economic energies so radically that not just war but a conquest of all Europe could be contemplated.

When that war began, a majority of Germans grew nervous, remembering too well the World War of 1914. The Wehrmacht's spectacular early success restored a giddy public mood. The Nazis found allies, supporters, collaborators, and self-designated "Aryans" in every country they invaded. Before the war they had enjoyed the support of small but vocal minorities in the future Allied countries, including the United States, most famously from Henry Ford himself. During the war, many French Jews were arrested and escorted to concentration camps by French police. Some first saw German soldiers on their arrival in Auschwitz. In recent years a number of European countries have been forced by new research findings to revise their traditional wartime histories of heroic resistance, and to confront instead the darker annals of willing collaboration.

Germany headed a wartime Axis of fascist and proto-fascist states, some of which, such as Italy, preceded the Reich, and territories run by local tyrannies such as Ustasha Croatia and other puppet nations set up by the Reich in its conquests. The Nazis could play liberator to the Bolshevik threat, blame their own crimes on Stalin's, blame everyone but themselves as the originators of the war.

Only with military defeats and the massive Allied bombardments of German towns did a majority of Germans begin to entertain doubts about the course their nation had struck, if only with regard to the outcome of the war. After the war, denial of the Nazi crimes was widespread, and not just among actual perpetrators. Some observers therefore wanted to damn all Germans for eternity. Others styled the German people into the victims of a small clique.[16]

All this still explains little about how and why millions of men (and not a few women) became active Nazis long before 1933, or what motivated and created the actual perpetrators of the atrocities. All the same, and even if the answers will always elude us, we must also ask the above questions in reverse: Once the vast majority of Germans had supported, accepted or adapted to the terror, why did a few still refuse it?

To the Reader

This book reveals important differences and similarities in the wartime histories of Ford and General Motors in Germany, and draws comparisons between them and other corporations.[17] The histories show what was typical and atypical about these companies and the use of forced labor at their plants. To avoid simplifications, we cannot compromise on the depth of detail or the breadth of context. We introduce a proverbial cast of thousands. The book, however, is meant for students, scholars, and all interested readers. Specialized historical knowledge is not required.

In the year 2000, fifty-five years after the end of the Nazi regime—under which some of the worst crimes in history were masked by a crazy confusion of authorities—even well-read students may be studying the Second World War in depth for the first time. And how all-encompassing is the history of the war! It is still the stuff of conflict among nations, of political anguish and criminal cases within nations, of nightmare to so many people who suffered and fought through its horror and tumult, or who lost those they loved.

Today, ten years after the end of what was called the "post-war order," the Second World War remains the defining conflagration of our age. It raised a specter of planetary destruction that has never since departed. In collective mythology 1945 is Zero Hour, and not only for Germany or Japan, but also for Israel, the whole of Europe, the victorious Allies, and many of the countries that emerged from the shattered European empires. The war was a crucible in which dozens of national identities were (re)shaped for the following decades. The two sides in the Cold War strove to derive legitimation for their later actions from their historic victory over Nazi Germany's ultimate threat.

Today, amid a never-ending cycle of commemorations of wartime events, ranging from the heartfelt to the merely official, the war remains a wellspring of metaphor for current politics. We are all familiar with phrases from its history: appeasement, isolationism, totalitarianism, fascism, collaboration, the banality of evil, the Good German, the silent majority. These are still daily invoked, and often abused, in long-running skirmishes of scholarship and spin.

We have tried to do justice to this great subject, to keep the history accessible to younger and non-specialist readers. Each author works discursively within the broader literature on the war and on industrial history. The reader will discover a wealth of background and biographical information in the text, boxes, footnotes and endnotes. The list of abbreviations, the glossary and the appendix provide a quick reference to key institutions within the Nazi state and its Reichseinsatz.

Throughout this book there is talk of finance and production. In our age of mega-billions, the 1940s figures may seem quaint. Currency changes, inflation, economic growth and technological revolutions prevent direct comparisons across decades. Such comparisons might skew our understanding, for example of restitution and reparation payments provided at different times, or of the significance of a few thousand trucks in 1940 as opposed to 2000. In 1927 there was one car for every 5.3 people in the United States, compared to one for every 196 people in Germany.[18] An American industrial worker, among the best paid in the world, was lucky to take home six or seven dollars a day. The U.S. produced 5.3 million motor vehicles in 1929. In 1932, during the Great Depression, production fell to 1.3 million.[19]

A few currency benchmarks: A 1938 U.S. dollar in terms of prices for international trade was roughly equivalent to $3.59 in 1976,[20] and since then the figure has again more than doubled. The official exchange rate of the strictly controlled reichsmark in 1938 was set at 2.5 to the dollar. The deutschemark started in 1948 at about 4.20 to the dollar.[21] In 1999 it traded between 1.80 and 2.00 DM to the dollar, as one of the currencies within the euro, which traded between 1.00 and 1.10 to the dollar. The German Reich's gross national product was at about 60 billion RM in 1933, having shrunk dramatically during the depression.[22] Nowadays the Federal Republic's gross domestic product hovers just below 4 trillion DM. The country is smaller, although the population is about the same.

PART ONE

PROLOGUE

The Pre-War Years

A maker of bicycles and sewing machines, the Adam Opel firm began producing automobiles in 1899. By the 1920s Opel was the largest European carmaker. Its home plant, in the Hessian town of Russelsheim, was the largest car factory in Europe. When operating at capacity, Opel Russelsheim employed 13,000 people. It was considered technologically advanced. An assembly line was introduced in 1925[1] and most of the machinery was purchased in the late 1920s. According to General Motors's analysis at the time, Opel had the best dealer organization in Germany.[2]

The period of family ownership need not be romanticized. Despite the general 1920s emphasis on rationalization and the hallowed goal of *Fordismus*, in 1929 production process in Germany and at Opel was still inefficient by American standards. The Russelsheim plant was divided into isolated departments, and the workers in each faced serious problems: poor sanitation, safety hazards, arbitrary penalties, low wages.[3] The market was weak. By 1928 the factory was operating below capacity.[4] German industry at this time generally operated below capacity. It might have been a good time for businesses to raise wages and create a mass market, but this course was not pursued.

For its part, Opel ran into difficulties managing its debt, and rechartered as a stock corporation (AG). General Motors, which became the world's largest producer through the acquisition and integration of other carmakers, purchased 80 percent of Opel shares in April 1929, a deal worth $26 million. GM acquired the remaining 20 percent in 1931 for $7.3 million.[5] At a time of great consolidation in the automotive industry worldwide, Opel was GM's most important investment abroad, and the largest American investment in Germany. GM placed American executives and engineers in the directorate and management, and at key posts throughout the plant. They remained there until the outbreak of war in 1939.

Russelsheim was reorganized on an American production-line basis, which raised efficiency but also led to serious labor conflicts (see Chapter 3). Because of the global depression that began in the fall of 1929, the car market did not develop as General Motors had hoped. Remembering the hyperinflation of the early 1920s, successive German governments pursued tight budgeting and deflationary policies. So dire was the crisis in Germany that the state in July 1931 banned transactions in foreign currencies.

Opel still managed by 1933 to increase its proportion of German car exports to nearly two-thirds, and of the domestic market to one-third.[6] Given the reduction in the German market, however, Opel's domestic sales amounted to a mere 31,000 new cars. By early 1933 Germany counted six million unemployed workers.

THE NAZIS ROSE UP from near non-existence in 1925 to win 13.7 million votes in the national elections of July 1932—a plurality of the electorate.[7] Although the Nazis lost ground in the following elections that November, all efforts to form a stable anti-Nazi majority failed. Many in the German establishment and military saw Adolf Hitler as a last resort for restoring stability, getting control over an unruly German labor force, and countering the threat of Bolshevism. The German elite naively believed that they could domesticate the Nazis, who had been unrelenting in their violence, by letting them share in the responsibility and burden of government.

Nineteen key industrialists and bankers, among them Hjalmar Horace Greely Schacht, Baron Kurt von Schröder and the steel magnate Fritz Thyssen, wrote President Hindenburg to recommend that he appoint Hitler to head a government.[8] Encouraged by these signals, the weakened conservative German National Peoples' Party, the DNVP, entered into a coalition with Hitler, who was named chancellor on 30 January 1933. The next day, Reichskanzler Hitler went on radio in a brief statement to announce a national revolution. Germany would be made great, there would be work for the people.

The Nazis thereupon seized dictatorial power with a rapidity and brutality that left even their dedicated opponents astonished. The Reichstag was dissolved on 1 February. Demonstrations were forbidden, the two million storm-troopers of the Nazi paramilitaries S.A. and SS received police powers and shooting orders. After the Reichstag arson of 27 February, which the Nazis blamed on the German Communist Party KPD (it may have been set by a lone Dutch council communist, or by the Nazis themselves), the elections of 5 March were held under a reign of street terror. When the new Reichstag convened, the Nazis excluded the Communist deputies and banned the KPD, achieving a majority.

The first concentration camp, at the town of Dachau near Munich, opened its gates to prisoners on 20 March, beneath the sign: "Work Makes Free." A few days later the Reichstag passed an emergency order to suspend the laws of the Republic, with only the Social Democratic Party (SPD) voting against. A total of one hundred concentration camps were opened that year.

The S.A. called a boycott of Jewish shops on 1 April, the Gestapo was established as a terror police on 26 April. Union leaders and activists were rounded up on 2 May, after which the German Labor Front (DAF) was founded under Robert Ley as the only legal, and in fact compulsory labor organization.

On 10 May, Nazi mobs lit bonfires with thousands of "subversive" books torn from the shelves of universities in Berlin. The SPD was banned on 22 June, all other parties agreed to their own dissolution by 5 July. The sterilization of "unworthy life" was made legal on 14 July.

HITLER'S FIRST MAJOR PUBLIC SPEECH as head of state was delivered on 10 February 1933, at the Berlin sports stadium. Playing on religious overtones, he brought the crowd into a tumult: "German people, give us four years time, then judge us."

The next day, Hitler spoke at the opening ceremonies of the Berlin "AA" motor show. There he announced a huge road-building program. Based on Weimar-era plans that had gone unfulfilled, this was to become the Nazis' largest non-military public spending item. Hitler lifted the tax on new car purchases, and promised that the motor industry would henceforth be organized as a key sector separate from the rest of the transport system.

At the next Berlin motor show, in March 1934, he revealed plans to create a *Volkswagen*–a car of the people that would sell for under 1,000 reichsmarks, and thus be affordable to most households.[9] This idea captured the imagination of a great number of the German people. Construction of the first *Autobahn* began that month, with Hitler briefly digging the turf as thousands cheered. The state hired hundreds of thousands of workers for its mobile construction squads. Starting in 1935, the Autobahns "linked Germany from border to border and were the first integrated network of express highways in the world." They "became a model for all future highway construction," as the automotive historian James Flink writes.[10]

Volksmotorisierung was the original centerpiece of Nazi economic policy. The military build-up was started in secret, so as not to antagonize the still-dominant Western powers, but "popular motorization" could be pursued with a maximum of fanfare. That motorization also had a military effect, whatever the intent, is clear. The products of the German auto industry would prove vital in powering the Blitzkrieg. The Autobahn was of secondary importance. Incapable of bearing heavy armor, during the war it was useful for shuttling supplies among German arms plants.[11] Otherwise, *Motorisierung* tremendously increased demand in the materials processing and supply industries, and stimulated their development. Three thousand kilometers of new road were completed and over three thousand bridges built by 1939.[12]

Quite beyond the direct increase in demand, these powerful and early signals encouraged the auto industry to invest and expand. The carmakers of Germany, at first uncertain about the Nazis' announced commitment to their industry,[13] were quickly won over by the results. Overall production of vehicles increased from about 52,000 in 1932 to 342,000 in 1938. By that time the motor sector employed 1.5 million people, representing one out of every twelve jobs.[14] The consumer market had expanded insofar as the country's gross national product more than doubled, to 130 billion RM in 1939,[15] and unemployment was wiped out. Starting already in 1934–1935, however, the emphasis in Nazi policy had turned decisively away from the mass market, and towards armaments. German car production in the late 1930s was still much less than a tenth of U.S. production in 1927.

As the largest German carmaker, and as a maker of small cars, Opel was a primary and early beneficiary of German motorization. Compared to a 1929–1933 average of about 24,000 units, domestic sales of Opel cars more than tripled by 1938, to 85,497 units. Exports rose from about 8,000 in 1934 to more than 33,000 in 1938. This was in addition to truck sales. Opel's operating profit shot up from a loss of nearly $3 million in 1930 to a peak of almost $14 million in 1938. In the same period General Motors doubled its plant investment, raising employment at Russelsheim to about 20,000 people.[16] Opel's success was a source of chagrin to its "fully German" competitors, for example Daimler-Benz.

A few words about Daimler, a company that plays a secondary but important role in the pages ahead: The motor enthusiast Hitler (who never learned how to drive) had struck up a friendship with Jakob Werlin, a Mercedes salesman who sold him his party's first official Benz limousine in 1923.[17] Werlin joined the SS and managed Daimler's extensive pre-1933 contacts to the Nazis. Daimler-Benz supported the Party by providing it with vehicle fleets at high rebates starting in 1931. Four of its top managers entered the SS in May 1933, joining the two SS men who were already on the board. Werlin was also appointed a top executive.[18] The labor at the company's many factories was subjected to an unrelenting discipline and barrage of nationalist propaganda. Nevertheless, Daimler made large cars, and was not nearly as efficient as American producers. Although its sales rose, Daimler lost car market share. Otherwise, as a mixed industrial concern with excellent connections to the Party, Daimler participated heavily in the arms boom, and from 1933 to 1939 quintupled its revenues.[19]

BY LATE 1934 the Nazis had consolidated their total control over all aspects of German politics and society. Regional parliaments were dissolved in January 1934. Hitler Youth was made into a compulsory state organization. The party leadership resolved its conflict with the "left-wing" Nazis, who demanded an anti-capitalist revolution, with the assassination of the S.A. leaders in June and July 1934. Many others fell victim to the purge. As one consequence, the SS began rising towards its later, dominant position as an independent military elite within the Party under Heinrich Himmler. It took charge of the concentration camp system and the police.

Hjalmar Schacht, the business favorite, was made Minister of Economics in July 1934. All members of the armed forces were compelled to swear loyalty directly to the Führer in August. A rigged referendum to give Hitler unconditional powers received a 90 percent "yes" vote on 19 August. That was the last official election result under 99 percent.

In the summer of 1935, the Nazis dissolved even the right-wing Freikorps paramilitaries left over from the Weimar era. They also banned the Freemasons. That September, during the huge Nuremberg Party rallies, they decreed the laws that made Jews officially into second-class citizens and banned "mixed" sexual relations, a further step in the total dehumanization, exclusion and expropriation of the Jews.

Already in 1934, the Reich's spending on the military far exceeded spending on transport, and after 1935 spending on all other programs combined.[20] Opel entered the booming arms business in 1935. At the behest of the armed forces, the company agreed to build a new truck plant in Brandenburg, south of Berlin. The Wehrmacht believed that only Opel had the resources and expertise to build such a large factory in the shortest possible time.[21] The Nazis had tightened the pre-1933 restrictions on currency remittances to foreign countries, and General Motors no doubt found it useful to invest Opel's growing liquidity in this fashion, selling off its German equity holdings in the process.[22] In January 1936, the largest and most efficient truck plant in Europe began producing the Opel Blitz, a line of light and medium-weight trucks usable as troop and supply carriers. Unit production rose from about 14,000 in the first year to more than 24,000 in 1939.[23] After the annexation of the Czech Sudetenland in October 1938, the Opel Blitz was sold almost exclusively to the German armed forces.

Opel's Russelsheim factory had a pre-1933 history of strong, Social Democratic unionism as well as periods of effective Communist organizing. It was the scene of various clandestine activities after 1933, although most of the underground was smashed by the Gestapo in a nationwide crackdown on resistance groups in 1935. The handful of groups who remained met in small, paranoid cells. A company network of informants reported daily to the Gestapo and the management. In the coach department, a brief strike was staged in June 1936, protesting low wages and poor conditions. All of the workers in the department were fired on the spot. Many of them were arrested. A few ended up in the camps. Any kind of labor action was by then exceedingly rare. Even years later, the more committed Nazis among the authorities regarded Opel (and the Americans involved in its management, who were often said to be under "Jewish influence") with suspicion.

During these early years of the regime, many a Nazi functionary tried to obligate the entire automotive industry to participate in the "common German project" of a Volkswagen. Most carmakers remained skeptical about the practical aspects, especially the possible effects of a Volkswagen on their own market share. The companies financed a joint study within the auto industry association RDA. This resulted in the famous design by Ferdinand Porsche. (A version of it captured the world's markets as the VW Beetle after the war.)

The carmakers were wary of each other, fearing that a competitor would either make its own Volkswagen or take over the Nazi project. The historian Hans Mommsen writes:

> With the exception of Adler Werke, the company representatives were unanimous in their decision to exclude Ford Werke [from RDA's Volkswagen planning in 1934]. In contrast to Opel, Ford was not considered a "fully German company." ... "Otherwise the fight against Ford until now would have been for

naught," as one of the participants put it. At the same time at Ford, however, the expectation still reigned that Ford would be involved in the Reich government's plans for a popular motorization, which was thought to be feasible only with American financing.[24]

In 1936, as they showed their best face to the world in preparation for the Berlin Olympics of August, the Nazis embarked upon increasingly obvious preparations for war. In its first open intervention abroad, the Reich dispatched its Legion Condor to fight on behalf of Franco and the fascists in the Spanish civil war. Berlin's expenditures on the Wehrmacht alone shot from 5.1 billion RM in 1935 up to 9.0 billion RM in 1936 (by 1939: 16.5 billion RM).[25]

A further intensification of the military build-up and a policy of economic autarky, intended to free Germany of any dependence on foreign supply, was adopted in the guise of the "Four-Year Plan" approved in September 1936. Hermann Göring, Reichsmarshal and head of the Luftwaffe, the number two man in the Nazi Reich, was designated its guardian. In violation of Germany's international treaty obligations, the popular former air ace had overseen an initially secret expansion in German aircraft orders from a few dozen in 1932 to the more than five thousand aircraft produced in 1936, half of which were warplanes.[26] Under the Four-Year Plan, the state established a large, publicly owned steel enterprise known as the Hermann-Goering-Werke. Among economic elites, the Four-Year Plan neutralized the role played until then by such old-school bankers as Schacht.

An increasingly influential role was played instead by I.G. Farbenindustrie, the chemicals giant by then under the dominance of committed National Socialists. The largest German cartel, a world-spanning conglomerate founded in 1926, IG Farben specialized among other things in the production of synthetic fuels. These ultimately kept the war machine running despite a shortage of oil. IG Farben became infamous after the war, when the world learned of its heavy involvement in slave labor and genocide at Auschwitz and other camps.

In place of the mass market initially hoped for by many businessmen, the Nazis had created an economy in which the state, as the buyer of armaments and military supplies, was the top customer of private corporations. Acknowledging the rights of private ownership, as long as it was "Aryan," the Reich still kept a firm rein on wages and hence on popular buying power. The armaments program became an economic stimulant from which Germany, if it was not to fall back into economic crisis, could never afford to back down. Schacht was later stripped of his remaining influence for making exactly that claim. The problem only intensified after the domestic consumer market peaked in 1938. After 1936 the Reich was therefore less hesitant in applying pressure on companies to conform to the needs of the war build-up, assigning them to exact roles in the division of labor within its armaments programs.

For businesses wary of state control, the three years before the war have been characterized as "the nervous years."[27] Contrary to the ideas of the more committed Nazi planners, the balance of economic power was never shifted towards state concerns, due to resistance even within the Party, and given the relative efficiency of the private companies. The relationship between state and corporate sector became one of mutual dependence. As the historian Neil Gregor put it, speaking of the management of large companies: "Under certain circumstances, pragmatism encouraged barbarism."[28]

With their businesses nonetheless booming by comparison to the crisis years, auto industry executives were hardly forwarding alternatives. They were more interested in neutralizing the Volkswagen project, which had run into financial difficulties. The industrialists secretly hoped the Volkswagen would be produced by a state concern, and also feared exactly that. Finally, in the spring of 1937, Hitler designated the KdF ("Strength through Joy") department of DAF as his desired carrier for the Volkswagen project.

Strength through Joy was the DAF branch charged with organizing recreation and travel for workers. The DAF had turned into the largest mass organization of the Nazi Party. It counted twenty-one million members in 1939, and assured a docile workforce, which in Nazi jargon was called "the Following" (*Gefolgschaft*). Company managers were referred to as "leaders" (*Betriebsführer*). At each workplace a political "Shopfloor Leader" (*Betriebsobmann*) was appointed especially by the party.[29] An archaic "leadership principle" was enshrined in company organization.

At Opel, as at other workplaces, the personnel were gathered about once a month at compulsory rallies, where hours of propaganda speeches were delivered by company and party officials. To get a job, a worker had to present his or her *Arbeitsbuch*. This booklet documented employment history as recorded by the employer and the authorities. The *Arbeitsbuch* was one of many means used to tie workers to their jobs in a tight labor market, although in practice companies tended to hire workers even against the rules.

After DAF took over the Volkswagen project, Porsche and DAF ignored the existing auto industry and created an independent, state-owned Volkswagen plant. Werlin became a general manager of the project. The company later known as Volkswagenwerk GmbH was founded in May 1937. "The building of the Volkswagenwerk was carried out according to American models and aimed at applying the most advanced techniques used at Ford plants in Detroit."[30]

Porsche's inspiration was Ford Motor's famous River Rouge plant, viewed as the bastion of modern mass production and Fordism. Porsche went on a pilgrimage to River Rouge in the fall of 1936. He sent a delegation there in 1937 to recruit German-speaking Ford engineers. A group of them became the core of Volkswagen's technical personnel.[31]

Germany suspended its payments on reparations under the Versailles Treaty in January 1937, and raised the volume on demands that its pre-1918 African colonies be returned. In keeping with the Nazi ideology, however, the real focus of the Reich's foreign policy remained on *Lebensraum*–ample "living-space" for the supposedly overcrowded German people, as called for in *Mein Kampf.* That meant central and eastern Europe, starting with Austria and Czechoslovakia, but going on to Poland and the territories of "the East." German foreign policy worked to achieve hegemony among the more primitive dictatorships and fascist-*völkisch* movements of central and southern Europe. In November 1937 Hitler ordered the Wehrmacht to plan for total war.

The next year accordingly began with renewed threats against Germany's neighbors. The Reich had in previous years reincorporated the Saarland after the people there voted to join Germany in a referendum, and remilitarized the Rhineland in violation of the Versailles Treaty. With the help of Nazi cadre in Austria and ample public support, that country was absorbed into the re-named "Greater German Reich" by way of a lightning invasion in March 1938. Democracy was smashed, the KZ system extended to Austria. A series of increasingly dire threats against Czechoslovakia, home to an ethnic German minority, finally led to the Munich conference of September 1938. The Western powers, fearing war and believing Bolshevism to be the greater threat, agreed to let the Reich occupy the Czech Sudetenland.

On 9 November 1938, after the shooting of a German consul abroad, the Nazis orchestrated a nationwide pogrom against the German Jews. Hundreds were killed, synagogues burned to the ground. Insofar as it had not already been established through dozens of decrees, the total exclusion of Jews from social and economic life was now completed. All Jewish property, which the Nazis had ordered registered in April, was expropriated and given over to "pure" German owners, a process known as "Aryanization." This had in reality begun years before, as banks refused to extend credits to Jewish-owned businesses, forcing the owners to sell at below-market prices.

A few months later, in March 1939, with its agents stirring up further unrest in Czechoslovakia, the Reich occupied the rest of that now defenseless country. Britain and France finally understood the pointlessness of appeasing the Reich, and committed themselves to the defense of Hitler's next likely target, Poland. Ever resourceful, the Nazis entered into negotiations with Stalin that would culminate in the Nazi-Soviet "non-aggression pact" of August 1939, allowing the war to begin in earnest.

The huge Volkswagen plant, the "German River Rouge," was nearing completion in Lower Saxony. The factory and the new city nearby were supposed to serve as models of Nazi industriousness and German superiority. A VW auxiliary plant, set up in Braunschweig, trained an elite of German production workers in a basically military regime.[32] This was appropriate, as most of them would end up on the front, not the assembly line. The factory would soon produce warplane parts and the Wehrmacht's trademark "bucket cars," based on Porsche's design. The majority of the workforce would be forced laborers.

Hitler had announced that the Volkswagen was to be called the "KdF-Car." The new town became known as the "City of the KdF Car" (which it was called until the British renamed it Wolfsburg in 1945). The DAF's propaganda offensives trumpeted the "KdF" savings scheme as the means for workers to purchase the cars that the Volkswagen plant would one day produce: "5 Marks a Week to Save–If You Want to Drive Your Own Car!"[33] As the number of people in the concentration camps and prisons swelled to 300,000 by April 1939,[34] millions of Germans dreamed of owning a KdF Car.

Only the Volkswagenwerk management knew that its price would have to be at least twice what was being advertised.[35] Intended to finance production once the plant was completed, the savings scheme was a swindle. The 280 million RM gathered from the 336,000 subscribers[36] served as the fodder for corrupt dealings within the DAF. Even after the war started, with the VW plant switching to military production and refusing car orders, the propaganda encouraged front soldiers to keep paying into the scheme. Production start of the KdF Car was originally scheduled for late summer 1939.

– Nicholas Levis

MAP 1: Europe in May 1942

Source: Colin McEvedy, *The Penguin Atlas of Recent History (Europe since 1815),* maps as devised by Colin McEvedy and drawn by David Woodroffe (London, 1982), 79.

(continued)

The map on the preceding page shows Europe under the New Order, a few months after the height of German military success. Nazi Germany (the Deutsche Reich) united with Austria through the Anschluss of March 1938, extorted the Sudetenland from Czechoslovakia in September 1938, and saw its military intervention in Spain (starting in 1936) culminate in the triumph of the Spanish Fascists in March 1939. Germany occupied the rest of Czechoslovakia in March 1939, dividing it into a Protectorate of Bohemia and Moravia and a nominally independent Slovakia. The Reich then invaded and conquered Poland in September 1939, prompting Britain and France to declare war. Western Poland was annexed to the Reich and Eastern Poland was occupied by the Soviet Union, as agreed in the secret codicil to the August 1939 Stalin-Hitler pact. The remaining third of pre-war Poland was put under the Nazi General Government. The Soviet Union went to war with Finland in November 1939, gaining territories in the peace of March 1940. Denmark, Norway, the Low Countries and France were defeated by Germany and occupied in the months from April to June, 1940. Alsace-Lorraine was annexed to the Reich; unoccupied southern France was placed under a collaborationist regime in Vichy. The Soviet Union occupied and annexed the Baltic states in summer 1940. Germany invaded and conquered Yugoslavia in April 1941; small territories were annexed to the Reich and to Italy, the rest carved into an occupied Serbia and a Croatia under fascist government. Greece, which had turned back the Italian attack of October 1940, was conquered by German forces in April 1941; most of it was placed under nominally Italian occupation and Thrace was annexed to Bulgaria. Germany launched war against the Soviet Union in June 1941, conquering Eastern Poland, the Baltic states and the western part of the Soviet Union, annexing further territories to the Reich, and carving out the new, Nazi-governed units of Ostland and Ukraine. At various times the Reich dictated boundaries and oversaw the addition of territories to its Axis allies, Hungary, Romania, Bulgaria, and Finland. Dotted lines indicate the Italian empire. As of May 1942, Switzerland, Sweden and Turkey are neutral, as is fascist Spain. Among European states, only Britain and the Soviet Union are still fighting Germany. The United States entered the war in December 1941 and is preparing a European expeditionary force.

Chapter 1

Airplanes for the Führer

Adam Opel AG as Enemy Property, Model War Operation, and General Motors Subsidiary, 1939–1945

Are large transnational corporations such as the automotive giants General Motors and Ford Motor Company so powerful and remote from public scrutiny that they can violate U.S. security interests at will? The U.S. Senate Committee on the Judiciary considered that question once, a quarter of a century ago. In the spring of 1974, its subcommittee on antitrust and monopoly, chaired by Senator Philip Hart, called hearings on "American Ground Transport." Among other issues, these zeroed in on the activities during the Second World War of General Motors's German subsidiary, Adam Opel AG of Russelsheim, and of the German Ford factory in Cologne. At the hearings Bradford Snell, a young Senate staff attorney, delivered a controversial report. After 1933, he claimed, General Motors and Ford had played important roles in arming Nazi Germany, long before the outbreak of war in 1939.

Snell wrote that in 1935 and 1936, "at the urgent request of Nazi officials who realized that Germany's scarce petroleum reserves would not satisfy war demands," General Motors agreed to share its synthetic fuel-making techniques with IG Farben. According to Snell, "General Motors and Ford became an integral part of the Nazi war efforts" after the German invasion of Poland in 1939. Snell claimed that without the technical prowess of the two American companies, especially Opel's expertise at aircraft engine manufacture, the Nazis never would have been able to pursue their war as successfully or as long as they did.[1]

In the United States, General Motors and Ford in early 1942 set up executive offices in Washington and started working exclusively for the Department of Defense. Snell alleged that the two firms "maximized profits by supplying both sides with the materiel needed to conduct the war." "GM's plants in Germany built thousands of bomber and jet fighter propulsion systems for the Luftwaffe at the same time that its American plants produced aircraft engines for the U.S. Army Air Corps."[2]

Most explosive was the charge that General Motors shared responsibility for the actions of the Opel management after the U.S. entry into the war. Snell argued that the same German executives who had managed day-to-day business in Russelsheim before 1939 remained in place throughout the war. In other words, the pre-1939 Opel directorate (*Aufsichtsrat*), dominated by American GM executives, had appointed the management board (*Vorstand*) who organized wartime arms production at Opel.[3] Snell further claimed that three of four Americans on the Opel directorate never formally resigned, although they stopped exercising their functions after Germany's 11 December 1941 declaration of war on the United States.

These accusations were leveled at none other than Alfred P. Sloan, the president and corporate architect of General Motors, whose stature in automotive history rivals that of Henry Ford—and at the GM vice presidents James K. Mooney and Graeme P. Howard.[4]

Jim Mooney, head of General Motors's overseas operations and hence GM's most important executive in Europe in the late 1930s, plays an important role in the early part of our story. In 1938 he accepted the "Grand Cross of the German Eagle." This was the highest Nazi honor for foreigners who had performed exceptional service to the German Reich. It was bestowed upon a total of four Americans, among them Henry Ford and Charles Lindbergh. After Mooney's last months in Nazi Germany, which are related below, starting in 1940 he helped run GM's arms program in cooperation with the U.S. government, simultaneously serving as an officer in the U.S. Navy.

Graeme Howard was the author of a 1940 treatise on *America and a New World Order*, later described by the U.S. government economist James Stewart Martin as "an apologia for the Nazi economic system that might just as well have been titled *You Can Do Business with Hitler*."[5]

The German Reich did not appoint an "enemy property custodian" (*Feindvermögensverwalter*) to assume control of Opel until 25 November 1942, more than eleven months after Hitler's declaration of war on the United States. Snell's report asserted that the custodian had no power over the majority of management board decisions. In his view, GM "was in complete management control of its Russelsheim warplane factory for nearly a full year after Germany's declaration of war" on the United States. And even beyond, thanks to formal restrictions on the custodian's authority. Snell cited U.S. State Department documents and Opel financial records, claiming: "Communications as well as materiel continually flowed between GM plants in Allied countries and GM plants in Axis-controlled areas, presumably in direct violation of trading with the enemy legislation," throughout the war.[6]

Snell's version of history did not go uncontested. General Motors's lawyers succeeded in discrediting his claims with the Senate committee as "totally false." Their rebuttal was published by the committee as an appendix to Snell's report. In their telling, all American GM personnel at Opel were called back to the United States at the beginning of the war in September 1939. "As early as October 1939, the German Government had prohibited the transmittal of financial or operational reports from Opel to General Motors. The last of GM's American employees who had been assigned to Opel departed from Germany in early March 1941." As we shall see, that most likely refers either to Cyrus Osborn or to Elias "Pete" Hoglund, at the time members of the Opel directorate. "A meticulous search has disclosed no communications whatsoever between Opel and General Motors Corp. after September 2, 1941"–a full two months before the United States became involved in the war. The "relationship with Opel was entirely severed" on 11 December 1941. "No Americans sat on the board of directors, even nominally, after that time."[7]

General Motors claimed that the enemy property custodian appointed by the Reich was the sole executive authority at Opel from 1942 until the end of the war. Further, "Opel, while under GM control, possessed no special aircraft product technology. The product development and engineering required for the production or assembly at Russelsheim of aircraft parts for the JU-88 medium range bomber, and, later the jet engine of the ME-262 jet fighter, was supplied by German aircraft and aircraft components firms. The German Government brought this German aircraft technology, including know-how, into the Opel plant to build the products of war."

After this confrontation the hearings were called off, the documents filed back into limbo. The GM subsidiary's involvements with the Nazis ceased to interest U.S. scholars and journalists.[8] Those involvements never became much of an issue in Germany, either. According to the version that was standard history in both countries until the 1990s, U.S. executives opposed Opel's conversion to arms production in 1939. Conversion was carried out at the Nazi government's orders. Immediately after the German declaration of war on the United States, Opel was quasi expropriated by the omnipresent trusteeship. It was subordinated utterly to the dictates of the Nazi Party and the State.[9] So the story goes.

Here we shall employ the available evidence in sketching a more complete history of the events at Opel's wartime operations: the successions in the management and directorate, the company's conversion to arms production, problems with production and personnel, the increasing use of foreign forced labor as the war progressed, and the evidence on General Motors's role in Opel before and after December 1941.

Although we do not wish to propose a definitive verdict in favor of either side of the 1974 dispute before the Senate, we shall see that Snell was right about several important items. Based on the findings here, it would be hyperbole to conclude, with Snell, that General Motors exercised "complete management control" at its Russelsheim factory during the war. Instead, to put it in legalistic terms: The Opel executives appointed by General Motors before 1941, and after 1941 by GM's German legal representative, Heinrich Richter, retained the same preponderance of control over day-to-day operations at Opel after 1941 as General Motors had exercised before the war, despite various official challenges to their authority; and they worked within the same system of Nazi workplace organization that had been built since 1933, during the period of GM's open presence; and their work was in the service of the arms market, which was the only one available. The transition from open GM involvement to these conditions was not abrupt, but occurred in the period from September 1939 to early 1941. What would have happened if General Motors had opposed the conversion to arms production in September 1939 is fairly certain: Opel would have been expropriated. But we have no evidence that any such effort was considered. In fact, the evidence suggests General Motors's willing collaboration in the conversion. There was no official German seizure of Opel or its assets under the Reich.

We will draw no conclusions about the charges that GM traded materiel or funds with Opel after 1941 in violation of the U.S. Trading with the Enemy Act. We do not speculate, as Snell does, about what General Motors or the Nazis would have done about Opel if Germany had won the European war. Given the importance of the Opel management question, the convoluted story of how and why an "enemy property custodian" was appointed for Opel is presented in detail.

We begin with the conversion of Opel Russelsheim to warplane parts production in the fall of 1939 and spring of 1940, and the simultaneous "peace mission" undertaken by Jim Mooney, who during this time met with both Franklin Roosevelt and Adolf Hitler. Of concern in the subsequent history are the conflicts among the German Opel management, Reich ministries, and Nazi authorities, the first in 1941 to 1942, over the appointment of an enemy property custodian; the second in 1942 to 1943, over the general restructuring of the war industry according to the Speer Ministry's principle of "industrial self-management"; and the third starting in early 1942, over how to boost production of Opel vehicles and aircraft parts, which were considered vital to the German war effort. Sections on the executive intrigues and developments in the overall management of the war economy alternate with sections concerning the situation at the plants and the fate of the foreign workers.

The case of Opel as "enemy property" reveals a confusing and confused to-and-fro behind the facade of unity in war. In an arrangement of power that has been called polycratic, authorities in the Nazi state and party overlapped and conflicted. Political influence was often based on a given leader's momentary standing and alliances, or his relationship to Hitler. Although "pragmatism" was mainly a means in achieving the goals defined by Nazi ideology, there were still clashes between true Nazi believers and practical technocrats. The technocrats gained ground in the management of industry as the war progressed.

A maze of legal regulations, bureaucratic frictions, competing Nazi Party and Reich ministerial interests, workplace loyalties, and maudlin National

Socialist "duties" had to be negotiated before the General Motors subsidiary became an absolutely reliable part of the Reich war machine.

James Mooney's Odyssey and the Opel Conversion

In October 1938 the German Luftwaffe approved a plan, ostensibly by Order of the Führer, to effect the most rapid possible "quintupling" of the German warplane fleet. This was to be accomplished mainly under the umbrella of the Junckers Flugzeug- und Motorenwerke AG (JFM), the maker of JU warplanes, which strove to become an industry-dominating cartel along the lines of IG Farben.[10] The planners faced the daunting task of organizing a massive increase over the national production of 5,235 aircraft in 1938.[11] As their conceptual model, Reichsmarshal Hermann Göring and Luftwaffe General Ernst Udet on 29 October 1938 agreed to adopt Opel's proven "American manufacturing methods."[12] Beyond that, the Luftwaffe command devised plans, in the event of a war, to incorporate Opel's Russelsheim factory and the Volkswagen KdF plant in the production of the mid-range JU-88 bomber.[13] Göring toyed with the idea of asking Opel to build an aircraft engine factory in Marburg, but dropped it after the costs were estimated at 40 million RM.[14]

At that point it is unlikely that the Luftwaffe plans were known to General Motors. A look at how GM's top executive in Europe described his activities a few months later, and in the first months of the war, offers a revealing contrast:

> A journey to Europe undertaken in March and April of 1939 to straighten out certain matters with the Nazi authorities of Germany, including the question of rubber for our German-manufactured cars, established a chain of circumstances which led to the strange request in October, 1939, that I try to mediate between Great Britain and Germany for the purpose of halting Hitler's war before it became a world conflagration.[15]

The writer is Jim Mooney, in his memoirs of 1946. He is referring to a 1936 rubber arrangement, adopted by General Motors under pressure from the German government, which was trying to achieve economic autarky under its Four-Year Plan. The U.S. parent company was required to finance in dollars rubber imports for Opel production, and in exchange the costs were liquidated by means of barter transactions and Opel car exports.[16] On his spring 1939 visit to Berlin, Mooney hoped to negotiate a termination of the burdensome rubber arrangement. Mooney discussed with various officials of the Reich his idea of arranging a large gold loan to Germany, possibly through the Bank of International Settlements in Basel. In exchange, Germany would terminate its export subsidies and the raw materials import restrictions under the Four-Year Plan. Beyond that, Mooney hoped that the Reich would grant new peace guarantees.

He went on to London, where he failed to arrange a meeting between the American ambassador to Britain, Joseph Kennedy, and Emil Puhl, the head of the Reichsbank. Later he brought Kennedy to his London hotel apartment for a meeting with Helmuth Wohlthat, Göring's main economic adviser on the Four-Year Plan. Wohlthat enjoyed good connections among German industrialists. His presence in London was revealed the next day by the press, however, and Mooney's gold-for-peace plan went under.[17]

This was the prelude to what Mooney describes in his memoirs as a "strange odyssey" undertaken on his own initiative in October 1939 to March 1940. During these early months of the Second World War, he seems to have employed company resources in carrying the expenses of his activities, and to have recruited at least a half-dozen of his fellow American, British and Dutch European GM executives in arranging meetings with diplomats and in relaying secret messages across war lines. Whether and which of his various interlocutors in Germany, Britain, and the United States regarded him as a private person committed to making peace, or as the head of General Motors's European operations, is an open question. His memoirs leave little doubt about his own perception that his mission could have changed history, and that he was acting on behalf of much more than General Motors, on the contrary: in the service of avoiding a massacre among the nations of the white race.

By the summer of 1939, the Luftwaffe was fighting against the Reich's other military branches in a losing battle for scarce raw materials. Internal analyses of the aircraft boom revealed that any slowdown in warplane production might induce a domino effect on the economy as a whole.[18] Of course, this was true of the guns-over-butter economy in general.

The historian Lutz Budrass describes the psychological subterfuge by which Göring solved the Luftwaffe's supply bottleneck. He arranged a big air show for an audience of one: Hitler. Then, on 22 August, Göring convinced the thrilled Führer to sign an order that effectively tripled resource allocation to the Luftwaffe.[19]

That same day Mooney, according to his memoirs, embarked on a ship from New York to Bremerhaven. He arrived in Berlin on the eve of the march into Poland. He records a depressed mood among the German people at the outbreak of war.

During the next two weeks in Berlin, Mooney conferred "with my business associates in Germany about the status of our properties … about the evacuation of General Motors's non-German personnel, and about the various measures possible for the protection of the corporation's investments within the Reich."[20] At least the first and third points would have involved GM's German counsel, the prominent Berlin lawyer Heinrich Richter*–a pertinacious character who played a pivotal role at Opel during the war years.

---

*Heinrich Richter, vice-president of the American Chamber of Commerce (ACC) in Berlin since the late 1920s, held power of attorney in Germany for various U.S. organizations during the war, including the ACC, the U.S. Catholic Church, the New York Times, the Associated Press, and National City Bank of New York. By his own account, his work for General Motors, which dated back to 1934, was the most time-consuming and politically controversial.[21] He was

Mooney's memoirs unfortunately reveal no details about his business-related discussions or possible meetings with the Luftwaffe or vehicle industry authorities in Berlin in September 1939. "After two weeks in Berlin," Mooney went to his German home in Wiesbaden, "to examine the position of our German automobile plant, the Adam Opel A.G.," located in the neighboring town of Russelsheim. On 21 September he "proceeded to Switzerland and Italy in order to be able to communicate freely with General Motors in New York."[22]

For many of the events at Opel during this crucial period, we are forced to rely on Mooney's postwar memoirs as the sole available source. No minutes of Opel directorate meetings are available, although many memos and letters can be found in German state records and at the Russelsheim town archive and museum. The Opel archives offer only fragmentary evidence on the war. Only a few General Motors documents were available for this study.[23] Still, it is easy to figure out a few of the items on the Opel agenda in September 1939.

The war brought an immediate and total crash in German private car sales. The Wehrmacht requisitioned every private vehicle it came across, if it was suitable for ordnance. Suddenly the carmakers had nothing to do. Millions of German men were drafted. Six thousand of the 22,000 Opel employees were called up in September. By the end of the year the company's personnel had been reduced to 13,000.[24]

The Luftwaffe's plans for placing Opel in the Junckers program were now activated. On 18 September, Göring and his Luftwaffe generals, Udet and Erhard Milch, met with Heinrich Koppenberg, the powerful chief executive of JFM, and General von Schell of the Wehrmacht. Schell was the "Plenipotentiary for the Vehicle Industry in the Four-Year Plan," one of the Reich's several overlapping authorities in the motor vehicles sector. The group agreed that Opel's Brandenburg factory should continue producing the successful Opel Blitz truck for the Wehrmacht, leaving the Russelsheim plant and the remaining 7,000 to 9,000 Opel employees at the disposal of parts production for JFM.[25] Volkswagenwerk would also be pressed into the JFM program.

The latter started out as a losing business, however, as Volkswagenwerk still had little to offer beyond its huge, mostly empty factory space.[26] Opel Russelsheim, by contrast, could not be converted to aircraft assembly, but commanded high tech facilities that were ideal for the production of small and specialized parts, cooling units, and engines. Its process expertise could be passed on to JFM and the other Luftwaffe contractors.

The concrete details of converting Opel's sprawling factory to JU-88 parts production were worked out on 19 September, one day after the brass met in Berlin, at the offices of the southern Hessian regional "Military Economy

---

taken prisoner by the Soviets in late May 1945, a subject of concern in the Mooney-Lochner correspondence after the war. They helped out Richter's wife with packages from the States. According to Bodo Fischer of Opel, Richter was sent to Siberia, where he died.

Inspectorate" for war production and resource allocation: Wehrwirtschafts-inspektion XII in Wiesbaden (henceforth: "Inspectorate XII"). At that meeting Opel was represented by Heinrich Wagner, the production director of the Russelsheim factory.[27] It is unclear what role might have been played in the negotiations by Mooney, who according to his account was in Wiesbaden, or by Cyrus Osborn, the U.S. national whom GM had appointed chief managing officer of the Opel firm.[28] At any rate, immediately after this meeting Russelsheim began converting to war production. Interestingly, on the two days after Mooney says he left for Switzerland, on 22 and 23 September, Opel purchased 10 million RM in German equities, an action approved officially by the General Motors "Policy Committee" on 16 January 1940, and presumably allowed by the Nazi authorities.[29] Whether that decision was forced, opportune, or related to production plans is unknown, although it does not suggest a company looking for an exit.

Thanks to Heinrich Wagner's consummate engineering talents, the conversion from cars to aircraft parts was overseen entirely by the Opel management. Wagner had come a long way since starting as an Opel shopfloor worker in 1922. The Nazis thought him politically unreliable, and he did not join the Party until 1941. But he was good enough as a technician that they were willing to risk the ideological heartburn.

Only external factors caused delays in the conversion.[30] Inspectorate XII entered "constant written and telephone negotiations" with eight other military inspectorates to "bring more machines and materiel" to Russelsheim, according to a report sent to the central inspectorate in Berlin on 25 September 1939.[31] Many companies were reluctant to surrender their machines to Opel, fearing production breaks, a loss of idle workers to the draft, even bankruptcy.

Poland capitulated on 27 September. The Wehrmacht began moving its forces to the Western front, where Hitler ordered the earliest possible offensive.[32] Many of the German generals were reluctant, considering it suicidal. In the meantime there began a "Phony War," with the two sides staring at each other across the Rhine and the Maginot Line, otherwise engaging in naval battles. This was to last more than six months, until the lightning invasions of Denmark and Norway in April 1940, and of the Low Countries and northern France in May 1940–when the concentration of the German armor at a breakpoint sliced through an opposing Anglo-French side who had a similar armored force, but whose tanks were spread out weakly among the infantry like hors d'oeuvres on a platter.

With the Phony War underway, Mooney returned to Wiesbaden in mid-October 1939, and was promptly called to Berlin by Richter. Richter had been contacted by Otto Dietrich, Hitler's press secretary, with a proposal that Mooney mediate negotiations between Germany and Britain, perhaps even informally on behalf of the United States itself. Uncomfortable about the possible legal consequences back home, Mooney first met with his good acquaintance Wohlthat, Göring's adviser, and then Göring himself on 19 October. For that encounter Mooney made sure to put on his Nazi medal, "which had been awarded me in my capacity of President of General Motors Overseas Corporation, and which, with the approval of the U.S. Navy, I had accepted not as a tribute to myself but to our company."[33]

Immediately after meeting Göring, Mooney related the conversation to the AP correspondent in Berlin, Louis Lochner, who typed up extensive notes. Apparently neither Göring nor Mooney mentioned the Luftwaffe or Opel, which was being turned into one of the Luftwaffe's key suppliers. They talked instead of a subject that Mooney addresses often in his memoir, the Asiatic threat:

> Mr. Mooney was impressed with Goering's sincerity in not wanting a war with England and in seeing no reason whatever why France and Germany should come to grips. Also, there was an obviously sincere liking for Americans.... Mr. Mooney put quite bluntly to Goering the question as to whether Germany was ready in principle to unite with the other white races of Europe (meaning of course principally England and France) in stemming the danger of the Asiatics overrunning Europe that lies in Germany's commitments toward Soviet Russia, an essentially Asiatic power (as Hitler himself has said), and Japan. Mr. Mooney hitting straight from the shoulder called Germany's tie-up with these two partners an "unholy alliance."[34]

According to Lochner's notes, Göring "emphatically said YES," protesting that Germany had been forced into the "unholy alliance" by the Western powers. Germany would be happy to make peace if Britain and France accepted it "into their club as a full-fledged member with equal rights." Göring then assured Mooney that solutions could be found for everything, with neutralized Polish and Czech states "enjoying complete cultural and administrative autonomy," increased religious liberty, and "a new start in the Jewish question in Poland.... They are to be given a square deal."[35] In 1946 Mooney, without a trace of irony, could still write: "[Göring] indicated that the Jewish problem would have to run its course, but that its final solution would have to await some more suitable time in the future."[36]

Mooney's memoirs also record his strong impression that Wohlthat and Göring both communicated to him, through gestures and body language, a willingness to sweep Hitler aside, if that was Britain's condition for a peace on Germany's terms, to "retire Herr Hitler to a kind of Valhalla or, as we might say in America, make him Chairman of the Board." However, "I want to emphasize that Dr. Wohlthat actually said none of these things in words that bear any resemblance to mine."[37]

> As I rose to leave, General Goering came around from his side of the huge desk, took hold of my arm and, shaking his finger in my face, said: "Now Mooney, don't get me wrong about this situation. I am asking you, for our government, to go over to see the British and find out what this war is all about. We have read Chamberlain's recent speeches and can't figure out whether he really wants to fight or not ... before we start, I think it is important to find out what we are really fighting for, and whether both sides really intend to fight."

Mooney attempted to fulfill this assignment, but when he went to London the Foreign Office shuttled him around, and finally dismissed him as an unwanted meddler, and his mission as a dangerous ruse. He returned in a circuitous way to Germany, and then spent a few weeks running around Italy and Spain, trying to arrange another appointment with Wohlthat, and getting the U.S. Navy to encode his reports to Washington and his request for a meeting with President Roosevelt.

Meanwhile, the Opel directorate and management convened on 19 December 1939 to discuss the ongoing conversion to war production and sort out their ranks. By then Mooney was back in the United States. According to the list published in the regional Commercial Register of the next day,[38] Osborn, still chief executive, was bumped up to the directorate, where he henceforth served as deputy to Chairman Wilhelm von Opel, the aging son of the company founder. Von Opel had joined the Nazi Party upon its accession to power in 1933.

Von Opel and Osborn, memorandum on the costs of conversion and war production, 7 February 1940:

1. All expenses arising from changes at the factory and its facilities will be charged to the government and repaid fully to Opel.
2. All extraordinary costs arising directly from the new production … will be charged to the government and repaid fully to Opel.
3. All capital investments for new tools, facilities, development costs, etc. will be repaid fully to Opel in cash.
4. At the end of the war Opel will receive full compensation [from the government] for all consumption of warehouse inventories, materials in processing, and investments and other expenses arising in the course of the war.[39]

Heinrich Wagner was designated the new chief executive, leading a management board of six Germans. The new directorate included five American GM executives—Osborn, Sloan, Mooney, Howard and "Pete" Hoglund, of whom however only Osborn and Hoglund, who were residing in Germany, were likely to be present at the meeting of 19 December. Other board members included Albin Madsen, director of the GM plant in Denmark, and a further GM executive from the Netherlands.

There were two German directors besides von Opel. Consul Franz Belitz was an attorney from the influential Dresdner Bank. Carl Lüer, the future "enemy property custodian," was also a Dresdner Bank executive. A professor of economics, Lüer had joined the Nazi Party in 1927 and served as a deputy in Hitler's first Reichstag. He took over the regional chamber of industry and commerce, the Frankfurt Industrie- und Handelskammer (IHK), in 1933. He was first appointed to the Opel directorate in 1935.

The conversion to arms posed no great technical challenge to Opel.[40] Russelsheim however was only first adequately supplied after receiving some machinery evacuated from the potential combat zone of the Saarland. (Still later, Opel received machines plundered from Holland after it was conquered in May 1940.) In February 1940, the plant started building suspensions, suspension frames, cockpits and interior paneling for the JU-88. Much of this work was accomplished on the assembly line, a feat no other German plant had until then achieved.

Mooney's "peace mission" entered its last phase. Mooney had met with President Roosevelt on 22 December, and again on 24 January. Roosevelt seems to have been courteous and noncommittal, holding his own cards close, and allowing Mooney to continue his efforts "under the guise of an ordinary business trip, such as I was in the habit of making."[41]

A few weeks later Mooney and the GM executive William Wachtler traveled to Germany via Italy, meeting Osborn and Richter in Munich on 14 February. Mooney briefed Richter and Osborn on his efforts during a train ride to Berlin. Richter helped him draft a letter to Hitler, requesting an audience. In Berlin, Mooney met with the "affable and courteous" foreign minister, von Ribbentrop, on 29 February, but he was snubbed by Sumner Welles, the official American envoy who was also in Berlin at the time. Their simultaneous presence sowed confusion in the talks, an effect apparently intended by Roosevelt.[42] Mooney finally got to see Hitler on 4 March. At that point the Wehrmacht's planned Western offensive had been delayed by logistical tie-ups, bad weather, and an intelligence failure, but not by a lack of resolve on Hitler's part.[43]

Mooney had met Hitler at least once before, in May 1934, on General Motors business. According to the German notes for that meeting, Mooney was supposed to receive assurances that the Führer would "allow no discrimination against foreign capital invested in legitimate business pursuits in Germany. That also applies, despite the special German interest in advancing the German motor vehicle industry, to the capital of General Motors and similar companies. He naturally expects that German capital abroad is just as secure."[44]

Hitler's promise had not been broken. Opel had been treated like a German company, and in the meantime received plenty of military orders. Of the March 1940 meeting, Mooney's memoirs emphasize that Hitler did not rant or rave but was "very coherent, well analyzed, and very direct." "Suffice it to say that the burden of his talk was that Germany had no war aims, wherefore it was necessary that her adversaries abandon theirs in order to make the restoration of peace possible."[45]

Mooney went on to another amicable discussion at Göring's estate and hunting lodge, Carinhall, where Göring swore he believed in the principles of free trade. Finally, with his mission having got nowhere,[46] Mooney met with the Opel directorate for the last time on 9 March 1940. General Motors was in the process of evacuating its American personnel from Germany, and Mooney himself left soon after:

> It was quite obvious after the failure of my mission … that America would sooner or later be drawn into the world conflict. Accordingly, in 1940 the General Motors Corporation relieved me of my responsibilities for … overseas operations

… and I was made chairman of a small group of directors of the company who were charged with converting the General Motors domestic plants from the production of passenger cars into the manufacture of airplanes, tanks, guns, and ammunition.[47]

Here Jim Mooney also leaves our story. He was active in drumming up opposition to Roosevelt in the presidential campaign of 1940. After the war he became president of the Jeep producer Willys-Overland and wrote up his memoirs, which Lochner edited for publication. When his old associate Bill Wachtler of General Motors read the manuscript, he wrote to Mooney on behalf of himself, Hoglund, and another executive who had been involved in Mooney's actions, Ed Zdunek, the postwar CEO of Opel. They urged him in the strongest terms not to publish:

> [We] were in the picture merely as aids to your main idea, and largely, as far as we were concerned, because we happened to be with General Motors. You called the shots, and whoever happened to be in that corner made the next play … The inclusion of such a large number of General Motors men in the story builds up a very definite tie-in between your plan and General Motors. The average reader, I am sure, could not conceive that all you describe was going on without the knowledge and backing of General Motors. They would not realize that General Motors as such actually was not involved in any way. Finally, in the manner of telling the story, an atmosphere of under-cover goings-on of big business in international politics is definitely created. For all of these reasons I feel that you shouldn't publish the book at all.[48]

According to Lochner's postwar correspondence with Mooney, the prospective publisher, Doubleday, was put off by the concluding third of the book, in which Mooney outlines his vision of international politics and what to do about it. For whatever reason, the manuscript disappeared into the Wisconsin State Archives, and Mooney went into retirement a few years later.

On 12 March 1940 General Motors's New York office granted power of attorney for GM business in Germany to Pete Hoglund.[49] He stayed in Russelsheim for another year, and represented General Motors, the only Opel shareholder, in the functions of owner and general assembly. Hoglund appointed Richter as his deputy in November, granting to Richter the full authority to exercise the same functions, including the power to appoint directors and managers. Hoglund left Germany in February 1941, declaring in a letter to the Reichsbank General Motors's adamant refusal to ever sell Opel, to "never unload—to anyone."[50] Deutsche Bank at the time was deliberating a plan to buy or otherwise get its hands on Opel.

Cyrus Osborn was likely the last American to depart, in the spring of 1941.[51] In any case, by May 1941 no GM Americans were left in Russelsheim. Heinrich Richter thereafter functioned as a one-man general assembly—as the sole and legal representative, in Germany, of all General Motors shareholders.

We shall now turn to events which Hoglund and Osborn may have witnessed during their last year in Russelsheim. On 15 March 1940, following an earlier proposal by General Udet,[52] Berlin ordered Opel to suspend its faltering export-car production and place all capacity at the Luftwaffe's disposal. Opel also began producing shell casings for the navy.[53] By 1941 Russelsheim became the largest supplier of aircraft suspensions to the Luftwaffe. In the period preceding the German declaration of war on the United States, Opel delivered 200 million RM in aircraft parts to Junckers. High profits were derived and dividends, which could no longer be repatriated, were placed in escrow accounts with the Reichsbank, earmarked for payment to General Motors after the war.[54] Opel Brandenburg made about 21,000 units in 1941, more than a third of all new military trucks delivered to the German armed forces that year.[55]

A War Economy without Workers

From the first days of the war Opel's operations lacked reliable sources of natural gas and coal. The labor shortage posed an equally serious problem. With an intensive lobbying effort, the Opel management succeeded in getting a few hundred of the skilled workers who had been drafted by the military in fall 1939 ordered back to Russelsheim later that year. With preparations for JU-88 hydraulics and bombing bay production running full steam, the company needed still more skilled workers, especially machine operators. In Wiesbaden, Inspectorate XII engaged in an unfruitful campaign to attract workers from northern Hesse to jobs at Opel. But at the same time the regional Arbeitsamt (Labor Office) in Mainz bombarded the Opel personnel department with a series of military recruitment lists. One week the Mainz Arbeitsamt demanded another hundred men for the front, a week later two hundred, then four hundred.[56]

Protesting that it was desperately short of labor, Opel called for a suspension of the draft at its Russelsheim factory, especially with regard to skilled workers. In the early months of 1940 the company personnel department exchanged many letters with the Reich Labor Ministry (RAM) in Berlin, the central authority coordinating the regional labor offices. On 2 April 1940 the company posed an ultimatum, claiming it could not guarantee on-time delivery of JU-88 parts unless 7,000 additional workers were assigned to Russelsheim by June at the latest.

The gamble backfired. RAM dispatched a "special commission" to snoop around in Russelsheim. They soon decided that Opel was employing too many skilled workers, and registered 1,350 men as "overcount." Six hundred and seventy of them were drafted immediately in a "combing action." Ironically the RAM commission made use of an internal Opel study of March 1939, titled "Outline of Our Following in the Production Departments." Although that report found that Russelsheim lacked 3,497 "special workers," i.e., trained machine operators, it also concluded that 3,500 of Opel's skilled workers were "not employed on the basis of their qualities or qualifications."

Both groups were missing after the "combing action," and the Opel management knew it was pointless to press the case any further with its antagonists at the Arbeitsamt, who had not and would never issue a decree excluding "special workers" from military service. The company therefore shifted tracks, and made use of good connections to officials at Inspectorate XII in Wiesbaden—especially with the influential Nazi banker, Wilhelm Avieny,* who held a post there. Opel suddenly claimed that its real problem was a lack of *unskilled* laborers. "This shortage has already led to substantial production bottlenecks," the management wrote to Inspectorate XII. "Unskilled workers and others suitable for retraining are not available in sufficient numbers. Women are the only reserve. Getting them involved is extremely important. Soldiers' wives are difficult to attract, since they see no incentive to work, given the high support they receive" from the state. Inspectorate XII agreed, and added: "It is generally an obstacle that the lack of goods to buy undermines the incentive to earn more money."[57]

Missing workers were not the Opel management's only headache. Many of the available ones were also causing problems. In the first year of the war the working day was lengthened repeatedly to make up for the labor shortage, although a wage freeze was imposed at the start of the war. Eleven-hour shifts with a working week of sixty hours became the norm after May 1940. Wages were cut even further via "new" piece-work rates. The first protests followed. On 1 June 1940, the company security forces discovered two wall slogans that had been up in a shop bathroom for hours. "Hitler speaks," one read. "I have abolished the 8-hour day for the German worker, but granted a 12-hour day with lower wages and more work in exchange. That is my Socialism for the Worker." And: "The Opel Worker is hard-working but cowardly, for he does nothing as his wages are robbed." Inspectorate XII interpreted this as a "serious" but "isolated" signal. Given the level of terror that the Nazis had established, even bathroom graffiti was a courageous, almost revolutionary act. A quality controller from the same department was denounced and arrested as the perpetrator, and sentenced to fifteen months imprisonment by the Darmstadt Sondergericht, one of the Nazi "special courts" for political cases.[58]

Gained through exhortations to the "Following" and wage deductions, Opel's output achievements were unstable. To the north, the Rhine-Ruhr mining and industrial regions were bombed by the British Royal Air Force for the first time in June 1940. This caused interruptions in coal deliveries to Russelsheim. Opel fell behind on its production targets. But Paris capitulated

---

*An SS group leader since 1933, chief of staff of Sprenger's *gau*, the militant anti-Semite Wilhelm Avieny had made his reputation by overseeing the Reich's expropriation of all Jewish property in Hesse, called "Aryanization." In his role as a businessman, Avieny was directorate chairman of the Vereinigten Deutschen Metallwerke and head of the regional Bank of Nassau.[59] But the most interesting of his many jobs, from Opel's perspective, was his executive position with the Inspectorate and Armaments Commando XII in Wiesbaden. In that function he was among the men who oversaw, starting in 1941, the delivery of French, Belgian, and Russian prisoners of war to Opel for use as forced laborers.

to the German armies later that month. The Gross-Gerau region surrounding Russelsheim, until then a designated staging area for military operations, was now deemed safe for stationing prisoners of war from the conquered Western countries. Among Opel executives, and among southern Hessian industrialists generally, the nearby presence of this potential labor force was seen as the first glimmer of hope in the wartime labor crisis.

The Army High Command (OKH) oversaw the Reich's network of prisoner-of-war camps, known as Stalag (*Stammlager*). Companies who used prisoners of war as laborers were required to maintain their own separate POW barracks, guarded by company security forces, entailing additional costs. Once OKH started stationing Western prisoners of war in Gross-Gerau, Opel wasted no time in building a prison camp in Russelsheim. The camp was completed in July 1940, whereupon Inspectorate XII arranged to transport 600 French and Belgian prisoners from Stalag Limburg to the "armaments operation" Opel.

The use of POW forced labor at Opel Russelsheim thus began at a time when American executives were still present to witness it. Did they? Later, when the U.S. was at war with Germany, and Hoglund and Osborn were asked by the U.S. military to report on Opel, they mentioned only the following:

> The only foreign workers employed by Opel are a group of 200 to 300 Czechs who were recruited by the German Labor Offices in Czechoslovakia and placed in the Opel Blitz Truck Plant at Brandenburg. These men have proved to be satisfactory productive workers but considerable trouble was experienced because of friction between these Czechs and the German workers. Consequently it has been necessary to keep the Czechs all together in certain departments and it has also been found necessary to erect barracks on the factory grounds to house them.[60]

The French prisoners of war were "paid" according to the uniform practice across the Reich. For each new prisoner Opel was expected each month to pay the Stalag 80 percent of the regional average wage for a German. That amount went down to 60 percent after one and a half years. But as allowed in the Quartering Provisions Law (Quartierleistungsgesetz), Opel deducted a part of its security budget and per diems for lodgings and food from the prisoners' "wages." The Opel finance department negotiated transactions in detail with the Stalag XII accountants in Mannheim. The documents for the years preceding 1943 have been lost, with the exception of a single letter from Opel, dated 28 September 1940, which cites the "increased rationing of cigarettes to the security personnel" as the reason for a deduction in payments to the Stalag.[61] Prisoner working times were ostensibly based on regional standards and physical ability, but "their labor power is to be stretched to the extreme," according to the decisive directive issued jointly by OKH and RAM.[62]

Opel also participated in the Reich's many campaigns to recruit civilian workers from occupied France, Holland, and Belgium, and from Slovakia and Italy. The parallel employment of prisoners of war and of relatively privileged civilian workers was a constant source of friction, as Inspectorate XII reported to Berlin on several occasions. The civilians complained about

What should a prisoner of war cost? In September 1941, Opel's branch in Berlin arranged to make use of a few prisoners of war who were staying at another company. Since the authorities required each workplace to maintain a company-owned camp for POW laborers, Opel Berlin drew up a modest budget proposal for a camp to house about thirty men. This was submitted to Russelsheim.[63] Adam Bangert of the management board wrote back to point out that the food item was overbudgeted:

Prisoners of War

… It should be noted from the start that we are of course fundamentally in favor of your employing prisoners. We also understand that you must see to their lodgings. We are in fact impressed that you were until now able to keep the prisoners who are working for you at the [other] camp. If you cannot set up your own lodgings for them, which would be very expensive, then we would also support your using another company. What we know about the matter suggests that if you take over the lodgings you may in the future be forced to hire only prisoners.

But of absolute importance is that you choose the most cost-effective way. Your proposed budget, for example, does not specify that you must pay the food for the guards; further, that you must provide cigarettes, or that the salary of Herr Litten will be included as a prisoner expense.

What we do not understand at all is how you calculated costs for food rations. To our knowledge the rule is uniform for the entire Reich…. I refer in particular to the [Reich guidelines] on "Remuneration for Prisoners of War" … and request you determine why the Berlin rates differ so much, which is also the reason costs for the prisoners there are far higher than here.

I request that you … above all be guided constantly by the idea that the prisoner must also make his contribution towards reducing the branch's losses, i.e. that the costs for him be kept as l o w a s p o s s i b l e .

their poor lodgings. Having French civilians working alongside French prisoners did not exactly enhance the shop climate. It was difficult to keep civilians and prisoners apart at the factory or after work. Unfortunately, no detailed documentation of the "labor deployment" of *Westarbeiter* at Opel has been found.

Although the number of foreign civilians at Opel remained stable at about 1,000 through mid-1941, turnover was disruptively high. Many of them didn't return from their holidays. A high escape rate was especially a problem at Opel Brandenburg, where over half of the Westarbeiter disappeared during their first three months of deployment. The Potsdam Armaments Commando recorded on 16 June: "Of the group of foreign laborers assigned on 1 September 1940, 58 left legally after their contracts ran out and 219 ran away. Of these, 74 were from the Protectorate [Czechoslovakia], 55 from Belgium, 51 were French…. On 28 Oct. 1940 there was a mass flight of foreign workers."[64] As for the prisoners of war, OKH would transfer whole groups to other companies or to municipalities and farms, wherever the need for them was thought to be more urgent.

Nevertheless, the Opel personnel department seems to have been satisfied on the whole with the new arrivals, especially the foreign "civilian workers" in Russelsheim. Their work morale was "good," Opel wrote to Inspectorate XII on 16 September 1940—even better than among the German workers, who were still complaining about longer working hours and lower wages. Summing up the events of November and December 1940 for Berlin, Inspectorate XII echoed Opel's view that the French and Belgian prisoners of war were working "well." As for the civilian workers, Inspectorate XII evaluated Slovakian civilians as "willing and skillful, assuming the work is not too demanding." Southern Italians were considered "less

---

The United States Strategic Bombing Survey summarized the Russelsheim factory's considerable contribution to the German air war in a 1945 report:

> [1940–1944]
>
> <u>Summary of Aircraft Assemblies Produced</u>
> Percentage of Total German
> Production of These Items
> <u>Produced by Russelsheim</u>
>
> 1. Power Plant Assembly for JU-88 50
>   (Medium Bomber)
> 2. Complete Landing Gear Assembly for JU-88 50
> 3. Rear Landing Gear Assembly for JU-88 50
> 4. Landing Gear Cowl for JU-88 100
> 5. Landing Gear Frame for JU-88 100
> 6. Landing Gear Connecting Strut for ME-109 60
> 7. Rear Landing Gear Assembly for Arado 100
> 8. Landing Gear Assembly for ME-262 80
>   (Jet Propelled)
> 9. Jet for ME-262 . . . .)
> 10. Jet Housing for ME-262 . . . .) 10
> 11. Jet Housing Carrier for ME-262 . . . . .)
> 12. Complete fuselage for JU-88 . . . . –
> 13. Canopy Roof for JU-88 100
> 14. Wing Extension for JU-88, 188 100
> 15. Wing Flap Reinforcement 80
> 16. Complete Wiring Harness for JU-88 75
> 17. Oil Pressure Pump for Junckers Motor 213 30
> 18. Engine Oil Container for ME-109 50
>
> Above information furnished by plant management.

Source: USSBS Munitions Division, "ADAM OPEL (RUSSELSHEIM)," Washington, 1945.

useful, lacking a concept of time." Northern Italians were said to be too particular about food. Those from Lorraine and Belgium were on the whole
seen as "good" workers, but the Dutch were generally too "demanding."[65]

By then the Opel work force numbered 15,000 Germans and non-Germans. Their high productivity, achieved through force, control, and rationalization, was reflected in high output. From March to July 1941,
Russelsheim produced 499 cockpits, 476 pilot canopies and 577 rear
canopies, 326 chassis, 224 A1 radiators, 426 air-charged radiators, 2,785 fuel
tanks, 1,163 A frames, 2,645 A4 radiators, 376 engine housings, 215 engines,
1,015 A4 frames, and 575 oil pumps for warplanes.[66]

Enemy Property and Executive Intrigue

Understanding the conflicts that arose among the Opel management and
directorate after the departure of the GM Americans requires some background information on "enemy property" under Reich law. "Enemy property" should not be confused with "property of the enemies of the people,"
i.e., that belonging to the Jews under the Reich's authority. All of that was
to be confiscated. Rather, enemy property referred to property in the Reich
that belonged to natural or legal nationals of an "enemy state." It was subject to regulations spelled out in a series of decrees issued by the Reich Justice Ministry starting on 15 January 1940.[67] These at first defined enemy
states as France, Great Britain, and the British colonies, but more countries
were added after Germany attacked them. One exception was the area of
Poland under the General Government. This was not "enemy," yet all property there was game for expropriation. Enemy property under Reich law
was thus a kind of due process bubble within a system that was routinely
lawless.[68] The legalistic approach was partly intended to protect German
properties abroad.

Legally independent corporations chartered in Germany were not automatically defined as enemy, even if the share equity was in the possession
of "enemies," as was the case with Opel after 1941. This loophole was left so
as not to disturb trade with neutral countries. Companies like Opel were
instead said to be "under enemy influence," and they were to be placed
under a trusteeship.

A trusteeship was not mandatory. Rather, the decision was made on a
case-by-case basis by a "Reichskommissar for the Treatment of Enemy
Property." The Reichskommissar was formally subordinated to the Ministry of Justice. If he determined that the legal prerequisites for placing a
company in trusteeship obtained, he would file a motion to that effect
with a regional court, and nominate a custodian.[69] In reality, the Reichskommissar answered to the needs of the Four-Year Plan and the Reich
Ministry for Armaments and Munitions. His decisions often as not were
based on a political consensus. What mattered most was the potential effect
on the war economy. If a company was thought to be functioning well, the

custodian was invariably someone proposed by the company, so as not to disrupt its management.

Under the law, the appointment of a custodian suspended the rights of a company's directorate, management board, representatives, and owners. The custodian became the sole legal embodiment of the company.[70] But this was also not mandatory. Just as the Reichskommissar could choose not to impose a trusteeship in the first place, he could also direct the court to limit a custodian's authority. He was free to appoint several custodians, to restrict them to specific functions, and to appoint an additional "advisory council" (*Beirat*) with veto and voting rights.

The Reichskommissar was even free to explicitly deny the "duties of executive office" to the custodian, effectively leaving the old management fully in charge. The mere fact of a trusteeship indicates nothing about whether the Nazi Party or Reich ministries intervened in a company's internal affairs. To determine what really happened, we need to explore the actual events at that company.

In short, thanks to the loopholes a custodian might even be mere window-dressing. This was exactly the case at Opel. The real reasons for the trusteeship are evident in the files of Dr. Johannes Krohn,* a career civil servant who held the post of Reichskommissar starting in October 1941.[71]

SOME OF THE DRAMATIS PERSONAE in the farcical theater that Krohn's meticulous and dry notes document have already been introduced: Göring, Krohn, and Schell among the Reich authorities; Wagner, Richter, Lüer, and Von Opel among the company men. Supporting roles were played by the managers of the Brandenburg Blitz plant. The director there was the *Wehrwirtschaftsführer* Gerd Stieler von Heydekampf, who had also joined the Nazi Party in 1933, and who was appointed to the Opel board in 1936.[72] During the war he served until 1942 as the head inspector of the Armaments Commando (*Rüstungskommando*) based in Potsdam, and thus he had the power to mobilize homefront resources on behalf of his plant. Heydekampf's deputy was the production expert, Heinz Nordhoff. Nordhoff never joined the party.

---

*Johannes Krohn, Ph.D. in Law, born 4 July 1884 in Stettin, died 11 July 1974 in Bad Neuenahr. Krohn studied jurisprudence from 1903 to 1906, and was appointed town councilor of Stassfurt in 1914, before joining the military in the Great War. He moved up through a series of advisory positions at the Labor Ministry in the 1920s and 1930s, culminating with an appointment as a state secretary at RAM in 1933. Owing to differences with the DAF, Krohn transferred to the Wehrmacht in 1939, but was incapacitated by a combat injury in 1940. In 1941 he was appointed "Reichskommissar für die Behandlung feindlichen Vermögens im Reichsjustizministerium." In April 1945 he personally surrendered his files to the Allies in Bavaria, and spent that summer and autumn completing his final "enemy property" reports for the new Military Government, a fairly exceptional action for any Reich official. But if Krohn was a smart and dispassionate man, which he seems to have been, then he might have realized years in advance that Germany was likely to lose the war, in which case the victorious "enemy" would get to closely scrutinize his treatment of their property. After the war, Krohn served as the chairman of the FRG's commercial board of arbitrators from 1948 to 1953.[73]

By the spring of 1941 all of the GM Americans had left Russelsheim. Richter and the German management were on their own. The climate between Germany and the United States changed dramatically during the course of that year. The Reich took pains to avoid tensions with Washington, but America's increasing support for Britain brought nationalist heat to bear on Opel. Anti-American demonstrations broke out in front of the main building in April, prompting "temporary repressions" by the regional Gestapo.[74] Speaking to a June assembly of "the Following," Lüer raised the specter of a "warlike situation with the USA."[75]

At first only among themselves, the Opel executives pondered who should become the company custodian if war broke out with the U.S., as seemed ever more likely. Wagner and his financial officer, Hermann Hansen, traveled to Berlin that spring to discuss Opel's future with officials at the Reich Economics Ministry (RWM). At that time RWM still held some sway over industrial politics, and was known as a hotbed of Nazi ideology to the detriment of economic expedience. Wagner and Hansen also visited the Foreign Office, and the deputy Reichskommissar for enemy property, Sperl. They received multiple assurances that "for well-known reasons, General Motors would deserve very favorable treatment." But they were told that Opel needed to place more stress on its image as a German company. Otherwise "it would be viewed as subject to American influence in the case of a war."[76] To their dismay, Wagner and Hansen heard that a group around General von Schell were devising their own, confidential plans for a trusteeship at Opel.

Germany launched its invasion of the Soviet Union on 22 June 1941. The Wehrmacht's demand for new trucks thereupon grew insatiable. At the same time the "Göring Program," which gave topmost priority to raising warplane production, was approved. Opel was vital to both objectives, and among the various parties concerned with the company it was thought urgent to settle the trusteeship issue in advance of a war with the United States, so as not to risk disrupting production at either Russelsheim or Brandenburg. Two main candidates for custodian emerged. The more prominent was Carl Lüer.* He was backed by his IHK, the RWM, and the influential Dresdner Bank. But his most prominent and loyal sponsor was Jakob Sprenger, the *Gauleiter* (Nazi governor) of Hesse and Nassau. Lüer also enjoyed some support within Opel–most significantly that of Heinrich Richter, the GM counsel.[77]

---

*Carl Lüer, b. 14 Aug. 1897 near Hannover, Professor of Economics, NSDAP member No. 71,637 as of Dec. 1927, member of the SS, NSDAP Reichstag deputy. In 1933 Lüer became president of the IHK Frankfurt and began collecting a number of additional posts with regional and national chambers of commerce. Appointed to the Opel advisory board by GM in 1935, he was made head of the Dresdner Bank Berlin branch in 1938 and designated a *Wehrwirtschaftsführer* on 30 Jan. 1938.[78] Later he was prominent in the creation of the "Gau Chambers of Commerce" (*Gauwirtschaftskammer*), a new lobbying structure aimed at strengthening the say of regional medium-sized companies and restricting the influence of the Armaments Ministry. Lüer started running for president of the regional Gauwirtschaftskammer as soon as its establishment was authorized in April 1942.[79]

Richter and the Opel management board supported Lüer, as they claimed, so as to prevent the appointment of a custodian "foreign to the company." That was a possibility. Göring, his "Industrial Council of the Luftwaffe," and General von Schell all favored Eduard Winter, since 1939 the owner of a parachute factory. With their help, Winter in April 1941 was appointed custodian for General Motors's properties in occupied France and Belgium. His candidacy for the Opel custodian's post, and his support from Göring and Schell, were seen as an affront to the Opel management.

Winter had worked for Opel as a sales executive starting in the early 1930s, and later represented the company at state agencies in Berlin. Rumor held that he started his fortune by defrauding the company. Opel terminated his contract with a high severance payment in the fall of 1939, because, as Lüer wrote: "It would have been impossible to have Herr Winter's personality interfering everywhere during the negotiations over the conversion of the plant to arms production."[80] In short, the real objection to Eduard Winter was not that he was "foreign" to the company. On the contrary, he was all too familiar.

Hoping to turn back Winter and improve Lüer's chances, Richter persuaded Wagner to resign his post as speaker of the management board. Lüer was inscribed as the new chief executive in the Commercial Register of 19 July 1941. Richter later stated to Reichskommissar Krohn that this appointment was approved by the American GM directors in writing, in May 1941, and that this was their last official intervention in affairs at Opel.[81] Lüer was also named director of production at the Russelsheim factory. However, Wagner stayed on as deputy chairman, and as the actual organizer of production.

The Ostarbeiter Deployment

That summer Russelsheim was crawling with dealmakers: high Party functionaries, military commanders, *Wehrwirtschaftsführer*. As part of the "Göring Program," the Reichsmarshal and a staff of his advisers known as the "Industrial Council of the Luftwaffe" wanted to make greater use of the Opel plant, now a proven "war economy operation," in the sensitive task of making propulsion systems for Junckers. Opel was also expected to produce torpedo guns. The Luftwaffe generals Milch and Udet visited the factory on 9 October 1941. They were charmed by the "serendipitous link between German companies and the big series factories in the USA" and duly impressed with the engine repair facilities, the assembly line, and the use of spot welding. Other aircraft plants were still riveting. Marshal Milch conveyed his thanks to the management in a letter of 15 October 1941: "Your example will serve to raise output at other German industrial plants, so that our Wehrmacht will have the weapons it needs to achieve final victory."[82]

The visit by the air force brass signaled a new phase in war production at Opel. Russelsheim was expected to launch series production of engines for the JU-88 in the winter of 1941–1942. As a precondition, it submitted to

Inspectorate XII an application for 6,500 additional laborers. Following the usual bureaucratic to-and-fro, a new "contingent of 750 French prisoners of war" was assigned to Russelsheim on 1 September 1941. An additional 1,000 prisoners were promised for October, with 1,200 to arrive in November. Believing this insufficient, Opel applied for permission to recruit civilian workers in the unoccupied southern part of France, then ruled by the collaborationist Vichy regime.[83] Soon thereafter this plan was postponed in favor of using forced labor from the newly occupied Soviet territories.

A "Decree of the Führer" (*Führererlass*) issued in the early days of the Eastern campaign banned the employment of Russian prisoners of war in Germany. However, with the Reich increasingly hard-pressed to come up with labor, the Wehrmacht High Command (OKW) in August 1941 published an opportunistic reinterpretation of Hitler's order: "The use of Soviet prisoners of war within the borders of the Reich is a necessary evil, and therefore to be kept to a minimum. They may be employed only at workplaces where they can be kept in complete isolation and held in closed columns while working."[84] The Reich leadership officially approved the "Russian deployment" (*Russeneinsatz*) on 31 October 1941.

The new policy endorsed and encouraged the use of Soviet prisoners of war as forced laborers, but required that they be maximally exploited, treated and nourished in the worst possible way, and put to death for the slightest infraction.

Companies and war production inspectorates began preparing for the deployment of Soviet prisoners of war in mid-November 1941. The documents reviewed here do not reveal whether Opel applied for, or was assigned a Soviet POW contingent. The Russelsheim factory was a highly sensitive arms operation, designated "Security Zone A." Opel would have likely avoided using Red Army prisoners in production, but might have employed them in transport or construction outside the factory. The daily war journals of Inspectorate XII note only that most Wiesbaden-area industrialists feared Russian soldiers would engage in sabotage, and therefore wished to avoid taking any at all. Many companies protested that the employment of small labor columns under armed guard was impractical on assembly lines. Inspectorate XII felt compelled to apply "a great deal of persuasion" in convincing some of the companies to accept Soviet prisoners of war.[85]

At any rate, the Reich's hesitant determination to exploit Soviet POW labor proved belated. By the winter of 1941, as many as two million of the Soviet soldiers captured in the first successes of "Operation Barbarossa" had succumbed to the Stalag treatment. Only a few hundred thousand survived past the end of the year.[86]

Deprived thus of most of their prospective new slave labor pool, the Reich authorities began debating in late 1941 whether they should instead "deploy" civilian forced laborers from the occupied territories of the Soviet Union. OKW, RAM and RSHA (the SS central agency overseeing Gestapo, S.D. and police) entered into several months of bureaucratic wrangling.

Reinhard Heydrich, head of RSHA, finally signed the *Ostarbeitererlasse*, a set of decrees authorizing the employment of Soviet civilian forced laborers, on 20 February 1942. On 21 March, Fritz Sauckel was appointed Plenipotentiary for the Labor Deployment (GBA). In this capacity, he oversaw the deportation to Reich territory of millions of people from their homes in Eastern Europe.

The RSHA guidelines on Ostarbeiter warned that Soviet citizens, including Ukrainians, "have lived for years under Bolshevik rule and have been systematically educated as enemies of National Socialist Germany and European culture." The "security requirements" were accordingly draconian. The decrees specified that Ostarbeiter were to be rounded up by force, brought to Germany in sealed boxcars, and kept in isolated barracks surrounded by barbed wire, under the strict guard of the Gestapo and an armed company guard known as *Werkschutz.* For easy identification, Soviet civilians were required to wear a large patch labeled "OST." Latvians and Lithuanians, called "Ostländer" (the Baltic states had been combined into a single Nazi administrative unit known as "Ostland") were supposed to receive slightly more generous treatment. Payment and food rations for Ostarbeiter were set far lower than for Western civilians, but higher than for Soviet prisoners of war.

The first transport of enslaved Soviet civilians to Military District XII (the Wiesbaden inspectorate) arrived in early May 1942. The first factory in the region to set up a "foreigner camp" for Ostarbeiter was Opel Russelsheim. Forty-four wooden barracks were built on the factory grounds along the Main River in May and June 1942. Opel workers dubbed this area "Stalinallee." Not all occupants were Soviet nationals, however. The complex included "an Ostarbeiter camp, a Western countries camp, a Russian women camp, a Czech camp, an Italian camp, a delousing barracks, and a commissary," where company security sold chewing tobacco and cigarettes. The food, cooked at the *Ausländerküche*, was also served in the commissary.[87] The camp administration was subordinated to the company "Social Department" under the Opel executive W. Hildebrandt, and managed on-site by the Opel employee J. Schembs. A multilingual "foreign woman" worked in the camp office, going through the mail received and sent by the foreigners and "reporting all incidents" to the Gestapo.

Unfortunately these reports have never been located, and we are forced to rely on testimonies given after the war in support of defendants at "de-Nazification" proceedings. At his 1949 proceeding, Hildebrandt, a former chief of staff of the Hesse *gau* and an Opel management board member starting in May 1943, claimed that the real authorities in the "Russian camp" were the Gestapo and the agent of Military Counter-Intelligence (*Abwehrbeauftragte*): Major Lachmann from the Gestapo unit in Darmstadt.[88] Rules were set by Gestapo and enforced by German "camp leaders." The "leader" of the "Russian women camp" from July 1943 until its dissolution was Anna Leitschuh. Like all other camp leaders, she was responsible for "order and security."

Not a party member, Leitschuh faced no charges after the war. She testified on behalf of Arthur Liebermann, the former NSDAP-appointed
"Shopfloor Leader" (*Betriebsobmann*) at Opel Russelsheim.[89] In his initial de-
Nazification proceeding, Liebermann had been classified a Nazi activist
("Category 2"). Accused of having hit forced laborers and of abusing them
in a "torture chamber" on the factory grounds, he was sentenced to six years
in an Allied internment camp. Later he appealed for amnesty, and many of
his former "party comrades" appeared to testify. As was not unusual in such
cases, they practically styled him into a resistance fighter. In her testimony,
Leitschuh claimed that violations against camp rules were not punished by
company employees, but directly by the Gestapo.

The company Werkschutz performed the footwork of keeping foreign
workers, forced laborers, and prisoners of war in line, as was generally the
case at German industrial plants during the war. A unit of SS members within
Opel company security was headed by the "Hauptsturmführer" Heinz Riller,
a former police major. He reportedly sent several people to KZ Osthofen
near Worms.[90] (Riller was arrested by the Gestapo for unknown reasons in
mid-1943, and died a few days later under mysterious circumstances.)

In the documents still available to researchers, the first hints of "difficulties" in the deployment of "Ostarbeiter" at Opel are contained in the daily
journal of Inspectorate XII for 9 July 1942:

> At the Adam Opel AG camp for Russian civilian workers the serving of food was
> suddenly refused. The investigation found that among other reasons the cause
> was a low food ration compared to the Latvians, whom the Russians have always
> viewed as their inferiors. The Latvians enjoy every freedom, and the Russians do
> not understand why they get such far lower food rations, given their far superior
> work performance in comparison to the Ostländer, as Opel itself acknowledges.
> Opel AG saw to it that calm was restored through a partial equalization of the
> portions and extra rations. The Gestapo was informed of the incidents.[91]

The first and only known Opel report on "the deployment of foreign laborers" in Russelsheim, unfortunately undated, was written around this time,
possibly in reaction to the Gestapo's investigation of the above incident. The
Opel memo gives a precise listing of foreign groups. Soviet prisoners of war
are not mentioned, suggesting that none were employed in production,
though they may have been used elsewhere. The Luftwaffe contact office at
Inspectorate XII submitted Opel's report to Berlin on 10 September 1942.[92]
Because such documents are rare, I shall quote it almost in full:

> Employed are   502 Soviet Russian male civilians
>   146 Soviet Russian female civilians
>   1539 French prisoners of war and
>   262 other foreign civilian workers

> It seems the Soviet laborers who came voluntarily were recruited with promises
> that cannot be fulfilled under the reigning regulations. This is a psychological
> mistake, which undermines trust and the will to perform. Experiences with the

Soviet Russian male and female civilian workers vary greatly. The industrial worker is very skilled, willing, and diligent, his capabilities and qualifications may on average be described as quite good; the will to work is at approximately 70 to 80 percent. The Soviet Russian farm worker is less suitable for industrial work since he yearns always for work in the country and for that reason tends to desire escape.

The health situation is unsatisfactory because many of the laborers arrive here sick with tuberculosis and nervous and venereal diseases, while the rest have been weakened by the food provided until now. A thorough medical examination of the laborers before transport to the Reich would save on transport costs and improve the food situation through less superfluous mouths to feed. We have succeeded in reducing the average sick rate to 5% at this time. But many arrived with lice and nits (122 of 125 women had lice).

The foreign workers usually arrive without shoes, underwear, or adequate clothing. Protective work outfits are urgently needed for reasons of safety and production, especially given that winter is imminent. Unfortunately that is not possible, as the collection of old clothes and rags did not go well. If the people are not clothed in keeping with requirements then there will be more sick and useless mouths to feed than can be justified given the food situation.

The Lithuanians and Latvians entirely lack discipline and are neither diligent nor particularly skilled in their work. They take to drink, are unfriendly among themselves, and tend to rowdiness and games of chance. The will to perform among the Ostländer is low, 60% at the highest. By no means do these workers deserve the generosity that is granted to them, they are a burden on the climate, and especially the Soviet Russian workers cannot understand why these inferior workers—who in the eyes of the Soviet Russian laborers are even worse than Jews—are receiving preferential treatment.

The work output of the French prisoners of war was initially good but has slackened over the course of time and can now be described on average as adequate at best. The drop in performance is attributable mainly to the exaggerated spiritual supervision, which he [the French worker] does not understand and views as a weakness. It is especially damaging that the French receive packages from home with goods that are scarce here, such as chocolate, candies, dates and cigarettes. They use these goods to bribe members of the German Following. Our German comrade-in-labor is disturbed to see the French eating rare goods completely unavailable to him. For his part, the French prisoner of war suffers because the French civilians who work with him may move about freely, but he, as a prisoner of war, is subject to limitations. He says: "As a soldier I took my own skin to market, and these shirkers here now run around freely with preferential treatment." It would therefore be better not to employ prisoners of war and civilian workers in the same operation. After a removal of the chronically sick the sick rate is now running at 2–2.5%.

The French civilian workers deployed at Opel are generally not in a fully usable condition (*Einsatzbereit*). Most of them are people whose labor-power (*Arbeitskraft*) is already very used-up. Their work output leaves a great deal to be desired, since they are incapable of the work rhythm that is self-evident at Opel. Their will to perform is at about 75–80%.

From Enemy Property to Self-Managed Industry

Carl Lüer had an appointment in Berlin as a supplicant to Reichskommissar Krohn on 8 December 1941.[93] The news that day would have been filled with reports of the Japanese attack on Pearl Harbor. As the chief executive of Opel, Lüer presented himself as the logical choice for company custodian, and tried to discredit his opponent, Eduard Winter. But during his brief period in charge, Lüer's incompetence, shrill style, and machinations with the SS had so dismayed his fellow executives that they were ready to support any alternative, even Winter.

Three days later, Hitler declared war on the United States. Richter now lobbied against any kind of trusteeship. On 7 January he sent a lengthy memo to Krohn, invoking the loopholes in the enemy property decrees, hoping to buy time. Richter pointed out that the legal definition of "enemy" had not yet been extended to cover the United States. He claimed General Motors "by its basic conviction" had never contradicted the policies of the Reich. He recalled Mooney's March 1940 visit to Hitler and "services and efforts during this war, as known to the Reichsmarshal and to the Foreign Minister." Most importantly, Richter argued that Opel's impressive production achievements obviated the need for a trusteeship. As a compromise, he offered to use his powers as the "general assembly" of Opel shareholders to officially purge the directorate of "the Americans," who were still nominally members, if only "for reasons of courtesy."[94]

Winter paid his own, rather enigmatic visit to Krohn on 10 January 1942. He presented himself as a long-standing good friend and pupil of the current GM president, William Knudsen, the man who was now mobilizing the U.S. company for the war, and even stated that General Motors bought Opel on his suggestion. Yet Winter also claimed he was the right candidate to oversee Opel's expropriation back to German ownership, under the aegis of Göring and Schell. Winter did not neglect to mention Richter's associations with a Jewish lawyer, and claimed Richter had called General Motors from Switzerland to warn them of an impending expropriation, at which point Richter supposedly received authorization to block it any way he could.[95]

Krohn, given these three proposals, was reluctant to impose a trusteeship on Opel. He feared American retaliation on German capital in the United States. Krohn tried to influence Göring and Schell accordingly. But their concerns were of a different magnitude. The German advance on Moscow had been halted by the Soviet counteroffensive of 6 December 1941. Badly overextended, the Wehrmacht barely avoided a complete dissolution of its defensive line. Thousands of vehicles were still being lost to the Red Army. Making up for this devastating loss of mobility would require unprecedented rises in production. Göring and Schell therefore clamored for an immediate trusteeship, naively believing it would give them the power to boost production at Opel.

The Party was loyal to its old-guard comrade, Lüer. Gauleiter Sprenger was especially insistent in endorsing Lüer to Göring, but Göring thought "the former tutor" Lüer was "pathetically clueless." After meeting with Schell on 13 January, Göring tried to bully through Winter's appointment. He conveyed an "apodictic order" to RWM, naming Winter the custodian. Göring singled out Sprenger for extra abuse: "If that's not to the Gauleiter's taste, then he should see to it that he gets lost." Meanwhile, rumors accusing Winter of corruption were circulating among SS circles, conceivably at Lüer's behest. Göring dismissed these. Even if Winter had "dirt to hide, he must be appointed, because the most important issue is that of productivity."[96]

Despite these strong words there was no legal basis for imposing a trusteeship on Opel in January 1942. Neither Göring nor Schell seemed to care about the legal clothing for their political decision. Krohn, however, demanded at least an official "Decision of the Führer" (*Führerentscheid*). Accepting Göring's order would set a precedent circumventing his authority as Reichskommissar.

Richter meanwhile feared that Lüer was out to help the SS "get their hands on" Opel. Richter and Wagner accused Lüer of currying support with the high SS official Hans Jüttner, and of cultivating relations at SS-WVHA, the agency running the concentration camps.[97] Lüer stoked their fears by raising doubts about GM's ownership of Opel.[98] Richter protested to the Reichskommissar: "Better to have Winter as the custodian than a candidate of the SS." He called for Lüer's "honorable return to the Dresdner Bank," or perhaps an appointment to a post with the Wehrmacht.[99]

Göring was undeterred, and pressed Krohn to appoint Winter. Krohn stonewalled. Lawyers from the Four-Year Plan agency stepped in to pacify the situation. They knowingly misinterpreted Göring's command as a desire to have Winter appointed custodian *after* the Enemy Property Decree was extended to cover American properties. This bought time for everyone—during which Schell fell out of favor with Hitler.

In the following months, up to late March 1942, Lüer failed to tame "the influence of the Gestapo at the plant," or to prevent "friction between the Gestapo and the DAF." Finance Director Hansen was arrested by the Gestapo. Lüer did not intervene. Hansen was released, but he and an assistant were removed from their posts "to satisfy the Gestapo," according to Richter, who described the two men as indispensable.[100] With the enemy property question temporarily on ice, the intrigues turned to the naming of replacement directors for the Americans. Lüer, von Opel and Gauleiter Sprenger all forwarded their own nominations of friends, party members and business associates. Sprenger favored the banker Avieny.

Richter opposed all of the nominations. With Krohn's explicit approval, he convened himself as the "general assembly" of General Motors on 31 March, "voted out" the GM Americans, and "voted in" the rest of the old board members: von Opel, Belitz, and the Danish GM executive Madsen. He also elected a new director: Heinrich Richter. Then he wrote a letter to his now fellow board members and Professor Lüer, to inform them of the results.[101] Richter therein proposed an additional advisory council to include

Reichskommissar Krohn, and indicated willingness to accept a limited trusteeship, assuming authority in production remained with Wagner.

Advanced in April 1942, Richter's gambit of a status quo directorate was in conspicuous harmony with the new trend in the war economy. The architect Albert Speer, long one of the key functionaries in the Nazi economy, took over the Reich Ministry for Armaments and Munitions after the death of Fritz Todt in a plane crash on 8 February 1942. Under Speer's direction, Armaments rapidly achieved the first real centralization of authorities in German industry, and consolidated its hold over the economy of occupied Europe. The ministry was renamed to cover "Armaments and War Production." Speer instituted the principle of industrial self-management,[102] under which manufacturers were granted operational autonomy in meeting the Reich's output goals.

Lüer and Richter openly attacked each other in the weeks that followed. Gauleiter Sprenger and the Gauleiter of the Mark of Brandenburg again demanded Lüer's immediate appointment as custodian, and called for the suspension of Richter's new directorate. But they discovered that Göring had abandoned the idea of a trusteeship altogether. The Reichsmarshal quietly made it known that it was time to "finally stop with the forced measures at Opel."[103]

Göring's sudden circumspection was related to the ongoing restructuring of the German war economy. The Blitzkrieg was history. The material losses of the failed winter offensive of 1941 had been tallied up, including: 31,100 Wehrmacht trucks destroyed or lost to the Soviets. That was equivalent to over half of all Reich truck output in 1941.[104] Without a radical boost in vehicle and arms production, the planned summer 1942 offensive was doomed. In the crisis, Göring's command over the economy as the guardian of the Four-Year Plan was restricted. Real power shifted to Speer.

During the next two years Speer oversaw a "miraculous" expansion of the German "total war" economy, until then thought already to be operating at maximum capacity. Vehicle production, for example, almost doubled from 1941 to 1943, although the numbers still proved laughable compared to Allied and especially U.S. output. Aircraft production was raised to 40,000 planes in 1944. The achievement was partly thanks to Speer's relative sophistication in the application of force. He took firm charge of the labor market, working closely with the Sauckel slave recruitment program, and saw to it that restrictions on using "inferior" foreign labor in Germany were further loosened. For the use of slave labor, especially, he displayed convincing regret at the main Nuremberg war crimes trial in 1946, and unlike most of the defendants Speer was sentenced not to death but to twenty years imprisonment, which he survived.

Speer's reorganization of German industry was led by "organs of self-management." In his view, industrialists knew how to manage and rationalize their own operations far better than military officers or ministry bureaucrats. He gave firms a financial incentive to raise efficiency by changing the ministry's pricing system from cost-plus to fixed-rate, leaving implementation to the companies. Under a merit system, the "best operations" among arms makers were expected to transfer their production expertise to the less efficient. The inefficient could be compelled to place their plants at the disposal of the "best." This was meant to streamline the multitude of competing models with non-standard spare parts. Industrialists from each sector of production were organized into a network of "main committees" of end-producers and subordinate "rings" that included suppliers, a structure later coordinated by Speer's Central Planning Board. The Main Vehicles Committee and the Main Airframes Committee, relatively inconspicuous bodies established earlier under Todt, were given new life and granted sweeping authorities in April 1942. Opel, now with improved status as one of the "best" operations, sat on both committees and was represented by its production experts, Wagner and Nordhoff.

The rise of the Main Vehicles Committee put an end to the "Plenipotentiary of the Vehicle Industry," General Schell, who lost all influence by June 1942. But as one independent meddler fell, another seemed to rise in his place. The concentration of authority in the technocratic Committee was complicated by the growing influence of the former car salesman, Jakob Werlin, who was appointed the Führer's "General Inspector for the Vehicle Industry" in January 1942. Werlin was also an SS officer. His new mandate as General Inspector in 1942 was technically limited to organizing repair and maintenance centers in occupied Eastern Europe. But he was cunning, and he interfered with the Main Vehicles Committee and the "Four-Year Plan," devising his own, half-baked schemes.

Under the aegis of the industrialists at the "Speer Ministry," as Krohn's notes attest, a trusteeship for Opel came to be viewed as an annoying but unavoidable evil, with the purely cosmetic function of draping a German image over an American company. Having plant directors who were able and ready to teach American series production procedures to Opel's German competitors was of far greater importance than keeping reliable Party comrades at the helm. The Reich needed rationalization experts, men authorized to step up war production with imaginative steps of their own initiative. Even at a hardline company like Daimler-Benz, Wilhelm Haspel, a technocrat who was not a Party member, in July 1942 took over the management board after the death of the chief executive and SS officer Wilhelm Kissel.[105] A similar development at Opel was indicated by the growing influence of Heinrich Wagner.

American property was legally defined as "enemy" on 9 April 1942. For Ford Werke, where there were no serious conflicts among the managers, Armaments asked Krohn to nominate as custodian the chief executive, Robert Schmidt, which Krohn duly did on 9 May 1942. The situation at Opel was complicated, and Armaments explicitly declined to recommend a custodian. Göring kept up his half-hearted support for Winter, while Lüer was now rallying a broad alliance of true believers in the Party, DAF, Gestapo, SS, and RWM. Werlin suddenly entered the fray in April 1942, demanding Lüer's appointment in light of "his honorable service to the

Movement."[106] Göring admonished him, and Werlin shut up as suddenly as he had spoken out. Richter and most of the Opel management held fast to the idea of no trusteeship, or of a limited custodian.

Armaments remained aloof from this pointless debate. Speer wanted only to raise output and turn the Opel Blitz into the basic type for all three-ton military vehicles. While a limited custodian was no obstacle to that, he considered it far more vital to establish an effective partnership with Opel's production experts on the Main Vehicles Committee: Wagner and Nordhoff.

Raising Production? A Blitz License for Daimler-Benz

The Opel Blitz had proven extremely useful on the front. Opel Brandenburg made 50,000 Blitz trucks in the three years from 1939 to 1942, covering 35 percent of three-ton truck production. Blitz models were often equipped with four-wheel drive. That was a novelty, and an advantage in the muddy Russian steppes or the deserts of North Africa. Daimler-Benz, Opel's main competitor alongside Ford, had a well-equipped truck factory in Mannheim, but was far less efficient in production. The Daimler diesels had performed poorly in combat conditions.

The Main Vehicles Committee and the Four-Year Plan administrators were therefore pleased at Opel's usual expressions of readiness to transfer its technical expertise to other truck producers. But they were reluctant to let an American company grow through the armaments boom. Although Opel held higher cash reserves than practically any other firm in Germany,[107] it had been barred from new investment since late 1939. Most recently, Opel had submitted a renewed application for expansion at Brandenburg in January 1942. Citing fallow capacity at other plants, Schell turned it down. The truck losses in Russia and production problems at Daimler, Borgward and Magirus forced a reevaluation, and softened the anti-Opel sentiments at the Armaments Ministry and RWM.

In this situation Lüer, ever the university economist, saw an opportunity to polish his image and disprove Göring's assertion that he had no idea of practical business management. On 21 February 1942, with General Schell on his way down and out, Jakob Werlin asked Lüer to re-submit the rejected expansion plans. Four weeks later, Werlin and Lüer entered into official negotiations, ignoring Opel's directorate and management. In a memorandum to Werlin, Lüer claimed an immediate expansion at Brandenburg could achieve a three-fold increase, from 2,000 to 6,000 trucks per month.[108] Perhaps this was the point when an impressed Werlin adopted Lüer's candidacy for custodian.

Historians would later mistake Lüer's fantasies for an official Opel statement.[109] That is not the case. Lüer's proposals were backed by Hitler, who at Werlin's urging on 10 May 1942 approved the plant expansion and a rise in Blitz production to 6,000 units a month.[110] But the Opel directorate, convening in Russelsheim one day later, firmly rejected the Brandenburg expansion as infeasible. Wagner, von Heydekampf, and Nordhoff all argued that Brandenburg had barely enough labor and raw material supply to maintain current production levels. Lüer ignored them, and kept spinning his case with Werlin. Hoping to ease their reliance on Hitler, Lüer and Werlin made use of their connections to the SS. Werlin told Lüer on 13 May 1942 that he had "spoken with the Reichsführer SS Himmler at the Führer's request, since the SS is especially well-placed for providing assistance in the expansion of Brandenburg,"[111] obviously as a source of unlimited KZ slave labor. Werlin was overestimating his influence with Hitler and, worse, had failed to clear his plans with Armaments.

On the same day, at Führer Headquarters, Speer told Hitler that Brandenburg was too vulnerable to bombing. They decided Opel should move into a large abandoned train-car factory in Riga. Contrary to the standard Reich practice of subsidizing operations in occupied Eastern Europe, they expected Opel to finance (and own) this new plant.[112] Accompanied by an official from the Speer ministry, Wagner and Nordhoff traveled to view the Riga site. They rejected it, however, for reasons unknown to me. The project was postponed, although the idea of building a new factory "in the East" was not given up.[113]

After its rejection of Riga, Opel needed to move quickly. After all, the Führer said he wanted 6,000 trucks a month. Lüer again saw an opportunity to redeem his battered image with Speer and Göring.[114] To the disgust of the other Opel executives, he declared that an expansion of Brandenburg output to 6,000 trucks a month was possible, assuming "additional labor" of the kind mustered by the SS. Lüer's was the only concrete proposal for immediate expansion in May 1942, and it had been rejected by a majority of both Opel boards. When it became known on 22 May that "the plans of the SS to take over Opel have taken on a palpable form"[115] and that Lüer might become the custodian of an SS-run factory, von Heydekampf resigned his board seat. Wagner went on the warpath.

Throughout the war years, Richter and Wagner were tenacious in resisting SS influence. Were Wagner's animosities directed more against the SS, or against Lüer personally? Perhaps he simply saw the impossibility of tripling production, for rather elementary reasons. Shortages in fuel and raw materials, especially rubber, were still dire. Opel did not have enough master craftsmen or fitters. Even with total support from the state, Wagner saw no chance of fulfilling Lüer's plans.

But perhaps Wagner simply didn't want to work with the SS. According to the available evidence, Opel was the only large German vehicle producer not to employ KZ camp prisoners in the period that followed, at either of its two production plants.[116] The company's tradition was conservative, and not at all anti-Semitic. Opel's forced laborers, both prisoners of war and civilians, were guarded by company Werkschutz. Concentration camp prisoners were guarded by SS henchmen. Their presence might have intensified the latent labor conflicts at the Russelsheim factory. Wagner may have also feared that a flood of unskilled and semi-skilled slave laborers, who were all in extremely bad shape, would irreparably damage Opel's productivity. Despite the highly rationalized production process, the proportion of skilled laborers at Opel remained higher than at other automotive companies, well into the 1940s.[117]

Whatever their motivations, immediately after the SS plans became known the Opel executives set course for what historian Karl Heinz Roth called one of "the most important licensing agreements in arms production in the Third Reich."[118] In late May 1942, Wagner visited his old buddy Gottlieb Paulus, director of production at the Daimler-Benz factory in Mannheim, to discuss the idea of Daimler building the Opel Blitz on license. Wagner did not inform the other Opel executives in advance, and also ignored Richter, but surely acted in collusion with Speer.

Paulus had run the Opel Russelsheim truck department in the mid-1930s. He and Wagner knew each other well. Their talks on a possible Blitz license hardly took place in a vacuum. Speer had placed "Type Concentration in Truck Production" on the agenda for the upcoming meeting of the Main Vehicles Committee. Wagner probably thought the fastest and cheapest way to fulfill Hitler's wish for 6,000 Blitz trucks a month would be if Daimler-Benz took up licensed production. This was not without precedent. "Type concentration" by licensed production was a classic rationalization strategy, dating back to the First World War. In the 1920s, many economists had advocated it as the cure for "industrial particularism." Opel had produced aircraft engines under license from BMW during the Great War, and passenger-car components for other General Motors units starting in the early 1930s.

Surprising the other Opel and Daimler executives, Wagner and Paulus revealed their plans of an Opel Blitz license for Daimler-Benz at the Main Vehicles Committee meeting of 27 May 1942. Speer thereupon raised the production goal to 9,000 units a month and recommended that Borgward and Magirus join a "production circle" of licensed Blitz makers. The Committee requested written positions from all of the companies in advance of its next meeting, scheduled for 22 June 1942. Nordhoff and Richter hastily wrote a memorandum of approval and submitted it to Speer, without waiting for an official vote of the Opel executives. Although still lacking a proper contract, the Daimler management board voted in favor of licensed production on 3 June, against Chairman Kissel's objections that Speer was intruding on his turf.[119] The other Daimler executives sensed an opportunity to compensate for their failures in the truck segment and pick up some American organization and process methods. Best of all, Daimler would be supplied with American-made machine tools as part of the deal.[120]

The Main Vehicles Committee met again at the Speer ministry on 22 June 1942. Top of the agenda: Who should build what quantities of Opel Blitz? Speer refused to modify his goal of 9,000 units a month. Daimler claimed it could build 2,000 to 2,500, Borgward intended to add 2,000. Magirus passed, and wanted to pull out of truck production altogether. Ford Werke had not yet decided, but claimed it was prepared to build its arch competitor's vehicles under license. How to cover the remaining 3,000 units per month? Speer revived his plans for a new plant "somewhere in the East," "which also would be highly desirable for political reasons."[121]

The powerless Schell was asked to put his signature under the official licensing decree on 25 June 1942. In the ensuing negotiations, Opel was represented by Wagner, Otto Jacob (a board member specializing in patent issues), Nordhoff, and, on occasion, Lüer. Wagner and Jacob signed the contract on 12 and 17 August, respectively. Opel received a one-time licensing fee of 800,000 RM from Daimler, plus 120 RM per vehicle produced under the license, however excepting those sold to the main customers: the Wehrmacht and the Waffen-SS.[122]

We shall note only that the production launch at Daimler was delayed until August 1944, and that Daimler made a maximum of 2,500 Opel Blitz three-ton vehicles through February 1945.[123] The companies of the Main Vehicles Committee were worried that licensing fees would raise their costs, Armaments that it might raise the price on Wehrmacht vehicles. Borgward pulled out in late August. Ford insisted on building its own three-ton and 4.5-ton vehicles, the Maultier, and in mid-1942 forced the Committee to agree. On 6 August 1944, the day that Opel Brandenburg was devastated in an Allied bombing raid, it was still the only factory that had ever produced an Opel Blitz: 18,262 units in 1942, 23,232 in 1943, and 16,146 in the first three quarters of 1944.[124]

A Custodian Is Appointed

In May 1942 Gauleiter Sprenger received word from Werlin that Armaments was considering proposing Heinrich Wagner as custodian of Opel, and that Göring had even invited Wagner to an interview in Berlin. Sprenger immediately launched a political attack on Wagner, accusing him of ideological anemia in a memorandum of 15 May 1942. Wagner had only joined the Party the year before, and he was mistrusted by many Nazis at Opel and in the Party. Admitting Wagner's competence as technician, Sprenger criticized him for "following liberal thinking" in the organization of production, and for granting preference to employees "without any connection to the Movement." Sprenger recalled that it took his own "personal effort" to put down the 1936 strike among the Opel "Following, which was utterly contaminated by Marxism." After the strike, in Sprenger's version, he and Lüer toiled for a very long time to correct the "deplorable state of affairs [at Opel], which had arisen over years." Appointing Wagner custodian would be a "direct and intolerable blow" to the Party, and Sprenger declined any responsibility for the "political consequences." "Among the Opel Following and the population of the entire region, Party Comrade Lüer is seen as a leading exponent of the Party and as the sole guarantor against a repetition of these earlier political difficulties at the Opel plants. Whereas Herr Wagner bears no mean responsibility for those troubles."[125] Sprenger was so disgusted by the pragmatism in

Berlin that he even offered himself as the custodian, just in case Göring was rejecting Lüer for personal reasons.

On 16 May 1942 the Opel directorate approved an investment of forty to 50 million RM for a factory to be built somewhere in the occupied East. Wagner's cooperation on that and on the licensing agreement with Daimler made a trusteeship superfluous. The company's efforts to intensify truck and aircraft parts production had obviated the argument that a trusteeship was the only way to raise output. The executives were being "pragmatic" in all things.[126] They believed Germany had stumbled into war with the United States only because of the Axis alliance with Japan, and saw no ideological necessity for placing American property in trusteeship. Only the Party, most of all Sprenger, continued to pursue anti-Americanism as a faith, and viewed a trusteeship of the largest "enemy property" as a symbol of the New Order.

The New Order was obsolete, and Göring believed he could swipe Sprenger away. In apparent harmony with Speer and the slogan of "self-management," Göring informed Sprenger "confidentially" on 29 May 1942 that he would "refrain from appointing any custodian for Opel," and instead ask for Wagner as chief executive. Lüer would be bumped up to the directorate. Göring called upon Sprenger to cease his resistance, invoking National Socialist discipline.[127] After a talk with Krohn on 13 June, Göring ordered Lüer to step down at Opel, and Wagner to resume official control of the company on 1 July 1942.[128]

Since Göring was implementing the line advocated by Richter, one might expect that Richter in particular was satisfied. Far from it. Richter on 7 July instead protested to Krohn that no law authorized Göring to tell a company whom to choose as its chief executive.[129] Richter, Lüer's harshest critic in the preceding months–he had described Lüer's activities as "malheur" just eight days before–suddenly championed Lüer's cause. He argued that demotion would insult Lüer, and that the Party would not accept his dismantling. He pleaded for having Wagner and Lüer take up the management of the company as equal partners. That would require a supervising authority to "mediate as necessary, but also intervene and decide."[130] As Sprenger had done one month before, Richter offered to take over the custodian's post himself.[131]

Suddenly everyone wanted to be custodian. Krohn once again shared Richter's line, and pleaded for the establishment of an advisory council, or for his own appointment to the Opel directorate. Sprenger made it known that he would not even discuss Wagner as chief executive. Wagner was ready to take over, but would not accept Lüer as an executive director. He claimed to have 95 percent of the personnel behind him, and that "at most 5 percent" supported Lüer.[132] Wagner could live with Lüer as director of finance. Richter vetoed that as inadmissible for legal reasons.

Wilhelm von Opel could not conceal "a certain pleasure in the developments."[133] He called for a meeting of the directorate on 24 July 1942 to sanction Göring's order through a formal vote.

Still the game was not lost for Lüer. He made the maximum use of his pull within Hessian business circles at IHK and in the new "Gau Chambers of Commerce," then in formation. RWM asked Göring to revoke his latest order. Göring was now in a dilemma. Speer favored Wagner, but Göring could not afford to snub the interests behind Lüer. Looking for a compromise, he invited Lüer to Berlin for their first meeting, on 21 July 1942. The two must have hit it off well. They promptly blamed all past "misunderstandings" on Schell. Göring claimed he could not reverse his decision, but he could "rehabilitate" Lüer.[134] One day before the Opel directorate meeting of 24 July, Göring telegraphed Russelsheim to postpone discussion on "returning Lüer to the directorate" until such time as "a contrary order is given."[135]

Wagner was voted chief executive, but the decision was neither announced nor published in the Commercial Register. Göring, who was now also getting fire for his decision from the indignant leader of the DAF, Robert Ley, invited Wagner to Berlin to sift through the alternatives. They agreed that Lüer and Wagner should sit down and come up with a solution that would diminish neither Wagner's authority nor Lüer's reputation. In other words, the final decision was passed back to Opel.

The two rivals cut through their Gordian knot in tandem. Early in August, Wagner and Lüer agreed to have Opel go into trusteeship under Lüer as enemy property custodian, but with the stipulation that Lüer was barred from impinging in any way upon Wagner's authority as the new chief executive. One of Göring's personal advisors was blunter in describing the cosmetic nature of the agreement: "The appointment of Professor Lüer as custodian is intended solely to avoid damage to his public reputation through the appointment of Wagner as general director."[136] On 31 October 1942, Göring ordered Krohn to initiate legal implementation of the Lüer-Wagner compromise. By a ruling of the Darmstadt court, the first two points of Göring's order passed into Reich law on 25 November 1942.[137] Point 1 suspended the Opel directorate and made Lüer custodian. Point 2 read: "The management board of the company retains its full authorities. The establishment of the trusteeship shall in no way be allowed to hinder the management board in the performance of its tasks, above all in that of raising production."[138]

Thus did Opel go into trusteeship, two weeks short of a year after the German declaration of war on the United States. The weight of the evidence contradicts the legend, upheld by Opel and General Motors, that the trusteeship was a repression imposed by anti-American Nazis. On the contrary, its final form was determined by internal deliberations at Opel. Lüer was not an outside autocrat but a GM-appointed directorate member since 1935, and his appointment to Custodian came with Richter's blessing. Custodian Lüer was not the legal representative of the company, and bound de facto and de jure to uphold the will of the management board. According to the ruling: "The Custodian is not authorized to represent the Company."[139] In the company's operational hierarchy, Lüer was demoted to a deputy director under Wagner, and he left that post in April 1943. He then lost any remaining influence as custodian to the "advisory council" appointed by Krohn, which was authorized to outvote Lüer, and which first met in May 1943.

The appointment of the advisory council involved a new and protracted round of bitter personal conflicts, much like those that preceded Lüer's appointment as custodian, which we need not go into here. The only legal difference between the old directorate and the new council was the latter's duty to cooperate with the Reichskommissar. Richter was on it, representing General Motors. The chairman was the banker Avieny, the favorite of RWM and the Party. Wilhelm von Opel was his deputy, against Sprenger's wishes, but with Lüer's support. Belitz got in, against the will of RWM, but with the support of Wagner and Richter.

The other three members were war industry big shots. Fritz teer Meer was a management board and "central committee" member of IG Farben. William Werner, who helped initiate the industrial self-management concept at Armaments and headed Speer's "Main Engines Committee," was with Junckers and Auto Union. Walter Schieber, chairman of the "Aryanized" Gustloff Werke, held a long list of imposing titles at the Speer ministry. He was a close associate of Sauckel, the plenipotentiary for "labor deployment."

Even if not intentionally, the right executive formula had finally been found. A management board of technocrats under Wagner raised efficiency in Russelsheim, while the well-connected industrialists in the advisory council secured material supply and political support.

The Fear of Mutiny

Opel Russelsheim was the target of an Allied air raid in the night of 8–9 September 1942. An aerial mine landed in the prisoner-of-war camp, adjacent to the factory. Twenty-one barracks went up in flames. Eighteen French prisoners died, eighteen were seriously injured. In its report to Berlin, the Opel management knew to blame the French for their own misfortune: "The prisoners did not go into the safety trenches." The next day about twenty non-commissioned French officers refused to work. Stalag Limburg dispatched Luftwaffe officers to restore order in Russelsheim. Refusal to work was punished by assignment to hard labor. The dead were buried at the town cemetery, with Wilhelm von Opel in attendance.[140] The company filed damage claims with the Reich, applying for 7.5 million RM in compensation. After a long exchange of letters this was rejected in 1944, on the grounds that Opel still belonged to General Motors.[141]

Further unrest among the French workers followed a reduction of the group piece-rate in November 1942, which management called a "rationalization measure." Reacting to the wage cuts and the increasingly repressive shop climate, more and more French prisoners used their relative freedom of movement (compared to "Ostarbeiter") to escape. When the Main River froze over in January 1943, many groups dared the icy crossing in the night. How many got away is unclear. The company complained of "heavy losses."[142]

The number of "Ostarbeiter" at the Russelsheim factory tripled in the months between the writing of the company report on forced labor reproduced above (presumably in the summer or fall of 1942) and December 1942. For the first and only time during the war, the company in September 1942 informed Inspectorate XII that it was "oversaturated" with "unskilled laborers." At least half of its new contingents from "the East" would have been women, one-quarter minors under the age of sixteen. Their number is given in Opel's "secret" annual report for 1942, delivered to Krohn. That lists a total workforce of 32,185 people in Russelsheim, Brandenburg, and all branches as of 31 December 1942. About 30 percent of the 26,295 "German employees" were actually in the Wehrmacht. The Russelsheim factory employed a total of 18,500 in production. Less than 20 percent of them were foreigners. Their numbers were specified as follows:

1,512 prisoners of war [no nationality given]
1,173 civilian Russians
  191 Ostländer [Latvians and Lithuanians]
  313 Belgians
  129 civilian French
   38 Danes and
   72 laborers from other nations

The 1942 annual report claims: "The new problems that arose with the arrival of the prisoners of war and civilian foreigners (lodging, nutrition, clothing, training, general supervision) have been mastered, albeit with great difficulty."[143]

At the same time Opel was using about 2,000 foreign laborers at Brandenburg. There they represented 52 percent of the workers. A memo sent to Russelsheim by the plant boss, Nordhoff, fixes the total Brandenburg "Following" (including foreigners) at 3,996 people. The foreign workers at his factory came from eighteen different countries, although 700 of them were "Russian civilian laborers" (*Zivilrussen*, the company's preferred synonym for "Ostarbeiter"). Nordhoff: "A large barracks complex was built to lodge the foreign workers right next to the plant. It is equipped with every desirable facility."[144]

Russelsheim took up series production of aircraft engines in January 1943—even as the Wehrmacht suffered devastating defeats along the Eastern Front and the trapped Sixth Army was decimated at Stalingrad. The Reich's rules on secrecy were tightened and applied more strictly to labor issues. Whether in the reports of Wehrkommando XII (Inspectorate XII; the inspectorate system had been reorganized and renamed by Speer) or in the documents of the Reichskommissar, written information about the use of foreign laborers at Opel becomes increasingly sparse after January 1943.

In a revealing contrast, Wehrkommando XII at the same time multiplied its output of advisories on preventing "mutinies and worker unrest" among prisoners of war and foreign laborers, its calls for "greater security" in the "Ostarbeiter" camps. An increased risk of labor trouble was diagnosed in spring 1943 as arising from "1) ... incitement on the part of the political commissars [among the prisoners], 2) the unfavorable war developments for Germany on the front, and 3) general dissatisfaction in the camps stemming from unfair treatment, poor and unsanitary accommodations, unfair wage deductions, and inadequate food." Wehrkommando XII recommended that companies take measures to militarize their security forces, that foreign labor camps be broken up into smaller and more isolated units, and that factories schedule longer breaks between shifts to avoid having the entire foreign workforce gathered in the same place at the same time.[145]

Security at Opel Russelsheim was beefed up in mid-March 1943. The guards were equipped with new rifles, carbines, and ammunition. That spring the SS perimeter guard, originally posted near the factory in 1936, was also expanded. Rules were tightened for German workers. Opel carried out a number of large-scale campaigns to remind the Following that "The Enemy Is Listening." German craftsmen and white-collar workers were strictly forbidden from entering work areas outside their own, or from talking to anyone about their work.

These preparations for suppressing revolt were the stick. The carrot was a cautious liberalization with regard to the Ostarbeiter. "Everything must be subordinated to the goal of winning the war," reads a "Notice on General Principles for Treating Foreign Laborers Employed in the Reich," dated 15 April 1943. "The foreign laborers ... are therefore to be treated in a fashion that maintains and encourages their reliability ... to keep their labor power serving the German war economy in the long run—yes, even to raise productivity!"[146] Companies were advised to improve support, food, lodgings and the working and living conditions of the foreign workers. Instead of force, targeted promotions and assignments based on individual inclination were recommended as the new tools in raising labor productivity. "The New European Order should be accepted by the Ostarbeiter," according to another memorandum from Wiesbaden.[147] Ostarbeiter under sixteen years of age were to receive six months of training from German skilled workers at special schools for Russians. There was even talk of allowing occasional "excursions" for Ostarbeiter on their day off. And Russians who died in Germany could now look forward to burial in a public graveyard.

The documents do not allow definitive conclusions about the reality faced by Soviet civilians at Opel after 1943. A bureaucratic guideline calling for better working conditions or food for Ostarbeiter does not automatically mean real improvement. "Questionable and inferior meat is preferably to be used for the rations provided to Soviet prisoners of war, Ostarbeiter, and prisoners of justice," according to a letter circulated to all labor camps in the Gross-Gerau region on 3 May 1943, about two weeks after the above liberalization guidelines. It was signed by the "Nutrition Office, Department B" of the regional administrator (*Landrat*). "Horsemeat may no longer be used for rations provided to prisoners of war."[148]

A few pages of "Opel Finance Department Guidelines" still exist.[149] Dated 12 April 1943, these detail the hourly and piece-work rates "paid" to

French prisoners of war since 29 July 1942–about 60 percent of the rates nominally due German workers.

> Especially capable and diligent prisoners of war employed for hourly wages can receive (… or be deprived of) performance bonuses, piece-wage workers can profit from the group bonuses for the entire labor column (and also lose them should performance drop off). The usual compensation for night work of an (additional) 10 percent is not paid to prisoners of war, also no bonuses for working on weekday holidays (Göring holidays).

Of their "earnings" the prisoners of war were supposed to get 70 pfennig per day. This was in "camp money," issued by the Russelsheim Volksbank and worthless outside the camp. The prisoners could use it to buy soap or cigarettes from the "commissary." The gross wage was paid to the Stalag in reichsmark, minus charges for camp money and expenses for rations and accommodations. Daily food rations were charged at 0.80 RM for normal laborers, 1.20 RM for those doing the heaviest work. A night in the barracks was charged at 0.20 RM per prisoner. Opel had to pay for work clothes and wooden shoes. That could not have been all too expensive. Inspectorate XII wrote to the company in January 1943 that supplies of wooden shoes had run out.

Under the Quartering Provisions Law, Opel was expected to pay the accommodations and food for the Werkschutz guarding the prisoners. In fact, the company demanded a daily "compensation" from the Stalag, equivalent to 0.40 RM for a soldier and 0.70 RM for a staff officer. From its Stalag payments, Opel deducted per diems for camp doctors (1.35 RM) and priests, paramedics and craftsmen (1 RM each). All other "direct overhead costs," such as stationery for the Werkschutz, the wages of the German "Following" working in the camp or "foreigner kitchen," the employer's share of social insurance, and so forth, as well as transport costs "for the prisoners of war received from the Stalag or the Arbeitsamt" were taken off the sum paid to the Stalag as the prisoners' "wages."

Opel Operations and the GM Connection

In May 1943 the Nazi leadership awarded to the Russelsheim factory the title of "Model War Operation," an event Opel celebrated with the usual bombast. Signed by Hitler, the official certificate towered above an image of massed Opel workers on the cover of the spring issue of *Der Opel Kamerad*, the company's DAF-approved "total homefront" magazine (see Photo Set A). Obviously Hitler's award had nothing to do with the "model treatment" of foreign workers. We have seen how Russelsheim raised warplane parts production in spite of frequent fuel shortages caused by Allied strategic bombardment, how Opel's "American" organization won favor with Speer, and how the Opel Blitz was the acknowledged best of the German truck fleet. Every third Wehrmacht truck had been made at Opel Brandenburg.[150]

Principal Diehl of the Russelsheim secondary school doubled for a time as NSDAP Town Leader (*Ortsgruppenleiter*). On 1 April 1943 he wrote a complaint about the presence of so many foreigners in town to his fellow party member, Russelsheim Mayor Müller:

Re.: Foreign Workers

As you certainly know, a large number of foreign workers are employed in Russelsheim. By now they are the only ones on the street. Mainly in the evening hours and on Sundays.

Now these foreigners, especially the "Ostländer," tend to spread themselves out and like to visit our Town Park. Mostly they are 18 to 25 year-olds of both genders. On a recent Sunday there were at least 100 of them, some of whom stretched out on the park paths with music (guitars and mandolins), or even sat down on the benches next to our fellow Germans and continued to play.

Energetic action must be taken against this disgusting state. For with the warm seasons coming, the Town Park of Russelsheim, with its beautiful facilities, flower beds, playgrounds, ponds, etc., serves as a place of rest for our women and children. The older residents and the armaments workers go there to seek a few hours of calm and recovery, all the more necessary if they have been working hard throughout the day in the total war effort. A place for recovery and for gathering new energies must therefore be available to our residents, and only to them. It is intolerable that the residents of our town should go into the park and be confronted with loud foreigners who cannot even move properly.

A German cannot be expected to sit down next to such a <u>lousy and dirty</u> foreigner. It is entirely unacceptable that these brothers should hold the benches while the German is left to stand and watch this gang's wheelings and dealings. Action must be taken immediately. It would be best when all entrances to the park had signs posted with the announcement: "Entry Forbidden to Foreigners."

Beyond that the local police must carry out more frequent raids, and if they find that one of [the foreigners] has snuck in, they should bring him forthwith to the appropriate place. The police could in every way finally be more "helpful" to the foreigners.

And in the restaurants and cinemas as well, the foreigners take the best places and the German worker can go home again, because the box office is already "sold out."

And what is going to happen in the coming b a t h i n g s e a s o n and the use of the swimming pool?

The Russelsheim population, mainly our mothers, children and soldier's wives, would particularly greet the measure of keeping the foreigners far away, thus banishing the possibility that they might even be harassed.

Party Comrade Müller, as the leader of the Town of Russelsheim you must take the necessary steps in this matter without delay, lest some unpleasant difficulties should arise.

Heil Hitler!

Source: Stadtarchiv Russelsheim, XXIII/1/49.

In fall 1942 Opel took over two of the front-line vehicle repair stations known as "K-Werke," in Warsaw and Riga. It also managed the "Werlin" war repair plant in Pleskau, the largest K-base of all, which served German Army Group North in the Soviet campaign. As of July 1943, K-Werk Pleskau employed 1,400 to 1,600 laborers, primarily "Ostarbeiter."[151] An Opel employee's 1943 photo album shows a few of the half-starved Russian workers at Pleskau, poorly clothed and sitting in the snow.[152] Much of the Pleskau plant was scheduled to be moved in the fourth quarter of 1943, to the tank repair station in Riga. But Soviet partisans blew up part of the Riga facilities, delaying the move. As of year's end 1943, the Riga location employed twenty-three Germans as foremen and managers, forty-nine Latvian workers, one Latvian soldier, 153 Russians, and three "Ostarbeiter."[153] Witnesses from that time say that Jews from the Riga Ghetto worked for Opel,[154] but no confirmation of this can be found in the Latvian archives of documents relating to Jewish ghetto slaves. The Riga operation was dismantled in June 1944 and moved to locations in the German Reich.[155] In December 1942 the Vienna branch office informed Russelsheim that a busload of "Gestapo prisoners" were being driven each day to work on an Opel construction site, but this was apparently a local initiative.[156]

Opel also held a 100 percent share of the Edmund Becker steel foundry in Leipzig. The company's balance sheets displayed such an immense surplus that RWM ordered Opel to stop publishing its business results for fear that the "liquid reserves" item–130.8 million RM in liquidity at the end of 1942–would "cause bad blood." Opel was swimming in more and more cash every month. Barred from investing in expansion, all it could do was save. The company applied for 21 million RM in projects for the Russelsheim factory in 1942, all of which were rejected by the authorities. Payments on loans from General Motors, some of them dating back to 1931, were blocked, further raising cash on hand. Dividends for the years 1939 to 1942 were "put in reserve" for payment to General Motors after the war. These were listed as an accumulated 14.3 million RM in the balance for business year 1942.[157] Opel continued faithfully collecting the dividends until the end of the war.

At first unbeknownst to the Reich authorities, General Motors in Detroit wrote off its entire investment in Opel as a loss on its U.S. federal tax return for 1941. Cyrus Osborn, in a postwar report: "In 1942 the Corporation's investment in Adam Opel of $34.9 million was written off against reserves previously provided. The write-off, which was allowable as an ordinary tax deduction, resulted in a tax reduction of approximately $22.7 million."[158] This was not a divestiture, rather, General Motors retained its shares in a company now technically valued at zero.

The Opel executives in Russelsheim were well aware of what GM had done. The write-off served them as ammunition in the next political dispute over Opel's future. In August 1942, officials at RWM began planning to expropriate or even "liquidate" Opel. Russelsheim fought this tooth and nail, but executives at Opel's Berlin office proposed founding a "second Opel company" to take over the production plants of the first.

Richter declared complete opposition to all such ideas. At RWM in Berlin on 30 January 1943, he warned that a second company would amount to an "implicit expropriation" of Opel, with dire effects on postwar production. He claimed that General Motors had never, since the original acquisition, repatriated more than 2 percent of Opel proceeds. A second company was superfluous, since "the General Motors Corporation has written off all Opel property, down to the last cent." He threatened that Detroit's true attitude to Russelsheim was one of indifference: "The interest in foreign business seems to have been restricted to a smaller group of personalities" among the Americans. The former GM president "Herr Knudsen, for example, is said to have always disapproved of expansions beyond American shores. One should not believe that a fait accompli" of expropriation could be combined with what even RWM called a "beneficent cross-pollination by America." An "expropriation from General Motors, regardless of the form it takes, would mean the irreversible loss of interest on the part of General Motors for all time." "It would be exactly the same with other companies," Richter concluded, perhaps in allusion to his other eminent American clients.[159]

All Reich plans for expropriating Opel were revoked on the same day by an "Order of the Führer."[160] The custodial advisory council later discussed General Motors's write-off of Opel plant and property on 13 May 1943: "The entire stock of machinery has been written off in the balance for 1941," according to the minutes of that meeting.[161]

The General Motors Corporation has always disputed having had contact with Adam Opel AG after the German declaration of war on the United States. But how did Richter know about Detroit's balance sheets in advance of the Reich authorities? We might construct convoluted hypotheses about Richter's intelligence contacts, but the straightforward explanation is that GM counsel Richter informed Detroit about the goings-on at Opel, and that General Motors gave Richter the information he needed to protect GM's interests. Carl Lüer officially "informed" Krohn of Richter's contacts to Detroit, as though Krohn had not heard the news, in a comic note of 4 January 1943. The Reichskommissar's permission was required for association with "the enemy shareholder or their representatives." Lüer: "The middleman for the enemy shareholder is Herr Heinrich Richter, Attorney-at-Law, Berlin, whom you of course also know personally," and who "in addition has for a very long time served Adam Opel A.G. as its company counsel." The Custodian kindly asked that the Reichskommissar allow him to continue communicating with his company's Counsel, and signed off with the customary, "Heil Hitler!"[162]

Contacts between Russelsheim and Detroit may have run through Albin Madsen, General Director of General Motors International in Copenhagen, who sat alongside Richter on the directorate until December 1942. Madsen was left out when the directorate became an "advisory council," but Richter remained, and he kept in touch with Madsen until the end of the war.[163] Belitz, who was well-connected with the German Foreign Office and authorized to travel to Switzerland, also maintained confirmed contacts to Madsen through the end of 1944.

Technically, the writing-off of Opel assets by General Motors in the United States meant that the Opel factories (not the AG) became subject to confiscation by the U.S. government. This was apparently no issue after the war, "when the United States government requested the Corporation to again resume control of Adam Opel," according to Osborn's postwar report. "On the basis of certain conditions … General Motors resumed control of Adam Opel AG on November 1, 1948." Osborn does not mention whether or when the accumulated Opel dividends were paid to General Motors. And what about GM's returning its 1942 tax break to the U.S. government? "In 1948 the Corporation's investment [in Opel] was recovered at a tax value of $4.8 million requiring a U.S. tax payment of $1.8 million"–about $21 million less than the company saved on its 1941 tax bill.[164]

COMPLICATING RUSSELSHEIM'S mounting "liquidity problem" during the war (i.e., the political problem of too much cash in "enemy hands"), Opel's operations regularly exceeded production targets. For the months of January, February and March 1943 the Reich demanded 660, 682 and 800 JU-88 engines, respectively; Opel produced 692, 690 and 820. The story was much the same with the many other production targets. Russelsheim took up parts assembly for the Arado 96 fighter in spring 1943.[165]

The working week averaged sixty-six hours in late 1942 and sometimes hit seventy-two hours in the weeks following forced interruptions. At the same time the draft was repeatedly stepped up, so that the proportion of German "male Followers" fell continuously until the end of the war. Their number was partly compensated through the "assignment of German women" and "Ostarbeiter women." At one point in 1943 the Opel council, a group of old men who lived in pretty villas in Wiesbaden and Mainz, met to consider a really tough question: How many hours of factory work are ideal in optimizing a worker's productivity? The gentlemen agreed on a working week of sixty to sixty-six hours as the ideal, noting however "how difficult it is to accelerate the work tempo of the foreign laborers." Seventy-two hours was no great imposition on the likes of them–or on the office workers, who "merely sat."[166]

The paramedic Martha M. looked back on the drudgery from a different perspective in 1987, when she recalled how workers came to her often with complaints of colic but would refuse to lie down in the clinic's rest area, as this might be interpreted as "refusal of labor" or "sabotage."[167]

As of 15 April 1943 the Russelsheim factory employed 9,742 male and 1,635 female German wage workers, 756 male and 584 female Ostarbeiter, 835 foreign male civilian workers (mostly Westarbeiter) and 1,323 French prisoners of war–down from 1,512 in January. A few older French POWs had been transferred, but many more had been reclassified as "civilian Westarbeiter"–i.e., the same men were kept at the factory and started receiving wages and benefits, such as bonuses for Sunday work. Most of the other French POWs were also redefined as civilians that summer, so that the number of "Westarbeiter" and "foreign civilians" rose to 1,913 by 30 September 1943.[168]

In no way did these re-categorization schemes ease Opel's constant fundamental problem: too few workers for too much arms production. The influx of "Ostarbeiter" largely ceased in 1943, as the Wehrmacht lost ground on the Eastern Front. Lüer to Krohn: "There were no assignments of Ostarbeiter, apparently no transport trains arrived [in this quarter]. Despite all our efforts to get more labor, we were unable to raise our personnel numbers."[169]

A core of 115 French military men, presumably the ones considered most dangerous, were kept as prisoners of war and transferred away from production areas in September 1943. They were replaced by at least 300 Italian "military internees." Hundreds of thousands of Italian soldiers had been taken prisoner by the Wehrmacht after the Italian surrender that month. The Allies had captured Sicily and were marching up the boot of Italy. Opel was to later receive still more Italian prisoners. The numbers of male and female "Ostarbeiter" in Russelsheim remained relatively constant at 730 and 570, respectively. What about the difference in September 1943, of twenty-six men and fourteen women less among the Russians as compared to April 1943? Perhaps this gives us a clue about conditions in Russelsheim. Lüer to Krohn, 28 October 1943: "Aside from transports back to the place of origin for health reasons, there are no escapes to report in this period."[170]

If Lüer stressed that no "Ostarbeiter" had escaped from Russelsheim, it was surely meant to distract from the "scandals" that summer in Brandenburg. The number of foreign workers there had risen to 2,100 as of April 1943; at which time over half of them were reported to be "Ostarbeiter," with the rest coming from twenty-three different countries. "The productivity and mood of the foreign workers [in Brandenburg] is entirely satisfactory," Lüer wrote to Berlin in April 1943. Reported at little more than 3 percent, the sick rate among the "Russians" would have been excellent. But news of the Soviet advances on the Eastern Front was filtering through to the "Westarbeiter." More and more of them wanted to escape Brandenburg before it turned into a war zone. Just a few weeks later Lüer wrote: "French workers who go on holiday no longer come home ... 217 workers disappeared in the last weeks. The production director has investigated ... and discovered that some have taken up work elsewhere, while others can no longer be tracked down." Neither Lüer nor Krohn knew how to stop the flight. Krohn: "The method used until now, of punishing a group of foreigners every time any of their countrymen fail to return to the factory, has proven counterproductive, as it lowers labor morale among those punished."[171]

Two hundred of the French POWs at Opel Brandenburg (who had also been redesignated civilian workers) broke out of their camp one night in late June 1943. Apparently many of them did not even try heading for France, but took an offer of better work at another factory supervised by the Potsdam Armaments Commando. This mass flight triggered a series of inspections at Opel.[172] As recorded in Krohn's files: "Of its total personnel of 4,000 men [sic] the Brandenburg factory lost 1,731 men from 1 July 1942 to 1 July 1943 through breach of contract, failure to return after holidays, sickness, death, arrests, forced recruitments to special labor programs, service obligations, and drafting into the Wehrmacht. This … represents a great burden and poses a serious threat to quality levels." Brandenburg thereupon hired Spaniards to replace the French escapees, but "90 percent of them had to be returned as unsuitable," according to Krohn.[173]

The Jäger Program and the Bombing of the Opel Factories

Starting in Autumn 1943, Russelsheim is kept busy with a series of new contracts. Opel is assigned to develop and build complete tail-ends for the new top-secret jet model, the JU-188, which the Allies called the ME-262. The jet plane is one of the radical new weapons systems still buoying false hopes among the High Command. The development and production departments spend months preparing and restructuring for jet components, working towards a production launch in summer 1944. Opel simultaneously develops engines for the TA 154 and FW 190 fighters. First deliveries of these are planned for April 1944. Then an order comes in for 300,000 parts for anti-tank mines a month, a level also to be achieved by April. Output of these hits 150,000 in January 1944.[174]

That year, in Germany as a whole, with the war lost, under Armaments' scientific management and with the labor of slaves, the war machine achieves the maximum development of its productive force. In early February 1944 the Allies commence a systematic bombing of the German aircraft industry. The loss of airplane factories, suppliers and half-finished planes causes an alarming decline in production. A series of heated crisis meetings between Hitler, Göring, Speer, and Milch lead to Göring's establishment of the Jägerstab, the "Fighter Staff," on 1 March 1944.

Under the operational supervision of Karl-Otto Saur, the Jägerstab is authorized to raise warplane production by any and all means. As their cure-all, its experts step up the bizarre strategy of circumventing the Allied air war by breaking up large factories and relocating them to underground sites in salt and gypsum mines, or to bomb-reinforced quarries. Whole armies of KZ laborers are sent below ground, never to return.

Opel's Russelsheim factory escapes two Allied air raids almost unscathed (13 March and 7 May 1944), but these are seen as a dire warning. Like other arms makers, Opel is expected to disperse its engine production to emergency locations. With a shortage of underground space in the region, the plan for Opel involves splitting production among locations in the sleepy country towns of Raunhein, Flörsheim, Gonsenheim, Worms, Saarbrücken. Precision parts are to be manufactured at a brewery in Pfungstadt, and at wine cellars in Mainz-Weisenau. The strategists of the Jägerstab inspect the silver mines at Bingerbrück with Opel in mind.

As it turns out, these locations are only ever used to produce insignificant amounts. Wagner repeatedly calls for modifications to the dispersal plans. For months, Saur accuses him of "proposing improvements" to delay relocation until it is too late. And then it is too late.[175]

The Russelsheim warplane parts factory is bombed by the U.S. Air Force on 20 July 1944, the same day as the attempted assassination of Hitler by a conspiracy of military men. One hundred and two U.S. 8th Air Force bombers with a full fighter escort fly over the factory in six waves and drop more than 400 high-yield explosives and multitudes of incendiaries. The French prisoner of war Pierre Cuillier writes in his diary: "The clocks at Opel stood still at 11:13 AM. The town lies in ruins."[176]

One hundred and twelve people die, according to the German report.[177] Engine Plant I and eight hundred of its machine tools are completely destroyed. Extreme suspicion is raised by the perfect timing of the raid, almost immediately after the start of tail production for the JU-188, and just before the final decision to disperse engine assembly to underground locations. The meticulous detail of the USAF report (title: "Bombers Baedecker for Russelsheim"), which includes marked photos of the central fire hydrants, reveals that the Americans were well informed about the organization of production at Opel. The bombing survey report will be written among others by Pete Hoglund, who took a position with the military government.[178] The Luftwaffe's birds have flown. The Americans are returning to Russelsheim, with a vengeance.

The Brandenburg Blitz factory is devastated by a bombing raid on 6 August 1944. In a secret report to the Nazi government, the Opel management estimates that the Allied bombing since 1942 has cost the company 156.5 million RM in material damage, mostly at the Russelsheim plant. As an American-owned company, Opel does not qualify for the usual compensation payments from the Reich War Damages Agency in Berlin. "The company's liquidity problem has solved itself," Heinrich Richter mockingly remarks. To his surprise, however, the Armaments Ministry in January 1945 grants 35 million RM in damage claims for the Brandenburg plant, 18 million RM of which is payable immediately. This allows production at Brandenburg to resume on a low level in the final weeks of war.[179]

The Royal Air Force finishes the job on the Russelsheim factory. A relatively small raid on 13 August is followed by a massive attack on the night of 25 to 26 August 1944. Four hundred and twelve aircraft hit the plant with 1,600 tons of explosives and incendiaries. According to the RAF reconnaissance, "Among the buildings severely damaged are 3 large Assembly Shops, the Research Laboratories, the Drop Forge Shop, 2 large Machine Shops, the main Body Building Shop, and the Aero Engine Shop." Of the labor camp (see Photo A17), the report states simply: "All 31 huts destroyed."[180] Pierre Cuillier writes: "A bomb fell on the dug-out for Russian women. We hear of 119 victims, a number that in reality is surely much higher."[181]

Late that morning, a transport of eight American prisoners of war, the crew of a B-24 shot down over Hannover two days before, arrive in Russelsheim under military guard, on the way to the Bad Homburg prison camp. Here the rail line is interrupted. They must march through the town to the other side. Two women see them and scream: "There are the terror flyers! Tear them to pieces! They destroyed our houses!" One of the Americans cries out in German: "It wasn't us! We didn't bomb Russelsheim!" A lynch mob gathers with the Nazi Party town leader, Josef Hartgen, at its head. The guards pull back, the prisoners must run a gauntlet. Three Opel workers arrive with iron bars and start beating the men to death to the cries of the crowd, with Hartgen firing shots in the air. The German-speaking American cries: "I have a wife and two children!" Two of the Americans immediately play dead; they will later escape from the cemetery. Six are killed. Pierre Cuillier: "They load the still living onto a cart and take them to the cemetery, where they are buried, without anyone bothering to check if they are still alive." After the war, a military government investigation convenes one of the first large group trials for war crimes. The prosecutor is Leon Jaworski. On 2 August 1945, seven of the lynch mob are sentenced to death. The judge commutes the sentences of the two women to thirty years in prison. Five men are executed on 10 November 1945.[182]

The later U.S. bombing survey arrives at a total of 315 Opel workers killed and 277 seriously injured in July and August 1944.[183] The three attacks on Russelsheim disabled about 2,500 of the factory's 9,000 functional, if worn, machines. Over half of these are repaired by the workers, however, and production of aircraft tails and engines is resumed at a low level, despite the lack of a roof and other serious difficulties. These feats of "final struggle" are described in Custodian Lüer's last report to Reichskommissar Krohn, dated 5 January 1945:

> By way of Sunday and extended Saturday hours the rebuilding was accelerated to the utmost limits of the Following's productive capacities. Nevertheless only a fraction of the delivery target could be met for the period of this report (3rd Quarter 1944). A monumental additional task was posed by the relocation of production forced by the air raids, for which no less than 21 outside manufacturing points are planned. About 30 percent of these relocations were carried out by the end of September.[184]

Aside from the production targets, the air raids demolish the system which differentiated a "German Following" from "Western" or "Eastern" civilians, Soviet or French prisoners of war, Italian "military internees." The barracks on Russelsheim's "Stalinallee" are leveled by a bomb carpet. An unknown number of forced laborers escape into the forests and beyond the Rhine. Many German workers stop coming to work. The rail lines are cut off. Opel altogether ceases reporting its personnel figures to Berlin. The last statement, describing the situation as of 30 September 1944, is limited to percentages: 79.99 percent German workers, 9.56 percent "Ostarbeiter," and 10.45 percent "other civilian foreigners."[185]

The Russelsheim parish priest:

Heavy shelling on 24/3/45. Many dead. My wife and my maid seriously injured. Much destruction. On Sunday, 25/3, after another hard night, the end is finally here, for us. Everyone is in the bunker. We have to watch out for low flyers. That means: they are here. The news is felt as pure salvation. It is awful to see our poor troops, young fellows, hardly past puberty, tired and speechless, marching past the bunker to the Flörsheim bridge, and by contrast the Americans, strong, mature men on their tanks, without a hint of exhaustion. Much was destroyed before the retreat. They blew up all of the bridges. All of the files at the mayor's office and at the city economics department were burned. The potentates, the local group leaders, the mayor, the executives of Opel, all of them left town in autos, taking food from the stocks as they went. We are really like a herd without a shepherd. There was a lot of shooting in the days that followed. I sleep in the bunker at nights. Everything is being plundered. The prisoners of war now turn into a terrible plague, thousands of them are here, Polish, Russians, Italians. I see that some among the Dutch, who always came to my mass, now come instead to my house to steal, having heard that Russians had already broken in. After all, there is a large Russian camp at the high school. Things are terrible there.[186]

As provisional mayor, the Americans first appoint an Opel executive who speaks English, but he is revealed as a Nazi and replaced forthwith by a Social Democrat leader.

Richter flees to Berlin. There, with the city crumbling in Hitler's last stand, he describes to a court official the last hours of German control at the Opel plant. The notes read: "The factory and the city of Russelsheim were shelled heavily for several hours, there was a great deal of structural damage. On orders from the Rüstungskommando, the factory was 'crippled.'"[187]

"Crippling" is in these weeks the common contravention of Hitler's final order, which was to leave nothing standing, to punish the unworthy German people by scorching the earth. The alternative of "crippling," which leaves machinery almost intact, is encouraged by the Armaments Ministry and the Inspectorates. In a metaphoric sense, it becomes Speer's last contribution to the postwar German economic miracle. Or, perhaps, it is the moment when the technocrats are reborn as "resistance fighters." According to the researcher Axel Ulrich, the destruction of the Opel plant is actually hindered by a resistance group that forms among the workers in the final weeks before the Americans arrive.[188]

Richter's report: "The Following was informed by way of a poster that Adam Opel AG was 'closed,' and that salaries and wages for the following periods could be picked up at the payroll bunker."[189] Richter describes seeing the management board, the factory's Nazi "Shopfloor Leader" Liebermann, and 130 other Opel executives run away, leaving Opel and its "Following" in the lurch.

Conclusion

The management of General Motors's wholly owned subsidiary was subject to political observation by Reichskommissar Krohn. The currency transfer ban prevented a direct repatriation of profits to the United States. The Reich also refused to provide the war-damages support normally paid to German companies. Despite these disadvantages, the company's literature is false in portraying Opel as the victim of the forced Nazi economy. The developments at Opel show that as the war progressed and production demands skyrocketed, the management's leeway and authority to make decisions grew at the expense of the Party's political and ideological authorities. Once Hitler's forces were bogged down on all fronts, the hour of "self-management" was struck. Ideological reliability was no longer decisive. Competence and organizational capacity were. The political rulers' grip on company management slackened—in no way does that apply to the workers! Companies' freedom of action grew, but obviously in a context that subordinated industrial initiative to the constraints of total war.

Industry, in this case Opel, put its entire capacity and innovative energy at the Nazi war machine's disposal, and objectively helped pursue and extend the war. In reality, the leading men at Opel, above all Wagner and Nordhoff, were refining the rationalization strategies of the Weimar period, updating for the Nazi era concepts such as "Fordism," the "Americanization of production," type concentration, and license agreements. Their "managerial qualities" made the Nazis dependent upon them, but the structures of operative decision making at Opel under "self-management" were not in themselves "National Socialist."

Richter died in Siberia. Nordhoff and Wagner survived the Reich's collapse and re-emerged as important West German business leaders. Heinrich Nordhoff, who never joined the Party but ran the Brandenburg Blitz plant starting in 1942, was named chief executive of Volkswagenwerk GmbH, the later Volkswagen AG, by the British authorities in January 1948. It was his idea to turn the Wehrmacht's "Bucket Car" into the VW Beetle. Heinrich Wagner, the most influential man at Opel during the war and the organizer of the conversion to arms production in September 1939, was as good as "de-Nazified" by way of Gauleiter Sprenger's hysterical attack. In 1948, Wagner took over as a plant director at Daimler-Benz AG, where he later advanced to chief executive.

– Anita Kugler

"Our Tank Armor," Der Opel Kamerad, January 1941 (A1)
After 1933 the Opel management published its factory magazine in cooperation with the press department of the DAF. By 1941 the bimonthly glossy (the paper got cheaper as the war went on) was distributed across Europe among the Opel workers who had gone to the front as soldiers and mechanics.

The other pictures here are secret Opel factory photos from the war. These lack exact descriptions, and we have no way of telling if the laborers in them are German or foreign.

Workers making bomb detonator casings (A2, above, 1943) and detonators (A3, below, 1942) at Opel Russelsheim.

"Work–Fight–Win!"

Der Opel Kamerad, December 1941 (A4)
Nazi ceremonies at the factory, such as the frequent military honors given to bosses and model workers, in lavish features. Bombastic appeals from "Company Leaders" urging the "Following" to work harder for Führer and Vaterland. Sporadic threats to shirkers and defeatists from "Shopfloor Leader" Liebermann. Tips for moonlight gardening to help "ease the situation on our meat market." "Victory on the Front," where the brave Wehrmacht foot-men are "saving the German race from Bolshevism and Jewish conspiracy," comes only through "Sacrifice at Home."

Backbone of the Blitzkrieg

Opel executives and representatives of the Nazi Party and Reich pose in front of the first Opel truck produced at General Motors's new factory in Brandenburg, 7 January 1936 (A5). Below (A6): "The Opel Blitz, reliable helper to our Luftwaffe," *Der Opel Kamerad*, December 1940.

Jedesmal, wenn der Opelkamerad bei mir eintrifft, erfüllt es mich mit großer Freude, denn hierdurch fühle ich mich mit der Heimat eng verbunden. Wir hier in der Beobachtungsabteilung wissen den Opelwagen besonders zu schätzen, denn ihm obliegt die angenehme Aufgabe, unsere Urlauber von Frankreich nach der Heimat zu bringen. Diese wichtigen Fahrten liegen bei unseren 3 To Opel-Blitz in besten Händen.
Zum Schluß möchte ich Euch noch für das Päckchen danken, in dem schöne und praktische Dinge waren.
Es grüßt alle Kameraden, besonders die Abteilung 704
Bild 6   Gefr. Otto Müller.

. . . Besonders freut es mich, daß ich auch jetzt im Kriege Opelwagen fahren kann. Habe bereits jetzt mit einem Opel-Blitz 45 000 km zurückgelegt, und wenn ich ihn brauche — er ist immer da!   Heil Hitler! Feldwebel Josef Keller.
B.-Id 7, 8 u. 11

An alle Opel-Kameraden die herzlichsten Grüße von
Bild 9   Arbeitskamerad Seb. Stützer.

Sehr geehrter Herr Betriebsführer!
. . . Mit Stolz und Freude kann ich Ihnen von meinem Opel-Blitz, der mich nun schon viele Monate im Feindesland begleitet und oft Tage mit mehreren 100 Kilometern zurücklegen mußte, ohne den geringsten Schaden zu haben, berichten. In unserer Kolonne haben wir mehrere Opel-Blitz, die auf Grund ihrer Zuverlässigkeit und Schnelligkeit immer gerne gefahren werden. Ein sehr erfreuliches Zeichen für die Qualität unserer Opel-Fahrzeuge, auf das wir alle stolz sein können. In diesem Sinne grüße ich Sie sowie alle meine Vorgesetzten und Arbeitskameraden   Gefr. Julius Habeth,
Bild 10 u. 16   Abt. 142/036.

. . . Wir sind mit unseren Opel-Blitz sehr zufrieden. Sie haben uns im Gelände noch nicht verlassen und kommen überall durch. Allen Kameraden herzliche Grüße.
Bild 12   Willi Beckhaus, Abt 551.

. . . Alle meine Kameraden können nur immer das eine sagen: „Es geht nichts über Opel Blitz."
Auf diesem Wege möchte ich allen meinen Werkschutzkameraden herzliche Grüße übermitteln
Bild 13 u. 14   SS-Sturmmann Herm. Bischof.

Die besten Grüße aus der Eifel sendet Hermann Flohr, Abt. 992—344. Ich wünsche der Firma und allen Arbeitskameraden für die kommende Zeit alles Gute und hoffe auf ein baldiges Wiedersehen.   Hermann Flohr.
Bild 15

Every issue, dozens of dogged, cheerful greetings from Opel workers at the front, with pictures like a vacation (A7). Invariably, testimonials to the hardiness of Opel vehicles, as proven over Libyan sands and Russian tundra. Theater, music, and Rhine steamer trips for "Our Soldiers' Wives," all courtesy of the DAF leisure organization, Kraft durch Freude (Strength through Joy). Reports on factory sport teams, the S.A. rifle squad, and the Opel shooting range. Always, a black-bordered page listing the "factory comrades who fell heroically for Führer and Vaterland."

Company Leaders

With the support of Gauleiter Sprenger (A8, above, center) the Nazi Professor Lüer (right) gained the post of "enemy property custodian" at Opel. But Lüer lost the struggle for real authority to the production technocrat Heinrich Wagner (left). Below (A9), Sprenger addresses thousands of Opel Russelsheim employees and the *Werkschutz* at a company assembly, 14 July 1941.

The Brandenburg factory personnel assemble to hear Lüer and the new plant director, Heinrich Nordhoff, call for "more trucks for the front," 26 June 1942 (A10). Below (A11), General von Schell, the Reich's vehicles plenipotentiary, hands a war service medal to Wilhelm von Opel, head of the company directorate, on the occasion of von Opel's 70th birthday, 15 May 1941.

The Following

At Opel Russelsheim eleven-hour shifts with a working week of sixty hours became the norm after May 1940. Seventy-two hours were considered acceptable for foreign workers or office employees, who "merely sat."

Wiring circuitry, 1943 (A12).

Series production of main landing gear for JU-88/188, undated (A13).

Assembly line for JU aircraft body parts, undated (A14).

Insulation for fuel tank (A15).

"We Welcome the Leader of Greater Germany!"–Hitler's train passes by the Opel factory in Russelsheim, 1938 (A16). Below (A17), USAF aerial reconnaissance of the Opel factory in 1943. The foreign workers' barracks are marked at left in solid black (#18).

CHAPTER 2

1945. HOW THE AMERICANS TOOK OVER COLOGNE–AND DISCOVERED FORD WERKE'S ROLE IN THE WAR

D irty Business" was the headline given to a sensational December 1998
report in *Newsweek* about the role of American banks and businesses in
Nazi Germany after 1933. "America had its own Nazi connection," the magazine wrote. "Chase, General Motors and Ford all had some links to Berlin.
And now they may have to face the consequences."[1]

Sold as a major revelation, this was not terra incognita to researchers.
American historians began already in the early 1960s to explore the policies
of the Ford Motor Company in Europe and Germany after 1933.[2] The
results are informative and important, but do not delve too deeply into the
politics and ethics of the company's role in German war preparations and
production. The use of forced laborers at the Ford Werke subsidiary in
Cologne is given little or no attention, even in Charles Higham's harsh cri-
tique of the support for Hitler.[3]

After the attack on Pearl Harbor in December 1941, when the United
States entered the Second World War against Japan and Germany, Ford
Motor became the third-largest American arms maker. The company saw
itself as part of the "arsenal of democracy." But during the prewar years and
in the first years of the war Ford Motor had raised production capacity at its
advanced automotive factory in Cologne and taken up military production.
The company headquarters in Dearborn, Michigan was well aware of Ford
Werke's importance to Hitler's "fast divisions." Was the U.S. parent management simply unscrupulous in lending support to a totalitarian regime,
one that was preparing war with the goal of a reactionary new world order?
Were Henry and Edsel Ford indifferent to the idea of a Europe under the
swastika? Or did they see only an opportunity to increase their own business power and gain a share in a new, single European market?

These and similar questions were asked repeatedly at the U.S. Treasury and Justice departments after 1939. During the war the two ministries looked into Ford's policy in France, and they investigated Ford Werke in Cologne right after the war. The inquiries produced informative reports, but in the end neither resulted in any political or legal consequences.

The following examines the U.S. government investigations of Ford in the spring and summer of 1945, while necessarily drawing a far broader context of the U.S. occupation and policy in western Germany, from the first days of victory amid a destroyed and depopulated Cologne to the quarrel over the revival of the German economy and the appropriate forms of "industrial disarmament" and control. The investigations did not occur in a vacuum of normality, but during a time of great transformation and sudden developments.

Shattered Cologne Falls to First Army

The advancing U.S. soldiers first crossed the border from Luxembourg into Germany, north of Trier, on the early evening of 11 September 1944, about one hundred days after the Allied landing in Normandy on 6 June.[4] Advance units of the U.S. 1st Army reached the outskirts of Aachen twenty-four hours later. The German commander of the town garrison was ready to surrender. In Paris, at the Supreme Headquarters of the Allied Expeditionary Force (SHAEF), the joint command for U.S. and British forces, it was anticipated that a rapid push forward might capture the city of Cologne before the end of the month.

However, the German Wehrmacht succeeded in rallying their disintegrating troops in the west, blocking the Allied advance. Eight thousand American soldiers were killed in a battle that stretched out over the next six weeks before Aachen was reduced to rubble and the garrison finally surrendered. Under the headline, "Aachen: A Test of Nazi Fanaticism," the *New York Times* warned in mid-October that this pointless and total resistance would have fatal consequences, above all for Germany. "What is happening [in Aachen] is bound to happen to other German cities if the nature of the war does not change."[5] To the east of Aachen, the German front held up under American pressure. In mid-December the Wehrmacht launched a counterattack in the Ardennes. The Allies were not to reach the river Rhine until late February 1945. This five-month delay entailed utter devastation for the Rhineland and especially for Cologne, the Western Allies' next destination on their way to Berlin.

Years of air war had already wrought havoc on that ancient city. Of the pre-war population of 772,000 people, 40 percent had by September 1944 fled or been evacuated. Despite this, Cologne remained an important center for military transport, industry, and supply. It was therefore once again designated a main target for the British and U.S. air fleets. From late September 1944 to early March 1945 upwards of 4,000 Royal Air Force and 7,000 U.S. Air Force bombers dropped their payloads there. The destructive force visited upon Cologne in these five months, a cumulative 30,000 tons of explosives, was over twice as great as in the preceding war years.[6] Much of the damage was impossible to fix or counteract in the short term, rendering meaningless the desperate efforts at repair.[7] In mid-November 1944 there were still 250,000 people remaining in the city. Seventy thousand of them departed in December, leaving 180,000 behind. Transport, communications, power and water systems were brought to a standstill, many until well after the end of the war. Nearly all of the key military producers—who had still achieved astonishing output numbers in the first three quarters of 1944—were forced to suspend operations. By the end of the year the city had ceased to function as a war resource.

The U.S. 1st and 9th Armies launched their decisive move towards the Rhine at Düren and Jülich on 24 February 1945. Their success was immediate and spectacular. Within days, U.S. war reporters were writing "of spreading panic, coupled with signs that the Germans are beginning to withdraw across the Rhine."[8] Nevertheless, with the horror of Aachen still fresh, SHAEF decided to smooth the conquest of Cologne by means of prolonged shelling and a final blow from the air.

Cologne came within range of U.S. artillery fire on 26 February 1945. Two days later the remaining 85,000 civilians—civil servants, police officers and fire brigades included—were ordered to leave the city. On 2 March, at 1000 hours, just as the local authorities and an SS unit began to force all stragglers to move to the eastern bank of the Rhine, downtown was paralyzed by the last RAF attack. "850 planes swept over the city diligently, block by block, using the RAF's technique of night-pattern bombing against a city under full daylight observation."[9] "More than 150 RAF bombers returned during the afternoon to repeat the blow. Airmen said Cologne's famous cathedral was standing, but that most of the rest of the city 'looked like a heap of rubble.'"[10]

A great flight of civilians ensued and "after the exodus came a period of waiting, during which there was almost no movement in the streets of the ruined city," except for isolated patrols of the squads who were supposed to mount a defense. An unknown number of German civilians, deserters from the Wehrmacht, members of the underground resistance, and foreign forced laborers hid in cellars, bunkers, and amid the ruins, waiting for the arrival of the victors.[11] The "Rome of the North" had been transformed into a depopulated and terrifying wasteland, "a perfect illustration of what modern war means—total destruction, with the survivors driven to existence in cellars and caves."[12] The war photographer Margaret Bourke-White remarked in March 1945 that Cologne was the first city of ruins she had ever seen. "It was a measure of the catastrophe that had befallen the Nazis."[13]

The British bombers were followed by U.S. infantry and tank divisions. Ground units moved in on the morning of 5 March 1945 and occupied the city west of the Rhine by the evening of 6 March. Allied fears of a new Battle of Aachen, or even a "Stalingrad on the Rhine," proved groundless. But their hopes of capturing an intact bridge over the river went unfulfilled.

The U.S. soldiers were astonished by the friendly reception from the remaining civilians. One of the first Americans to enter the city on 5 March, tank corps Sergeant Mitchell, was sent back to SHAEF in Paris to report his experiences at a press conference. His description turned so euphoric that the journalists began doubting whether the U.S. Army's ban on fraternization with the enemy was being upheld.

The Americans were treated practically as liberators, the sergeant said. The Germans, of whom disproportionate numbers were children or elderly people, at first waved white flags and held up their hands. They broke into joy and relief the moment they realized they were out of danger.[14]

As American intelligence units confirmed, the sergeant was not describing an isolated case. "The first interrogators in Cologne noted without exception, as they went through the town in the wake of the combat elements, the 'terrific' welcome given to American troops. Free beer and wine were offered by several beerhouse proprietors.... Civilians showed an inclination to pat soldiers on the back and addressed jokes to them. Everywhere a spirit of 'liberation,' genuine or synthetic, was in evidence and tanks were stopped by civilians, who in broken English or in plain German simply said: 'Endlich seid Ihr gekommen, seit Jahren haben wir auf Euch gewartet.' (At last you have come, for years we have been waiting for you.)"[15]

The enthusiasm faded in the days that followed. "Nevertheless, a sober sense of release, akin to 'liberation,' is reported to exist still in Cologne. Much of this is patently false; expressions of enthusiasm and smiling goodwill have always come easily to the people of this area. The opportunists reveal themselves inevitably by their eagerness to 'spill the beans' or 'put the finger' on the remaining Nazis left in the town.... Quite obviously, the shoe is now on the other foot."[16]

THE AMERICANS' ELATION at encountering minimal resistance gave way to mounting sobriety with each new discovery of the crimes of the Nazi regime. "Of Cologne's normal Jewish population of 16,000, all but 100 were deported, members of that remnant reported," *New York Times* correspondent Gladwin Hill cabled his editors on 7 March. "They hid out in the city, constantly hunted by the Gestapo like criminals, for fear of being sent to execution camps."[17] On the same day a first unit of the Military Government liberated the inmates at two of the city's most notorious torture centers, Klingelpütz Prison and the Gestapo Headquarters at EL-DE Haus near the Cathedral. Right up to the moment they took flight the Gestapo agents at both sites had tortured and executed political prisoners.[18]

The eighty inmates liberated by the Americans, women and men of various nationalities, had been left behind by their guards because they were too weak to move. After the Gestapo withdrew, the prisoners spent five days in their cells without food or water before being rescued. It took three days for the Americans to bury the dead and make arrangements for the sick and dying. At Klingelpütz and EL-DE Haus the U.S. medical officer, Captain Moreland and his assistants found tools of torture and parts of a gallows designed for executing several prisoners simultaneously. They discovered that mass executions had been carried out in late February, just days before the city fell. Several dead prisoners were still in their cells, where they had been buried by rubble during the bombing and shelling.[19]

U.S. and British reporters were given an opportunity to speak with the liberated prisoners on 10 March. "Many wept–men as well as women. Others laughed.... Some could scarcely walk. More than 20 had already been taken to a hospital.... Each story of the reasons for their imprisonment was different, but in each story was some heroism, great or small. A Frenchman forced to work in a Cologne restaurant had given food to Russian slave laborers. A Belgian woman of 22 had refused to do espionage. A young Dutchman had listened to BBC broadcasts and had reported news to friends.... Odette, 19 years old, had spent nearly 20 months in prison for helping French prisoners to escape from Paris, where she was living when the Gestapo seized her. Her home was in Charleroi, Belgium." The youngest of the prisoners, the reporter found out, "was a French boy of 16, who had been seized for slave labor when he was fourteen, and later imprisoned for attempting escape and suspicion of espionage.... Seeing these people, you could begin to comprehend what the Nazi system meant. This was only one of many such prisons. Here lives were shattered by terrible, organized cruelty."[20]

That day the journalists also visited the first camp set up by the new Military Government of Cologne to accommodate the many thousands of "displaced persons" (DPs). Most of them were foreign nationals who had been used as forced laborers at companies on the west bank of the Rhine, and who had gone into hiding amid the ruins in the first days of March.[21]

MILITARY GOVERNMENT DETACHMENT E1H2, pinpointed for Cologne, officially assumed its duties on the morning of 9 March 1945. During the next hundred days, in which the unit took responsibility for the city and county (*Regierungsbezirk*) of Cologne, its staff grew to fifty-two career officers and thirty-three noncommissioned officers and recruits, making it one of the largest Civil Affairs units in the U.S. Army at that time. E1H2 had earned a good reputation for its service in the Aachen region in the fall and winter of 1944 to 1945. Its officers were chosen carefully, and had backgrounds as engineers, doctors, businessmen, civil servants, and lawyers. Six of the twenty-one men who formed the core of the Cologne MG had attended the U.S. School of Military Government from 1943 to 1944. Eleven others had taken special preparatory courses at elite colleges and universities.[22]

The detachment came to Cologne with five primary tasks. They were expected to stem the acute typhus epidemic, establish a supply of drinking water and minimal energy needs, build a functioning German administration, shelter and feed the liberated political prisoners and foreign forced laborers, and revive the city economy. Under the command of Lieutenant Colonel John Patterson, E1H2 soon succeeded in containing the typhus and in mastering the repair of ruptured water and power lines.

They also established contact with Konrad Adenauer, who had been the High Mayor of Cologne from 1917 until 1933, when he was removed by the Nazis. Adenauer (who in 1949 became the first Chancellor of the Federal Republic of Germany) served first as an advisor to E1H2 and was then appointed by the Americans to his old post as *Oberbürgermeister* on 4 May.[23]

During the one hundred days Cologne was ruled by Americans, E1H2 headquarters became the nerve center of the paralyzed city. It attracted numerous British and American correspondents, high ranking politicians and military officers, Allied intelligence units, and field teams from specialized American and British services. George Orwell, who visited Cologne in March on assignment for the British *Observer*, drew a conclusion that would be seconded by many in the weeks to follow: "When the Americans first entered, many of the streets were quite impassable until the bulldozers had swept them clear. The town has no piped water, no gas, no transport, and only enough electrical power for certain vital jobs such as keeping the electric ovens of a few bakeries working. However,... the Military Government—in this area a purely American concern—is tackling the job of reorganisation with praiseworthy energy."[24] The daily reports of E1H2 (completely preserved by Patterson) bear convincing witness to the unit's exceptional engagement, effectiveness and improvisational talent.[25]

Foreign and Forced Laborers in Cologne

When the thunder of Allied artillery was first heard to the west, in mid-September 1944, about 30,000 foreign nationals were still working in Cologne. The largest contingent of DPs, representing over 40 percent, were Soviet citizens, mostly Russians and Ukrainians. There were also large groups of French, Italians, Belgians, and Dutch. Nearly all had been rounded up by force and expelled from their countries for "labor deployment" in Germany (*Reichseinsatz*). Almost eight million foreign workers were so "deployed" in German agriculture and industry, most of them as cheap laborers, as of autumn 1944. The regime was desperate to alleviate the growing shortage of labor, especially in the arms industry where production was at full tilt.[26]

As they approached the Rhine, the Western Allies liberated 100,000 "Allied and neutral deportees in German territory, generally referred to in the British [and American] Press as slave labour, but known officially as Displaced Persons.... By the first week in April [1945] the number had risen to about 1,000,000, and it is now thought to be round about 2,000,000, with the prospect of many more to come; for there are at least 7,000,000 of these people in Germany and German-held territory...."[27]

The officers who were in charge of solving the DP problem knew little of the history or practice of "foreigner deployment" (*Ausländereinsatz*). Even the U.S. Psychological Warfare Division (PWD) experts were unable to investigate it in detail until they were on German soil. PWD issued a first report, based on information from "forced labor groups, mainly from Belgians who worked in various parts of the Reich," in late December 1944:[28]

> In most places foreign workers were separated into three categories, each of which was always referred to as 'voluntary' by the Nazis: (1) Western workers (French, Belgian and Dutch)–these were allegedly treated like German workers and received the same pay; (2) Polish workers–these wore a large square yellow insignia with a "P" on it. They were paid according to the German wage scale, but were made to return a considerable amount through the device of a heavy *'Ostabgabe'*. In public places and transport they were subject to many restrictions. (3) Russian and Ukrainian workers–these were clearly the worst handled category, recognized by their large blue square bearing an 'O' for *'Ostarbeiter'*. They received a little spending-money, but this could not be spent legally since they were not permitted to enter any stores or other public places. The money was used mainly to purchase items on the black market run by Western workers.– Both Russians and Poles were treated on a sub-human level.... In some places, it is reported, Eastern workers were systematically starved.

Whether with "Ostarbeiter" or "Western workers," the Germans had acted like a master race, as the Americans discovered. "Belgian workers ... claim that despite their membership in the first category they were treated as second-class persons." On public transport and in the movies "they were forced to give up their seats to Germans and 90% of all restaurants were closed to them. Industrial workers, who were obliged to wear a badge marked 'A' for *Auslaender* (foreign) suffered more severely from the slogan *'Feind bleibt Feind'* (Once enemy, always enemy) than workers in rural districts. Here it should be noted that conditions of foreign workers vary largely from area to area, and even from plant to plant. During the recent past, the Party [NSDAP] has issued various guidance notes to correct excesses of both generosity and cruelty. There is a fair amount of evidence that foreign workers were treated kindly by German fellow-workers and by well-disposed civilians, particularly women, who would secretly slip them some extra bits of food."[29]

Poles and French deployed to agricultural work may have represented the majority of foreign laborers from 1940 to 1941, but the number and importance of civilian workers from the Soviet Union increased with each year of the war. In Cologne the trend was obvious in the workforces of the major state and private military producers. A catalogue of the labor and prisoner-of-war camps in the city, derived from a survey of companies carried out in 1949, lists 107 camps in 1943 and 1944, all of which were located at or near businesses and organizations of vital military importance. Seventy-one of these camps held civilian laborers, thirty-four were for prisoners of war. The survey arrives at a cumulative camp occupancy of 21,000. Many of these figures were too low. For example about 2,500 foreign workers were deployed at Ford Werke in mid-1943, and about 2,000 at Klöckner-Humboldt-Deutz (KHD); whereas the 1949 camp catalogue lists only 2,000 for Ford and 1,100 for KHD.[30]

According to a more recent estimate, there were at least 250 labor camps in Cologne. In June 1944 the local Labor Agency (Arbeitsamt) counted

28,198 "Ausländer" and "Ostarbeiter" among the total of 170,000 workers then registered in the district of Cologne.[31] Whatever its shortcomings, the 1949 survey allows a ranking of operations employing foreign and forced laborers at the high point of war production efforts in the years 1943 and 1944, before the bombs of fall and winter 1944 crippled the city's industry and transport. Besides private companies, foreigners were employed by the Reichsbahn (the railway authority), Organisation Todt (a special labor army established for the construction of infrastructure and military installations), Kommando Reichsautobahn (highway building and maintenance squads), and the Deutsche Arbeitsfront (DAF, the Nazi labor front). The 1949 catalogue names forty-seven companies in all, with foreign labor forces ranging from 20 to 2,000 people. Measured by approximate camp occupancy, the Reichsbahn topped the hardly flattering list of Cologne's "slave-masters" with an estimated 3,600 forced laborers–followed by Ford Werke, where in mid-1943 about 50 percent of the workforce were from abroad. At the same time the number of foreign workers in the German automotive industry amounted to about 31 percent.[32]

In the case of Ford, the indispensability of compulsory labor to the intensified German war production effort is made clear in the minutes of the company's advisory council (*Beirat*) of 17 August 1942. "The war program until now ran at about 4,000 units per quarter. The authorities have ordered a rise in output to about 7,000 units per quarter. That requires a more intensive use of prisoners, especially Russians, who already make up nearly $\frac{1}{4}$ of the personnel."[33] At that time, total personnel was at around 4,000, meaning about 1,000 were "Russians." The mounting losses of the Wehrmacht demanded an ever higher tribute in the form of male German conscripts, exacerbating the labor shortage. "Military recruitment is no longer sparing our key people. The gaps in the factory, in purchasing, and in other departments are growing, and the hired foreigners no longer suffice. This is another matter causing major worries at the Ford plant."[34]

The "labor question" became a constant theme among Ford's top executives. The managing director and wartime custodian, Robert Hans Schmidt, reported to the advisory council on 1 July 1943 that "about 50 percent of the employees are now foreigners, and of these about 1,200 are Russians, mostly women." Schmidt:

> Insofar as they already were industrial workers, the Russians are reported to have familiarized themselves with their work in surprisingly rapid order. But the training of the agricultural workers was very difficult. The capacity (*Arbeitskraft*) of the average Russian is at about 90 percent of a normal German worker's, while that of the German personnel has declined to about 75 percent as a result of the air raids. This trend is unfortunately exacerbated by the need of having the people work 54 to 60 hours per week, a constraint imposed by the so-called 'combing-out' commissions.

These were roaming conscription squads who drafted laborers they judged redundant, and "whose will cannot be denied, if even more workers are not to be lost."

The excessive number of hours is counterproductive. More can be achieved with 48 hours at a plant like Ford, but that could only be implemented gradually. The sick rate is rising dramatically, amounting at times to 17% of the personnel, with the women showing the highest rates. Everything is being done to assure that unnecessary sick calls are avoided through the use of company doctors, but we cannot ignore that this level of output cannot be expected from a labor force compelled to spend two to three hours in a bomb shelter every night, though their spirit and will are astonishingly high. The foreign workers are getting their own specially cooked meals. They are housed in a now completed, separate barracks city. Five different kitchens have been set up according to nationality, also birthing wards, homes for babies, and other measures of this kind.[35]

In the second week of June 1943, during a business trip to Spain and Portugal, Robert Schmidt visited the U.S. embassy in neutral Portugal, where he reported, among other things, that "approx[imately] half of the employees were females; the male workers are mostly foreign, Russians predominating with a scattering of Belgians and other nationalities. The employees are fed in a tremendous mess room at the plant; three different types of rations are distributed according to the heaviness of duty performed; overtime was partly paid in an increased food allowance."[36]

Schmidt seems to have avoided figures, and his report on food and pay did not touch on the different fates the foreign laborers suffered, depending on their country of origin.[37] By 1943 the situation on the eastern front had turned clearly against Germany. Schmidt apparently hoped to demonstrate Ford Werke's good treatment of its forced laborers, knowing that in a not too-distant future he might be held responsible for their fates. Why did he choose the U.S. embassy in Portugal? Possibly Schmidt had learned from Ford representatives he met in Spain, on his way to Lisbon, that the embassy there would be willing to transmit his message.[38]

The vast majority of foreign workers at this stage of the war were adolescents and young adults, men and women working against their will, even if the company was offering "five different kitchens," "birthing wards" and "homes for babies" in the barracks camp on the plant grounds. Even in the "underdeveloped East," word had by then spread about the true status enjoyed by "Ostarbeiter" in Germany, how they were fed and accommodated, and how many hours they had to work each day for a few pfennig at best.[39]

Rescuing the Displaced Persons

Before the occupation of Germany, the Allies were in the dark about how many foreign workers and refugees they would have to shelter and feed, possibly without advance warning. Following a mid-May 1944 press conference with senior U.S. Civil Affairs officers at Allied Headquarters, then still in London, the *New York Times* wrote of "some 16,000,000 displaced persons in Europe, who at the first inkling of German surrender probably will attempt to rush like an ant horde over the Continent to their former homes.... The problem further is complicated by the physical and economic conditions of the homeless souls. A great percentage is known to be under-nourished, ill-clothed and diseased. Many from eastern Germany are reported to be typhus victims. No army in history ever faced such complex problems in the field of civil affairs, as those to be met on the continent."[40]

After the first regions of Germany were occupied, the press obtained more realistic information. Reports in the winter of 1944 to 1945 revolved around "only" nine million DPs, of whom 7.7 million were presumed to be in Germany. That was still more than enough to pose one of the main problems facing the occupiers. For this reason SHAEF emphasized, in its "Handbook of Military Government," that commanding officers were responsible for looking after foreign nationals. Displaced persons from Allied countries were to be gathered "in Assembly Centers until they can be repatriated in an orderly fashion." Securing food and shelter for the DPs was defined as an absolute priority, to be met if necessary at the expense of the German population. Presumably the most important message in the handbook's twenty-five paragraphs on displaced persons was that combat forces were *also* required to view the DP situation as a priority.[41] SHAEF in the following months issued more precise instructions, based on experiences gathered in liberated Western Europe.[42] Six thousand officers and 12,000 noncommissioned officers (NCOs) were assigned the "breathtaking" task of housing the DPs, by then estimated at 4.5 million people, in 1,500 camps for 3,000 people each.[43]

Untold thousands of foreigners were thought to be awaiting liberation in the industrial city of Cologne. Three DP detachments were assigned to the E1H2 Military Government. They had a commitment for support from U.S. Army transport units, but in the first weeks of the occupation the burden proved far lighter than anticipated. The German forces had herded the majority of foreign laborers to the regions east of the Rhine just before the Allies occupied the main part of the city on the western side.

The Americans within a week of their arrival established the first "Assembly Center for Displaced Persons," on the outskirts of the city. They there provided shelter for about five hundred people, most of them liberated foreign workers from Russia, France, Poland, Belgium, Italy and several other countries.[44] As the number of incoming DPs rose, two more camps were set up in late March. There was a camp for Soviet citizens, one for Poles, and one for French and Italian nationals. Food for the refugees was drawn in equal parts from local stocks and U.S. Army supplies. By 7 April 1945 the three camps sheltered 12,000 people, and the initial food shortages had been overcome.[45] However, the most dramatic phase of the DP crisis still loomed.

The German front collapsed in mid-April 1945. U.S. forces occupied the regions east of the Rhine, setting off a westward flood of freshly liberated DPs. "The city is overrun with forced laborers, and the situation will be getting much worse in the next days when other areas are liberated. The food situation is acute, and at the moment the Military Government is not functioning except for the police. The eastern end of the Hohenzollern Bridge was closed off in order to keep Displaced Persons from moving into western Cologne."[46] Groups of liberated *Ostarbeiter* looted throughout eastern Cologne, spreading fear and terror among the German population. "Numerous incidents of plundering and acts of violence by Russian and Polish Displaced Persons have been reported during the last 24 hours. These include damaging machinery, attacking German policemen and looting civilian homes."[47]

E1H2's good preparation and cooperation with combat units proved vital in overcoming the crisis. Bread production was centralized and equipment stocked up at the three existing camps.[48] Working with Russian and Polish contact officers, E1H2 on 21 April found in the suburb of Dellbrück a barracks complex suitable for a new camp to house the several thousand Russian DPs from the areas east of the Rhine.[49] A further center, this one for *Westarbeiter*, was set up just across the river from the Cathedral. Many of the French, Belgian and Dutch nationals who gathered there clamored to go home. U.S. Navy boats brought them across to the western bank, and Army trucks drove them to Brauweiler in the west of Cologne, where they could set off on their own. Two more camps were opened in early May for Western Europeans and Poles.[50]

In the parts of Germany controlled by the Western Allies, May 1945 witnessed the high point of migrations towards the west. The "repatriation rate" for Western Europe, running at 35,000 people per week in April, jumped to 200,000 a week. By June only about 5 percent of the former "Westarbeiter" still remained in Germany.

The return of over two million Russian DPs began in late May. Like most of their fellow sufferers from the West, they were sent home on cargo cars. By the end of August 95 percent of the Russian DPs had been transported out of Germany. The Allied forces and their military governments had mastered the massive logistics of repatriating several million foreign and forced laborers. The last large group to be brought into motion were the Poles, for many of them were hesitant to return to their country now that it was dominated by the Soviet Union.[51]

Germany in Ruins? "A Policy of Hard Realism"

About one third of the E1H2 officers sent to administer occupied Cologne in March 1945 were responsible for economic matters.[52] All they knew of Cologne in advance was provided by SHAEF intelligence: pre-war maps, scattered data on companies and industrialists, a series of aerial reconnaissance photos that gave an idea of the destruction. After months of preparation, they arrived in Cologne to discover that very few experts of any kind were still left in the city.[53] The first written information the officers received from Germans were two lists of Cologne companies that were still in operation before the carpet bombings of 2 March 1945. The first representatives of a local company they met were "two officials of the Ford plant."[54]

"A preliminary survey of one of the most highly industrialized sections of the city" was made on 10 March 1945. "This included twenty-four of the largest plants in the area. All of these factories were in very bad condition and the indications are that the extent of the damage in most cases is almost 100%."[55]

The officers inspected twenty-nine companies during the next week. They focused on plants where a resumption of production was allowable under the guidelines of the military occupation, which read: "You will instruct the German authorities to reactivate such plants as may be absolutely required for the production of supplies or for the maintenance of public services as may be immediately necessary in the support of military operations.... You will take no other steps toward the economic rehabilitation of Germany."[56]

The first report from early March certainly raises the impression that the bombing had put an end to the local economy: "Plant was damaged 100%,... was burned and 100% destroyed,... is 90% destroyed,... was 75% destroyed by fire and bombs,... only slightly damaged,... 95% damaged,... is 40% burned,... is undamaged,... was badly damaged,... was 80% destroyed,... was completely destroyed,... was completely destroyed,... was completely demolished,... 100% destroyed,... completely destroyed,... in fair condition,... not damaged,... completely destroyed,... 80% destroyed,... 90% damaged."[57]

Washington Post correspondent Marquis Childs drew the conclusion: "Germany is finished as a modern industrial nation for at least 30 years. I am convinced of that after seeing the destruction in Aachen ... and other towns in the Ruhr and Rhine valleys—and now this once populous city." "According to the estimate of engineers on the staff of the Allied Military Government, 90 percent of Cologne's industry has been destroyed. That may be a high estimate, but ... the job of reconstruction is plainly overwhelming." "Public opinion in both England and America has solidified in favor of stern treatment of the conquered nation, and we have begun to plan how this shall be meted out. Who will be left to rebuild Germany, where will the energy come from, where will the capital come from?"[58]

Childs was voicing a fear shared by many U.S. officers and politicians: that an excessively hard policy in a destroyed Germany would rouse bitterness and resistance against the "barbaric Americans." In the United States the long-running argument within the Roosevelt Administration about the future of an occupied Germany, in which liberal-reformist "hardliners" faced off against business-oriented "realists," was entering its decisive phase.[59]

JOHN MCCLOY, the assistant secretary of war, traveled to the Rhineland in early April 1945 to gather an impression of the state of affairs. E1H2 Commanding Officer Patterson briefed him in Cologne. In his diary McCloy wrote: "There were the usual problems—sewers, water, power, food and displaced persons.... There were reserves of food but when these reserves have gone there was going to be real distress. —Not one of Germany's enemies could wish for a more complete sight of destruction than the town of

Cologne. Every home seems to have been hit–rubble throughout the town, and still people living in it." McCloy was overwhelmed by the extent of destruction he saw in the whole region. "Here was this beautiful [Rhine] valley–prosperous, industrious and seemingly contented ... and now it is a wasteland in large parts. Its industry mostly destroyed, its towns laid waste.... I do not see how this country can ever recover. All Europe hates her and harbors well seated grudges. The slave labor under which she operated is now gone and the prisoners [of war] will not return perhaps for years. How are the crops to be sown and gathered? They will have to go back to a medieval existence and, even so, they will starve. There has been nothing like it since the Thirty Years War and I have an idea that was mild compared to this."[60]

Back in Washington, McCloy on 26 April spoke with the press. One reporter wrote: "In presenting a grim picture of the situation inside the country, ridden by famine, desolation and hatred, the Assistant Secretary revealed that food stocks captured by the Allies in the sectors he visited will be exhausted in thirty to sixty days. 'The problem is going to be food and manpower,' he declared.... Everywhere he saw 'complete destruction' and 'dissolution of society–complete collapse of social and political economy.'"[61]

Whatever the threat of starvation in Germany, the American public in those weeks was far more absorbed with the crimes of the Nazi regime, the scale and horror of which were just becoming clear to the Allied soldiers and journalists.[62] "The most devastating experience of the war for most of us was the first visit to a concentration camp," a senior intelligence officer later recalled.[63] The pictures from Buchenwald and Bergen-Belsen were radicalizing the mood of both the eyewitnesses and the people back home. "The newsmen hold to the view that the uncovering of almost countless examples of Nazi sadistic cruelty and brutality in prison camps has convinced the troops that they are fighting a nation steeped in evil instincts, and that this knowledge is preventing fraternization on anything but a very minor scale."[64]

Thus, the advocates of a moderate and pragmatic occupation policy in Germany saw themselves faced with a horrified public who apparently had nothing against a severe peace and a rigorous security policy of restriction, supervision and reform. "Topic 'A' in the Press during the week was the way we are treating the Germans," the press officers at SHAEF noted with dismay on 26 May 1945. "Quite a hot blast was directed against the Allies by the U.S. and U.K. newspapers, and there is obviously more to follow. Although peace has come to Europe, the Allied public are uneasy about apparent weaknesses in our grip on the Germany of today and newspapers have been quick to emphasize the danger of any soft attitude to a defeated but still dangerous people. –'Don't let them get away with it' is a fair summing up of what the Press is saying."[65]

The overall occupation authority, known as U.S. Group, Control Council (USGCC, reorganized in the following months as OMGUS, the Office of Military Government for Germany, United States) was forced to take account of the reigning mood. General Lucius D. Clay, deputy military governor for General Eisenhower and head of USGCC, called a press conference on 15 May to announce "a policy of hard realism for the American zone in occupied Germany," to "be applied through a military government of twelve departments." His top priority, he promised, was "to smash whatever remaining power Germany may have for making war and the elimination of the Nazi party."[66] Responding to questions of why the anti-Nazi regulations had at times been interpreted leniently, Clay said "that 'men with a Nazi viewpoint and who have been active in the Nazi Party will be purged, and purged quickly.' He also promised that although some Nazis might be used to 'get electricity on'—a favorite phrase of Military Government officers—the history of every applicant would be carefully considered."[67] Clay introduced some of his advisors and a few department heads, but the press had to wait until the end of the month for more hints about the program and more detailed information about the future decision makers. On 26 May, Clay announced that German cartels would be abolished and future exports strictly supervised. Further: "Plants which cannot be converted to production of essential civilian goods will be destroyed."[68]

The published details about the "leading American civilians and Army officers appointed to help carry out the policies of the United States and Allied authorities in controlling Germany's economy" proved more instructive—and triggered immediate criticism. "The Americans just named as advisors to the U.S. Control Council include top executives of steel, automobile manufacturing, copper, oil, explosives, lumber and investment firms.... In many cases, the persons just named have long represented American industrial interests in Germany and bear heavy responsibility for the industrial practices pursued in Germany during the inter-war years."[69]

A critical USGCC internal paper named the men responsible for the recruitment of "big business officers" to control the German economy: "This pattern of recent appointments had been shaped by the industrial representatives already in military government, notably General Draper of Dillon Read, Lewis Douglas of General Motors and Mutual Life, and Graeme Howard of General Motors."[70] Assisted by senior War Department officials, these men* influenced American occupation policy by selecting personnel

---

*Lewis Douglas, head of the Mutual Insurance Company of New York since 1940, also accepted directorships in other major corporations, of which the most prominent was General Motors. Douglas "became a strong advocate of German economic reconstruction as the key to promoting European recovery and curbing communism." He played an important role in accomplishing these objectives as the U.S. ambassador to Britain (1947–1950). Graeme Howard represented General Motors in Germany starting in 1929 as the regional director for Europe. He formally remained a member of the Opel directorate until March 1942 (See Ch. 1). In 1944 and 1945, as a colonel with the U.S. Army, Howard influenced postwar planning and personnel appointments in the U.S. occupation authority: "Colonel Howard was in charge of the Economic Planning Group at Bushy Park, England, and was later assigned to the U.S. Group CC (Germany). He returned to the United States 20 March '45 ... and worked ... in recruiting personnel for the Economics Division, U.S. Group CC [USGCC]." In 1945 and 1946 Howard again served as General Motors's vice-president in charge of Europe. He then took a new job with Ford Motor in 1947, and accompanied Henry Ford II to Europe (and Cologne) in February and March 1948 as a consultant on overseas matters. (Henry Ford II was the grandson of

for key positions. It is astonishing how smoothly and successfully John McCloy, as assistant secretary of war, and General William H. Draper, as designated head of the Economics Division, modified post-war planning and recruitment procedures during the very early stages of the occupation to gain a greater role for the War Department and its representatives in Germany.[71]

The recruitment of economic officials undertaken by McCloy and Draper in April 1945 focused on "outstanding civilians" and experts from big business. A contrary effort was backed by the secretary of the treasury, Henry Morgenthau, who favored a lasting weakening of Germany's war-relevant industries. One of Morgenthau's long-standing advisers, Bernard Bernstein, had been appointed acting director of Finance Division USGCC. In March and April he assembled about forty people on his staff, mainly anti-trust specialists from Treasury and Justice now focusing on German industries and cartel investigation. No wonder that Colonel Bernstein's group was viewed with suspicion by General Clay's political advisers.[72]

U.S. occupation policy in the spring and summer of 1945 was shaped by directives comprising both punitive and "elastic clauses." It was influenced by the unexpected death of President Roosevelt, growing anti-German feelings at home, and by planning for the upcoming first postwar conference of the victorious Allies, at Potsdam in July 1945. U.S. policy became a confusing mixture of strongly worded announcements and instances of tough action against selected German industries, even as most of the key positions in Clay's military government were filled with "pragmatics" arguing that first of all "German economic activity must be restored."[73]*

Henry and the son of Edsel. He became chief executive after the death of Edsel in 1943 and of Henry in 1947.) A New York Times article of 27 May 1945, "U.S. Board Named for Reich Control," remarked that of six further managers just named to the occupation authority, two had histories with General Motors. "Edward S. Zdunek, formerly head of General Motors at Antwerp" was appointed to supervise the MG Light Machines Production Department, which oversaw vehicle production in the U.S. zone. The GM Vice President "Peter Hoglund, on leave from General Motors and an expert on German production" was appointed "to serve as Colonel Boyd's deputy" in overseeing industrial production. Elias "Pete" Hoglund had held power of attorney for GM's businesses in Germany, i.e., Opel, from February 1940 to February 1941 (See Ch. 1). Edward Zdunek had been employed continuously by GM since 1925 and became regional director for Europe in 1946. He later took over as chief executive at Opel.

*"For your secret information, Lew Douglas has just sent back a message to Secretary of War Stimson.... Douglas emphasizes the basic necessity for central control and the urgent necessity of avoiding during at least the next eighteen months any limitations (except the obvious ones covering the production of armament and material of this character) on the productive capacity of Germany already badly smashed, necessary to the essentials of life. He goes as far as insisting that temporarily we should use whatever German production of synthetic oil and synthetic rubber we can, confident that when the strain is over we will be able to take the decision to liquidate these industries. In other words, the trend here is that our hands should not be tied by a rigid directive in the economic field. –General Clay is working out well and I think we can count on him for intelligent and effective cooperation." Eisenhower adviser and "pragmatic" Robert Murphy, letter to Emile Despres, Chief, Division of Financial and Monetary Affairs, Department of State, 3 May 1945. (BA Koblenz, RG 260, POLAD/737/26–28).

THE INITIAL REPORTS of "total destruction" were overdrawn, as became clear already in the first weeks of the occupation. The U.S. Reparations Commission sent economist Moses Abramovitz on a tour of fourteen west German cities in early May 1945. He was cautious: "No reliable evaluation of the present condition of industrial facilities is now available in any quarter. It is generally agreed that, given transport, coal, certain other raw materials, a usable monetary system, and government authorization, the recovery from the present desperately depressed condition could be rapid and substantial." Abramovitz emphasized that the evidence the group encountered "varied in extreme fashion. A preliminary survey of facilities in Cologne made by MG showed that most establishments were completely destroyed.... A similar survey of plants in the Duesseldorf area employing more than 250 workers showed few plants destroyed, and the rest either undamaged or partially damaged."[74]

Even in Cologne, the dramatic conclusions of mid-March 1945 gradually gave way to a more optimistic appraisal. At the start of their industrial survey the MG officers were astonished to discover two large plants had both withstood the bombing nearly untouched: the chemicals producer Glanzstoff-Courtaulds, and, not far from it, Ford Werke, the largest factory in the city west of the Rhine. A survey was made of the Ford plant on 11 March 1945. The office building was burned and destroyed by the evacuating Germans, but "with the above exceptions, the plant was undamaged by bombs or shell fire and is in excellent condition. The stock room was in very bad disorder from the activity of our own troops—many parts of motors and much desirable material have been wasted."[75]

The Americans found the company's chief executive was waiting for them and eager to answer their questions:

R. H. Schmidt, General Manager of Ford Motor Co., made [an] initial report as follows: (a) Capital–32,000,000 RM. (b) 52% owned by Ford Motor Co. in Detroit. (c) 6% owned by Ford Motor Co. in London. (d) Balance–42%–by unknown German nationals. (e) Prewar output 20,000 trucks, 20,000 passenger cars yearly. (f) Output third quarter 1944: 5,000 trucks, 20,000 motors, 4,000 tons spare parts. (g) Employment: (1) Third quarter 1944, total of 5,000, consisting of 800 on Salary roll, balance of payroll–2,000 Germans, 2,200 foreigners of which 800 were Russians, 400 Italians and balance Dutch, French and Belgian. (h) Production, February/45–250 trucks, 500 motors. Decreased production due to loss of energy and supply of parts. (i) Financial condition: 12,000,00 RM (approx.) in Reichsbank and Dresdner Bank on deposit. 20,000,00 (approx.) bank credits. 16,000,000 due from German Govt. (j) Since October/44 approximately 80% of machinery has been moved east of the Rhine to points from ten to twenty miles from the Rhine. Some machinery is still on freight cars near the plant. (k) About sixty key employees have remained in Cologne. Approximately 300 foreigners, mostly Italian, are still in Cologne.[76]

The above report was useful but far from complete. Schmidt failed to mention the chemicals empire I.G. Farbenindustrie, a major shareholder in Ford Werke, and did not indicate the full extent of his factory's military output or the higher number of foreign and forced laborers used during the peak periods of war production in 1943 and 1944.[77] But the MG officers were not charged with examining Ford Werke's role in the war. They were instructed to focus on Schmidt's optimistic conclusion: "A considerable number of trucks can be produced within a short time when conditions permit."[78]

The discovery of an intact automotive factory, one of potentially great use to the U.S. Army, was welcome news amid the depressing impressions of the Military Government's first days. It was also a bombshell for the journalists. The "war correspondents who called today," E1H2 reported on 14 March, "were particularly interested in the Ford plant, which escaped damage in the air raids on Cologne."[79] The reporters' curiosity was understandable given the thousands of Allied bombers that had flown over and past the large car factory many times on their way to other targets in the Cologne area. Had the planners of the bombing campaign against Germany's automotive industries been unaware of the plant's importance?

An Allied military intelligence report on Ford Werke, dated 29 May 1943, had left little doubt: "Principal wartime activities are probably manufacture of light trucks and of spare parts for all the Ford trucks and cars in service in Axis Europe (including captured Russian Molotovs)." "There may also be some production of light Army vehicles and especially of engines for them. The addition during the war of three new buildings suggests that the works are operating at a high level." The paper argued that destruction of Ford's large machine hall, which housed many hundreds of irreplaceable tools that had been made in the United States, might immediately halt production.[80]

Ford Werke was designated Target Category 1 ("major plants in industries of major importance") by the British Ministry of Economic Warfare, but no action was taken until early October 1944, one and a half years later. "Intelligence sources (10-5-44) state Ford, Cologne, was never bombed, was working full speed, is protected by barrage balloons and produces 1000 3-ton trucks per month."[81] The tone of this later report suggests that the failure to raid Ford may have been causing discontent among those involved in choosing targets. The Allied foot soldiers landing in Normandy in June 1944 had been astonished to see that the enemy's favorite truck brands were from Ford and General Motors.

In the course of the war, both sides had learned that precision attacks were especially effective against plants with complex production processes, as in an automotive factory.[82] The Ford factory grounds were first included in "area attacks" on northern Cologne on 2 and 3 October 1944. The 2 October attack left craters on the plant grounds and in nearby fields, and hit barracks in the forced labor camp, causing casualties there. Ford Werke was specifically targeted in USAF "precision attacks" by daylight on 15 and 18 October 1944 but was not hit in the raids.[83] No further bombings were scheduled, although aerial reconnaissance only days later verified that the attacks had failed. Definitive evidence to explain why this important production plant was not again targeted has yet to surface.[84]

Production at Ford Werke nevertheless declined precipitously in fall 1944, when massive bombings in the Ruhr and Rhine valleys often shut down transport and energy supply.[85] "September and October 1944 became the worst months of bombing raids and our production came to a complete standstill from October 1st through November 16th," Schmidt reported in late May 1945 to Lord Perry, the head of British Ford in Dagenham. "From then onward on a reduced schedule compared with the monthly average of 1944 production was kept up until the occupation of Cologne."[86]

In 1943 the Reich Ministry for Armaments and War Economy had set high production targets of 24,000 Ford trucks.[87] Mainly because of a "lack of material," Ford-Werke AG fell short of that by some 20 percent in 1944, producing about 40,000 trucks in the two years 1943 and 1944 combined, but also covering unscheduled orders for 10,000 Maultier half-tracks (military transporters with caterpillar tracks in the rear).[88] Armaments Minister Speer had to make do. After the destruction of Opel's truck factory in Brandenburg on 6 August 1944, Ford in Cologne and Daimler-Benz in Mannheim were the most important remaining suppliers of the vital three-ton transport and supply vehicles.[89]

The lines of the Cologne plant stood still on 28 February 1945.[90] With the exception of 290 Italian military internees, the foreign and forced laborers left in the Ford camp were evacuated east of the Rhine, just before the U.S. 3rd Armored division occupied the factory grounds on 6 March 1945.[91] In the weeks after the occupation and before the Rhine front collapsed, "several hundred shells hit the roof of our premises so that practically no glass was intact. The roof was holed in hundred[s] of places. The structure, however, was not damaged to any extent."[92] Because 80 percent of the machinery had been moved since mid-November 1944 to five dispersal factories in the surrounding region, neither the German shells nor the vandalism of the U.S. combat troops were to cause Ford any lasting concern.[93]

U.S. Treasury vs. Ford Motor Company

When SHAEF in Versailles received word that Ford Werke had been taken intact, a team was dispatched from Military Intelligence (G-2) Economic Section. Arriving at Ford Werke on 13 March 1945, the men spent five days searching for papers and questioning the top management and Schmidt's secretary, all of whom "gave information willingly and were helpful in our obtaining considerable economic data." The G-2 men blew a safe at the factory and twice visited Schmidt at his house. On 20 March, having removed a number of documents and prepared a report, they left the plant. The target presented "no further interest" to them.[94]

This may have given impetus to a far more ambitious probe being prepared under the auspices of Colonel Bernstein and the Finance Division USGCC. Morgenthau's associate, Colonel Bernstein, had proposed in the summer of 1944 "that the Military Intelligence (G-2) Services adopt a program to investigate Germany's international assets and to uncover and prevent transfers through searching the files and interrogating the personnel of the large German firms." Military Intelligence at first gave serious consideration to the idea but decided against participation on the grounds that it lacked enough qualified personnel. Finance Division therefore assumed the responsibility for planning "a program of financial investigations" within USGCC, aimed at the heart of the country's industry and finance.[95]

U.S. Attorney General Francis B. Biddle, a staunch defender of the New Deal antitrust and reformist factions, put their programmatic stance in plain words:

> The German Government and the German people as a whole have never accepted the doctrines of economic liberalism which run through American history. The monopolistic firms of Germany have survived in that country through two wars and constitute a definite menace to the future peace of the world. As long as they survive in their present form it will be exceedingly difficult to develop independent industry outside of Germany.... [Therefore the victorious allies should] break the power of the German monopolistic firms. The purpose of such a program would not be to destroy German economic life in its entirety, but to put its industries into a form where they will no longer constitute a menace to the civilized world.[96]

Bernstein had spent several weeks in Washington in February 1945 to recruit experts from the Treasury and Justice departments. He worked out his plan with senior officials from the State Department and from the War Department Civil Affairs Division.[97] In principle there was agreement on the goals of reordering the German economy and imposing effective controls and enforcement measures towards "industrial disarmament," as official policy held in 1944 and 1945.[98] The "realists" at War and State, however, were mainly concerned with "securing German potential," in part due to the presumed threat of a more powerful Soviet Union. They therefore favored a rapid reconstruction of the German economy, and opposed anything that might endanger it. From the beginning they attempted to keep Colonel Bernstein and his "trust-busters" under control.[99]

The influential "pragmatist" Robert Murphy, the political adviser to Eisenhower and Clay, wrote on 11 April that while the State Department was "sympathetic to the view that large corporate combines should be disestablished and that there should be elimination of interlocking directorates," nevertheless "a well-conceived program for this purpose should contemplate the establishment in Germany of vested interests which would prevent the reconstruction after withdrawal of Allied control of such combines and interlocking directorates." "The Department of State believes," he concluded, "that such a program should not be formulated and executed solely by the Finance Division but should be the joint responsibility of all appropriate Divisions in the Control Council. The Department adds that if possible the program when formulated should be referred to Washington for final approval."[100]

Murphy was only partly successful. A "Committee on German Cartels," called forth by Clay in early May, included both hardliners and realists. The pressure of events forced its suspension, however, and a further reorganization followed in June.[101] There was growing criticism in the United States of the German occupation policy for being too soft, and the government felt compelled to send a clear signal. On 5 July General Clay ordered the seizure of all I.G. Farbenindustrie properties in the American zone. Looking to the upcoming Potsdam conference, he announced that the German "industrial empires" would be broken up. Don Whitehead in the New York *Herald Tribune*, 6 July 1945: "This would mean the end of the great combines, such as Krupp's, IG Farben, Siemens, Hermann Goering Stahlwerke, which have poured steel, armaments, chemicals, rubber and aluminum into the maw of the German war machines and given Germany the industrial domination of Europe." Whitehead's readers could have easily drawn the conclusion that Morgenthau's hard line had taken hold among the makers of U.S. occupation policy. That was not the case. Morgenthau, who had argued that "a weak economy for Germany means that she will be weak politically and … won't be able to make another war," tendered his resignation on 5 July 1945. The protagonists of his political credo lost their stronghold in the reshuffling of the Truman Administration.[102]

THE STRUCTURE OF THE MILITARY OCCUPATION was still being defined during the months from March to September 1945. This was a period of constant new tasks, inconsistent directives, political uncertainties and a general shortage of personnel. Under these circumstances Colonel Bernstein found he had a lot of room to maneuver. By early April 1945 a team of civilian professionals from Treasury and Justice prepared a list of 230 "leading financial houses and industrial firms in German iron and steel, chemicals, electrical equipment, aircraft components and motive power, machinery, optical equipment." The directory served as a travel route for several "file searching teams with a group of interrogators." One set of teams covered "the major financial houses and firms important in iron and steel and related industries," the second "the major chemical firms and their financial houses."[103] Group No. 1 began its search in the Rhine-Ruhr industrial region. Its list of objectives for Cologne included two banks and nine industrial enterprises, including Ford-Werke AG.[104]

Why did Bernstein and his investigators view Ford as a primary objective? Besides Ford Werke's importance in German rearmament and war production, the long-running antagonism between the company and the Roosevelt Administration surely played an important role.

In the 1930s, the autocratic founder of the Ford Motor Company was among the most aggressive opponents of President Roosevelt's New Deal and anti-Hitler stance.[105] From 1921 to 1927, Henry Ford publicly propagated an extreme anti-Semitism through a number of self-financed publications. He made no secret of his admiration of the Germans and their Führer.[106] That would have sufficed to make plenty of enemies within the Roosevelt government. Two events in the late 1930s served to galvanize the aversions against Ford. On the occasion of Henry Ford's 75th birthday, Hitler bestowed upon him the "Grand Cross of the German Eagle." This was the highest honor reserved for a foreign supporter of the German Reich, and came with the Führer's personal congratulations to the pioneer of automotive engineering. Celebrated with great pomp on 30 July 1938, the medal-pinning, carried out in Dearborn by a German consul, set off a storm of indignation in the United States. A growing number of Americans were disgusted to see Henry Ford accepting honors from a regime that had established totalitarian conditions and was openly preparing to wage war on its neighbors.[107]

The criticism did not prevent Henry Ford from withdrawing, in mid-June 1940, his company's participation in a deal negotiated between Washington and London, under which Ford Motor Company would have produced 6,000 aircraft engines for the British government. At that point the Wehrmacht had conquered a half-dozen European countries. Hitler was parading into Paris and the Luftwaffe was gearing up for the Battle of Britain. Looking to soothe the renewed surge of outrage against him, Henry Ford published an editorial in the London *Daily Mail* of 26 June 1940, in which he conceded to the British and Canadian members of his corporation the right to pursue their patriotic duties, but without reversing his decision: "Ford Motor Canada and England are using their facilities to the utmost for production of military equipment for defense of the British empire and will continue to serve their countries as they should do. While I am against war nevertheless I believe our facilities in America should be preserved for American defense when and if so required."[108] Ford's article kept quiet about the activities of German Ford.

That week the same incident was also causing headaches for Ford executives in Germany. The chairman of the Ford Werke directorate, Heinrich Albert, who was loyal to Henry Ford and to the Nazi government, was confronted with a false report circulating among Wehrmacht High Command (OKW) officers: that Ford Motor Company in Dearborn *was* delivering war material to Britain. Albert fired off a defense to General Zuckertort of OKW: "These kinds of rumors always come up. We assume that they originate with American competitors who are uncomfortable with Henry Ford's stance. They have always been proven wrong ... the rumor is refuted in detail."[109]

Henry Ford and Adolf Hitler

In his article on Henry Ford in the 1999 edition of *American National Biography*, the automotive historian James Flink writes: "Apart from Ford's increasing callousness toward his work force—from key executives to floor sweepers—the main blot on Ford's reputation was his blatant anti-Semitism. Ford's magazine, the *Dearborn Independent* ... began publishing anti-Semitic articles in 1920. Between 1920 and 1922 Ford reprinted them in four brochures and in a more comprehensive book, *The International Jew*, which was translated into most European languages and widely circulated throughout the world. Among other things, Jews were accused of controlling the world's banks, starting World War I, and plotting the destruction of Christian civilization."

At the time of these publications, Ford the carmaker was regarded by millions as a kind of pope of the modern age. He was receiving thousands of letters a month from admirers and advice-seekers. A reading of *The International Jew* alongside the sections about the Jews in *Mein Kampf* (1924) reveals a largely identical content: a diffuse nation of Jews, pretending to be based on a religion, "getting" instead of "making," as the secret power within every country, running high finance, labor unions, Communism, liberal press, gangsterism, pro-sex ideology, atheism, internationalism, jazz music and modernist art. Ford called upon the white race to take up the fight by "Naming the Enemy."

Of course, Hitler and Ford were both drawing from the same broad European anti-Semitic tradition and, more specifically, from the "Protocols of the Elders of Zion," an early-century forgery by the Czarist intelligence. Contrary to Flink's assertion, Ford is not mentioned in the edition of *Mein Kampf* available to us. However, Flink is correct in writing: "Ford was considered a 'great man' in the Nazi pantheon of heroes. A picture of Ford was displayed in a place of honor at the National Socialist party headquarters.... By late 1933 the Nazis had published some twenty-nine [by 1942: thirty-seven] German editions of *The International Jew*, with Ford's name on the title page and a preface praising Ford for the 'great service' his writings on the 'World Jewish Program' had done to the world." At the main Nuremberg war crimes trial, Baldur von Schirach, the leader of Hitler Youth, testified that he picked up his ideas at age seventeen from Ford's book.

Privately, according to his associates, Ford also saw Jews behind General Motors and the banks that were "out to ruin him." In the democratic United States, Ford came under political pressure for his publications, and the company was subjected to a boycott. Henry Ford publicly retracted *The International Jew* in 1927, and arranged for the destruction of all copies that could be gathered. He made no further public statements against Jews. The bad press did not let up, however. Despite his failure in politics, Ford seems to have continually applied a pathology of total control at his company. In his classic on *The Automobile Age*, Flink writes (p. 125): "Citing the Ford Motor Company as the world's outstanding example of an industrial dictatorship, the *New York Times* on January 8, 1928 called Henry Ford 'an industrial fascist—the Mussolini of Detroit.'" Henry Ford set up a troop of company informants and strongmen called the Ford Service Department and led by the boxer Harry Bennett, who came to be Henry Ford's most trusted associate. "From Edsel Ford on down, the Ford executives came to fear and despise Bennett as his influence grew, and by the mid-1930s Ford workers wondered whether Hitler had derived the idea for his Gestapo from Bennett's Ford Service." That trivializes the Gestapo, but the company joke is revealing.

Ford and Hitler were not necessarily conspiring together, but they seem to have shared important traits and behaviors. Many writers mention, however without a primary attribution, the rumor that Ford presented Hitler with high cash gifts every year on the latter's birthday. In December 1932, with the Nazis preparing their decisive move, *Berlin Tageblatt* reported rumors that Ford was financing Hitler, and submitted an official protest to the American embassy in Berlin. For all this, whether and which of the Ford Motor Company's activities in Nazi Germany were related to Henry Ford's personal beliefs, or were a function of "business as usual," or were forced by the regime, is a question for case by case scrutiny.

Today, Henry Ford remains a legend. He was named "Businessman of the Century" by *Fortune* magazine in November 1999. Of all of the above, the magazine saw fit to mention only: "In his latter years he surrounded himself with goons, spouted ugly anti-Semitic bile, and left his company in terrible shape." In this case, "anti-Semitic" is a euphemism, as though it were a private fault. If we are to remember Ford for his accomplishments in business and engineering, then we cannot at the same time de-emphasize his highly public political persona. (RB/NL)

Collaboration with Dearborn's Consent

Many people in the U.S. government who reviled Hitler never forgot or forgave Ford's unwillingness to help the besieged British ally—or his company's business-as-usual policies in Axis Europe before and after 1939. Social reformers and opponents of Hitler saw in Henry Ford the epitome of a reactionary capitalist, a man who pursued his own foreign policy outside democratic control, and who seemed not at all disconcerted by the thought of a Europe united under the Nazis, as long as his own empire remained intact.

In spring 1943, Treasury investigators paid a surprise visit to Dearborn and demanded to see the personal files of the company president, Edsel Ford (son of Henry), and the vice-president, Charles E. Sorensen, neither of whom were informed of the reason for the investigation.[110] The agents hoped to find out about Ford Motor's "relationship and its control over its French subsidiary."[111] They discovered many letters and telegrams sent back and forth between Edsel Ford and Maurice Dollfus, the managing director of Ford SAF in Paris, in the period from the German conquest of France in June 1940 to September 1942, when contact was interrupted.[112]

Randolph Paul, acting secretary of the treasury, encapsulated the findings to Morgenthau in May 1943 as follows: "From the fall of France to July 1942—the date of the last letter in the files from Ford of France to Ford of America: (1) the business of the Ford subsidiaries in France substantially increased; (2) their production was solely for the benefit of Germany and the countries under its occupation; (3) the Germans have 'shown clearly their wish to protect the Ford interests' because of the attitude of strict neutrality maintained by Henry and Edsel Ford; and (4) the increased activity of the French Ford subsidiaries on behalf of the Germans received the commendation of the Ford family in America."[113] The seventy-page report of the Treasury investigators in every way confirms these points.

In late August 1940, Dollfus informed Dearborn that Ford of France had begun producing trucks for the Wehrmacht and would be raising output in the following weeks, "which was better than ... our less fortunate French competitors are doing. The reason is that our trucks are in very large demand by the German authorities and I believe that as long as the war goes and at least for some period of time all that we shall produce will be taken by the German Authorities." Dollfus appears to have been enthusiastic in serving the new masters once Berlin issued assurances that the conditions of ownership would not be changed. "In order to safeguard our interests–and I am here talking in a very broad way–I have been to Berlin and have seen General von Schell himself [the "Reich Plenipotentiary for the Vehicle Industry under the Four-Year Plan"], who is the highest executive responsible for the motor industry both from the military and civilian points of view. I will satisfy myself by telling you that my interview with him has been by all means satisfactory, and that the attitude you have taken together with your father of strict neutrality has been an invaluable asset for the protection of your companies in Europe."[114]

Dollfus returned to the last point on 27 November 1940. "Even in the case of a completely victorious German peace, the rights of the shareholders will be protected … and your right of control will remain." "If we admit the possibility of a German victory, in my opinion, we certainly must (a) maintain the independence of the French company and eventually that of the British company; (b) have a company or organization … comprising representatives from every country, all the more so that then the United States of Europe will be contemplated, and each state will have to be represented there. In that company you should have independent men of your own choice, and not satellites placed there to protect Cologne's interest."

Edsel Ford answered by telegram and letter: "Appreciate your efforts to continue development Ford interest France. Hope it unnecessary to change status of company control." In his next letter, Edsel Ford hinted where his own priorities lay: "It is gratifying to learn of the efforts you have made to continue the Ford manufacturing program which began prior to hostilities and especially to know that you have been able to get the cooperation of various interested parties and to make some progress towards the completion of this program."[115]

Ford SAF's cooperation with the German occupiers began to bear fruit. By August 1941 the Paris factory was producing 1,000 units a month. Six months later, Dollfus informed Dearborn of net profits on the year 1941 of 58 million francs. But Robert Schmidt and Heinrich Albert, the heads of Ford Werke, were by then causing Dollfus great worries. They were out to establish a European Ford corporation under German control. Edsel Ford showed sympathy for Dollfus's distress, but kept quiet about his own views.[116]

Despite the ample evidence that Ford managers in Paris collaborated with the Germans with Dearborn's consent, Randolph Paul and John Lawler (the author of the 1943 Treasury report) saw no grounds for an indictment under the Trading With the Enemy Act, since the United States had not been at war with Germany until 11 December 1941.[117] Years later, in July 1945, Dearborn would even cite the Treasury investigation in defending Ford against charges that it acted illegally by doing business with Hitler.[118]

Historian Charles Higham's bitter commentary, forty years later: "No attempt was made to prevent Ford from retaining its interests for the Germans in Occupied France, nor were the Chase Bank or the Morgan Bank expressly forbidden to keep open their branches in Occupied Paris. It is indicated that the Reichsbank and Nazi Ministry of Economics made promises to certain U.S. corporate leaders that their properties would not be injured after the Führer was victorious. Thus, the bosses of the multinationals as we know them today had a six-spot on every side of the dice cube. Whichever side won the war, the powers that really ran nations would not be adversely affected."[119]

Colonel Bernstein's Revenge: Investigating Ford Werke

The contacts Colonel Bernstein had forged at SHAEF while preparing his large-scale investigation started paying off as early as March 1945. He learned of the documents which Military Intelligence had secured in Cologne. These were examined carefully by one of his teams. The head of the Finance Division was called on short notice to other concerns, however. Military Intelligence had secured a large store of documents belonging to the Cologne bank J.H. Stein, a private firm which was considered one of a group of "some of Germany's most aggressive combines, among them I.G. Farbenindustrie A.G. ... and Krupp of Essen." In early April, Bernstein dispatched a large group of investigators to Cologne and a second one to the IG Farben plants in the Frankfurt area. IG Farben became target No. 1, and most of Bernstein's field teams ended up involved in the campaign against Germany's largest and most powerful industrial complex.[120]

The Ford Werke investigation therefore had to wait until early June, when the U.S. Army officers responsible for the plant had already left for the American zone and the Cologne area was about to pass to British control. The field team assigned to Ford Werke was centered on a civilian expert, Henry Schneider. After searching for documents and questioning the wartime executives, they arrested Schmidt and took him to their headquarters in Frankfurt, where he was held and interrogated for three months. Once the most powerful Ford manager in German-occupied Europe, Schmidt was compelled to write fifty-two statements (of varying quality) on himself and other executives at the Cologne plant, production schedules, wartime products for the Wehrmacht, the history and politics of Ford in Germany, and the brief European empire of Ford-Werke AG. Schmidt provided a great deal of information to his interrogators, helping to structure their final report but also influencing its content by the way he used his knowledge.[121]

The "Ford Boys"—as the team was dubbed by a superior officer at the Finance Division—finished the inquiry in late August 1945. They submitted their "Report on Ford Werke Aktiengesellschaft" on 5 September. Colonel Bernstein passed it on to General Clay four days later.[122] The main text was just eight pages long, but the notes ran thirty pages, and 221 exhibits were included. Schneider's investigators did not learn about a further set of meaningful documents kept by Johannnes Krohn, the Reichskommissar for the Treatment of Enemy Property, whose office had been responsible for overseeing Ford Werke during the war.[123]

Nevertheless, the conclusions in the "Report on Ford Werke" proved highly reliable. Schneider and his team presented the case like charges in an indictment:

- "The Reich used German Ford and its cooperative parent in Dearborn as a direct means of stockpiling the raw materials needed for war." "Even prior to the War, German Ford arranged to produce for the Reich vehicles of a strictly military nature.... This was done with the knowledge and approval of Dearborn.
- "When war came German Ford stepped into the position of a major supplier of vehicles for the Wehrmacht." In addition "as much as 7 or 8% of total output during the war years consisted of more specialized war material."
- "As was common in other German enterprises Ford increasingly resorted to use of prisoners of war and other slave labor" who had to live "behind barbed wire." "The foreigners employed rose to over 40% of its labor supply in 1944. The usual Nazi discriminations in wages and working conditions were practiced."
- "Because one of the Ford companies was located in Germany, absorption of its other members in continental Europe into the Nazi war economy and utilization of their resources by the Reich war machine were simplified." Consequently "an organization of most of European Ford under hegemony of German Ford was accomplished during the war."[124]

Exhibit 1 in the "Report on Ford Werke" was a memorandum from Heinrich Albert, dated 25 November 1941, concerning the question "as to whether a complete Germanization would be necessary or advisable." Writing at a time when hostilities with the United States seemed imminent, Albert was arguing preemptively against those who might wish to see "enemy property" expropriated by the Nazi state. Ford Werke, he claimed, was a fully German company that also enjoyed the privileges of membership in a global corporation. The benefits to Germany were obvious in the country's current accounts, which profited by Ford Werke's exports.

Albert recalled how Ford arranged to import vital raw materials into Germany before the war: "All needed foreign raw materials were obtained through the American company ... to cover the production needs of the German plant and above that, in part for the whole industry." "Already during the peace the American influence had been more or less converted into a supporting position for the German plant." Albert claimed that Ford's international network would be invaluable in resuming German export sales after the war, and that new American models would be made available for production by Ford Werke at no development cost. To Germany, Ford had and would again offer invaluable "insights into the American methods of production and sales."[125]

Upon discovering Albert's memorandum in June 1945, the investigators submitted it to Colonel Bernstein's deputy, Orvis Schmidt, a Treasury director. Orvis Schmidt flew to Washington later that month to testify at Senate hearings on "German penetration into the industry and finance of foreign countries," presided over by Senator Harley Kilgore.[126] Describing the aggressive conduct of German banks and companies between the world wars, Orvis Schmidt stressed "the extent of the investments by American firms in various types of German industries and of the types of American concerns which are known to have had substantial interests in German industry."[127] He did not mention Ford by name. That task fell to a widely syndicated columnist, Drew Pearson, who exposed the Albert memorandum for the *Washington Post* and other newspapers under headlines like, "How Ford Helped Nazis" and "Ford to be Used as a Cloak." The column was published on 17 July 1945, the same day Truman met Stalin and Churchill at Potsdam to discuss how to deal with defeated Germany. Pearson made a clear link between the revelations on Ford and the "Berlin talks":

> Senators probing the question of the extent to which American business helped Hitler have unearthed a very interesting document written by Dr. H. F. Albert, chairman of the Ford Auto Works in Germany ... in which he urges upon the Nazi government the importance of cooperation with American business. This whole question of whether American business will continue to cooperate with Germany after this war as after the last, is sure to lurk in the background of President Truman's Berlin talks. There is a definite school of thought in both Britain and the United States which advises building up Germany again as a buffer against Russia. Unfortunately the presence of representatives of Standard Oil, the Mellon interests, J. P. Morgan, and other powerful business corporations now in American uniform does not allay these Russian suspicions.[128]

Surprised and worried by the surfacing of the Albert memorandum and the public accusation of having helped Hitler, Dearborn struggled to formulate a credible defense. Since Albert had been known as one of the company's most important representatives in Europe long before the war, the statement on Pearson's column, written at Ford Motor headquarters and dated 26 July 1945, did not criticize the incriminating paper or its author, but instead emphasized the legitimacy of the "common business procedure" Dearborn and Cologne executives followed up until the United States entered the war.[129] If Ford had arranged for imports into the Reich of otherwise unavailable raw materials beyond Cologne's own needs, then only because the

> alternative was to close down our Cologne operations or to sell out the Ford interest to German capitalists, with little or no chance of being able to convert the proceeds of this sale into dollars due to German government exchange controls. At the time this export-import arrangement was submitted to our German company officials and referred to us by them we investigated the matter very carefully and had an authoritative opinion by an attorney specializing in matters of this kind. Although ... it was not satisfactory from a business standpoint, the entire transaction, however, was common business procedure as carried on by many other American manufacturing organizations and banks and was strictly within the provisions of a ruling made by the U.S. Treasury as by Treasury Department Release 9-25 dated December 23, 1936. It was a case of having a substantial investment in a country and attempting to protect it in hopes that eventually the general situation would improve so that we could continue our business in a more satisfactory manner.[130]

There was no serious reservation towards the new regime but only concern that Ford might lose the struggle for German market share to competitors with better connections among the Nazis.[131] Moving out of Germany was never an option, in part because Ford did not want to show weakness in the face of its true arch-enemy, General Motors, and furthermore it was expected that the German market would offer good business opportunities. The German Ford management had issued a jubilant annual report for 1933: "The predominant feature of the business year 1933 was the revolutionary change of the conditions prevailing in the automobile market. The repercussions of the crisis of 1932 were still being felt in the beginning of 1933 when the energetic measures taken by the Government with a view of motorising Germany, and especially the exemption of passenger vehicles from taxation, caused an exceedingly increasing demand for passenger cars and trucks resulting in the revival of the automobile industry."[132]

After 1933 Dearborn increased its equity in the Cologne company, supported almost all of its Cologne executives' initiatives to improve cooperation with the German authorities, and enjoyed success. Production and turnover increased rapidly in 1935, and in 1936 Ford-Werke AG reported its best operating result in Germany to date. In the meantime production had been aligned to use more materials produced in Germany; the number of domestic suppliers rose dramatically. In addition Dearborn gave permission for the Cologne daughter company to produce the high performance V8 engine, which had up to then been produced only in the United States.[133]

Dearborn supplied Cologne with raw materials, parts, and machines that were difficult or impossible to obtain in Germany. In 1937 Ford managed to once again greatly raise production and was the only carmaker in Germany to do so other than Daimler-Benz.[134] The regime honored this cooperation by officially naming Ford a "German company," but at the same time demanded that Dearborn provide additional deliveries of raw materials and machines. Albert issued one of his dramatic appeals to Ford Motor: "If you leave Cologne in the lurch, the effort of an increased program breaks down—not only for 1937, but also for 1938 as the negotiations with the authorities about the again increased program for 1938 are based on your readiness to provide us with pig iron."[135] Again and again Dearborn consented, paving the way for large and lucrative state orders. After years of lobbying the German authorities, Ford in Germany finally became a major Wehrmacht contractor.[136]

To cope with the growing requirements of the military Albert, who had replaced Lord Perry of British Ford as the chairman of the Ford-Werke AG directorate in June 1937, proposed setting up additional truck production at the Berlin factory of the automotive supplier Ambi-Budd. This was at the military's behest. Although one U.S. Ford executive criticized the proposed vehicle as "war munitions," Dearborn decided in favor of the project. "In principle we have no objection to the plan," Ford Motor Vice President Sorensen wrote to Albert, and he traveled to Germany in April 1938 to get the project going.[137] "Sorensen had no qualms about working for the government," Wilkins and Hill write. "He scoffed at the danger of war and felt that orders from the regime would simply help the company."[138]

With the German armaments effort at a fever pitch, the danger of war in Europe became increasingly obvious. This failed to prompt any eleventh-hour reservations at Ford. By approving the new factory in Berlin, Dearborn was communicating to the Germans that Ford Motor had no problem either with armaments or Germany's threats of war. The "Report on Ford Werke" comments: "The relatively unimportant productivity in specially designed vehicles in no way detracts from the fact that even before the War a portion of German Ford had with Dearborn's consent become an arsenal of Nazism, at least for military vehicles."[139]

Ford Werke sales zoomed, as did year-end results. Revenues rose by 400 percent from 1934 to 1938. Since the profits had to be used in Germany, they mainly served to raise capital and expand production plant. Although it now retained profits, rather than repatriating to the U.S., and had switched to "German vehicles" with "German parts," Cologne remained dependent on Dearborn. Starting in 1935, according to one of Schmidt's statements, the Cologne managers and many suppliers traveled regularly to the United States to learn about the latest technology from their American counterparts. Licenses and patent rights were granted and a few of the contacts led to new business for German suppliers.[140] In 1938, after considerable plant extensions and installations of more high-end machinery from the United States, the Cologne plant ranked as the second most advanced auto factory in Europe. Ford Werke was fourth on the German market in passenger car sales after Opel, DKW and Mercedes, and second in trucks after Opel.[141]

In the same year the rubber arrangement, "which in 1937 had already been utilized to cover imports of non-ferrous metals and 5,000 tons of pig iron was extended to include such strategic material in express terms. The Reich Ministry of Economics conditioned its consent upon German Ford's increasing its export of vehicles to 10,000 out of a total production of 40,000 and exacted for its own disposition not only 30% of the rubber imported by German Ford but also 20% of the pig iron so imported." The incredulous comment of the "Report on Ford Werke": "This did not deter Dearborn from supplying these raw materials to Germany."[142]

Summing up 1938, Cologne informed Dearborn that business with the authorities had developed so well that demand could only be met by importing a considerable number of American trucks. When the Reich ordered 3,150 trucks in June 1938 for the planned occupation of Czecho-slovakia, Dearborn secretly delivered pre-built components to Cologne for rapid assembly in special night shifts.[143] The "Grand Cross of the German Eagle" was bestowed upon Henry Ford the following month.

In the summer of 1939 a top executive from Dearborn visited the plant and endorsed a further expansion of the factory, as strongly recommended by the Cologne management.[144] At the end of July the company received the "Germanized" new name it bears to this day, Ford-Werke AG. When the war started in September, German Ford joined fully in the German homefront effort. Within ten months it had assumed control over most of the Ford subsidiaries on the Continent.

Dearborn does not seem to have been seriously disturbed by Germany's invasions of its neighbors in 1939 and 1940. Cologne continued drawing materials and machine tools from the United States. In late 1940 Dearborn approved Albert's proposal to raise equity by 12 million RM, to 32 million RM. Despite its high profits, Cologne needed additional capital to satisfy Wehrmacht demand. Even in 1941, the headquarters sent vital machinery from the United States to Cologne, helping to expand the plant's capacity for war production.[145] The German plans for a new European economic order after victory seem to have been of little interest to anyone at the company. "It is, of course, somewhat early to discuss what should be done after the war," Albert wrote to Edsel Ford on 18 September 1940. "But not only in official quarters but also in business circles, the opinion prevails that a radical change will take place after the war economically and that the German sphere of interest will be immensely enlarged whatever the political settlement may be. It is assumed that the greater part, if not the whole, of Europe will economically form one unit and that import and export will be possible only according to a uniform plan and that also in the motorcar business a united program as mentioned before may have to be set up for the whole of Europe, Germany taking the lead."[146]

Wartime Operations and the Domination of Ford Companies on the Continent

Anticipating that the United States would enter the war, Schmidt and the IG Farben director Carl Krauch,* who served as Albert's deputy on the Ford Werke directorate, wrote to Reichskommissar Krohn in June 1941 to claim that Ford Werke was "a purely German company, and has taken on the accordant obligations with such success that the American majority share—quite apart from the for us favorable political attitude of Henry Ford—has even sometimes functioned as an asset for the German economy." Schmidt and Krauch listed the many services Ford rendered to the Reich, citing much the same points that Albert later brought up in his memorandum of November 1941: "The product is made entirely from German materials (insofar as the required material is not only available abroad, such as rubber or copper)" and by a "German workforce." Ford's "maximum growth in

---

*Carl Krauch, a top I.G. Farbenindustrie AG manager who later chaired the Farben directorate, was one of the most influential industrialists in the apparatus of the Nazi regime. In 1936 he was named the Reich's Plenipotentiary for Special Questions of Chemical Production as part of the four-year plan implemented that year under Hermann Göring. Krauch and many of his technical employees were committed followers of the Nazi Party. Found guilty of "enslavement" in connection with Farben activities and sentenced to six years imprisonment by a U.S. military court in 1948. He was released in 1950. (USGCC, Finance Division, *Ermittlungen gegen die I.G. Farbenindustrie* [Nördlingen 1986], pp. 17f.)

TABLE 3: Ford-Werke AG in Facts and Figures, 1932–1945

| Year | Production | | | German Motor Veh. Industry | | Export | | Capital Stock & Annual Accounts in Reichsmark (RM) | | | | | Work-force | Management (*Vorstand*) | Directorate (*Aufsichtsrat*) |
	Passenger Cars	Sched.	Trucks & Trucks Halftracks (3 ton)	Trucks for Wehrmacht	Trucks & Pass. Cars	Trucks	Turnover Export	Capital Stock	Turnover Engines & Parts	Turnover Total	Net Profit	Divi-dend	Employees & Workers	Managing Director & Other Board Members	Chairman & Deputy
1932	2,214		867		320			15,000,000				–		Edmund C. Heine (1926–28 May1935)	Sir Percival Perry (16May26–11Jun37)
1933	3,795		1,161		163					17,740,000		–			
1934	7,638		2,097	1,764	160		775,000			30,020,000	3,825	–	1,139		Prof. Dr. Carl Bosch (1934–11Jun37)
1935	8,126		4,210	7,053	311		3,359,000	17,000,000		42,570,000	62,778	–	1,707	Dr. Erich Diestel (1 Jun35–14 Dec38)	
1936	13,0297		7,763	7,284	1,048		15,408,000	20,000,000		64,993,000	368,900	–	2,297		
1937	22,039		9,681	12,739	7,325		19,421,000			94,317,000	1,014,303	–	3,383	RH Schmidt, E Vitger (11 Jun37–16 Jun41)	Heinrich F. Albert
1938	23,969	19,000	12,145	22,792	9,051		25,282,000			120,970,000	1,213,358	5%	4,262		Prof. Carl Bosch (11Jun37–27Apr40)
1939	17,374	18,000	*17,886	32,558	3,810		17,406,000			140,260,000	1,287,876	5%	3,847		
1940	4,735	16,000	*13,423	63,296	3,000					118,830,000	1,716,603	5%	3,871		Prof. Carl Krauch (27Apr40–15Mar45)
1941	927	16,000	15,361	62,400	2,500			32,000,000		128,108,000	1,809,185	5%	3,476	Robert H. Schmidt	
1942	41	16,000	14,591	81,279	1,500				45,000,000	132,774,000	2,082,460	5%	Aug.: 4,182	Erhard Vitger	
1943	–	24,000	*23,472	109,085	500				75,000,000	184,340,000	2,169,385	5%	July: 4,986	Alfons Streit	
1944	–	24,000	*19,015		–				57,000,000	152,274,000		–	Feb.: 5,742	Hans W. Löckmann (16Apr41–15Mar45)	
1945	–		3,100							15,000,000		–	Dec.: 2,600		

By Reinhold Billstein

*Figures for 1939 and 1940 include command cars built at the Berlin plant, those for 1943 and 1944 include halftracks (*Maultier*) built as part of a special program.

Sources: Report on Ford-Werke AG (as in Ch.5, Note 85), Exhibits 21, 22, 27, 29, 34–36, 41–49, 51, 52, 57, 61, 89–91, 94 and 204; Reichskommissar für die Behandlung feindlichen Vermögens, Bericht über die Verwaltung der Ford-Werke AG, 1 Aug. 1945 (BA R87, 2606); Minutes of Ford Werke AG advisory council meetings (as in Ch. 5, Note 33); United States Strategic Bombing Survey, Munitions Division: German Motor Vehicles Industry Report, 3 Nov. 1945 (NA, RG 243, Box 883); Wilkins and Hill (as in Ch. 5, Note 2), pp. 330f. and 436f.; Rosellen, "und trotzdem vorwärts" (as in Ch. 5, Note 36), pp. 174, 240–45.

Note: The financial decline discerned by Simon Reich starting already in 1943 (*The Fruits of Fascism*, p. 123f, based on Palumbo, "Germany 1943: Economic and Political Review." Ford Industrial Archives) is no longer convincing in light of the currently available company documents.

export and provision of raw materials beyond its own needs" helped the country's current accounts. "The plant is in every regard an armaments operation" and it was integrated in the war economy from the start. "Even before the war, it helped the army on the occasion of its march into Czechoslovakia with large deliveries from abroad."[147]

After the outbreak of war the top Ford Werke executives became more independent of Dearborn and assumed more clearly defined roles within the company's hierarchy. Schmidt officially became the chief executive. He received the title *Wehrwirtschaftsführer* and was named company custodian under the Reich Enemy Property Decree. In 1943 Armaments Minister Speer delegated to Schmidt the task of organizing the European Ford program. On 1 April 1941, Albert wrote to Edsel Ford: "The plants in Antwerp and Amsterdam in particular require a good deal of his [Schmidt's] time. We shall have to appoint two assistant managers: Mr. Streit who is at the head of the production and Mr. Loeckman who takes care of the purchasing department, substituting at the same time [for Schmidt] in his general functions when he is away."

Erhard Vitger, in 1939 still a managing director like Schmidt, until his demotion in 1941, was later characterized by the British Control Office for Germany as "a Danish national with strong Nazi sympathies though not a member of the Nazi party." In the Schmidt/Krauch memorandum of June 1941, Schmidt's financial manager was described as follows: "Vitger is Danish, but he has lived in Germany and worked for the Ford company for 20 years. His basic conviction and way of life are purely German, and he has remained on the board with the approval of the responsible authorities. He covers finances and has nothing to do with operations."[148]

Schmidt and Krauch did not mention Schmidt's membership in the Nazi Party as an argument to impress the Reichskommissar, but the notorious Baron Kurt von Schröder* did so in a letter to the Legal Office of the Führer (Kanzlei des Führers) in February 1942.[149] Von Schröder served the Ford Werke management as a banker and financial adviser. He was also a key

---

*In spring and summer 1945 Bernstein's investigators pieced together a report on "a small, select group of Germany's most prominent industrialists," the so-called Keppler Kreis, named after one of Hitler's economic advisers. These men "gathered monthly under the leadership of SS-Brigadeführer Baron Kurt Freiherr von Schröder for the express purpose of furnishing 'our most revered Reichsführer, Heinrich Himmler' with necessary funds," as Colonel Bernstein reported to Lieutenant General Clay on 8 September 1945 (NA, RG 260, USGCC, Box 1). The money to Himmler "was paid into a special account 'S' Bankhaus J. H. Stein, Cologne, in the name of Kurt von Schröder.... The 1943 contribution was RM 1,100,000, and that for 1944, RM 1,015,000."

"Baron von Schröder is the dominant figure in the J.H. Stein Bank of Cologne. The bank is one of a group of eight banks which have played the outstanding role in German big business and industry." Kurt von Schröder joined the NSDAP in early February 1933. A few weeks later, the finance minister in the Hitler government appointed him as the German delegate to the Bank for International Settlements in Switzerland, which was known at the time as the "bank of the central banks." Von Schröder later joined a small group of economic advisers who met regularly with Hitler's secretary, Martin Bormann. It is likely that in Cologne he was the person with the best connections to the Kanzlei des Führers.

economic adviser to the NSDAP and a senior SS officer close to SS chief Himmler's inner circle. Von Schröder lobbied actively for the appointment of Schmidt (with Albert as the second choice) as the wartime administrator of Ford-Werke AG, and against a custodian from outside the company. The Kanzlei des Führers agreed, and submitted a concurring opinion to Reichs-kommissar Krohn: "Due to the German character of this factory, the appointment of a special administrator is unnecessary, especially since there are employees there who will guarantee the protection of German interests."[150] On 15 May 1942 Schmidt became "enemy property custodian" of Ford Werke for the duration of the war.

Compared to the capacities and production of Ford factories in the United States, Ford Werke's absolute production numbers (or those of any other German producer) seem modest. As a proportion of the German military's needs during the rapid occupation of ten countries and the conquest of the Soviet Union up to the gates of Moscow, they were indispensable. According to a 1946 Allied report, in 1938 "Ford was responsible for 48% of the total German output of 2–3-ton trucks, while in 1942, when the Cologne works were concentrating on the production of medium trucks for the German armed forces and were producing 1,200–1,600 trucks per month, they are estimated to have made 35% of the total German medium truck output."[151] During his interrogation Schmidt wrote: "This company was the second largest producer of trucks in Germany," estimating that 95,000 trucks had been delivered directly to the Wehrmacht during the war years. Another 90,000 civilian Ford trucks were requisitioned by the Wehrmacht in Germany and in the occupied countries. "Of the 350,000 trucks which the motorized German army possessed in 1942, 100,000 to 120,000 were Ford built. Of the Wehrmacht's total of 650,000 mobile units of all kinds, 15 to 20% were built by Ford."[152] In addition, the company produced tens of thousands of replacement engines and countless spare parts.

While its main role was in motorizing the Wehrmacht and keeping its trucks running, Ford Werke was also involved in the production of high-end munitions. The Schneider report revealed details of a secret arrangement, made in a late-1939 meeting between Ford Werke representatives and OKW, under which "German Ford agreed to assume full responsibility for production of munitions and armament of the kind and to the extent deemed necessary by the High Command." At the same time, "Cologne was permitted to retain the appearance of continuing to produce only its standard Ford trucks (all destined for the Wehrmacht)." For this purpose a cloak company, Arendt GmbH, was set up by Ford Werke in December 1939 to manufacture munitions "throughout the war at a yearly turnover of 1,500,000 marks."[153]

Albert was pulling the strings in an affair Dearborn apparently knew nothing about. As he wrote to General Zuckertort, his contact at OKW: "The solution of producing the war material under a different name from Ford and outside the Ford factory has been a complete success. The small subsidiary created for this purpose [Arendt GmbH] has absorbed excess material and personnel from Ford and is producing the war material you have ordered at full capacity."[154]

Curiously, "German Ford did not think it necessary to use this or any other cloak for its 1939–1941 production of the command cars [by its Berlin factory]; nor for the 1940–1944 production for the Luftwaffe of 505 motors for boats and landing barges; nor for the 1940–1941 production of 20,000 gears for a Junkers aircraft plant; nor for the production of the 10,000 half-tracks begun in 1942 or 1943, nor for its participation in an army repair shop program from 1942 to 1944."[155]

Business at Ford Werke had never been so good. Revenues in 1943 stood at 184 million RM, about six times 1933 levels, and nearly double those of 1938. Net profits had also nearly doubled since the start of the war. The collapse of production in the fall and winter of 1944 and 1945 did not cause a corresponding collapse in the balance sheets. As Schmidt revealed to Lord Perry in May 1945: "Our finances were quite good even after the big bombing raid in September and October of last year, and the consequent downfall of production. Where we stand to-day we are not quite sure. Indications are that the financial position is still good although much material must be considered lost."

"In order to cover the costs of decentralisation," meaning the program of dispersing production machinery among various locations to avoid bombing, Ford Werke "had obtained an advance from the German Government which will cover the decentralisation as well as re-centralisation costs. The amount we still have to receive from the Government for trucks and parts is fairly small since we had cashed every possible invoice before the occupation." Neatly passing over the matter of forced labor, Schmidt added that "rates of pay, both for pay- and salary roll have not changed during the war, only in the cases of promotion or demotion."[156]

ACCORDING TO THE "Report on Ford Werke,"

> Robert H. Schmidt, wartime administrator of German Ford by Reich appointment gained stature with the expanding German borders.... In addition to Schmidt's appointment as Administrative Custodian (Verwalter) of German Ford he also became Kommissar of Ford in Belgium, Verwalter in Holland and for a period of 6 months acted as Kommissar of the French Ford plant, his successor being Albert. With all these powers, Schmidt and Albert were able to juggle machinery and productive capacity to serve the best interests of their Nazi rulers, to continue domination of German Ford's original territory in Austria, Czechoslovakia, and Hungary and to extend German Ford interests in other continental countries. There is no indication that the German management ever was so bold as to lay plans for taking over Dearborn. It is a fact, however, that an organization of most of European Ford under hegemony of German Ford was accomplished during the War. In the peace to follow, immediate objectives were to bolster this control over 'the European Greatspace' and effect German domination over British Ford and the few other Ford organizations in Europe not yet fully controlled.[157]

In the conquered countries, a "Kommissar" was appointed by the military command, a "Verwalter" (custodian) by the Reich's civilian occupation authorities. Either type of enemy property custodian had much the same powers. In July 1940 Albert and in September 1940 Schmidt reported to Dearborn in detail on Cologne's efforts to integrate the Belgian, Dutch and French Ford companies into the German war economy. Albert claimed the measures were in keeping with the Hague Convention and in the interests of both Germany and the Ford family.[158] Edsel Ford answered in October 1940:

> We have a fairly complete impression of the present status of the Ford Companies in Germany as well as the other occupied territories. It is quite evident and very gratifying that you and your organization are looking after our interests successfully and we appreciate your efforts on our behalf. I am glad to hear that the outside plants are beginning to operate, as it is the only way for rehabilitation to take place, and after all there are many people financially interested in these properties besides ourselves. Anything that can be done constructively to keep these plants in operation will be a great help for the future.[159]

"You have a very difficult task to carry out with regard to the companies that have come into your jurisdiction," Edsel Ford wrote two weeks later to Schmidt, "and I feel sure that you will have cooperation from the other continental organizations in looking after the best interest of the Ford organizations as a whole."[160] The expressions of fealty seem heartfelt and mutual. Albert wrote confidentially to Schmidt in December 1941 about his negotiations in Berlin with General von Schell. Schell's office had suggested merging Ford Werke with Volkswagenwerk, Hermann Goering Werke, Mercedes, or Auto Union. Albert to Schmidt: "For us it would go without saying that we would stick wholeheartedly and to the last minute to the American partnership, to the fact to be part of the Ford concern, to build up a German domination within the Ford concern as far as Europe was concerned."[161]

Had the Finance Division investigators seen the files of the Reichs kommissar, they would have known that they were by no means underestimating the extent of Cologne's operations and control over the European Ford units. In addition to the countries mentioned in the passage above, Schmidt also controlled Ford Athens. He pulled all the strings at the Ford Werke subsidiary in Bucharest, although Axis Romania had placed that under a custodianship of its own. Cologne imposed rationalization programs in France, Belgium, and the Netherlands, reorganizing production and supply among these plants to enable them to carry out self-sufficient manufacture for the Wehrmacht and reduce the burden on Ford Werke.[162] But production at Cologne was always the top priority. As Schmidt confessed to Lord Perry in May 1945, during the occupation 232 essential production machines were taken from the Ford plants in France, Holland and Belgium and shipped to Ford Werke.[163]

Schmidt expounded on the "satisfactory" process of "adding the non-German European Ford factories to the war potential" during a meeting of the Ford Werke advisory board on 1 July 1943. He noted that Ford Copenhagen was building gas-powered generators and that Ford in neutral Sweden was occasionally supplying parts to eliminate bottlenecks. Schmidt was especially thrilled that Ford affiliates in neutral Switzerland had been convinced to supply about 2,000,000 RM in replacement parts.[164]

During his imprisonment in summer 1945 Schmidt signed three statements on Ford Werke's influence in Switzerland, one of which read:

> Switzerland ... was Belgian Ford territory, but even prior to the war German Ford was quite a factor.... After Belgium was occupied, German Ford paid the staff of Belgian Ford in Switzerland and its expenses. The Belgian staff cooperated with Schmidt. He developed the idea of buying Ford spares in Switzerland both for German Ford and other European Ford companies. The German Government guaranteed payment. German Ford's sales also were increased. Moreover, it aided the German government's deal with all Swiss dealers in all makes under which the Swiss dealers agreed to repair 2,000 Army trucks and convert them into gas producers.[165]

Always on the Side of the Winners

After six years of feverish war activity on all fronts, of exploiting forced labor and collaborating in every way with the Nazi regime, Ford Werke and its management at first suffered nothing more than shell damage to the plant buildings during the Wehrmacht's pointless last stand. On 18 April the men of the Military Government of Cologne (specifically E1H2 Property Control Section) returned to the Ford plant for their first look since mid-March. The U.S. Army officers were disturbed by the new rubble, but the resourceful Schmidt was not worried. He announced that "500 trucks could be produced within a short time if he is permitted to conserve material which is available."[166] Schmidt knew that most of the plant's machinery was safely stored at dispersal points on the other side of the river. MG Cologne promptly made arrangements to allow plant employees to start cleaning up the grounds, and on 28 April "tentative plans were made to visit the various subsidiary Ford factories east of the Rhine to determine the feasibility of resuming operations here in Cologne."[167] The resources of the U.S. military were put to the task in the next days,[168] and Charles Thacker, former stock superintendent of Ford of England, was called in to take over the factory. He decided to immediately resume production.[169] Ford Werke became the first large factory in Cologne to do so. On 8 May 1945, the day of Germany's unconditional surrender, an American documentary team set up its cameras to record the sight of the first post-war truck coming off the Ford Werke assembly line.[170]

In September factory personnel was back up to 2,500 and by the end of the year Ford had built 2,438 trucks.[171] "It was a notable achievement, for raw materials were in short supply; steel and tires were at a premium and semi-finished goods were frequently unavailable because suppliers had not resumed production."[172] Of course, very little conversion work was required for peacetime production. All along the factory had "only produced trucks."

These no longer transported German troops and materiel, but they were needed to carry supplies into the city, start the displaced persons on the way home, and haul rubble.

THE MILITARY GOVERNMENT OF COLOGNE began allowing companies to resume production more freely after Germany's unconditional surrender. In Cologne a company could apply for a permit to the new municipal department for economics and labor. Later the task was taken over by the reconstructed city chamber of commerce and industry (Cologne IHK). Even then, companies with more than five (later ten) employees needed permission from the E1H2 Trade & Industry officers. Applicants were required to swear they had never been members of the NSDAP, SS or S.A. Decisions on industrial operations, and on what energy sources would be made available to them, were met by the military government alone. But as the E1H2 reports make clear, the military government was intent on avoiding any superfluous delays. By the end of May 1945, E1H2 had forwarded seventy-seven approved applications to the U.S. 15th Army command.[173]

Soon the German institutions were playing the key role in reauthorization. The military government's supervision of the process cannot be described as strict, except that E1H2 remained very persistent about not compromising its anti-Nazi policy. Patterson emphasized Eisenhower's strict orders and mentioned bad experiences due to leniency in Aachen.* Exceptions were granted only when higher U.S. Army staff overruled the Cologne detachment. Because it was directed against *all* "party comrades" and not just "ardent Nazis," the Patterson line called forth great agitation and expressions of outrage, above all from the industrialists who had been involved in the Nazi war economy. As Swiss General Consul von Weiss noted on 18 April: "Industry plans diplomatic overtures to Marshall Eisenhower through Mayor Adenauer or the Bishop Count Galen, in order to amend the current regulation so as to acknowledge a distinction between decent and wild Party comrades."[174]

Bernhard Hilgermann, the newly appointed chief executive of the city chamber of commerce IHK Cologne, commented on the attitude prevalent among his countrymen as follows: "Most of the Germans believed that everything past would be forgiven and forgotten with the cessation of hostilities; as after a boxing match, one reaches out for a handshake in an act of

---

*Ernest O. Hauser, a war correspondent who witnessed the establishment of the military governments in both Aachen and Cologne, summarized the origins of the "soft" Aachen and "hard" Cologne policies in the *Saturday Evening Post*, 2 June 1945: "The appointment of Nazis to administrative jobs under MG was left from the start to the discretion of individual teams. All the book said was that 'ardent Nazis' were not eligible, and the Aachen team experimented with some 'nonardent Nazis' until the Allied press communicated the scandal to the world. Thereafter, MG adopted a policy which was pioneered by Lt. Col. John K. Patterson, the military governor of Cologne. It disqualifies all former members of the Nazi Party. This new deal, which constituted a victory of Allied public opinion over MG's experimental frame of mind, created some difficulties."

friendship. After all, preparations are now being made for a peaceful reconstruction." "The businessmen feel that they have a completely clean record,
since they were only members of a party that was coincidentally called
NSDAP."[175] Hilgermann was one of the rare Germans with an insight into
the other side's thinking. "The officers were trained for their missions, but it
was not easy for them to cope with the exceptional conditions. They needed
the cooperation of the Germans. But these Germans were to them the originators of this long war, the inventors of the extermination camps, the mur-
derers of many millions of people; on purely personal grounds they rejected
them. At first this attitude was very clear in direct conversation. They did
not extend hands to Germans. The ban on fraternization underlined this
attitude. Only when alone with a German would they ask him to take a seat,
assuming they had come to like him."[176]

With only a few exceptions Germans, if they even came into contact with
the occupying power, were far too occupied with themselves to see the difficulties that the Americans faced. "In practice the detachments of the Military Government are running into a great variety of problems, complicated
by the temporary helplessness of the German civilians, by the unrestrained
loss of control with which the displaced persons are enjoying their newly
won freedom and releasing pent-up rancor against their former German
masters, and often enough by self-doubts among members of the military
government, about whether they will succeed in walking the narrow ridge
between strict justice with regard to the Germans and the urgent need to
reestablish at least a minimum of administration and economy."[177]

In reality the Rhineland business community had little cause for complaint. The American economic officers were competent, pragmatic, and
completely free of socialist influence. The general American policy was
based on private property and a predictable rule of law. The Americans
were making a massive logistical effort to transport home the frightening
army of now-superfluous foreign and forced laborers—away from their
camps near the factories. Even under Patterson's hardline enforcement of
the rules, a common distinction was by then being drawn between a strict
policy of de-Nazification for office-holders and a moderate one for trade and
industry.[178] "The finance and economic officers that we dealt with back
then," Hilgermann later recalled, "were often bankers from the Midwest or
businessmen obviously trying to get production moving to the extent allowable within their authorities."[179]

Given all that, Robert Schmidt may have felt he was on his way in late
May 1945, when he helped Thacker to reorganize the Cologne plant and
sought Lord Perry's absolution. That was foiled by the arrival of Bernstein's
investigators, who arrested him.[180] Vitger, who had stood by Schmidt's side
throughout the war, encountered no such difficulties. Vitger was made plant
custodian in September 1945 and hired on as the new boss of Ford Werke
after Dearborn normalized its control. Ford also kept Heinrich Albert, but
in a subordinate position at the company's Berlin office. Albert had made
himself unpalatable through the secret munitions production under the

cover of Arendt GmbH. Schmidt had his difficulties in getting cleared, but after a successful de-Nazification in 1948, he was back with Ford Werke in 1949. He became a top executive again in 1952 and stayed with the company for the rest of his life. (Schmidt died in a car crash on the way to lay a cornerstone for a new factory in Belgium in 1962).[181]

In their history of Ford's international businesses, Wilkins and Hill stress that "the European companies operated at a handsome profit in all years except 1945 ... [the last] chiefly due to the impending collapse of Germany," and that the Ford family's net paper profit for the war years stood at about $11 million.[182] But they suggest the Cologne subsidiary paid a stiff price because it was compelled to use German materials and to standardize according to German guidelines. During the war, exports plunged, profits had to be kept in Germany, and the Reich forced truck development along military lines. "The iron hand" of the Nazi regime "gripped Cologne firmly, although the velvet glove of approbation and profits (which eventually might be taken) made it fairly acceptable."[183]

This seems like an overcomplicated explanation for the activities of Albert and Schmidt during the war. Rather than seeing them as victims of some "iron hand," it would be far simpler to think they were activists, true to the regime, with a double allegiance that proved opportune amid the shifting winds of the war. A decorated civil servant, Albert was typical of many non-Nazis whose conservative loyalties to the Reich and its Wehrmacht in particular were obviously more important than oaths of office taken during the "legalistic period" of the Weimar Republic. The energetic Schmidt was also more than a "willing helper" of the Nazi regime, although his task involved producing and selling motor vehicles, rather than implementing the party's politics. As a *Wehrwirtschaftsführer*, Schmidt belonged to a caste of about 400 directors and industrialists who swore allegiance to the Führer and to the goals of the Wehrmacht. They held substantive and official authority as necessary to meet that responsibility.[184]

After the war Ford Werke went through a few years of difficult business but reestablished its prewar position as one of the top European carmakers. Ford cashed in $1 million for its war-related damages from the U.S. government in the 1960s. For fifty-three years, it upheld a rigorous silence about the forced laborers who had helped make its German unit so profitable during the war.

Epilogue

The presentation of the "Report on Ford Werke" to General Clay on 9 September 1945 did not result in any consequences for either Ford Motor or its German subsidiary.[185] The writers of the report avoided a legal interpretation. Even Colonel Bernstein did no more than assert that: "The activities of Ford Werke AG may serve for comparison with the activities of German owned or controlled subsidiaries located in the United States or elsewhere in the United Nations."[186] That was the end of the matter as far as General Clay was concerned. The "Report on Ford Werke Aktiengesellschaft" was filed away as confidential.

How did Ford Motor deal with the damaging accusation that it had helped Hitler? The answer is simple. The company as far as possible avoided any public discussion of the matter. Ford Motor's only known position regarding the accusations in Drew Pearson's *Washington Post* column from September 1945, a memorandum by the company counsel that apparently was never publicized, stressed the legality of Dearborn's activities.[187] The lawyerly argument sticks to the purely economic aspects of the involvement, and points to the many other U.S. companies who also stayed in Nazi Germany.

The political and ethical dimensions go unmentioned: not a word therein is lost on the company's policies, no regret was expressed. This was only possible because the accusations raised against Ford were largely ignored by the U.S. media. First of all, as many publishers and editors would have argued, we must try those who are *directly* responsible for the Nazi regime's military aggression and countless crimes against humanity.

Eleanor Roosevelt took up that issue when she used her popular column "My Day" to promote the findings of Bernstein's investigators, only ten days after the report was submitted to General Clay: "I hope a great many people read the story about the Ford plants in Germany, published in one of our newspapers the other day, with its record of the action permitted to these foreign plants by the majority stockholders in this country. Although the story dealt only with the Ford empire, there are many other great industrial concerns in the United States whose plants f u n c t i o n in many countries throughout the world." She made what seems to be an oblique reference to the Lawler Report from spring 1943: "I recall hearing, after France fell and after we went into the war, that the heads of a big industry in this country cabled congratulations to their managers in France because the latter were keeping the plant going–although they were keeping it going by making what the Germans asked them to make." But she avoided concrete details: "Business complications do strange things to our patriotism and to our ethics!"

"It is important that every now and then we stop and examine what we have done and what resulted from our actions. In the carefully documented case of the Ford German plants, it was quite evident that Hitler and the Nazis profited by the attitude of the stockholders in this country."[188]

Mrs. Roosevelt's appeal–to confront the activities of American companies in support of the Nazi regime sooner rather than later–had little effect. Whether in the United States or in Occupied Germany, time was working against the critics of Dearborn and its Cologne subsidiary. With Morgenthau's resignation the advocates of a hard peace, especially with regard to the German war industry, had lost their most important backer in government. During a reorganization of the U.S. Military Government in late September, General Clay stripped Colonel Bernstein of leadership of the

Finance Division. Clay offered to make Bernstein the director of the Division of Investigation of Cartels and External Assets (DICEA), a post that had been created with Bernstein in mind. Bernstein refused, and returned to Washington.

DICEA was soon demoted to a Decartelization Branch and assigned to General Draper's Economics Division. The reformers still left in the "branch" were not quite yet defeated. The quarrel over the extent of structural reform and reconstruction in Germany continued. In February 1947 Decartelization Law 56 and the similar British Ordinance No. 78 enforced new arrangements within their respective branches. Intensive investigations were initiated of conglomerates such as Henschel, Siemens, Bosch and Gutehoffnungshütte. But when the trust-busters submitted their cases for approval and filing in March 1948, the Military Governor Clay blocked them, citing economic reasons and the poor physical condition of industry.

West Germany's economy withstood the critical post-war years without suffering any lasting damage. The automobile industry was one of the beneficiaries of the victory of the "pragmatics" and "realists" over the "hardliners." After the end of the occupation, the carmakers repeated their grandiose rise of the 1930s, this time in a democratic republic and without need of a war program. The upward trend was of duration, as Ford Werke's further history clearly demonstrates.

Today Ford-Werke AG is one of Germany's twenty largest industrial corporations, with revenues of 27.8 billion DM in 1998 on European sales of 1.1 million vehicles.[189] The European headquarters of the Ford Motor Company in 1998 was moved from the British town of Dagenham to Cologne. On the brink of the twenty-first century, the whole Ford family of corporations is said "to have a chance of becoming the biggest car maker in the world, a position it lost in the 1920s to General Motors.... The company will be 100 years old in 2003. World leadership would be a fitting way to celebrate."[190] It sounds like a good time, surely, for the company to finally rid itself of a history of denial and equivocation by admitting openly the full story of Ford Motor's and Ford Werke's activities during the twelve years of the Nazi regime.

– Reinhold Billstein

DISCOVERIES

Troops of the U.S. First Army advancing into Cologne, 6 March 1945 (B1).

U.S. soldiers watch military parade at a Cologne stadium, 11 March 1945 (B2).

Cologne after years of Allied bombardment, 24 April 1945 (B3).

View from the Cathedral, 7 March 1945 (B4).

11 May 1945. Aerial photo of Ford Werke plant (center, standing) with camouflage cover for parking lot in foreground and barracks in the background (B5).

A German edition of *The International Jew: A World Problem* (B6). "The first American book on the Jewish question, edited by Henry Ford," 2nd ed., published in Leipzig in 1921. After seizing power, the Nazis put this book through 29 editions by late 1933. Below (B7), the author of *Mein Kampf* (1924), Adolf Hitler, views the Ford stand at the 1936 Berlin motor show, next to the Ford Werke chief executive, Erich Diestel.

FORD

Werkzeitung

Werkzeitschrift der Betriebsgemeinschaften FORD, KÖLN u. BERLIN 2. Jahrg., Okt./Nov. 1939

Deutsche Fortwagen auf polnischen Straßen

"German Ford vehicles on Polish roads." – *Ford Werkszeitung*, October 1939 (B8).
Exhibit 93 in the U.S. Finance Division's 1945 "Report on Ford-Werke AG."

Ford vs. Ford

Outside Kharkov, Ukraine, February 1943 (B9). German Ford V3000S kitchen truck serves the crew of a Wehrmacht Panzer III M.

German Ford Maultier half-track caterpillar with 2 cm anti-aircraft flak gun (B10).

Canadian Ford F60 captured by the Wehrmacht, used in missions behind enemy lines (B11).

Liberation

On the eve of VE Day in Cologne, Polish women and U.S. soldiers celebrate, 7 May 1945 (B12).

A Polish woman and U.S. soldier celebrate VE Day (B13).

Liberated French and Belgians wait for trucks to take them to a DP camp, the first stop on their journey home, 4 April 1945 (B14).

Walter Rietig (B15).

Walter Rietig (second from left) marches with International Workers Welfare in Langen, 1932 (B16).

CHAPTER 3

WALTER RIETIG AND THE
EFFORT OF REMEMBRANCE

W alter Rietig was just thirty-six when he was murdered, in December
1942, by the authorities of the German Reich. He was sentenced to
death by the Volksgerichtshof, the so-called People's Court in the Berlin district of Plotzensee. Many of the judges who delivered verdicts there regained
high posts and judicial authority after the war. They never had to answer for
their misdeeds. Their victims were relegated to the historical scrap-books of
the Federal Republic, the recollection of them fading with time.

A short street in the town of Russelsheim is named after Walter Rietig.
Despite such scattered symbolic gestures, people after the war more often
preferred to do away with the concrete evidence of the Nazi era. This tendency has survived into our own times. The old house at Schäfergasse 20,
where the last Jewish residents of Russelsheim were imprisoned in
cramped quarters before being transported away, was demolished just a
few years ago.[1]

Many Germans, even when they are open about the Third Reich in general terms, prefer to avoid dealing with specific Nazi-era events in their own
towns. Local studies, which have become common in the last twenty years,
tend to reveal the entanglements of individuals in the system. The local
approach to history raises questions of personal responsibility. Many people, both young and old, prefer to avoid such questions in their own lives,
or wish to conceal feelings of complicity. Some among the old may even be
hiding a direct participation. Many Germans who lived through the Nazi era
later claimed that they had been apolitical, or "inner emigrants." This manner of self-exoneration might appear dubious when contrasted against
examples of people who stood up to the Nazi tyranny.

Walter Rietig was not an outstanding political figure of the German
Resistance. He was just a man who remained true to his anti-Fascist

beliefs, in spite of the Nazi terror. By not adapting to the New Order, he showed that assent to the Nazi regime was not simply a function of yielding to irresistible force.

Walter Rietig, born 1906 in Breslau, worked on and off at the Opel factory in Russelsheim starting in 1929. He and his wife moved to the nearby town of Langen in 1931. In the 1920s Walter Rietig was a member of Socialist Worker Youth, as the youth organization of the Social Democratic Party of Germany (SPD) was then known. In 1929 he joined the Langen chapter of the "Friends of Nature," a nationwide association of hiking and travel groups within the workers' movement.[2]

The last years of the Weimar Republic saw an increasingly dramatic street-level confrontation between the trade unions, the SPD and the Communist Party of Germany (KPD) on one side, and the National Socialists with their million-plus paramilitary stormtroops on the other. In the Gross-Gerau region, as in many other places, the Nazis gained the support of a plurality of the rural population and of the middle classes. In other words, they won over the former voters of the bourgeois and conservative parties.[3]

Parallel to this life-or-death struggle, the years of the Great Depression also brought polarization within the workers' movement, between an SPD-oriented reformist wing and a KPD-influenced revolutionary wing. The KPD attempted to mobilize a united "Red Front" of all workers in an extra-parliamentary struggle of "class against class." Social Democrat politicians, often in government on the local level, instead felt compelled to uphold due process and the rule of law, if necessary against their own political goals. SPD-led town councils had to enforce the harsh emergency measures imposed by the series of conservative national governments who held power in Berlin during the late Weimar period. Communists, who organized demonstrations against cuts in social benefits and against wage reductions in compulsory work schemes, more often than not aimed their political fire at SPD-led municipal bodies, rather than at the conservative national governments.[4]

As the crisis intensified, the SPD came to be associated with workers who still had jobs, while the KPD became a party of the unemployed and the poor. Communist leaders viewed the SPD as their primary opponent. At Moscow's behest, they accused Social Democrats of being "social fascists." This hyperbole caught on with the KPD rank and file, who were incensed that SPD-led town councils and works councils were enforcing austerity policies. Whatever its superficial rhetorical appeal, the KPD's insupportable accusation of "social fascism" was simply self-destructive, all the more so because the true fascists were preparing to seize power.[5]

Events at Opel in the years 1929 to 1930 illustrate how the incipient division in the Weimar-period workers' movement turned irreconcilable. Shop-floor influence in Russelsheim traditionally was wielded by DMV, the metal workers' union. Social democrat in orientation, DMV was challenged in the Opel works council election of February 1929 by the

KPD-organized "Revolutionary Union Organization" (RGO). In their first ballot-box effort, the Communists captured 39 percent of the votes cast by the Opel personnel.

Despite the factory's advanced production process and technology, Opel, like most companies, faced a serious crisis as the global system of credit and payment collapsed. A family business until the late 1920s, the Adam Opel firm was converted to a stock corporation. Sensing a bargain, General Motors bought 80 percent of Opel shares in 1929. During its first year of control, the U.S. auto giant implemented a strict labor regimen and work speed-ups, and reduced personnel at Russelsheim from 10,000 to 6,500.

Until then, DMV leaders had viewed rationalization schemes positively, believing that higher productivity allows higher wages for those workers who escape redundancy. But General Motors instead forced a new shopfloor agreement to lower wages. The Communists were expelled from the works council for stirring extralegal opposition to the wage cuts. RGO thereupon launched a wildcat strike, on 12 February 1930, without the support of DMV. The action was suppressed immediately by a brutal police crackdown, and denounced by the Social Democrats as the "Opel Putsch." Following this failure, RGO was nearly wiped out in the Opel works council elections of spring 1930. Within two years the Nazi shopfloor organization, the NSBO, gained by election a majority of the seats on the company council for salaried employees. The NSBO also captured a strong foothold on Opel's blue-collar works council.

In the wake of these developments, the Social Democrats came to regard the KPD as no better than the NSDAP, while the Communists believed that their theory of "social fascism" had been confirmed. At that point neither side really imagined what would happen once the Nazis were in power. As a direct result of the "Opel Putsch," Communist and Social Democrat organizations across the nation broke off all but a few isolated points of contact. One of these was the Friends of Nature, within which the conflicts between SPD and KPD were continued on a smaller scale.

Walter Rietig may have felt himself trapped between the two camps. Most of the Langen "Friends" were social democrats. They adopted the anti-KPD policy set by the central headquarters of the Friends movement, and expelled a group of KPD members. The expelled Communists joined the Friends of Nature in nearby Egelsbach, who refused to toe their national organization's line. On the contrary, the Egelsbach Friends were among the few groups who still sought to bridge the splits and unite working people in a common political struggle against the Nazi threat.[6]

It is unknown if Walter Rietig was himself expelled from the Langen Friends, or if he supported the expulsions. But he did take part in a 1932 demonstration of the KPD-oriented "International Workers Welfare" in Langen. That allows for two interpretations:

1. Like many Social Democrats, Walter Rietig had turned away from the SPD and towards the KPD, or

2. He was following the lead of those who hoped to reunite the workers' movement.

Either way, it seems that the young Walter Rietig, like many other Friends of Nature, stood between the SPD and the KPD. It seems likely his convictions were individual and deep-seated, and that he would not have surrendered easily after the Nazi seizure of power in early 1933.

In his surveys of the minority of Germans who resisted the Nazi regime after 1933, the political scientist Axel Ulrich found a disproportionate number of young people who had been in the Friends of Nature, who had stood between SPD and KPD, or who were disillusioned with the SPD and leaning towards the KPD in the final years of the Weimar Republic. Ulrich presents ample evidence that, soon after the Nazis seized power, a clandestine resistance group formed at Opel, with members from both SPD and KPD.

In the first days of May 1933 the Nazis smashed all independent trade unions and rounded up labor leaders and activists, establishing the NSDAP German Labor Front (DAF) as the sole shopfloor organization, with compulsory membership. Ulrich: "Several resistance groups arose in the following years, mostly comprising former trade unionists—Social Democrats, Communists, Christians—and members of the disbanded Friends of Nature." These underground groups were generally tolerant of different political orientations. Communists played a dominant role, in part because they already had the most experience in clandestine activity.[7] Having seen the political disaster of 1933, the KPD was prepared to reorganize its Communist Youth Association (KJV) along heterogeneous lines, and to bridge the ideological rifts of the late Weimar period.[8] Various old grudges were overcome to form an incipient common resistance, with the Communists in charge.[9]

This was not a secret to the Gestapo. In February 1935 they launched a nationwide crackdown on resistance groups. The Darmstadt Gestapo reported on the regional results as follows: "119 persons were arrested just in the three Hessian counties of Offenbach, Gross-Gerau and Dieburg.... It is curious that in Mainz, the reorganized KJV took hold among the dissolved organization known as the 'Friends of Nature,' which before the coup consisted mostly of members and followers of the SPD. It may be inferred that in rebuilding the illegal KJV the KPD is pursuing the goal of a unified front with the SPD, especially with young Social Democrat workers."[10]

Witnesses who lived through that time confirm involvement by Friends of Nature in several resistance groups in the county of Gross-Gerau—and at Opel.[11] It is known that Walter Rietig joined an illegal group of Social Democrats and Communists in 1933, but nothing is known about the group's activities.[12] After all, opponents of the regime did not keep written records. They were under constant threat of imprisonment, torture and death, and forced to work illegally. This reveals one of the biggest problems in researching the Nazi-era resistance. Axel Ulrich points out the paradox that historiography has generally accepted Nazi documentary sources as reliable, as though the authorities were all-powerful and all-knowing, while the spoken testimonies of resistance fighters, and even their original documents, are usually treated with far greater skepticism.[13]

With the crackdown of 1935 the Gestapo succeeded in shattering the majority of resistance groups in the Gross-Gerau region. Many Opel workers were arrested. Walter Rietig was not among them. A new, especially paranoid phase began, during which most activists shunned all but the most informal resistance contacts.

The labor situation at Opel got worse in the years that followed. In June 1936 the workers of one department staged a fifteen-minute strike to protest a cut in pay and terrible working conditions. Two hundred strikers were fired on the spot. Thirty-seven were arrested, several of them ended up in concentration camps. Company security and Gestapo thereupon recruited an extensive network of informants, with the design of alerting management and secret police immediately of any organizing or expressions of discontent. In reaction the isolated resistance groups at the Opel plant gave up entirely on their often foolhardy written propaganda, and adopted stricter rules of conspiracy. Only after the outbreak of war, in September 1939, did they cautiously resume their organizing efforts.

Our next concrete information about Walter Rietig dates from 1942. Most of our knowledge about the events leading to his death was gained by Peter Schirmbeck of the Russelsheim Town Museum in interviews with Fritz Zängerle, a resistance activist who worked at the Russelsheim body plant, and who became the first leader of the Opel works council after the Second World War.[14] Fritz Zängerle was the contact man to Walter Rietig: "Actually our cell consisted of just a few people. It was supposed to never be more than five. There were I believe seven of us. One of us had the connection to the next highest level. None of the cells was supposed to know about the others...."

Since they were greatly restricted by the Nazi terror, their activities at first consisted in listening to foreign broadcasts. The mere possession of an unauthorized shortwave receiver was a serious crime. At the factory the conspirators met regularly at a metal-grinder to whisper news beneath the roar of the machine.

> That was practically our headquarters, everybody would bring something to grind, and we would circulate the news, whatever was going on, how things looked at the front, or that the English [prisoners of war in Russelsheim] were being given this or that as rations.... Walter Rietig was also a member of the cell. He wasn't an active member, but more someone who would give and get information. He was the contact man to the prisoners of war, to the French.... That's how he ended up under the guillotine, Walter Rietig, a Friend of Nature from Langen. A good acquaintance of mine, whom I saw every day.

> Of course, the Nazi shop stewards asked me what Walter Rietig was doing there every day, at my place. I said I had known him from the Friends of Nature, that

we had both been in it and had a few things keeping us together, such as that every week he brought me my laundry from my mother. The Nazi stewards had been assigned to find out who Rietig was meeting every day, and of course it was a big mistake that he came to me every day.

Fritz Zängerle recalls the day when "Rietig came to me and said, 'Fritz, they're making me give up my DAF card.'" Rietig had been interrogated by the Gestapo in connection with the spreading of defeatist rumors. Zängerle urged him to take flight: "I told him, Walter, if they're canceling your DAF pass, then you must get out. You can get connections, you can surely escape to Switzerland or France. But he said: 'No, I won't do that, what could happen to me? In three years at the most, the war will be over.' But he had misjudged his situation."

Walter Rietig was arrested and convicted on the testimony of three coworkers. They each received payments of 100 RM. "That was a lot of money back then," Fritz Zängerle says. "The top wage for a foreman was 1.25, 1.35 during the war. That was a small fortune that each of them got, just to make a statement in Berlin."

The Gestapo paid a visit to the Opel plant on 13 July 1942, interviewed the informants, and arrested Walter Rietig. He was brought to the State Police Prison in Darmstadt. There he confessed, apparently after torture. He later recanted, but that was of no consequence. Walter Rietig was transferred from Gestapo custody to the Darmstadt Regional Prison on 23 July, where he was kept to await trial. On 13 October he was taken to Alt-Moabit Prison in Berlin. He was tried by the Volksgerichtshof on 26 October 1942. His retraction was ruled inadmissible.

Herbert Bauch, in his study of Walter Rietig's death, quotes the Reich Lord Prosecutor: "In the following case, the accused has retracted his confession, and claims that the police is incriminating him unfairly on the basis of a nervous breakdown." Bauch writes: "The Berlin judges entertained no doubts. In Walter Rietig they saw 'a very secure personality, someone who would not lose his composure, even in the course of a rough treatment from the police—as may have been made necessary by his behavior.'"[15]

In her history of Nazi-era Langen, Heidi Fogel writes: "The lay jurors who assisted the two judges in the case of Walter Rietig were all functionaries of the NSDAP. Each held a high position in the Party. The court heard the three informants. They repeated their original testimonies. Walter Rietig objected that the main witness against him was acting on a personal grudge. This was swept away with the observation that the witness did not give the impression of being capable of such an action. No witnesses were called on Walter Rietig's behalf."[16]

Walter Rietig was sentenced to death for "weakening the inner front of the German people through Communist recruitment speeches" and for a "traitorous promotion of conditions conducive to the enemy, in combination with plans for high treason." The court did not uphold the original accusation of "forbidden communication with prisoners of war." Appeals for clemency and a resumption of the case were denied.[17]

The Reich Interior Ministry saw fit to consummate the sentence in the month of December 1942. The war was by then obviously turning against the Wehrmacht, and the German people were waking up to a grim reality. The secret S.D. "Situation Report" of 29 December 1942 reads: "A degree of disquiet has been roused [among the people] by Wehrmacht reports of difficult battles at Velikiye Liki [in Russia]. This town was believed to be far behind our lines, and one might therefore infer from the reports that the Soviets have advanced along this part of the front. The rumors that divisions are surrounded by the enemy at Stalingrad have also intensified, and are in part causing serious worries."[18]

The mood among the Opel workers was also causing "serious worries." Fritz Zängerle:

> The so-called factory roll-calls—nobody wanted to go there anymore! [The company security forces] would run through the factory departments, yelling: "Get up, let's go, why are you sitting around here? We are having a gathering back there!" [The personnel] had to be pushed into attending the roll-calls. They really only took place under pressure. And the Nazis were really angry about that. Something had to be done, to get all these defeatists to shut up, so that no one would dare say anything he might have heard in an enemy broadcast.

Walter Rietig's execution was intended to set an example, as the reading of the sentence confirmed. "As a deterrent," he would receive the highest penalty: "It is a clear danger that the poison of discord, which the defendant has spread among the personnel of the Opel factory, will continue having its effect, and may seriously impair the will to work at this vital military operation."[19]

Walter Rietig had underestimated the punishment he was likely to face, and this proved to be his doom. Perhaps he was thinking of earlier, similar cases at Opel. In the first years of the war, several Opel workers had been convicted for making statements critical of the regime. These were no worse than the statements of which Rietig was accused. Most of the offenders were sentenced to one or two years in prison.[20]

But the times had changed, and the Nazis apparently thought it necessary to set a more drastic example to the Following. Walter Rietig was killed by the guillotine in the night of 22 December 1942. On the same night, the Nazis executed the members of the legendary "Rote Kapelle," a group of dozens of well-placed Germans who had transmitted intelligence to Russia over some one hundred radio transmitters throughout Europe.

Despite his modest wishes for a cremation, as expressed just hours before his execution in his final letter to his wife and son, Walter Rietig's family was denied a decent funeral. His body was given instead to the anatomical institute of the University of Berlin, an act that expresses exceptional contempt.

The Interior Ministry ordered news of Walter Rietig's execution suppressed, except for a single announcement: a large red poster was put up at the Opel factory to inform the workers of the death of their colleague.[21]

"In my life I did my duty, as I had to do, my life was work and duty.... Now I take farewell, my love. Do not forget me, I will accept my sentence with the courage of innocence." Walter Rietig circumvented the censor in his letter with the ambiguous wish "of an imminent, just victory for the German people over their enemies, that they may gain a better place in the sun, work, contentment and happiness." That wish did not come true. The German people proved unable to overcome their Nazi barbarism on their own.

– Bernd Heyl

PART TWO

CHAPTER 4

FORCED LABOR AT FORD WERKE IN COLOGNE

In reply to our request [for information on the use in Cologne of forced laborers from concentration camps] Ford Werke in Cologne-Niehl stated that reliable documents from that time are not available, and they therefore must depend on information from company employees. According to reports, forty to fifty people, believed to have been prisoners from the Buchenwald concentration camp, worked on the factory grounds for about three months. There were no deaths, according to the factory doctor and the deputy of the company security force at that time; at any rate, neither of them could recall any such cases.

Cologne Office of the Registry, October 1949

I still remember well, when we workers from Ford were sitting in the canteen at midday, how the young Ukrainians always came over the roof, driven by hunger, and watched us while we ate. There were always colleagues who would open the skylight and pull the boys in. But there were also sadistic people from the company security forces who would guard the canteen, so that no foreign workers, as they were called at that time, could come in.

Fritz Theilen, retired Ford worker, September 1995

Perhaps you can't imagine it, but the tears flowed from my eyes while I wrote. I couldn't recall the camp, the bombings, the humiliations and the return home without breaking into tears.

Stepan Saika, former forced laborer at Ford
during the war, February 1995

The three efforts to remember the past cited above each stem from a direct participant, but the way they remember seems to differ greatly. In 1949, the factory doctor and the security officer claim they can no longer recall what happened a few years earlier.[1] Fifty years later, the retired Ford worker Fritz Theilen, who had been active in the resistance against the Nazi regime, says he remembers clearly.[2] For Stepan Saika, a former forced laborer, looking back on the years at Ford-Werke AG in Cologne is a painful process.[3]

German society is afflicted to this day by the rationalizations of its Nazi-era perpetrators, by their denial of crime and complicity. But questions of entanglement in Nazi crime also haunt the countries overrun by the German Reich in the war, the victorious Allies of the anti-Hitler coalition, and the countries that tried to stay neutral. The present controversy over wartime forced labor at the Ford auto factory in the Cologne district of Niehl reveals how tortuous the effort of memory remains, fifty-four years after the end of the war.

Historiography in Brief

For decades West German historians mostly ignored the Nazi practice of forced labor, until it was "rediscovered" in the early and mid-1980s. In those years, many researchers abandoned earlier, over-theoretical approaches to the Nazi past, and set out to examine events at particular localities in closer detail. Many histories of Nazi-era events as witnessed in towns, at workplaces, and at sites of persecution have since been published, and quite a few of these concern the use of forced laborers. Ulrich Herbert's *Fremdarbeiter. Politik und Praxis des "Ausländer-Einsatzes" in der Kriegswirtschaft des Dritten Reiches*, first published in 1985, is now considered the standard general study on forced labor during the Nazi era.[4]

The corporations that made use of forced labor during the war met any and all accusations in later decades with a defense borrowed from the Nuremberg Trial defendants. They argued that the Nazi state forced companies to accept slaves, that businesses were left no choice and no influence in the matter. A long series of studies have exploded this myth.[5] The debates triggered by important critical works, such as the two books on Daimler-Benz published in 1987 by the Hamburg Foundation of 20th Century Social History,[6] have encouraged a shift towards a more complex view, even at pro-corporate institutions like the Society of Entrepreneurial History (GUG) in Frankfurt am Main.[7] However, many companies today still refuse to open their wartime archives, especially to potentially critical historians.

Several works have examined in depth the Nazi-era history of Daimler-Benz and Volkswagen, including their use of slaves.[8] Less extensive studies deal with other carmakers, such as BMW, Adler, Auto-Union and Borgward. The forced-labor involvements of the U.S. auto giants General Motors and Ford, through their German subsidiaries, have not inspired quite as much scholarship among German-speaking historians. In fact, most of it is gathered in this volume.[9]

The issue of Nazi-era forced labor returned to the political agenda after 1989, following the transformation in Eastern Europe. The vast majority of the German Reich's slaves had been rounded up or recruited in the Soviet Union and Poland. Returning home after the war as "Displaced Persons," many of them were treated as "collaborators" or even deported to the Gulag. For decades, the erstwhile slaves suffered discrimination from the

Communist authorities and from their countrymen, and fell silent about their wartime experiences.

On the other side of the East-West divide, the 1953 London Debt Accords between the Federal Republic of Germany and the former Western Allies included a clause postponing individual restitutions for forced labor until after the signing of a "final" peace treaty for the Second World War. Citing that passage and various technicalities, the Federal Republic and its courts systematically turned away claims to compensation from former forced laborers.[10] But in 1990 the 2+4 Treaty joined the German Democratic Republic to the Federal Republic, with the approval of the four powers that had occupied the two Germanys since the war. Since then 2+4 has been interpreted as a peace treaty by German courts—although this is not yet conclusive—suggesting an incipient lapse in the 1953 stipulation. Meanwhile, the political shift in Eastern Europe has allowed former forced laborers living there to organize associations and pursue their claims more openly. They have used the new opportunities for communication and travel in part to forge links to German groups investigating the historic sites of their persecution. That has fueled further research, in Germany and elsewhere.

In Cologne, a grassroots initiative in the mid-1980s began to research the largely forgotten history of the many labor camps and concentration camp (KZ) satellites that had existed in the city. This "project group" later named itself after the largest of these camps (*Lager*), which was located at the public fairgrounds known as the Cologne Messe. "Projektgruppe Messelager" gradually established contacts to Messe camp survivors in Western and Eastern Europe, and invited several of them to a 1989 symposium in Cologne. This originated a visitors' program that, ten years later, remains unique in the Federal Republic. Each year, former forced laborers, prisoners of war, and KZ inmates receive invitations from the mayor of Cologne to visit for ten days at the city's expense. They return to their former prisons, camps and workplaces, speak to gatherings, and are interviewed at length about their experiences on behalf of the city's Nazi-era documents center, NS-Dokumentationszentrum der Stadt Köln, which keeps the transcripts in a public archive.[11]

The visitors program for 1995 specifically concentrated on forced labor at the Ford factory. Eight survivors from the Ukraine and Poland returned to Cologne and told their stories at a public gathering. Ford-Werke AG was persuaded for the first time to allow program visitors to tour the factory. Ford also provided photos and visual materials for a small exhibition on "Forced Labor at Ford," but made clear that no further documents could be contributed by the company. One executive wrote to Projektgruppe Messelager in July 1995: "In reality we comb carefully through our archives in response to such requests, today as in the past, and we speak with employees who might still remember that time. Never have we found documents or other information in Cologne about forced labor at Ford. We have had no occasion to press the issue ourselves."

Ford Werke otherwise declined to participate in the 1995 gathering, and rejected the project group's proposal that it finance a study of its Nazi-era history. The company claimed it would instead confront the problem of "forced labor in Cologne in the Third Reich" as part of a "common effort by Cologne companies."

After the 1995 visit, Projektgruppe Messelager published the transcripts of several interviews along with a collection of documents and photographs from the exhibition.[12] The book was intended to show that the company's history in Cologne demanded more study.

THE FORD MOTOR COMPANY plays a major role in any telling of automotive history,[13] and some U.S. publications have examined allegations that it collaborated with the enemy during the Second World War.[14] But we lack a general history of Ford Motor's wartime activities in Europe. No study published to date set out to examine as a whole the policies of the Ford Motor headquarters in Dearborn, Michigan, the connections between Cologne and Dearborn before and after the United States' entry into the war in December 1941, and the wartime events at various European Ford units in relation to Cologne and Dearborn.

The only comprehensive approach to Ford in Germany during the Nazi era, in a book by Hanns-Peter Rosellen, deals mainly with production and models.[15] Peter Lessmann explored Cologne's management of Ford Paris in German-Occupied France. Stephan Lindner treats Ford as a case in his dissertation on the "Reich Commission for the Treatment of Enemy Property." Johannes Reiling examines a key figure of the 1930s and 1940s in his biography of Heinrich Albert, the chairman of the Ford-Werke AG directorate in the years 1937 to 1945.[16]

The lack of a comprehensive business history of the European Ford units has handicapped research on forced labor there. Since much of the useful material on the topic has yet to be examined by scholars, the most important primary sources so far are the interviews with the former forced laborers.[17] I devoted a chapter to the Buchenwald satellite labor squad "Aussenkommando Köln-Ford" and its fifty prisoners in my book on the Buchenwald KZ satellites in Cologne.[18] Very few of Cologne's municipal records escaped destruction in the war.[19] Ford-Werke AG has stated that it possesses no documents of relevance. More thorough research is required to pick up the trail of documents which apparently still existed in 1945.[20] Important sources such as the thorough Military Government report written by Henry Schneider right after the war were kept confidential until very recently (See Chapter 2).

Thus the following account of forced labor at Ford during the war relies on a fragmentary documentation. It provides a context for the statements of the former forced laborers themselves. We may hope that the current wave of new research, begun by Ford in response to a class-action lawsuit, will tap new source material from European and U.S. archives towards creating a more complete history.

"Keep These Plants in Operation"

In 1931 the Ford Motor Company moved the head office of its German subsidiary from Berlin to Cologne, where a new, advanced vehicle factory was built to assemble cars for the German market. The company was still in the red in 1933, when the NSDAP seized power in the German Reich. The German Ford management and directorate thenceforth worked to shake off their image as an American company and to please the new regime, to take part in Hitler's "mass motorization of the German people."[21] Starting in the mid-1930s, Ford actively entered bids for Wehrmacht contracts. Ford enjoyed support within the Army High Command (OKH) and was able to position itself well, despite the opposition of its German competitors. The military recognized early on that Ford Werke's production capacities were vital "in fulfilling the pressing tasks of motorization in the country's defense."[22]

Ford's direction was set for the years to come: service to the Nazi regime, participation in German rearmament. Ford Cologne adapted its personnel and business policies accordingly, with the full knowledge and approval of Dearborn. The subsidiary's name was changed to support its public campaign of "Germanization." In 1939 Ford Motor Company Aktiengesellschaft became Ford-Werke Aktiengesellschaft.[23] Ford Werke share capital was raised from 20 to 32 million reichsmarks (RM) in summer 1941, at which time Dearborn cut back its share from 75 to 52 percent.

In the course of these efforts Ford apparently forged a partnership of mutual protection with the chemicals giant I.G. Farbenindustrie, one of the Reich's largest industrial combines. According to a Ford management statement to a Reich agency in 1941, IG Farben held about 6 percent of Ford-Werke AG equity. Unless this was false, Farben must have bought massively into Ford-Werke AG in the years that followed. A 1943 tax audit by the Reich reveals Farben's share at 42 percent, with the remaining 6 percent held by Ford of Britain. Ford Werke had effectively turned into a joint venture with IG Farben. Back in the United States, Ford Motor Company held a substantial interest in Farben's U.S. subsidiary.[24]

Following the outbreak of war, several heavyweight German industrialists were recruited for the Ford Werke directorate (*Aufsichtsrat*). Dr. Carl Krauch of I.G. Farbenindustrie became the deputy chairman and Dr. Wilhelm Bötzkes of Deutsche Industrie Bank also joined in 1940. Hans Hünemeyer, the vice-president of the regional Chamber of Commerce (IHK Cologne) joined in 1941. But Dearborn was still well-represented. Edsel B. Ford, the son of Henry Ford, had been on the directorate since 1925, his associate Charles E. Sorensen since 1929.[25]

The chairman of the directorate, starting in 1937, was Heinrich F. Albert, a Privy Councilor (*Geheimrat*) who had served the Company as legal counsel since 1928. Formerly a high-ranking civil servant, ministerial secretary, and, briefly, Minister of the Treasury, Albert had since 1933 maintained the company's contacts to high Nazi functionaries, with Dearborn's knowledge.[26] He played a key role in Ford's endeavor to run up high revenues in Nazi Germany while maintaining American ownership.

After the German conquests in western Europe in 1940, Albert arranged for the Reich's appointment of Robert Hans Schmidt—chief executive of Ford Werke since 1938—as the "enemy property custodian" of the Ford units in Belgium, the Netherlands, and France. Edsel Ford sanctioned Cologne's takeover of these independent Ford companies in a letter of 10 October 1940:

> We have a fairly complete impression of the present status of the Ford Companies in Germany as well as the other occupied territories. It is quite evident and very gratifying that you and your organization are looking after our interests successfully and we appreciate your efforts on our behalf. I am glad to hear that the outside plants are beginning to operate, as it is the only way for rehabilitation to take place, and after all there are many people financially interested in these properties besides ourselves. Anything that can be done constructively to keep these plants in operation will be a great help for the future.[27]

Cologne was well aware that the United States might soon become involved in the war. In that event, the Reich Commissioner for the Treatment of Enemy Property (hereafter: the Reichskommissar) would be empowered to impose a trusteeship on all companies owned wholly or even partly by U.S. citizens.[28] The Ford Werke management therefore strove to reach a friendly arrangement with the Reichskommissar in advance. They argued that Ford Werke was "Germanized" and fully integrated in the Nazi war machine. The management and directorate wrote the Reichskommissar in June 1941 to list in detail Ford's many services to the Nazi Reich. By raising exports, they said, Ford Werke had helped improve the Reich's current accounts. At the Reich's behest, Ford arranged imports of scarce raw materials for other German manufacturers. The company supported the German occupation of Czechoslovakia in March 1939 with "large deliveries from abroad," according to the letter. The Cologne factory was converted entirely to war production after the invasion of Poland: "The plant is in every regard an armaments operation." Cologne also oversaw the conversion to Wehrmacht production of the Ford plants in the occupied Netherlands, Belgium and France, the letter notes.[29]

At a time when Henry Ford was still refusing arms contracts from the U.S. government, Ford Werke Cologne had become an important partner of the German Wehrmacht. Revenues increased from 17.7 million RM in 1933 to 118.8 million RM in 1940.[30] "As elsewhere, the demands of a war economy were the decisive factor in our concluded business year 1940," the management reported in spring 1941 to the last general assembly before an enemy property trusteeship was decreed for Cologne. "To our satisfaction, we saw Ford vehicles from Cologne standing by the Wehrmacht everywhere in the hundreds—as helpers tried and true."[31]

Normally a foreign company that evidenced willingness to cooperate with the Reich was neither confiscated nor liquidated, but placed under the trusteeship of a custodian from the company itself. The Nazis did not sub-stantively attack Ford after December 1941.[32] Ford Werke's chief executive, Robert Schmidt, was appointed custodian by order of the Reichskommissar on 15 May 1942. Schmidt had started out at Ford's Berlin sales department in 1926, and worked his way up to General Director (CEO) in 1938. His appointment as custodian was supported by no less a Nazi than Baron Kurt Freiherr von Schröder, a primary financial backer and an architect of the Third Reich, the organizer of the "Friends of Himmler." Ford transacted some of its business through Schröder's Bankhaus Stein.[33] Schröder called the Legal Office of the Führer (Kanzlei des Führers) to urge Schmidt be appointed, and followed up with a letter to the Kanzlei on 7 February 1942. Therein he wrote that Schmidt enjoyed his full confidence as a "Party Com-rade and Wehrwirtschaftsführer." The latter title ("Arms Economy Leader") was a Nazi honorific for loyal industrialists. The Kanzlei des Führers was a nerve center for the euthanasia program and the Holocaust. Its support sealed Schmidt's custodial appointment.[34]

The directorate was thereupon dissolved. Albert, Krauch, Bötzkes and Hünemeyer–the Germans on the directorate–were appointed to a new "advisory council" (*Beirat*) without the two Americans.[35] In practice, the trusteeship had little impact on management at Ford Werke. Schmidt's "certificate of appointment" empowered him to represent the company for all legal and business purposes. He was free to delegate to the management board all of its old powers, although a change in mandate required the Reichskommissar's approval. Otherwise the Reichskommissar held a veto over actions that might expand, divest, or shut down Ford Werke in whole or in part (including its properties, shares in other companies, branches, etc.) The files leave no doubt that Schmidt's activities met with the Reich-skommissar's approval throughout the war. In difficulties Schmidt even called upon the Reichskommissar's support. Only on one occasion did the Reich Economics Ministry (RWM) block one of Schmidt's moves–his attempt, in late 1944, to found a Vienna-based GmbH for doing business in Slovakia.[36]

Officially, all contacts to Ford Motor Company in Dearborn were cut off after the U.S. entered the war and Schmidt was appointed custodian. Whether and how Dearborn was informed about Ford Werke's subsequent operations in the Reich, and to what extent it exercised influence on Cologne's policies and operations, is a major question for future research. Contacts may have been maintained through the branches in France, or in Denmark, where Ford Werke developed and built generators with help from IG Farben. Or in Switzerland, where Ford dealers repaired about 1,000 Wehrmacht vehicles in 1940 and supplied the Wehrmacht with about 2 million RM in replacement parts in 1943.[37]

It can be stated that Ford Werke's course in the 1940s was followed with the full knowledge and support of the Ford Motor Company in Dearborn and its ownership. By making business with the enemy, Ford became an accomplice in the crimes of the Nazi regime.

The Several Groups of Forced Laborers at Ford Werke

The outbreak of the war on 1 September 1939 caused an immediate collapse in the passenger car market and plunged Ford Werke and other automotive producers into a crisis. The regional military authority for war resource allocation–the "Armaments Commando" (Rüstungskommando) of Cologne–reported on 15 September 1939 that "Ford will be letting go of about 200 to 300 salaried employees and 1,200 workers within the next 10 days, as business in passenger cars is reaching a standstill. Most of the layoffs can be avoided insofar as mobilization orders for trucks now get going...."[38] Ford took on a small number of munitions production and similar military contracts,[39] and joined Daimler-Benz and Opel as a main supplier of three-ton trucks to the Wehrmacht for the rest of the war.[40] According to one estimate, of 350,000 Wehrmacht trucks in 1942, 50,000 had been built by Opel and 120,000 by Ford.[41]

As the war went on, Ford lost more and more of its male German workers to the draft. Foreign laborers were needed to meet the constantly rising official production quotas. The "labor question" became a long-running subject at meetings of the company's custodial advisory council. The council's minutes of 17 August 1942 read: "The war program until now ran at about 4,000 units per quarter. The authorities have ordered a rise in output to about 7,000 units per quarter. That requires a more intensive use of prisoners, especially Russians, who already make up nearly $\frac{1}{4}$ of the personnel."[42] The situation had worsened by January 1943: "The labor question has gotten extraordinarily difficult. Military recruitment is no longer sparing our key people. The gaps in the factory, in purchasing, and in other departments are growing, and the hired foreigners no longer suffice. This is another matter causing major worries at the Ford plant."[43]

From the first days of the war, the labor shortage in the German Reich was constant and ever more severe. As a result, the supply of food within the Reich might have fallen off disastrously in winter 1940, if not for the two million foreigners working at German farms. If not for foreign labor, war production would have collapsed after fall 1941.[44] In August 1944, a total of 7.6 million non-German laborers accounted for one-quarter of all workers in the German Reich. The proportion of foreign workers at arms makers at that time averaged about 50 percent.[45] Most of the companies displayed great initiative in attracting laborers through their own campaigns abroad, but above all by lobbying the three main sources for forced recruits: 1) the Arbeitsamt (Labor Offices) for "civilian workers" from the occupied countries, 2) the Wehrmacht and its Stalag prison-camp system for prisoners of war, and 3) the SS-WVHA, the bureaucratic administration and economic agency of the SS, for concentration camp prisoners.

Foreign groups were divided into a strict hierarchy: "Westarbeiter," "Ostarbeiter," prisoners of war, KZ prisoners. They were subject to a legal structure of discrimination that specified rules for every detail of their lives, defined their food rations and lodgings, their wages, and the make-up of the security forces guarding them. Drastic sanctions were approved and enforced in keeping them down, for they were viewed as a threat to domestic security. The basic framework for the treatment of forced laborers was set by various official decrees (*Erlasse*) such as the "Ostarbeiter Decrees" of February 1942. In the course of the war these were modified and reinterpreted, in some ways tightened, in others loosened. But the actual conditions under which forced laborers lived and worked varied greatly from company to company. The companies had a decisive influence upon factors such as the food, medical care, lodgings, and workplace treatment. Companies had an even more important leeway in deciding how many forced laborers they would use, and from which of the available sources they would draw their forced laborers.[46]

The first group known to have worked as forced laborers at Ford Werke, according to the available evidence, were a contingent of French prisoners of war assigned to Niehl at some point in 1940.[47] That year, many of the war businesses in the jurisdiction of the Cologne Armaments Commando began clamoring for assignments of POW laborers. Groups of prisoners were finally distributed among the companies in July and August 1940.[48] The Wehrmacht and the German Reich thereby acted in violation of the 1929 Geneva Convention, which prohibits the use of prisoners of war as laborers in military production. The treatment of the POWs also violated the Convention's requirement of "due respect for their persons and dignity."[49]

The French prisoners at Ford in 1940 were presumably sent by Stalag VI in Bonn. No French POWs from Ford have been interviewed, and practically no documents from Stalag VI still exist today, so that very little is known about their numbers or the conditions under which they lived and labored at Ford in 1940-41.[50] It is confirmed that Stalag VI later provided Ford with Italian "military internees" in 1943, as reported by the former Italian prisoner, Mareno Mannucci. The Italians were kept in a part of the Ford camp with the sign "STALAG VI G, ARBEITSKOMMANDO 619" posted at the entrance.[51]

Forced laborers of other nationalities report that the French at Ford in 1942 lived under relatively privileged conditions, with better food and lodging than the other groups. They were reportedly allowed to leave the camp area after work and on weekends. We may therefore infer that the first French prisoners of war were gradually redesignated "civilian workers," or replaced by other French nationals.[52]

By 1942 at the latest, Ford employed 400 to 500 "civilian workers" or "Westarbeiter" from France, the Netherlands, and Belgium. Some of the "Westarbeiter" were no doubt voluntary recruits, who may have come to Ford with the idea that they could earn good wages there. But the Reich occupation authorities often recruited labor in the conquered Western countries by compulsion. Yvon Thibaut was compelled to sign up for work by the occupation authority in Belgium in October 1942. He was told that otherwise, his brother or his father would be taken by force. Thibaut was one of seventy to eighty Belgians at the Ford camp in Cologne.[53] Dutch nationals are also mentioned as laborers at Ford, in a letter written by Schmidt.[54] Among the foreigners, the Western "civilian workers" clearly received the best treatment, with better food, lodging and pay, and a degree of freedom including holiday privileges.[55]

Five hundred Italian soldiers were brought to Ford in November 1943 as "Italian military internees" (called "IMIs") and used as forced laborers. They had gone through the Stargard (II D) prisoner camp and the camp at Meppen, where they received numbers from 15,001 to 15,500, before being brought to Ford.[56] Captured by German forces after the Italian surrender, IMIs were considered traitors and called "Badoglio pigs."[57] Their treatment in the Reich was especially brutal in the first few months. They were redesignated as civilians in September 1944, at which point their food improved and security measures were loosened.[58]

The first contingent of forced laborers from the Soviet Union came to Ford in April 1942. Called "Ostarbeiter," they soon made up the largest group of "foreigners" at Ford Werke.[59] Russian, Ukrainian, and Belarussian workers occupied some of the lowest rungs in the Nazi racist hierarchy, and accordingly received the worst treatment of the groups at the factory. They faced draconian rigor under the Reich's Ostarbeiter decrees of February 1942,[60] which ordered that they be "strictly" isolated from the German population. Sex with Germans was prohibited. That was normally punishable by death. "Ostarbeiter" were subject to a night-time curfew. They were banned from making use of public transport or recreational facilities, attending cultural events, or riding bicycles. Their mail was censored. The "Slavs" were in every regard relegated to the status of "subhumans."

Ford also kept a smaller group of Polish forced laborers. Poles were subject to similarly rigid rules under the "Polish Decrees" (*Polenerlasse*) of 8 March 1940.[61]

According to the testimonies of the survivors and company sources, the majority of the 1,200 enslaved Soviet nationals at Ford as of summer 1943 were female adolescents. Aged sixteen or seventeen, most of them had been taken summarily from their villages and towns, by force. Anna Nesteruk describes her abduction:

> The soldiers of Fascist Germany marched into our territory in the first days of the war [i.e., the invasion of the Soviet Union in late June 1941]. But we were carried off to forced labor, as it is called, on 3 June 1942, driven by blows from rifle butts to Starokonstantinov in the region of Chmelnizky. We weren't even given a chance to say goodbye to our families. Armed soldiers went from house to house. They were the local police, commanded by the German occupiers. Hiding was pointless because they could shoot whole villages. And so we sat and waited for the fateful hour when they would come for each of us. Like a herd of cattle we were driven forth on foot, but where and why we scared little girls and boys did not know. We hoped that we weren't being taken to be shot, because a great many Jews, Poles, and other nationalities had already been shot in Starokonstantinov for various offenses, as defined by the German occupiers, in the months from June

1941 to June 1942.... We were so many, mostly children and adolescents. Then we were put in cargo cars, bars on the windows, and taken to Germany.[62]

Anna Nesteruk's transport went straight to Cologne. The Cologne Arbeitsamt distributed the young women among companies "like a commodity," as Klawdia Podobed put it. Other enslaved civilians arrived at Ford through one of the intermediary camps serving the labor offices of the Rhineland, or after a period at a different workplace. Inna Kulagina reports that she and a group of young women were picked out personally by a Ford employee at the Wuppertal intermediary camp.[63]

One-quarter of Ford personnel as of August 1942 were foreign laborers, about 1,000 people in all, mostly prisoners of war and enslaved Soviet civilians.[64] The labor bureaus cooperated with the armaments commandos in assigning "Ostarbeiter" wherever they would best serve war production.

For the third quarter of 1942, the Wehrmacht prioritized production of Ford's "Maultier" (mule) trucks. Developed especially for the German armed forces, these three-ton trucks had a center axle to allow the addition of caterpillar tracks in the rear. The assignment of Soviet laborers to Ford was raised to help increase Maultier output.[65] By June 1943, about half of the 4,985 Ford employees were foreign nationals. The largest group consisted of 1,200 "Ostarbeiter."[66] Overall personnel rose to 5,742 by the end of 1943, so that Ford was running one of the largest labor camps in Cologne.[67] These figures do not account for labor at Ford's estimated 350 suppliers.[68]

Life at the Ford Camp and Factory

The assignment to a group within the Nazi hierarchy of "foreign peoples" was decisive in determining a forced laborer's living conditions. At Ford, the racist order was expressed architecturally in the "Ausländerlager," built right next to the factory on Henry Ford Strasse.[69] The camp was divided into three separate areas: a "Russian Camp" for Soviet forced laborers, a "Westarbeiter" camp, and (starting in 1943) one for Italian military internees.[70] The three areas were named after German Ford models, so that the "Russian Camp" was also called "Taunus."[71] A portrait of Hitler hung in the barrack where meals were served to the Soviet civilians. As if in mockery of the inmates, it bore a sign in Russian: "Hitler the Liberator."[72]

The "Ausländerlager" was built in 1942, and covered twice the area of the factory production halls. Ford spent 830,000 RM for the barracks, 530,000 RM of which was tax-deductible.[73] The size of these investments suggests that the company was reckoning with a long-term deployment of the foreign workers. Armed policemen with dogs patrolled the perimeter of the camp. The forced laborers had to show identification on entering or leaving the camp. The sole gate for "Ostarbeiter" ran through the inside of the security barrack.[74] Prisoners of war were never allowed to leave without guards. The Cologne police had orders to arrest immediately any prisoner of war spotted alone on the street.[75]

Kamila Felinska, a Polish national, was at first mistakenly assigned to the Russian camp and later taken for French, so that she spent time in both camp areas. She describes the difference between the two camps as one between "heaven and earth."[76] As a rule, Soviet civilians were not allowed to leave the factory or camp. Tamara Nosik, then a Soviet national, relates that the people in her transport to Ford were placed in an eleven-month quarantine immediately after their arrival in summer 1942. Afterwards small groups could request permission to leave the camp on Saturdays.

Barracks in the Russian camp were furnished with three-level wooden bunk beds and mattresses filled with sawdust. Each barrack held 250 to 300 people. There was no privacy. Several families, who had been abducted from the Soviet Union together, were lodged in a "family barrack." The very sparse furnishings stand out in Kamila Felinska's mind: "There was nothing there, only a large room, and in the middle there was a very long table." By contrast a couple in the French camp could even get a small room of their own with a cabinet, a table and two chairs.

Wherever they were, all of the interviewees recall that it was very cold. The small ovens in the barracks were inadequate, with frequent fuel shortages.

The forced laborers were guarded by company security, police, and sometimes soldiers. The commandant in the Russian camp was Police Officer Wierschheim, an older man usually called "the Boss." He was assisted by two Ukrainian deputies.[77] The inmates received a "company identification" with their camp number. The Soviet civilians were required to wear a badge with "OST" for "Ostarbeiter" in very large letters. The Italians wore a sign with their work number on their chest, and gray uniforms with an "IMI" label on the back.

Identification by number was the seal of deindividualization and degradation. The forced laborers were required to recite their numbers at roll-call and on other occasions. The memory of this particular humiliation still hurts today. "We had no name, we were only a number. We were a labor unit, not people," says Inna Kulagina. The camp order was, as Anna Nesteruk says, "very strict." "Ostarbeiter" were constantly reminded of their general helplessness and of the many rules devised for them. Inna Kulagina: "We had to sign a paper promising we would have no relationships with the Germans. And that anyone caught having a relationship with a German would be shot. I signed that myself." Stepan Saika: "The guard could at any time rap or punch someone on the head. There was no one to complain to, no right to complain, you were just livestock."[78] According to Saika, guards carried out unannounced inspections at any and all times, inside the barracks and out.

From the barracks the prisoners went to work in columns and under guard. They were used in nearly every department, on the production line, in quality control, loading and unloading, and maintenance and construction around the plant grounds. The usually heavy work was carried out in twelve-hour shifts, day and night. The young women were often exhausted. Risk of injury was especially high on night shifts. Inna Kulagina once fell asleep in the bathroom. Her supervisor found her and beat her unconscious.

Much of this labor would normally have been performed by qualified machine operators and trained craftsmen. Stepan Saika received only a quick explanation of how to turn on the machine that made cylinder heads. "I looked at these machines. Where could I have seen such machines in the village? I thought, they will take off my head!" Overwhelmed and fearful, the young man grew apathetic and stopped taking care of himself. His condition improved only after he was transferred, about a month later, to an easier job brushing metal rods.[79]

The forced laborers at the factory were at the mercy of the German personnel. Many Germans seem to have helped them by secretly giving them food. Some supervisors are described as friendly people. A few acts of sabotage were specifically intended to slow down the pace of work for the forced laborers. But the company security forces never rested in their efforts to prevent contacts between their "fellow Germans" (*Volksgenosse*) and the "foreign peoples" (*Fremdvölkische*), by harsh punishment if necessary. One German worker caught giving food to a foreigner was promptly sent off to the front.[80]

The interviewees also report that many of the Germans made use of the opportunity to issue commands and harass the foreigners with impunity. "You could do anything you liked to a Russian or a Pole," one German who worked at Ford relates. "They were fair game."[81] The NSDAP encouraged inhumane treatment by propaganda actions that constantly invoked "the clear line separating our fellow Germans from the foreign peoples, a line drawn in blood."[82] Anna Nesteruk describes being beaten on several occasions, once for stealing potatoes. "We all felt the rubber truncheon. We were constantly afraid.... But we also had moments of happiness, as when a German foreman shared his piece of bread with us or gave us a buttered roll. Those were moments of unlimited joy and gratitude. But there were other moments, when we were humiliated and called 'Russian pigs', when we were struck with rubber truncheons."[83]

Despite the heavy manual labor, the food was terrible. Reich authorities had established a nationwide table of rations for each foreign group. These were so low that they even roused criticism from German agencies. As the Cologne Armaments Commando reported in September 1942: "Food rations for the Ostarbeiter are completely insufficient. Especially with such a low intake of fat, it must be doubted whether the Ostarbeiter can keep up the demands placed on them in the long term."[84] The forced laborers are unanimous in recalling constant hunger and weight loss. Mareno Mannucci lost over ten kilograms in three weeks. He is all the more grateful to the colleague who secretly gave him bread. The interviewees all stress that they could have hardly survived those years without the extra bits of food that came their way.

Finding ways to get more food was a necessary survival skill. The French received packages from their families or the Red Cross. The Soviets had no such privileges. Malnutrition drove many of them to desperate measures. They needed inventiveness, luck, and courage. Those caught stealing from the canteen were beaten. Nadja Schubrawa was locked up in the camp prison for stealing a turnip. Below we shall see that many attempts to get food ended in arrests by the Gestapo. The company management and personnel were hardly unaware of these conditions: Leaflets decrying the "bread-begging of the Ostarbeiter" were passed out at the factory.[85]

Sanitary conditions and medical care were also terrible. According to a former German worker, Ford "did just enough to prevent epidemics, nothing more."[86] The medical care in the camp was limited to absolute necessity. Injuries sometimes went untreated. Lidija Solotarjewskaja tells of how she once had her finger slammed very hard by her supervisor. She had to bind her hand herself. Her finger was crippled. According to Mareno Mannucci, every two months the Italians were subjected to selections. The sick were exchanged for new prisoners from the Stalag in Bonn.

A closer study of known deaths from the Ford camp hints at the living conditions. The Westfriedhof cemetery in Cologne has the graves of three babies from the Ford camp. They were aged six, nine, and thirteen months. Nothing is known about the causes of their deaths.[87] There were at least eleven other deaths due to unknown causes among the Polish and Russian forced laborers at Ford. Conspicuous in most of these cases is that they were very young, seventeen to twenty-one years old.[88]

The Birthing Ward, Children's Barracks, Abortions

One of the most difficult stories is in the treatment of pregnant women, babies and children. Anna Obuchowskaja, one of the interviewed Soviet nationals, gave birth to a girl on 14 November 1943. She did not see a doctor or a nurse during her pregnancy. She delivered her baby in the barracks, and was forced to return to work soon after. She was allowed to go to the camp to breast-feed her child. Children at the camp were attended by German and Russian kindergarten teachers. A company document from 1943 creates the impression that Ford showed great concern for families and built maternity facilities and a home for babies.[89] However a controversy that arose in 1947, when Ford Werke re-hired Carl Wenzel, the head doctor at the factory during the war, gives rise to doubts about whether the earlier description was truthful.

Having joined the NSDAP in December 1931, before the Nazis took power, Wenzel enjoyed the status of an "old fighter" under the Nazi regime. He was let go from his factory doctor's post in December 1945, and put through de-Nazification proceedings. There he produced a number of character witnesses. The former paramedic of the "Ausländerlager" wrote, in a November 1947 deposition, that Wenzel was responsible for especially good sanitary conditions at the Russian camp, and added:

> He saw to the lodgings and clothing, nutrition, mental recreation and so on; and took exceptional efforts to arrange for a birthing station with a children's barracks, and did then set it up. Every child had a pretty little bed, strollers were

bought. It was a joy for everyone when they could go out for a stroll with the child. He treated women who were pregnant or post-natal and children just like Germans, granting them the same care, extra rations, and time to rest.[90]

Wenzel's own remarks serve as a curious counterpoint. Accused of having carried out racially motivated abortions on "Ostarbeiter" women at the camp, he argued these were humanitarian actions, given the dire straits of the pregnant women, who were usually sick, and given the "impossibility of raising children."[91]

Pregnancies among "Ostarbeiter" were a kind of abomination to the Party and much of the public. Until 1942 pregnant Soviet women were sent back home, but later a movement arose towards legitimating abortions for pregnant Polish and "Ostarbeiter" women, as their labor was considered too precious to lose. A general order of 11 March 1943 allowed abortion for these groups on the woman's request, given an approval by the local medical association.[92] Kresse, one of the doctors appointed for the Russian camp by Wenzel, claimed that many Soviet women applied for abortions following the publicizing of this order. At first the procedures were carried out in a Cologne hospital ward set up for the purpose. The medical conditions there were catastrophic, Kresse said. The operations were done without anesthetics. Many women returned to the Ford camp with infections, and had to stay in bed for weeks.[93] According to Wenzel's testimony, there were later ten cases in which abortions were carried out at the Ford camp by either Kresse or himself, but always at the woman's request.

Wenzel's claims that his motives were humanitarian and that the women aborted voluntarily were contested at his de-Nazification procedure. His former nurse, who on ethical grounds had refused to help him perform the abortions, raised serious accusations. The de-Nazification commission of Cologne took the following minutes of her testimony:

> In questioning, Mrs. Str. said 2 abortions were carried out within a short time on the same person, who was about 40 years old. The woman's health suffered greatly. According to the same testimony, an abortion was carried out on a Russian woman who was six months pregnant. Mrs. Str. would find it regrettable if Dr. Wenzel were to return to the company. With regard to nutrition at the Russian Camp, Mrs. Str. stated that Dr. W. did not exercise a minimum supervision. She claims to have often complained to Dr. W. about the poor nutrition for the children and the adults, but Dr. W. never took action.[94]

Based on these accusations, the de-Nazification commission asked for a statement from the Cologne Medical Association.[95] Determining that there had been seventy births in the camp as opposed to ten abortions (the abortions at the hospital were not taken into account), the Association wrote:

> It would contradict medical experience to see 10 indications for discontinuation, based on health, out of 80 pregnant women of average health.... The ratio of 70 healthy births to 10 abortions does not confirm Dr. W's assertion that abortions were carried out rarely and only for health reasons, but on the contrary demonstrates that other motives were surely decisive. Such motives could include: 1.

Racial policy or a desire to minimize absence from work. 2. Regard for the surely difficult situation of the expectant mothers, i.e. social indications.... We are closest to the truth if we do not view one of these motives, but the sum of them all, as decisive in the decision to abort.

Surveillance and Repression, Wages and Profits

Throughout Germany, company security forces (*Werkschutz*) played a key role in supervising and disciplining all personnel and especially the forced laborers.[96] Company forces consisted of both full-time guards and part-time recruits from among German personnel. Under the Ostarbeiter decrees, the Werkschutz were expected to work closely with the Gestapo. They took an increasingly paramilitary cast from year to year. A general order to Gestapo offices, dated 20 February 1942, requires all companies making use of Soviet workers to appoint a political "counter-intelligence representative" (*Abwehrbeauftragte*) to supervise the company security force. The same order urged the assignment of full-time Gestapo units to sensitive workplaces.

The Gestapo was, among other tasks, specifically charged with "fighting insubordination." They investigated "plots by enemies of the Reich" and cases of "sexual intercourse with Germans." The latter was to be punished by deportation to a concentration camp or "special treatment" (*Sonderbehandlung*). That was the euphemism for murder. "Less serious cases" were left to company security, who were granted full authority to carry out beatings: "In breaking acute resistance, the watchmen are also allowed to use physical methods on the laborers."[97] Company security forces, which were already bound to follow Gestapo and military orders starting in March 1939, were officially placed under the exclusive supervision of the Gestapo in October 1943, completing a close intertwining of the state and company disciplinary structures.[98]

"Company leaders" (*Betriebsführer*) were urged to work closely with Party, State and Gestapo in assuring the discipline and productivity of the foreign workers. The counter-intelligence representatives received regular propaganda schoolings from the Gestapo.[99] The first counter-intelligence representative at Ford was Wilhelm H. Buchwald. His deputy in the counter-intelligence hierarchy was none other than the "Company Leader" himself, Robert H. Schmidt. Schmidt's official "counter-intelligence" authorities were identical to Buchwald's. Buchwald reported regularly to the Cologne Gestapo.[100] To date, no information is available about the size of the security forces at Ford, but a guideline issued by the Cologne Armaments Commando urged that 30 percent of the male German workforce be incorporated into the forces in full-time or part-time capacities.[101]

Several cases are known of forced laborers from Ford who were turned over to company security or the Gestapo on suspicion of theft, misappropriation, or "plundering." Two of the still-existing case files show that the accused was released after an investigation.[102] Another case went badly.

Kambur Gonki left the camp to search for food. On his return, he was captured by a security patrol and turned over to the police. After a brief imprisonment, they sent him to the Gestapo for assignment to a "work education camp."[103] Run by the Gestapo, these camps were in many ways comparable to the KZs.

In another case, the police held two laborers from the Ford camp for theft from 13 January to 6 February 1945, and later deported them to KZ Buchenwald.[104]

The basement of the Cologne Gestapo Headquarters, in the so-called EL-DE Haus not far from the famous Cathedral, was a prison. Several hundred people were interrogated and tortured there during the war. Today, EL-DE Haus is home to the city's NS Documents Center and a permanent historical exhibition on the Nazi era. On the walls of the former cells, little more than brief narrow passageways into which dozens of prisoners would be crammed without room to sit, the many inscriptions carved by the inmates still evoke their hopes and terrors.[105]

Cell 8 is full of inscriptions by Nikolai Bulotschnik, a man from the Ford camp who was caught and turned over to the Gestapo for stealing:

> *Nor is the one happy*
> *who shall return.*
> *No lucky day*
> *awaits him.*
> *He will be forced*
> *to steal again*
> *and once more*
> *boys*
> *the prison.*

Another Russian inscription, inside a heart, makes known the death of Nikolai Bulotschnik:[106]

NIKOLAI
BULOTSCHNIK
FORD

sleeps a PEACEFUL SLEEP
City of STALINO
LIVED FOR 21 YEARS
ETERNAL REMEMBRANCE AND ETERNAL PEACE
WAS HANGED WITH THE 3rd GROUP

Nikolai Bulotschnik's execution cannot be dated, because those murdered by the Gestapo at EL-DE House were all buried in unmarked graves.

More is known about Michail Latipow, 32, a Russian, and Piotr Satew, 21, a Ukrainian. They were sentenced to death by a "Sondergericht," one of the Nazis' summary political courts.[107] On 30 August 1943, Latipow and Satew, both forced laborers from Ford, took clothes from the basement of an unoccupied house that had been destroyed some weeks earlier in an air raid. They wanted to bring these back to the Ford camp. Back out on the street, they were confronted by a passerby and soon after arrested. On 7 September 1943, Sondergericht 3 of the Landgericht Cologne, with a Judge Sudholz presiding, sentenced the two men to death for the crime of plundering. Their plunder was a bunch of dirty rags. A clerk with the Justice Ministry named Meissner wrote, a few days after the sentencing: "As foreign workers the condemned men treated in a base way the last belongings of our injured fellow Germans. We see no extenuating circumstances to justify a milder treatment. I therefore propose not invoking the right of reprieve, but allowing justice to take its free course."

The men were both married. Their wives were also forced laborers at Ford. As the authorities documented, they had acted in desperation. Piotr Satew wanted the clothes for his wife, who was pregnant and in her eighth month. In a last letter, addressed to the Russians at Ford, he begged his countrymen to take care of his wife, and to break the news of his fate to her gently. Latipow's wife was also expecting. In his last letter, he asked that his child be named after him.

The letters were never sent, but added to the case files with the following note: "The contents make these letters inappropriate for delivery, since the story as told by the letter writers will call forth unrest among the Ostarbeiter."

Latipow and Satew were executed at Cologne's Klingelpütz Prison on 4 October 1943. "Satew was taken from his cell at 15:15 and brought before the Prosecutor for the announcement of consummation of his sentence. He was very upset. He did not admit his guilt and claimed he had been unjustly condemned. He begged for religious counsel. He remained upset, until the execution."

On the next day, the Municipal Publicity Office put up 330 posters to announce the executions, all around the city. There can be no doubt that the news made a lasting impression on the "Ostarbeiter."

Three other forced laborers from the Ford camp fell into the Gestapo's custody in fall 1944. Many "Ostarbeiter" took to hiding amid the ruins of the bombed-out city. They armed and defended themselves against the police and Gestapo. The Gestapo reacted to the loss of control with brutal crackdowns, round-ups, executions. In November 1944, the Gestapo arrested two "Ukrainian civilian workers" in the Ford camp on suspicion of plundering. They announced an upcoming "major action" at the Ford camp.[108] Later that week, possibly in the course of this "major action," there was a shoot-out at the Russian camp. A third "Ostarbeiter" was arrested by Wehrmacht soldiers on suspicion of "gang membership," and turned over to the Gestapo.[109]

Escape was almost impossible, especially for the Soviet laborers. In his 1992 interview, Ivan Ananitsch was asked whether he had ever thought of escaping from the camp. The question seemed so odd that he had to laugh: "You could probably get away, but where would you go? No one paid attention to me. They let me through the gate, but it was pointless to run. If I had gotten away, they would have arrested me in the city, and sent me back."

Fugitives of course faced worse dangers than being "sent back," as the forced laborers well knew. Stepan Saika tells the story of a group of French men and two Russian women who hid in a train headed from Ford Werke to the Russian Front. At the Polish border the train was searched, and they were sniffed out by the dogs. The men were shot on the spot; the women were sent to a penal camp.

GIVEN THESE CIRCUMSTANCES, it is not surprising that the Russians comprised the most reliable and efficient group of laborers at Ford Werke in the summer of 1943. The advisory council minutes of July 1943 note that the "labor-power" (*Arbeitskraft*) of the Russians was "at about 90 percent of a normal German worker's." The "labor power" of the average German worker was said to have fallen off to 75 percent as a result of the many air raids on Cologne. German morale was further undermined by the rise in working hours, from fifty-four to sixty a week. Their sick rate was running at an extraordinary 17 percent.[110]

The "Westarbeiter" were by then causing many problems at Ford. About a third of the French, Belgian and Dutch civilians had escaped during the air raids, or failed to return from vacations. The situation among the French was considered critical. Seventeen out of one group of nineteen who went on holiday never came back to Ford.[111]

Instead of recruiting workers who "then disappear at the first opportunity," Ford now took up the strategy of transferring assembly and parts manufacture to Belgium, or to other occupied territories.[112] Robert Schmidt had started taking steps in that direction from the moment he was appointed commissarial custodian of the Ford Motor Company units in Belgium and Holland. Ford Motor Company of Antwerp was placed under Schmidt's administration on 29 May 1940, after which Cologne devised the production plans for the Antwerp plant, and gradually integrated Antwerp into its arms program. The mostly Belgian personnel jumped from 312 on 1 October 1940 to 1,080 on 31 December 1941, finally reaching 2,200 in 1944.[113] Schmidt was crafting his postwar scenarios at a very early stage, as reported in the company magazine, *Ford-Werkszeitung*, in summer 1941: "As the Commissar for Ford operations in the Occupied Territories, Wehrwirtschafts-führer R.H. Schmidt is preparing Ford to take the measures required in the interests of a European economy after the war."[114]

The overwhelming majority of forced laborers at Ford received very low wages or none whatsoever. KZ prisoners got nothing. Companies were required to pay a fixed per diem to the SS for each KZ prisoner (four RM for so-called assistants, six RM for skilled workers). In the month of November 1944, for example, Ford paid 5,220 RM to SS-WVHA for its KZ satellite commando.[115] Almost no other documents concerning costs or wages for forced laborers at Ford survive. Here we shall review the reigning general practices, as supplemented through oral reports from former forced laborers at Ford.

Prisoners of war received no wages. A fixed per diem, derived as a percentage of a German worker's average wage, was paid to the command of each "Wehrkreis," the regional defense district that administered the Stalag POW camps.[116] Mareno Mannucci was brought to Ford as an "Italian military internee" in 1943, and later given "civilian worker" status. When he was transferred away from the Ford camp, he received 50 reichsmarks as the wages for over one year's work. By decree, wages for "Westarbeiter" were lower than those for German workers. Actual net pay was in part determined by the companies, which deducted variable amounts from wages to cover the costs of a laborer's food or lodging.

The wages paid across the Reich for "Ostarbeiter" were so low that companies were embarrassed to pay them, as Armaments Commando VI reported in March 1942:

> The deployment of civilian Russians of male and female gender has by now begun at a number of arms makers. The companies are satisfied with their work enthusiasm and conduct. They are worried about the very low wages, however. The companies have been reluctant so far to pay these amounts, in the fear that the low rates will act as an immediate damper on work enthusiasm.[117]

Again, in paying wages companies made use of a large leeway to deduct for food and lodging. The payroll accountant at Ford testified, soon after the war, that after withdrawals for taxes, insurance, lodging and food the "Russians" received less than half the wages due them under the regulations.[118] This may explain why former "Ostarbeiter" from Ford report unanimously either that they got no money or, according to Stepan Saika, only worthless "camp money."

At the end of 1943, looking back on the past year, Reichskommissar Johannes Krohn expressed his satisfaction to Robert Schmidt "that the enterprises you administer contributed even more towards raising our arms potential in the year 1943 than in 1942."[119] Ford's revenues were indeed impressive, having reached 128 million RM in 1941, 132 million RM in 1942 and a peak of 184 million RM in 1943.[120] Even in 1944, with the Allies approaching and bombing from all directions and causing repeated production stoppages, Ford still turned over 137 million RM in the first three quarters.[121] Production bogged down only after the total collapse of the city's infrastructure in the devastating attacks of fall 1944.

The conspicuously high profits registered by "enemy companies" caused disputes between various Reich ministries. The Ministry of Economics (RWM) was especially keen to grab the profits.[122] A high-level tax inspector named Hiller was sent out in September 1943 to audit several foreign companies, including Opel, Ford, Hollerith, and Kodak. He observed an impressive growth in assets at all of the companies. He found that Ford-Werke AG assets had grown from 14.8 million RM in 1938 to 36.7 million RM in 1942, and that net liquid assets had in the same period risen from 10 million RM to 28 million RM. Hiller attributed this phenomenal growth above all to a rise in revenues through Wehrmacht contracts and the consequent operation of plant at full capacity. As a third reason, he cited the use of cheap labor, such as prisoners of war and "Ostarbeiter."[123]

Supported by the Foreign Ministry and the Reich Finance Ministry, the Reichskommissar put up a stubborn and successful resistance against RWM's designs on Ford's profits.[124] The dividends due to Ford Werke shareholders from "enemy states" were not paid during the war, but also not confiscated. They were left to Ford-Werke AG, and logged in the accounts books as loans from the shareholders or new equity.[125]

The Buchenwald Satellite at Ford Werke

In the final two years of the war, even with the Wehrmacht falling back on all fronts, Ford and the rest of the arms industry continued producing for the Nazi Reich's last stand. The Western Allies landed in Normandy on 6 June 1944 and liberated France that summer. On the Eastern Front, the Red Army on 22 June launched an offensive that smashed the German lines and reached the gates of Warsaw that autumn. No doubt remained that the Nazi Reich would suffer total defeat.

In August 1944, Ford set up a new camp near the factory in Niehl. The KZ slave-labor squad known as "Aussenkommando Köln-Ford" moved in to the camp on 12 August 1944.

The use of KZ prisoners in truck production came late in the war, and only after Armaments Minister Speer had applied sufficient pressure on the other authorities. Following a decree by Hitler in July 1944, Heinrich Himmler ordered that 12,000 KZ prisoners be made available for truck production. It was in this connection that Ford also received a KZ squad. Ford's squad comprised fifty men selected from KZ Buchenwald: thirty-five Russians, ten Czechs, two Germans, two Poles, and a stateless man. They were guarded by a unit of sixteen SS troopers.[126]

Ford's contacts to the SS went back much further than that. Prisoners from Aussenlager Messe, the KZ satellite camp set up in September 1942 at the Cologne Fairgrounds, had often been assigned to work at Ford.[127] Kazimierz Tarnawski was among a Messe group who traveled to Ford and back every day. If no transport car was free, they took the several kilometers on a forced march. At the company's docks on the Rhine, they loaded up ships with boxes headed to the Ford branch in Bucharest. Another "Aussenkommando" with KZ prisoners built bunkers on a field to the north of the factory.[128]

The Messe camp was withdrawn from Cologne in May 1944. Apparently upset, the municipal authorities led a lobbying campaign for a renewed assignment of KZ laborers. Three small commandos were thereupon assigned to the largely leveled city in late summer 1944: one for the municipality ("Aussenkommando Köln-Stadt"), one for Westwaggon, and one for Ford.[129]

In relative terms, the Ford KZ labor commando was a very small satellite camp. To take three examples from the automotive industry, Daimler, BMW and Volkswagen employed thousands of KZ prisoners under the worst conditions imaginable.[130] Compared to that, the conditions at KZ Aussenkommando Köln-Ford were better. But the deployment of SS resources signals a new quality compared to Ford's use of forced laborers until then. All KZ satellite camps practiced selection. Prisoners who were no longer able to work were exchanged for healthy ones from the main camp. Returning to the main camp, the sick faced a likely death of hunger and neglect, or execution. Even if no one died or was killed at the Aussenkommando itself, companies who made use of such squads were complicit in the National Socialist policy of annihilation. The example of Opel (see Chapter 1) furthermore shows that it was possible for an arms producer to avoid such direct use of SS "labor resources."

Marian Gazinski, twenty-four years old at the time, was an automotive locksmith by trade. In his telling, the barrack for him and the other KZ commando prisoners was located seventy to one hundred meters from the factory grounds. Their fenced-in camp was painted green and kept spotless. The center section of the barrack held rooms for command and guard posts, the kitchen, and baths and toilets. Either wing was furnished with a commissary and enough three-level wooden bunks for twenty-five prisoners each.

The SS men led them to Ford and watched as they worked. Their shift ran from six in the morning to six at night. KZ prisoners were kept well isolated from all other workers. Marian Gazinski was assigned wherever he was needed each day. He operated a lathe, made engine parts, tested ignitions. The number of skilled workers among the prisoners of the Ford Aussenkommando is conspicuously high.[131]

The camp commandant was twenty-seven years old. Mr. Gazinski describes SS Oberscharführer Josef Gergel as an "arrogant" but not a brutal man. The SS men did not mistreat the prisoners, but were "very concrete and determined," according to Mr. Gazinski. "We always behaved very properly, because we had this discipline. We knew you could lose your life for a trifle, so we stuck to the rules." In his recollection, the worst part about his time at Ford was the food, which he describes as worse even than at Buchenwald. Breakfast was coffee and two hundred grams of bread, dinner spinach and three potatoes or a white turnip soup. He still remembers a plate of lentils as the best meal he had. No food was served during the fifteen-minute break at midday, no extra rations were given for heavier labor or special occasions.

Four prisoners escaped from the Ford commando.[132] Nine more were assigned from Buchenwald and two transferred in from Kommando Köln-Stadt, so that Ford's group numbered sixty-one. One died of unknown causes and five were sent back to Buchenwald for unknown reasons.[133] With the city destroyed and the Americans nearby, Ford Werke shut down operations altogether on 27 February 1945. The Aussenkommando was dissolved. The remaining forty-eight prisoners were transported back to Buchenwald, where the death march began in early April 1945.[134]

Siege and Liberation

Although Ford Werke was a very important producer in the German war effort, it was not included in any Allied bombing plans until 2 October 1944. The U.S. Air Force flew two raids on Ford, on 15 and 18 October 1944. Instead of the factory, the bombs hit the barracks of the forced laborers.[135] The "Plan of Factory Ford-Werke AG," drawn up for the occupation government one year later, shows five barracks having burned down during the war. Of the plant itself, only a few smaller buildings are marked as having been hit.[136] One of the USAF attacks was witnessed by Franciszek Wój- cikowski, a prisoner in KZ Aussenkommando Köln-Stadt who was working at Ford. As he remembers it, on that day, after the first sounding of air raid sirens, the factory gates were opened, and the people ran out and hid wher- ever they could. The Soviet civilians ran to their barracks. After about a half hour, the bombers appeared and dropped incendiaries on the barracks. At first a few people ran out of the barracks and back to the factory. Then no one could get past the flames. An unknown number died. "The barracks with the people inside. There was such a screaming! A terrible screaming."

The intensive bombings of fall 1944 were the most impressive sign of the coming end of the war for Cologne. A few of the forced laborers at Ford, among them Mareno Mannucci, were assigned to the labor army of the Armaments Ministry, known as "Organisation Todt." They built tank traps against the advancing Allies, who in October 1944 reached the town of Aachen, just 60 kilometers west of Cologne. In the month that followed, most Cologne authorities and companies moved to the "safer," eastern side of the Rhine. Ford Werke began relocating in mid-September 1944.[137] Its machine capital was transported to various "dispersal locations" in the sur- rounding country. Afterwards most of the forced laborers were moved to overcrowded and under-supplied camps east of the Rhine.[138] On 1 March 1945 the Gauleiter of Cologne (the Nazi district leader) ordered a supervised evacuation of the whole city west of the Rhine.[139] Five hundred forced laborers from the Ford camp were brought to one of Ford's dispersal plants in Duemmlinghausen, a village in the upper Bergish Country near Gum- mersbach, on 3 March 1945.[140] About 1,000 of the Ford laborers were held in the Cologne suburb of Bergisch Gladbach, east of the Rhine.[141]

Of course, production at the dispersal plants never got started in the mad confusion of the last days of war. In early 1945 the Reichskommissar for Enemy Property in Berlin lost all contact to Schmidt, who was presumed missing or dead. A new custodian for Ford was appointed in Berlin. He somehow got through the collapsing transport system to take a tour of the Gummersbach location. Meanwhile, the Gauleiter of Cologne, in his addi- tional role as a "Reich Defense Commissar," appointed his own custodian for Ford's dispersal locations. The second custodian was bent on getting pro- duction running at the dispersal plants by the end of March 1945, by what- ever means. This was hopeless. In April the Wehrmacht collapsed altogether, and U.S. forces crossed the Rhine. As in the rest of the Reich,

Nazi hardliners ordered all of Ford's machinery destroyed. The Ford managers circumvented this and instead followed a deviant order from Albert Speer's Armaments Ministry, to disable, but not destroy, the machines.[142]

The Ford Werke factory grounds had been occupied along with all western parts of Cologne six weeks earlier, on 5-6 March. The U.S. troops liberated a group of 290 forced laborers who stuck it out at the bunkers in Niehl.[143] The majority of forced laborers, who had been evacuated east of the Rhine, remained in constant danger of being killed in the hostilities until their own liberation in mid-April. Mareno Mannucci still calls the thirteenth of April, 1945, the happiest day of his life.

The Myth of the Model Camp

After the war, Ford Werke and the great majority of its executives benefited from the "dual loyalty"[144] they practiced under Nazi rule. During the twelve years of the "Thousand-Year Reich," they took every effort to look and act like a loyal German company. As soon as the U.S. troops arrived, they turned into the courageous protectors of American property. The Ford Werke management immediately pledged their loyalty to the U.S. Military Government (MG), which in turn provided Ford Werke with decisive assistance in resuming production. American military units helped ship the almost intact machinery back from the dispersal locations, and transported Ford's German workers back from their evacuation. In the last days of the war, Schmidt had ordered the sinking of Ford's riverbound spare-parts warehouse. The Military Government raised the ship from the bottom of the Rhine; enough parts were salvaged to allow three months of truck production. On 8 May 1945, the day of Victory in Europe, the first new truck rolled off the assembly line at Ford Werke.[145]

The continuity in management was remarkable. The U.S. authorities in April 1945 appointed as the new company custodian Erhard Vitger, the same Danish executive who had served as Schmidt's second-in-command since 1937. He was joined on the new management board by Ford executives from Britain. Of Ford's 2,600 German employees, a total of forty failed their initial de-Nazification procedures, and were fired in the course of 1945.[146] Some disappeared, like the "Shop Leader" (*Betriebsobmann*) Brunkhorst, a notorious and feared Gestapo informant. But many of the Nazi-era executives had joined the NSDAP fairly late or not at all, and were exonerated in their de-Nazification procedures as Category V: "incidental members."[147] They were neither punished nor required to atone in any way. Of those who were fired, many returned to the factory, after a decent break of two or three years spent in effecting their rehabilitation. The former "Wehrwirtschaftsführer" and "Company Leader" Robert Hans Schmidt and the factory doctor Carl Wenzel were among them.

The re-employment of the factory doctor was controversial.[148] He had been fired in December 1945, but later placed in Category IV. A "storm of indignation" broke out among the workers when they heard that he would be allowed to resume his old function on 15 September 1947. The works council, the newly elected representatives of the company personnel, voted to stage a work stoppage on that day. An assembly of the personnel adopted a resolution against re-hiring Wenzel, with just two abstentions. The workers refused to accept medical care from an old "Party Comrade," all the more so since he would be involved in setting their sick time and rest periods. They argued that Wenzel's professional conduct under the Third Reich had proven that he cared much more about the company's interests than the welfare of the personnel. The investigations set off by these protests then discovered evidence of Wenzel's wartime abortions.

The strike delayed but did not prevent Wenzel's return. The doctor's case is exemplary of a curious process after 1945, by which hundreds of thousands of active Nazis and Reich supporters mutated overnight into "persecuted opponents of the regime." Wenzel had once been a member in Germania Leipzig, a right-wing nationalist dueling fraternity prohibited by the Nazis. His telling practically turned it into an opposition movement. He used every argument in discrediting the main witness against him, and apparently also got his friends to pressure her. The Ford "Ausländerlager" was stylized into a model camp. Wenzel provided the de-Nazification board with a number of the exonerating third-party testimonies known popularly as "detergent certificates" (*Persilschein*). Wenzel found three former "Ostarbeiter" who attested to his general helpfulness, a "Political" whom he had adopted as a protégé just before the end of the war, and a co-worker who testified that Wenzel had "helped Jews." As for the details, the recipient of the help was a "half-Jewish" woman terrified that her parents would be deported to the death camps. Doctor Wenzel promised that before that happened he would provide her with the poison they needed to kill themselves.

The debate over Wenzel's wartime conduct lost any factual dimension in the winter of 1947 and 1948, as it turned into a proxy for other conflicts brewing between labor and management. Wenzel successfully portrayed the accusations as a personal smear campaign. The municipal appeals commission ruled in his favor on 13 April 1948, writing: "[We] on the contrary are of the view that a part of the personnel are attempting to have workplace issues resolved to their favor by making use of the de-Nazification offices."

Robert Hans Schmidt was a far less controversial figure among the "company community," but he also had to fight for his return.[149] He served the U.S. Military Government with eloquence and readiness from the moment of their arrival in March 1945. MG Headquarters in Frankfurt ordered his arrest in June 1945, however, and he was interrogated for two months about Ford-Werke AG and I.G. Farbenindustrie AG. By the time he was released and returned to Cologne, the city had been taken over by a British MG as part of the British Zone in the Allied organization of Occupied Germany. They slapped Schmidt with an employment ban, citing his honorific as a "Wehrwirtschaftsführer," the title he had held since April 1941. Under Allied guidelines, this was grounds for immediate firing.

In the ensuing de-Nazification procedure, Schmidt reinvented himself as an internationalist and pacifist opponent of the Nazis. Not unlike Wenzel, he told of a "half-Jew" and of a "political victim" whom he had helped. But his first attempt at rehabilitation still went awry. The commission caught several false statements on his interrogation form. He neglected to mention his job as a "Reichskommissar" for Ford properties in Belgium and Holland, and his articles with a Nazi tone in the Ford company newspaper. The examples he cited of his "persecution" by the Nazis all turned out to be conflicts with individual NSDAP members that arose in the course of his efforts at building a private fortune. In a concurring statement, the British MG also balked at clearing Schmidt: "It is hard to believe regarding the carefulness with which the OKH and the NSDAP have selected their collaborateurs for responsible and leading positions that a completely politically unreliable person, as claimed by Schmidt, was selected for the positions stated above."

Rejected, Schmidt went searching for more exonerating material. In his appeal motion of 10 September 1946, he pointed to his exemplary conduct towards the forced laborers:

> My basic attitude in all social and wage issues naturally extended to the foreign workers, who were as decently treated, clothed, and fed as was at all possible under the very strict regulations. I often directly violated legal regulations in order to ease the lot of the people who had been taken away from their homes by force, insofar as this was possible. And here the limits of the possible were pushed far further than was generally the case.

Schmidt had seen how the war would turn out well in advance of the Allied victory. Instead of fleeing Cologne, he stuck it out at Ford Werke in March 1945. Now he claimed to be a resistance fighter who had defended the company's interests from the clutches of the Nazis. His argument was helped by a letter from the NSDAP district leader of Gummersbach, dated 12 March 1945. Therein, Schmidt is accused of sabotage for delaying the transfer of Ford's production machinery to the dispersal locations. This had helped thwart the Party's plans to destroy the machinery, and was very positively received by the personnel committee at Ford. It also helped that no documents confirming Schmidt's membership in the NSDAP had come to light. The commission never saw the only available source in which Schmidt is described as a "Party Comrade." That he had been a "Wehrwirtschaftsführer" was considered at least as serious, however. Schmidt deflated it by pointing out that his title was conferred only by General Leeb, head of the Army Weapons Procurement Office, and not by Reichsmarshall Hermann Göring. In no small part thanks to a recommendation from the Ford Werke works council, Schmidt was placed in Category V on 25 October 1947.

By the mid-1950s, with Ford Werke once again firmly and openly under the control of Ford Motor Company, most of the key executives from the Nazi era had moved back into leading positions. Six of them occupied posts on Ford Werke's eight-member board of managers as of 1956. Chairman Erhard Vitger and Deputy Chairman Robert Schmidt were joined by their long-term associates, Hans Grandi, Ernst Sagebiel, Hans Schmidt, and Max Ueber. Schmidt was promoted into the directorate in 1958, and remained associated with Ford Werke until his death on 24 October 1962.[150]

There is no doubt that the upper management at Ford was at least informed about the general living conditions of the forced laborers at their plant during the war. All manner of eloquent statements about their "foreign workers" can be found in their de-Nazification files, dating from 1945 to 1948. In their efforts towards exonerating each other, they helped constitute the company legend of the "model camp," in which the "foreign laborers" had lived particularly well. This legend not only found its way into the literature,[151] but has been kept alive among the majority of retirees who witnessed the war years at Ford.

Conclusion

Under great legal and public pressure, a few major German industrial corporations finally brought themselves, in the course of 1998, to consider setting up compensation funds for Nazi-era forced labor. These announcements may be part of the companies' attempt to foil the enforcement of the former labor-slaves' legal claims, but they also constitute an admission by the companies that their former defense—that they were simply compelled to follow the orders of the Nazi regime—has become untenable in light of the facts.

That Ford-Werke AG in Cologne did make extensive use of forced labor, and that its forced laborers were subjected to degrading conditions, is no longer subject to question. Even if the available sources are meager on many points, Ford Werke cannot credibly claim that it was involuntarily assigned forced laborers to meet dictated production numbers. No evidence suggests that Ford Werke made an effort to limit its production capacity to avoid employing forced labor. Much evidence shows that the American-owned German Ford unit actively and independently pursued an expansion of its operations at all times under the Third Reich, so that it became one of the most important suppliers of vehicles to the Wehrmacht.

That the Ford subsidiary in Cologne stood under the supervision of the Reichskommissar for the Treatment of Enemy Property starting in May 1942 does not, on closer examination, relieve the Ford Motor Company of its responsibility. Long before then, already in 1940, Ford Werke was employing French prisoners of war as forced laborers.

The company's policy in the years from 1933 to 1941 is evident: Ford-Werke AG, with the knowledge and support of the Ford Motor Company in Dearborn, integrated its operations into the Nazi war economy and set off on the course that was followed after 1941. Strikingly, Ford returned to business as usual very quickly after the end of the war, and in doing so relied heavily on its well-tested managers from the Nazi period. This apparently smooth transition, with almost the same leadership from one era to the next, is tantamount to a sanctioning after the fact by Ford Motor Company of the activities pursued by these men under the Nazi regime.

After the war the Ford Motor Company did not just reassume control of a factory, but implicitly assumed responsibility for its history. Through the lawsuits filed by the former forced laborers, Dearborn is today confronted with more than five decades of its sins of omission. Apparently no one at Ford Motor Company was interested in casting light upon this part of history, not even to explicitly proclaim a distance from the practices of Ford-Werke AG during the Nazi era.

— Karola Fings

RETURNING TO COLOGNE

Soviet *Ostarbeiter.* Four of the tens of thousands of forced laborers in Cologne during the war (C1, C2). Note "OST" patch on the woman's sleeve, top left.

French civilian forced laborers in front of their barracks (8) at the Ford camp (C3).

Fritz Theilen at age 15, in the uniform of a Ford apprentice, April 1941 (C4).

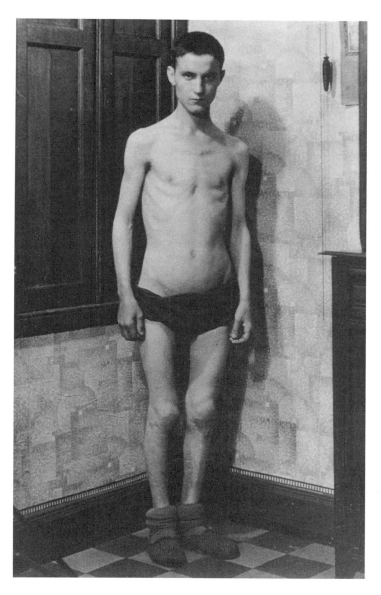

Yvon Thibaut after liberation from Buchenwald concentration camp in 1945 (C5).

Soviet forced laborers in front of their barracks at Ford in 1942. Above (C6), second row, first from right: Elsa Iwanowa. Sixth from right: Inna Kulagina. Below (C7), fourth from left: Tamara Nosik.

Elsa Iwanowa-de Meyer (left) and Inna Kulagina visiting Ford Werke in Cologne in September 1995 (C8).

Above, 1943 Ford Werke Gefolgschaft ID-card photos of Kamila Felinska (C9) and her husband (C10). Below, Kamila Felinska at Ford Werke in September 1995 (C11).

Kazimierz Tarnawski in the cellar of the former Gestapo headquarters in Cologne, September 1995 (C12).

Anna Obuchowskaja (right) visiting Ford Werke in September 1996 with her daughter, Mery (second from right), who was born into confinement at the Ford camp in November 1943 (C13).

Former Italian military internee Mareno Mannucci speaking to a gathering in Cologne, September 1998 (C14).

Returning former forced laborers Anna Nesteruk (center) and Nadia Shubrawa (right) present a gift to the mayor of Cologne as Stepan Saika (left) looks on, September 1995 (C15).

Former forced laborers at Ford in Cologne (from left) Kamila Felinska, Kazimierz Tarnawski, Klawdia Nikiforowna Podobed, Nadeschda Machtejewna Schubrawa, Anna Wasilijewna Nesteruk, Stepan Iwanowitsch Saika, Inna Efimowna Kulagina, and Elsa Iwanowa-de Meyer, with a researcher from the NS Documents Center and a representative of the City of Cologne (back), and a Ford spokesperson (right), at the entrance to Ford Werke headquarters, September 1995 (C16).

CHAPTER 5

"AND THEY TOOK THE 38 OF US TO FORD"

Interviews with Former Forced Laborers

The years were 1993, 1995, and 1998. The visitors came to Cologne from the Ukraine, Russia, Poland, Italy, and nearby Belgium. They met each other, got acquainted with their hosts, spoke to gatherings of sympathetic listeners. They returned to their former workplaces, where labor camps once stood. Perhaps to an old prison cell. Afterwards, in a room at the city's NS Documents Center, each visitor sat down with a German interviewer and an interpreter. On the table there were pictures, aerial photos, maps. Questions were posed in German. The subjects spoke in their mother tongues. A tape recorder was running.

The NS-Dokumentationszentrum der Stadt Köln provided us with German transcripts of nine interviews with former forced laborers. The interview with the former German Ford apprentice, Fritz Theilen, was arranged by Projektgruppe Messelager, the group of researchers who initiated the visitors' program.

Excerpts from the ten transcripts have been arranged by chronology and topic. The English translation sticks closely to the spoken word. Most questions have been deleted. Remaining questions are in bold. Summarized passages and additional information are in italics. Interpolations by interpreters are in parentheses, those by the editor in brackets. The long bracketed passages in Anna Nesteruk's testimony are taken from her 1994 letter to the NS Documents Center.

Kamila Felinska grew up in the Sarny district of eastern Poland, which is today part of the Ukraine. She describes her childhood, and how the war began for her. In September 1939 Germany invaded Poland, but allowed the Soviet army to occupy the eastern regions of that country.

KAMILA FELINSKA: I was born on 16 February 1923 in Sarny, in the region of Wolyn. I was the oldest. We were ten children in all, three girls and seven boys. We lived on a farm, an estate (*Folwark*). I looked after my siblings, because I was the oldest. We had a cow, a couple of pigs, some land. My mother had to take care of all that, because my father worked for the *starost*, the town administrator. I attended seven years of school. In 1939, when the war broke out, the Germans came. We thought the Germans would stay, but then the Russians came. After a few days of negotiations the Germans withdrew and we stayed under Russian authority. The wealthier families were taken off to Siberia. The sister of my mother was sent there, and the brother of my father. Our family was also supposed to go there, but my father fled and so we stayed put. He hid in the forest and came to the house at night, then he would get some food. Or he hid in abandoned buildings, so that even the neighbors did not know where he was.

On 22 June 1941 the Reich launched an invasion of the Soviet Union, within days overrunning Soviet-occupied eastern Poland.

Kamila Felinska: The Germans immediately began choosing young people from families with a lot of children. They were sent off to forced labor, and I was among them. By 5 May 1942 I was already in [the German town of Mechernich-] Antweiler. I was the oldest in our family, the other children were still young. We were informed by letter that we had to appear before a commission in Sarny, where we were put through medical examinations. There they said that I was healthy. There was nothing wrong with me, and so I had to go to Germany. They told us that we would be going to Germany. A great many people from surrounding villages and towns appeared before the commission. We were examined and everyone got an appointment, a date when he had to appear at the train station....

My fiancee, his family had only two children, so he was not chosen to go to Germany. But I was chosen. Because [he and I] had a relationship, he wanted to come with me, no matter what. I was just going to the train when I saw him, standing there with a suitcase. I asked him: "Where are you going?" And he said: "I'm going with you." ... So the journey began, with the train. It was a cargo train, because there were a great many people there. I knew no one. My husband came along voluntarily, but at the time he was not yet my husband....

After about a hundred kilometers I had a chance to run away from the train, but I had been told before leaving that my papers were already in Germany, and that if I didn't arrive there all members of my family would be killed. I thought that my family should be left in peace, and if anyone should die, then I alone. And so I stayed on the train. In Warsaw a Polish railroad worker offered to hide me in Warsaw, but I was afraid, because I was still young. I didn't know the man, and I was afraid of him.

We were all together on the train, girls and boys. Later the boys were brought into another car, and we girls remained. We got nothing to eat or drink, but we had been told in advance that we should bring something. I had a big ham and a loaf of bread. We also didn't ask for anything, because we had some food. We went through Berlin. We arrived at a distribution point in Germany, and we were given another medical examination. I can only remember that there was a stage everyone had to go through. The hair was shaved off, if someone had lice, all the hair would be shaved off, and we were given baths. As far as I know this was the procedure for all transports. It was all very well prepared, organized, there were quite a lot of doctors there waiting. Two people each would go to the baths and then straight to the examination.

After that there was a commission that determined where each of us would be assigned, to what kind of work. Because I was thin and small, I was assigned to a factory as a laborer. My fiancee was supposed to go somewhere else, but because we had the same name, he said that he was my husband, and that he wanted to go with me. I was asked if this was true. I stayed true to him and lied to them, and they believed that we were married. I had a passport in the name of Felinska and my fiancee was called Felinski, so the Germans believed that we were married.

We were sent straight to the brick factory in Antweiler. I have the address here. Perhaps one hundred of us, but when we arrived many Russians and Ukrainians were already there, and there were also Jews. They were Jews from Warsaw, they spoke Polish.[1] At the time I couldn't speak any German yet. I thought, what do I do now? Because I can't speak German. At first, the German soldiers were still there. The Jew from Poland did not want to admit that he spoke Polish, and said nothing. After that, when the soldier went away again, we couldn't understand each other, so the Jew spoke to me in Polish. He said: "I understand you, actually," and asked me whether I knew what was happening in Warsaw. I told him that they were building the ghettos. Actually I didn't know that for sure, but back at our town in Sarny there was a ghetto, so I assumed that ghettos were being set up elsewhere.

It was the Jews [in Merchenich-Antweiler] who taught us everything, how to do our jobs. My husband baked pipes at the brick factory, which were brought to the fields, and the Jews taught him how to do that. They were Polish Jews who spoke German very well, because they had already been there for three years or more. They had to wear the Star of David. At first I thought they were German Jews, but then it turned out, when he spoke Polish to me, that he was from Warsaw.

Do you know what happened to them afterwards?

Kamila Felinska: I don't know. It was only about a month's time, during which the Jews taught us. Afterwards they put older Germans to work on the machines. I had to help them by throwing the sand or the clay into the machine and then bringing [the bricks] to dry. These big bricks, weighing about twenty-five kilos and five kilos for the mold, meaning about thirty kilos altogether. I had to carry them to the drying room. The work ran from seven in the morning until seven in the evening, for twelve hours we worked. Naturally we didn't get very much to eat, because it was wartime. Whatever we got we were very happy about. Each person got a quarter loaf for two days, and a bowl of soup. There was no dinner, just coffee. I had to live off the bread for two days, but if I was hungry, then I would eat the whole bread as soon as they gave it to us. In the beginning I still had some of the food, the ham I had brought from Poland. That saved me. Later the Jews were sent somewhere else and all of us worked on the machines.... The worst part was the sleeping rooms, which were set up in an old barn. They had platform beds there. We were locked in. In the middle of the room there was a bucket, that served as a toilet. After work we could wash in the factory....

While in Antweiler I was hit so hard once that even today I cannot hear well in one ear. There was a rule there that the women, when they had their period, did not have to work for three days, because it was very physically demanding work. I had my period and I didn't go to work, and then the SS came with dogs. There were several women who weren't working on that day, I was not the only one. We were all led to the dining room. We were asked why we were not working, and then the rule was abolished. Everyone had to always work, and I was hit with a rubber truncheon.

Kamila Felinska recalls she was able to exchange letters with her parents in the normal way, through the post office.

Kamila Felinska: From my village there were two girls, they were older than me, about twenty-five, twenty years old. They were also forced laborers, but in Dusseldorf. I had contacts to them later. [The Germans] were sometimes censoring, to see what was in the letter, but sometimes there were no controls. You could see that easily, because the letter would come, but it was already open.

Inna Jefimovna Kulagina was born in the southern Russian town of Rostov-on-the-Don in 1925.

INNA KULAGINA: My parents were relatively well off. Father was an accountant, mother did not work. Their first children had died. My sister was a year older than me. Mother was afraid that my sister might also suddenly die, and so I came into the world soon after her. Mother was already forty years old. That is why I was born. And we sisters both survived. In 1933, when I started school, Russia went through a year of famine. Everyone back then lived very poorly. I studied well, I was always best in my class and before the war began I finished the ninth grade. In '41 the war began. The front approached the city of Rostov very quickly. Rostov was first occupied [by the Germans] in November '41. It was only for ten days, and then the front pulled back. I was sixteen years old. I began training as a nurse, to help out in the hospital or somewhere. Those courses were started during the war. But in June '42 the German army marched back into the city. And

I could no longer study and complete these courses. I stayed with my parents. I could not let myself be evacuated because my parents were old and there was a sister there. We could not yet do anything. We stayed in Rostov.

Elsa Iwanowa was also born in 1925 and grew up in Rostov.

ELSA IWANOWA-DE MEYER: We went to school and had no problems with each other. Mama, Papa, Grandfather and my brother, we are twins. Father worked in the offices of a sanitarium. He was responsible for supplying the Black Sea health spas. We were actually triplets, one brother died when he was ten months old, and one brother and I remained. We went together to school. Mother and Father worked, Mother as a bookkeeper. Grandmother would come every morning and keep our whole house, wash and cook for us.

I can't give you an interview, I already said so. I can't give an interview, I'm not at all talkative (interruption)....

When the Germans marched in [during the summer of 1942], Father wanted to evacuate us. Father came to get us, to bring us behind the Urals. Mother and Grandmother sewed the whole day long. What should we take with us? We had to take something with us, didn't we? And then in the evening the military doctor came. He was also coming, like Father, to fetch his family, but he said: "Comrade Iwanow, the bridge over the River Don has been destroyed!" What should we do? We had to stay, we couldn't go on foot. And I hugged my father: "Daddy, I'm going with you!" (cries). He couldn't get out of my arms. "I don't want to stay with the Germans!" He says: "What should I do with you in the barracks?" My brother, he was also sixteen, he was taken into the army. "And you," he told me, "stay with Mother!" He couldn't take me to the barracks with the men. He was in the army. And we didn't know yet that the people would be taken to Germany. And so I stayed with Mother and Grandmother.

Anna Vasilevna Nesteruk and Nadeshda (Nadia) Mahteyevna Shubrawa were both born in 1925 and grew up in two neighboring villages in the Chmelnizky region of the western Ukraine. They were both taken to Germany for forced labor in June 1942. They met during their transport, and have stayed friends ever since. They were interviewed together.

NADIA SHUBRAWA: I live in one village, she lives in another village. We were together for something over three years, we were like a family.

ANNA NESTERUK: I was born in what was called the Kamensk-Podolski region in 1925. Father died. I lived together with my mother. I had a difficult life. In 1933, the famine came. My brother starved to death. Times stayed hard after that. Mother was always alone, and I was alone with Mother. I went to work when I was twelve. I went to work in the fields, in the collectives.

[I was barely seventeen. We were practically children, we had seen very little of life in comparison to young people today. We had traveled nowhere and knew little. Our knowledge was limited to elementary school, some of us had completed fourth grade, some seventh grade. At that time the adults were afraid of the domestic authorities, police, secret police, NKVD. Surely you know of this. The young people therefore knew practically nothing about the political situation in the country. And we, the children of the 1920s, had no foreknowledge of how quickly Germany would descend upon our country—which until recently was called the USSR, but is today known as Ukraine, Russia, Belarus, etc. That is history already. Many books were written, many documents collected. I admit to you honestly that it is very hard to describe that time.]

Nadia Shubrawa: We were born in the country, in a village. In 1933 there was a great famine, and the years were very hard: hunger, collectivization, the people were driven into the collective farms (*kolkhoz*). Earlier people had their own land. Then everything was taken from us and we worked in the *kolkhoz*, like today. I went to school for three years. The fourth grade I did not finish, I went to work. I was twelve years old when I started working. We planted beets, sugarbeets.

[*When the war started* ...] I also fertilized beets, using a little barrel with two openings. I led the horse from the front, and in the back there was another woman and we fertilized the beets. Then it was made known [that we had] to go to Germany. '42, on 16 June, the eldest of the village told us that we would be going to the [German] farmers for the harvest. We were not told that we were going to the factory. It was said, to the farmers, for a half-year, for the harvest.

Anna Nesteruk: In '42 Sergei, the policeman, and a German came with a member of the German military to our house. And he said to my mother: "The daughter must go to the village soviet tomorrow morning. But if the daughter does not come, anyone who does not come to the village soviet will be shot, he will be no more." That was how the order was: "If she does not come, then we will *schiessen machen*," so the German said. We were all very frightened, we were young girls. From our village thirty-six people, girls, were taken away. So we went home to eat, and then we were taken away. And my mother stayed alone.

[We were carried off to perform forced labor—as you call it—on 3 June 1942, driven by blows from rifle butts to the town of Starokonstantinov in the area of Chmelnizky. We weren't even allowed to say goodbye to our nearest relatives. Armed soldiers went from house to house. They were the local police, commanded by the German occupiers. It was pointless to try to hide, because they could shoot whole villages. And so we sat and waited. Like a herd of cattle we were driven forth, but where and why we scared little girls and boys did not know. We hoped that we weren't being taken to be shot, because a great many Jews, Poles, and other nationalities had already been shot in Starokonstantinov for various offenses—as determined by the German occupiers—in the time from June 1941 to June 1942.]

Anna Nesteruk: We were taken to Starokonstantinov with the horse carriage. We arrived and we were kept there in barracks. We spent the night. We weren't allowed to go, not before....

Nadia Shubrawa: (interjects) Horse carriages arrived from the whole area.

Anna Nesteruk: We were locked there in the barracks, and the young people were brought there from the whole area. This was not long, about a week. The young people were brought there, all of us were then forced to go to the train station. We were put into livestock wagons, then these were locked. We had nothing to drink, but some of us had brought some food from home. We were put into the wagons, they were locked up, and then we heard the signal to go. Oh, mother ...

Anna Nesteruk: As the train got going the German soldiers played a funeral march, so that the mothers would not wail. On the way there was a railway accident.

Nadia Shubrawa: We arrived in Brest-Litovsk and the train stood at the station. An airplane flew over us and a bomb fell directly under the train, but did not explode.

Anna Nesteruk: [Near Cologne our group were placed into trucks, brought to the city of Cologne and kept in a barracks. We spent the night there and the next morning we were brought to a camp. The camp was fenced off with barbed wire and was patrolled on the outside by policemen. We worked in a factory where trucks and autos were made, called "Fordwerk." The factory was called "Fordwerk."]

Stepan Ivanovich Saika was born in 1925 in a village in the Chmelnizky area of the Ukraine. In summer 1942 he was transported in a livestock car to Germany. There he was assigned to Ford Werke in Cologne. He was deployed in the construction of the Ford factory barracks.

STEPAN SAIKA: The first thing they asked me at the Ford plants in the summer of 1942 was what I had done back home. I said that I kept cows and geese. They sent me to work on the building of the camp. I helped build barracks. Those hadn't existed when I got there, at the camp for Ford. Now the people from the Donbass region were the first ones who were brought there. And then came others from the Poltov area, from Sumy, Kharkov and Saporozhe. And later the people from Nikolayesk.

You had to build your own barracks?

Stepan Saika: Yes. The supervisor there was Fritz. He spoke very broken Russian. He said that he had been at the Dnepr hydroelectric plant in 1932, when that plant was being built. And once we had built the camp, and it was finished—I can remember it as though it was today—then there was a trailer, I was sent there, and I heard the name called: "Franz!" A very big man came out, and I worked with this German for two months. Not everything was all built up around the area, like we saw at Ford [today, in 1995]. There was a big smoking room, it was made of metal constructions and glass all around. And then they bring me to the construction shack, he says: "Franz!" A German comes out, he had such giant shoes that children could play in there. Later I found out he was a foreman. And then two other Germans come out—Jupp, he was 76, and Josef. And the work we did was like this: hot asphalt was brought in, they poured it out, and I spread the asphalt with a roller. And then I say: "I'm going to the camp, midday." I wanted to go to the camp to have soup. And one time Jupp comes out of the shack and says to me: "Stalin! Come here!" And these Germans gave me something to eat. Franz brought me these big pears, he lived in the country. And Josef brought potatoes.

Once the barracks were completed, Stepan Saika was among the first to move in.

Stepan Saika: There was a barracks for men, a barracks for women, and another one for families. There were many barracks, because there were about 1,500 people there. There were about 350 to 400 people to a barracks. These had three-level platform beds, with an aisle along the middle, and there would be two or three ovens. In the winter these were heated with briquettes. There was nothing else. You could sit on the beds. There were about two stools per compartment [for six people]. There was nothing else, just the ovens. There was no washroom in the barracks, there was one on the camp grounds. The toilets were on the street. In the barracks there was no water. There was a canteen, a hall. Everything was made of wood. There was a hatch through which we were served out of a big pot. There were two overseers, called police, in the camp. They maintained order. But we would be called to work by a German policeman, who came around especially for that purpose.

Anna Nesteruk and Nadia Shubrawa began working for Ford in the summer of 1942. During their first months at Ford, while the barracks were still being built, they slept at a nearby "silk factory."

Anna Nesteruk: *Ja, eine Barack.* We lived in barracks, we wore numbers. Everyone had a number, my number was 872.

Nadia Shubrawa: 894.

Anna Nesteruk: We had "OST" sewed on the chest, on the left side. We were taken to work under guard.

Nadia Shubrawa: First we were kept at the silk factory. What was it called? I've forgotten. Olga was at this factory.

Anna Nesteruk: We did not live at that factory for long.

Nadia Shubrawa: We lived there for as long as there were no barracks at Ford. We would go (from the silk factory to Ford) on foot–there and back.

Nadia Shubrawa: We went straight to work at Ford. There were no barracks there yet. And then the barracks were built, and we were moved there. Then we did not have far to go. A foreman came straight to us. We were many girls who worked together with me in one department–seventeen, eighteen, nineteen years old. That was an assembly line, where cabins were welded together. Then that was placed onto the assembly line. We inserted the glass, and over there they did something else and over there something else. And then that goes to control, they check whether it's good, and then to the 14th department. And there they did another job, they put the body on, and the autos came out finished. When we arrived, the Germans were only making thirteen to fifteen autos, trucks, daily. There were no workers left. And when we were brought in, we all worked. We all worked. They showed us how to do it and we worked. About 130 to 140 autos were built there each day.

What number did you have?

Stepan Saika: 456. They had all the numbers listed at the guardhouse. The policeman came, he would call a number, never the first or last name. As though he was calling your name. Maybe it was on a list somewhere, the name, where I come from and so on. But in the camp no names were used.

I was working at the cylinder block. A cylinder head, you know that? It's made of cast iron, and heavy. I was assigned there, but the foreman there was crazy evil. When he came to us at work, he wore a yellow uniform and an armband with the swastika. I didn't know exactly, but he must have been in the party. The first time I saw those machines! I looked at these machines. Where could I have seen such machines in the village? I thought, they will take off my head! The supervisor only showed me how to flip the switches. It was a half-automatic machine. It had as many drills as there were holes on the block. They drilled into the block, and after that they went up again.

I worked there for a month. I was so dirty, I stopped washing and I stopped bathing. When I had worked for a month, [the foreman] kicked me a couple of times to the side, and he brought me to Department 3.

Stepan Saika was assigned to an easier job in another department.

Stepan Saika: Freshly cast metal rods had to be worked over with brushes. That was easy work. And across from me there was a machine with white emulsion running over it. That is where, if I remember right, Jupp worked. He had a big belly and looked at me because I was so dirty. I had begun to piss in my pants, I was completely neglecting myself (cries). He looked at me, and towards evening he said: "Come with me." I thought: "Where does he want to take me?" He took me up to the upper level, where I saw that they had a good washing room. And he took me to the locker room, gave me soapsuds and soap and said: "*Waschen.*" I took a shower there, came back to the hall, and all the Germans laughed, since I came in looking so clean after the shower.

Yes, and then I worked there. I had stopped washing myself, because no one cared if I was clean or dirty. There were good people here, but there were of course also bad ones. That was a regime. There was a German who worked with me, for example, who would warn me. "Stefan, watch out: a fascist." So that I wouldn't say anything in [the fascist's] presence, because you could end up in the KZ. That was how it was. Not all Germans were like master race. But there were some who were, how should I say, influenced by national socialism. I met [Russians] who worked at the [German] farms. Some farmers had people for three years, and they were never allowed into the house. Others let the people eat with them, together at the same table.

Kazimierz Tarnawski grew up in Rovno, then in eastern Poland, today Rivne, Ukraine. Tarnawski was deported to a forced labor deployment in Germany in July 1942, at first in the town of Gelsenkirchen.

KAZIMIERZ TARNAWSKI: I was born on 26 June 1925 in the town of Rovno. Until 1939 I lived with my parents. In 1940, my father, who had been a soldier, came back from imprisonment. He had fought [*in 1939 and been captured by the Germans*]. I then went to middle school until 1941, when the next war began. Then the region where I was born and the entire Wolyn region was occupied by the German troops. Until 1939 it was Polish, then it was Russian, and then from 1941 again German.

At that time I could no longer go to school, I had to start working. In 1942 we got a notice. I had to register to work, otherwise my whole family would be taken to a concentration camp. All the young people had to register. Everyone between sixteen and thirty years of age had to register for work. And in July 1942 I was transported to Germany. Gelsenkirchen.

The transport was terrible, there was little to eat and two soldiers stood as guards in every train-car. I wanted to run away, but I could not, because they were constantly guarding us. I wanted to jump out whenever the train slowed down, but I didn't make it. It was very dangerous, the guards were ready to shoot at any time, and I wanted to live. My comrades, who were transported with me, were very afraid.

So I arrived here in Gelsenkirchen. Here I worked in a glass factory. It was heavy work and there was very little to eat. I was absolutely required to wear a "P." Once, when I didn't wear it, I was forced to pay a fine of twenty-five marks, and I had no money for it. Luckily my foreman said that I should stay calm. He would pay the twenty-five marks if I would work all the time in his garden. This I then did.

August 1942. A few weeks after the Germans occupied Rostov ...

Elsa Iwanowa: We had to register at the Arbeitsamt, that went by the alphabet. Everyone had to go there. Then I ran away with a friend, her uncle lived somewhere in a village. We got there and started working. We harvested watermelons. We wanted to stay there. One day I was coming back from work, and I saw Mother standing in the road. I said: "Mother, what are you doing there?" And she answered: "You must go back, because the Germans came to our house." They had gone to my friend's house and to my house and asked: "Where is your daughter?" [Mother] ran away [to us]. A lot of people were going through the villages then, trading for a piece of bread or something. In the city there was nothing. Everything was destroyed. The shops were empty.

They would have transported my mother in my place: "If the daughter does not come back...." My mother was so weak, and she came all this way on foot to find me. We went back to Rostov on foot, and we went to register. My group was already gone. I had the letter I, and then came K like Kulagina, A, B, W, and so on, I, K. My letter was already past, the people were gone. And so I didn't go with the first transport, but with the sixth. And later I heard that ten transports left Rostov with two thousand each. Twenty thousand girls.

Inna Kulagina was deported from Rostov to Germany in October 1942. During the transport she met Elsa Iwanowa.

Inna Kulagina: Russians generally are very great patriots. And naturally, there was our enemy. They had invaded our land, to conquer it. That was the relationship. We had heard a great deal. It was reported about how Jews were being exterminated, we had all heard about that. The German army was barely [in Rostov] before all the Jews were rounded up. Many Jews were evacuated. Rostov is a very big city. Then signs were posted, everywhere, everywhere, announcing that everyone had to go to the labor agency, to the German Arbeitsamt. And of course some among the Russians helped the Germans. Russian police would check who was appearing at the Arbeitsamt. Anyone who went there got a certificate, saying either he was to be released or to be taken. If I didn't possess such a document, it meant that I absolutely had to appear. These signs also announced that anyone who tried to hide would be shot.

Everyone was afraid: Where are they taking us? We were still children, sixteen years old. We seemed to already be grown up, but we were still children. My sister got a certificate, a document stating that she was the oldest child and had to help our parents. But I was taken.

On 6 October '42 we were brought to the train station and we were put into cargo cars, pullmans. You know pullmans, don't you? Such cargo cars were they, dirty, without anything. We were put in there, we lay right on the floor, and we were brought to Germany. We were locked up. From all of Rostov, it was two thousand people on each train. And there were ten of these trains, so 20,000 people. I was in the sixth train. I delayed a little bit. Alphabetically I would have had to go sooner. We were collected from various districts. First I belonged to the letter K, Kulagina, but by the time I went it was already the people with the letter P. I always delayed. I thought: "Maybe I can still somehow get myself released." And this is why Elsa and I met each other in a train car.

Everyone was put together, men and women. Now we had brought a little bag, we had some clothing with us. Our parents said to us: "Where are you going?" Everyone was weeping and calling "Mama!" as they said farewell.... And there were no windows, no doors in these cars. We were locked up and it was only opened when someone had to get off or there was something else. It was a terrible feeling, because we were transported like animals, everyone in the space. We wore coats. It was already October, it was cold. We slept with our clothes on. We would wake up and no one could wash, nothing, everything was dirty. In the truest sense like livestock. And we rode for a very long time. There were stops in Poland, usually at night so that we wouldn't be noticed. There were points there where we were given something to eat, one time. We were probably traveling for twenty days.

Elsa Iwanowa: They had said, for six months. "Then," it was said, "you will come back and others will be sent." That is what they said. But that was untrue, they took us away for ever.... We were supposed to appear on the sixth of October at the train station with our bags. Not the main station, somewhere outside the town, Rostov-Berge or something like that. There were cargo cars and we were all put in, but we just stood there at first, probably four or five hours. We couldn't start, our people were there: the Russians bombed. And Mother stood there and Grandmother, they had accompanied me [to the train].

We each had a small bag. We got in the car, everything was empty, cargo cars. We put down the bags, we slept on the bags. I slept on the bag for three weeks. The whole time everyone slept on the bags, if they had one. A little window was open, they would open the car at stations. In every wagon there was a soldier with a rifle. We would ask, he would say: "I'm going on holiday." German soldiers, when they went home for one or two weeks on holiday, they came with these transports. I still remember, they always stood there with the rifle.

[At stations] we would jump out of the train to drink, many fell off the train. The people crawled under the train. There was no toilet. Many who crawled under the trains were killed. The cars started, there were many ways, a lot of people died. (Begins to answer some of the questions as soon as they are posed, without a translation.) When we came to a station or (in German) a *Wasserbacke*, a crane, there would be water there. They gave us nothing to eat, nothing to drink, nothing. What mother gave us, we ate. Three weeks.

We arrived in Wuppertal [a town in the Rhine-Ruhr region]. But on the way we stopped somewhere in Poland. We were driven out like livestock, we had to take off our clothes, and stood there naked. We were only girls, we were ashamed. And there was a table, and Germans sitting at it, a doctor, and some woman. And we had to go past, and they went "snip snip": "*desin-fizieren.*" They thought we had lice, but we got lice in Germany.

Inna Kulagina: After [the transport] we were brought to Wuppertal. That was a camp from which everyone was sent to different places. These were barracks without beds. There was nothing there at all, and again we slept on the floor. Wuppertal is in a valley, and it was already October, it was raining. We had to always line up outside at four in the morning, and stand there in the rain until we were "bought." And it took a few days, we were not only there for a day. Four or five days. Drenched, without clothing, we slept right on the floor. Like livestock. I think they treated the livestock better. It was, you understand, terrible. We weren't people any more, just animals–dirty, slept on the floor, cold and drenched. It was just terrible!

In the mornings we would line up (and German) farmers and people from the factories would come to "buy" us. Around noon, when a few were brought away, we would get bread. Oy, that was no bread, I can hardly say what that was: black, and for some reason it was very sweet. I think it was made from sugar beets. And then some kind of soup, who knows what, water with some cabbage swimming in it. It was very bad, and we were hungry the whole time. And when we were taken away we were happy that we were going somewhere else, that these conditions would change. We didn't know what was expecting us there. And the thirty-eight of us, all from Rostov, they transported to the factory of Ford. We were all from the same train. We kept together and said to each other, "let's go, the main thing is that we stick together." We were put into trucks covered with tarpaulins and taken to Ford.

When we arrived at Ford and saw the many barracks standing there, the … what surprised us–everyone was dressed in black.… Back then women didn't wear any pants, back then in '41, it was: "Oh! Women in pants!" Dark blue jackets, "OST" on the chest, and wooden shoes and dark blue pants. We were at first kept in a small barrack with two-level plank beds. Only the people from Rostov were there. The barrack was small. There were large barracks there, but this one was small, and our group was kept there.… We were happy to get mattresses at least stuffed with straw. We weren't in this barrack for long, because another group came from somewhere in the Ukraine, and then we ended up in a barrack where it was mostly three-level beds. The people there from Russia were only those from Rostov, while all the others were Ukrainians, from Kamenez-Podolsk, from Poltava. But we got along well together. I slept below, and Elsa slept in the middle or above. I don't know anymore.

The barrack was built like this: doors–beds, doors–beds. In the middle of the barrack there was an iron oven. At night it was locked up and some iron bucket would be set up [on the floor]. That was our toilet. There was an outhouse, but they didn't let us out [at night]. Around the camp there was a barbed wire fence, guard posts everywhere, so that we wouldn't run away.…

We were sent straight to work. I was brought into the department where the processing was done.… I had never been in a factory in Russia. I had never even seen one. I processed spark plugs for the motors. I polished them with an emulsion. The foreman brought me around, showed me how to do it. I was small. I could barely reach the machine, so I got a bench to stand on. We worked twelve-hour shifts. But Elsa had to do very heavy work. She drilled openings in the motor hood. She was in the next section over.

Elsa Iwanowa: There were some cast parts with holes, and I had to drill in more little holes. And next to that there were metal cutters. That was hard, that was all out of cast iron … For big autos and small, light tanks. The factory produced big autos.

What were these metal parts exactly?

Elsa Iwanowa: I don't know, they didn't show us where they went. *"Arbeite und schweige! Schnell, schnell, arbeiten!"* From seven in the morning until seven in the evening. And the next week from seven in the evening until seven in the morning. For lunch we were taken to the camp for a half-hour. *Balanda* ("water soup"). I don't know what it was. Everything. In the morning we got three slices of bread, black bread like today, but it was made of red beets. And a pat of butter, no margarine—really thin. And that was breakfast. For lunch, *balanda*. And again for dinner … There was never cheese or sausage, only bread with margarine. We were hungry like a bear.

During work I sat there and cried. I couldn't stop. And the whole time I dreamed of a piece of a bread, I saw nothing else and couldn't think of anything else, only a piece of bread. Then I thought: "Oh, Grandmother made pancakes." It was hard to work nights. Still we were happy about it because when we went back in the morning we could sleep the whole day. We got there at seven [in the morning], went straight to bed and slept the whole day until the evening, to forget the hunger. We were young, we always wanted to sleep and the work was very hard.

In the night we were taken to the German canteen, probably around midnight. We went up the stairs. A policeman took us to the canteen and there was an extra meal for Russians. There were Germans there too, workers. And sometimes, when we saw a good German, we would ask him for a little bottle with a sweet, thick orange liquid. We begged: "Give us a little bottle!" Sometimes they gave us one. It was like lemonade, but very thick. Very tasty. It was filling, as though you had eaten. And there was a large pot, and next to it a very big policeman, a fascist. He had a fascist badge and a ladle in his hand. He stood there and we went past with our empty bowls. He filled the bowls. The soup was foamy, it had bubbles. It was sour, it was the leftovers from lunch. The soup stank because it was sour. The soup stood there from midday until night, and it was very hot inside the factory. We called that *balanda*. Sometimes we got potatoes with beets. Or a beet soup.…

One time in the nightshift, a man was tired and went to sleep in the machine. This machine cut some kind of iron parts, there were cuttings. It was off, at night it was not used. And he fell asleep there. In the morning the shift changed, a worker came, but he was still sleeping. The other guy turned on the machine, and he was ground up. And everyone in the factory: "Oy, oy, the man was ground up!" He was from our barrack, from the first. A Russian. The man starting work didn't know that someone was sleeping there. At seven, shift change, some were going and others were coming. The factory was operating day and night.

Inna Kulagina: When we got there we had to sign a paper in which we swore that we would have no relationships with Germans. And that anyone caught having a relationship with a German would be shot. I signed that myself. Young people, naturally ... A few [of us] were older, and regardless of what happened, there was love. Never with Germans! They said that it was wrong to mix Aryan blood. That is what Hitler said. [Among us] there were older ones, twenty-two, twenty-three years old, and still more of the twenty-five year-olds. We were the youngest—sixteen, seventeen years old, born in '25, '26, and '27. We were still half-children, there was still no talk of love.

There were many more women than men in the Russian camp, how many I cannot say. The only men there were those who had not gone into the army. In Russia, when the Germans started with the round-ups, all the women were available. The men of eighteen and up were largely gone, in the army. Only male minors, boys, were taken to Germany, and older men, who for whatever reason had not yet been mobilized. Germany needed labor, and they took whoever they could. Meaning the women.

There were no rapes. Germans and Russians together!? I never heard anything like that. There was nothing like that. You know, possibly, because we were all the same age, we were all somehow friends with each other, rapes didn't happen to us. I heard nothing of such things. Perhaps there were such things and I didn't see it. Of the camp I do remember this: hunger, cold, and that bucket. We were locked in, and every morning we had to empty it outside. And how we had to line up, call out our numbers. We had no names, we were only a number. We were a labor unit, not people. Our camp leader, a German, was not such a terrible man.

Anna Nesteruk: The barracks at Ford were surrounded by a barbed wire fence. On top there was barbed wire, so that we couldn't run away. The mattresses were filled with sawdust. These were three-level plank beds.

Nadia Shubrawa: The barrack was large, there was an aisle in the middle and on one side, and on the other there were twelve three-level plank beds: here three and there three. And here there stood two little cabinets and little curtains, we made a Spanish wall out of that, and it was like a little room. They closed like doors. Two ovens stood in the middle, in the aisle. We would steal potatoes in the factory, come back, peel them with a little knife, put them on the oven and roast them.

Anna Nesteruk: So that the police wouldn't see. There were police. We keep a look-out at the door. If a policeman comes—we hide right away! We were led to work under guard. But then they let ten people at a time go to the city.

Nadia Shubrawa: We wore "OST" on the chest.

Anna Nesteruk: In the first year they didn't let us out at all.

Anna Nesteruk: Yes. And there were guard posts, police. In all four corners [of the camp] there were stations, so that we didn't run away.

Nadia Shubrawa: In the beginning it was so strict, but we got used to it. The soil was sandy, we pulled the barbed wire apart a bit and went through, went away.

Anna Nesteruk: We went to the village [presumably the nearby town of Merkenich] and begged, some gave us potatoes, some gave us a piece of bread. But sometimes you would go and no one gave you anything. So it was.

Nadia Shubrawa: A whole year long we weren't allowed to go into the city, nowhere. We just sat there.

Anna Nesteruk: And for a whole year we were led around under guard. We always had to line up in fours, and were led around under guard.

Nadia Shubrawa: *"Antreten, vier!"*

Anna Nesteruk: One policeman stood in the front, and the other behind him.

Nadia Shubrawa: So we were led back from the factory under guard. Later, older German workers came from the factory to get us…. And then a year went by, and we all went alone. We already knew which way to go to work, so we got up and went there.

Nadia Shubrawa: They gave us such jackets and skirts. Sometimes the Germans would put out clothes, we would go and search out anything that was still good…. We made towels out of the oil cloths from the car seats. The seats were covered with an oil cloth. And this oil cloth we would attach to the assembly line … And once the line had turned around once … A nice material came out, it was orange colored. And we would dye it black. Oil cloths in the cars. We secretly attached it on there, and then it came back out. We sewed something out of that. After all you have to cover yourself with something.

Inna Kulagina: We were always hungry. There was only soup in a little bowl. We called it *balanda.* It was water and cabbage. We often left the grounds, we would crawl under the fence and go to the nearby village—there was a village near on. We begged from the Germans who lived there. They often gave us potatoes, but we couldn't cook these anywhere. But there was one room where the laundry was boiled, where we washed our clothes ourselves. We would wrap the potatoes in a heavy towel, tie them up and cook them there. And from the canteen … In the kitchen there were potato peelings, I remember this well, we would beg: "Give us something!" Then we would go to the barracks, stick the potato peelings on the oven and eat them then. The whole time we were hungry.

Stepan Saika: There was a laundry house, but there was no modern standard there like today. They stuck briquettes under the kettle, the laundry was put in and it was washed. Wood was taken. And if you somehow got potatoes, you could cook potatoes like this, using a little sack. A pouch, throw the potato in, and everyone stands there with his pouch [holding it in the water]. And you held it on a cord, because when the police came, then everyone pulled his sack out and hid!

Anna Nesteruk: The Germans helped, they gave us bread. Say a German is on his way back home from work, and his butter bread is left over. He sees that we are hungry. You understand? And in going away he gives us a piece of bread, or he puts it down somewhere and points to it lying there, because he was afraid. The boys roasted potatoes that we had got in the factory. Potatoes were taken up to the German canteen with the lift, and that's where I would steal them. There was an emergency exit, through an office. I would bring them to the camp, to roast the potatoes. And others also wanted something: "Give us!" "No, I won't give them to you."

Nadia Shubrawa: There was once a soup. Soap was transported in so that the work clothes could be washed.... In the factory the floor was cleaned with this. The soap powder was brought in sacks and poured out. And then these sacks were filled with potatoes, and that was brought into the camp. And these potatoes were cooked for us, given to everybody, but this was with the soap, and everyone was poisoned, the whole camp had to lie in.

Anna Nesteruk: I didn't get it, I hadn't gotten there yet. When I got there the people were already lying, sick. "What happened?" "We've been poisoned," they said. Betty, the Polish woman, had been ladling out the food.

Nadia Shubrawa: There were four or five potatoes for each, some got three potatoes with this sauce. We ate everything, you could hardly leave anything on your plate. The potatoes were in the sauce and that poisoned us, but no one died.

And how was it when you menstruated?

Nadia Shubrawa: We would find something for us.

Just any old rags?

Anna Nesteruk: Yes, no one gave us anything. There weren't any medicines there. If you were sick in the factory, the foreman would lead you away.... Among us there was one fellow, Stepan. He often fell over, he was an epileptic. When they gave him work, he would fall over. The Germans didn't pay attention to this, they kicked him instead. And then it stopped happening.

Inna Kulagina: We were occasionally led off to the "*Bania.*" There was also a sink, a primitive kind on the street. You know, under such conditions people just adapt somehow, regardless how, there is a possibility to wash, to dress.

Fritz Theilen was born in 1927 and grew up in Cologne. He began an apprenticeship at Ford as a tool maker in October 1941.

FRITZ THEILEN: My father was at Ford, and so it was clear that I would also be at Ford. My father had been employed there ever since the plant opened, in 1931. I had problems getting the apprenticeship, although I had already passed the entrance examination. But I wasn't in Hitler Youth. I had been thrown out of that because of "insubordination." I was allowed to start at Ford on 1 October 1941, because my father knew a lot of people at Ford.... That was already a miracle, that I got in. About a half year after that, the bad reference from Hitler Youth finally came in. From that moment I was a marked person at Ford. Anytime anything happened my name would be mentioned, whether I had anything to do with it or not.

In 1942 Fritz Theilen took up contact with the anti-Nazi underground youth gangs known as the Edelweiss Pirates. He also had first contacts with the forced laborers at Ford.

Fritz Theilen: The French weren't treated so badly, but Poles and Russians and Yugoslavs, those were the so-called subhumans. Everything that had a Slavic element, that was "subhuman." The Russians were especially labeled. Prisoners of war all had "PW" on their backs. And then the Polish, they had the small "P," the others–Russians and Ukrainians–had "OST" on them. When the civilians came, they got that too. Only, something I should still mention: there were a few Ukrainians who were helping the security forces. They had a different status from the other Ukrainians, I think they were volunteers, but I can't recall so clearly, I only knew they had a different status. They would also be in their own group at the canteen for the midday meal, but there weren't many of them. Most of the forced laborers were Ukrainians, then the Polish, a lot of Poles.

The [Poles and "Ostarbeiter"] were on nearly all the machines, in the machine hall, in the engine hall, they were everywhere. You can imagine it: the longer the war went on, the more of them we got. There were a lot of them later on. There was no part of production without them, they were everywhere. Some of them were skilled workers. It was more likely for you to have contact to one of the skilled workers, because they would operate machines. Of course we couldn't just talk to any of them on the production line, that wasn't allowed. In machine making it was possible to talk with the Russians who were there as craftsmen.

Fritz Theilen was sent into the Russian camp as an apprentice.

Fritz Theilen: We put in these iron stoves.... We installed and repaired ovens and chimneys. They had two beds on top of each other in the barrack, and a couple of large tables with long benches, like a barrack normally looks. I got to know these kinds of barracks, I was in a camp later myself. They would get food in the so-called "bucket" of the NSV ("National Socialist People's Welfare"), meaning the food was brought in on an electric trolley driven into the camp.

A few boys who were as old as me or a little bit older, they would come over the roof into the canteen. In the summer the windows were all open. [The boys] would always come, whenever we had soup. They knew that we wouldn't eat the barley soup, because we thought it was disgusting. Friday we had soup, and then they would come. Then we would open up the windows even more. But at the front, at the door, there was always some plant security, and there was one guy, he was called S., he had one eye and one arm. The one eye he had lost in the First World War. When the Russians came, he would look at them with his eye. But I think he could also see with the glass eye! This was his specialty. He was a sadist. And when he caught them, he would push their faces into the soup. Those were lead bowls, he would push their faces into the soup and then hit them on the head. I mean, there were other plant guards who would just look the other way, they didn't disturb things. But him, he was really fierce. You have to imagine that, the boys, they were hungry. They would just stick the whole bowl to their mouth and swallow whatever they could. We were happy when they sucked it up fast.

Who do you mean "we"? You and your friend?

Fritz Theilen: At the meal there were many who didn't exactly say, "give it to them" or "give it to him," but they looked the other way. They also found it quite amusing, the way the boys would vacuum it all up. But the boys would constantly be caught. That wasn't so bad, when they were caught, if they had already eaten. The bad thing would be to get caught before they had eaten anything. Or we would throw bread to them through the window onto the roof. There were always rolls when we had soup.

When this man from plant security pushed the faces of the forced laborers into the bowl, did anyone interfere?

Fritz Theilen: Yes, especially the older people, they interfered, but I think he also denounced people. He reported whatever they said. He wasn't a Nazi, but the Nazis without a party badge, now they were the worst ones. And he was a bad one, S. I recalled his name this week again, S. was his name. I saw them all again, all in their old positions. I saw them all again, at the factory after the war!

Inna Kulagina: Police in German uniforms, it was German police. And the administration was German. Gestapo, I think, it was a black uniform. And then we also had our Russian warders. (Views photo: C6). And here in the picture, that's me. That's me, there was Elsa too, but she's missing.

Oh, there she is, I see so poorly. And this one and this one there, they're Ukrainian policemen. Nikolai, and that one is Ivan. I don't remember their last names. And there is somewhere another man, a paramedic. He was one of us, a Russian.

Yes, everyone of us had a number, and when we lined up, so we could go to work, we went in closed columns, calling out like this: "First! I, second! I, seventy-three!…" Everyone is there. And then we were led in columns to work.

Yvon Thibaut grew up in the Belgian town of Charleroi. He was an active member of Jeunesse Ouvrière Chrétienne, a Christian workers' youth group, and wanted to become a priest. Belgium was occupied by Germany in May 1940. In October 1942 he was eighteen years old.

YVON THIBAUT: Before I went to Germany I was a student. I had finished the humanist gymnasium at a Catholic school in Argenteuil called "The Clergymen of Work." Argenteuil is a small community in the town of Hoins, not far from Waterloo. That's where I finished school. But then the school had to close, because of the supply situation, there was not enough food. The students couldn't stay there anymore. As the son of a worker I had no money for tuition at the boarding school. So I went back home and a few weeks later I got a notice from the "Recruitment Office" in Charleroi, an office of the German Arbeitsamt. I was drafted to go to Germany as a forced laborer. They told me there that if I didn't go, my father or my brother would have to go in my place. Because I didn't want that, I went to Germany, to work there.

I was assigned to Munich. My brother-in-law knew people who didn't go to Germany, who hid out in the Ardennes or at farms, but this was not yet well organized at the time I had to go. About a month later it would have been easier to organize. On 28 October 1942 I was transported from the train station in Charleroi. There I had to sign papers that I was going voluntarily. Of course! The train left with a group of people, and in all the big towns other troops of young workers were on their way too.

Disembarking at the Aachen train station, Yvon Thibaut's group were thirsty. He and another man were sent to get beer with a bit of German money they had brought from home. When they returned they could no longer find their group.

Yvon Thibaut: We went to the office. There they insulted us every way they could think of, called us *Scheisse* and *Schweinehund.* But they didn't hit us! That not! But it was close. There was one who wanted to hit us, but his boss said, "No." They told us: "Okay, you're going to Cologne, to rot there," they said, "rot in the ruins." And I said to myself, "Okay." When we got to Cologne, we had to register at an office on the Ring Street. They asked me: "What can you do?" I said: "I'm a student." "Oh, a student, student. And what about work?" "I can't work." "You can't work!?" So I said: "I was in school, but I did not work." They said: "Okay, then we will teach you how to work." They sent me to a school in Cologne-Mülheim.

The school was a fenced-off camp with a half-dozen barracks. Together with Russians and Poles, who were not allowed out of the camp, Yvon Thibaut was trained to work metals with machine tools. Westerners were paid small amounts when their performance was judged good, Russians and Poles in camp money. After three months Yvon Thibaut was assigned to work at Ford in early 1943.

Yvon Thibaut: When I got to Ford I was sent, because I was now a lathe operator of sorts, to a department where I had to shape little pieces for the rear axles of trucks. I had five machines. There was the first machine. The piece was big and it had to be stamped. The second machine stamped it further, and the third further and the fourth and the fifth finished it. Then there was a control machine. You stuck it in there to make sure it was okay, and then it was put in a box. You had to make, I don't know how many, six, seven, eight hundred a day. I don't remember exactly. I know that it was a lot, and there was little time for breaks during the twelve hours ... from seven in the morning to seven at night. That was a constant back and forth between my first and my fifth machine. Just as I was ready with the fifth, hop, hop, it started all over again and I had to be ready to place a new piece. Then I took it out of the first machine, and had to put it in again, five times, the whole time. The parts were attached to an assembly line and that took the part to where it had to go. That was well organized, it was really not badly organized. But still you had to work. Often we set the machines to go faster for a while so that afterwards we could relax for an hour or two a day....

There was also sabotage. There were prisoners of war who worked on the machines. Now and then one of them would come to me and say: "Do you want to take an hour off?" "Oh, of course!" "Good, but don't say anything." And he would take a bit of sand and throw it in the gears of the machine. He took a part off, I don't know how he did it, he filled it up [with sand], and two or three minutes later it went "crr, clack!" and it was over. And then: "*Oh, kaputt Maschine! Kaputt Maschine!*" Then I would get the big boss and I'd say: "*Oh, Maschine kaputt!*"–"Yes, why?" "I don't know." Then the German engineers would come and stand around the machine. I would explain it, they would see nothing. Then I would have an hour off while they repaired the machine, and I could walk around the factory. But they never figured out why my machine wasn't working. I thought, they must be able to figure it out....

It was like that in other departments, like the engine blocks. That was how it was. They didn't earn much from employing foreigners in Germany, because the foreigners sabotaged everything they could. The smart ones, of course, who weren't caught! Because if you were caught sabotaging, then you were sent to the penal camp. We had a colleague who was sent to a penal camp. He came back six months later, he weighed 65 or 66 kilos before and when he came back he weighed about 29 or 30 kilos. That was terrible, terrible. He had the place next to mine, and then he would be given breaks because he could no longer work. That was impossible. We had to carry him. And then he got better, at least he got better. Then he started working again, but he was assigned to the lighter work. I was also doing light work.

Later that was over for me. I was punished. I don't know anymore what I was doing when the inspector came. I was not at my place, I was talking to a prisoner of war or somebody. They looked for me and lost time doing so. To punish me, they assigned me to the engine blocks. The engine block of a truck is divided into four parts. I don't know anything about engines, but I do know that those were engine blocks that we were lifting and placing and attaching to the machine. And there were one, two, three, four, five such parts. You didn't have much time to catch your breath, because when you got to the fifth, you had to start again with the first and so on. It was a kind of mechanical turnstile....

The Russians and the Poles couldn't leave the camp, and of course the prisoners of war were also kept in. A French prisoner of war couldn't leave either, they had a small camp of their own. We would sneak in there sometimes, spend an evening with them. Or we would switch clothes. I would put on the prisoner's clothes and one of them would take mine. That depended on the size, of course. Then he could go out and I would stay there. Because there were always these control calls. And since there were a lot of us, the overseers didn't recognize me right away. The number had to be right. That was the point, that was the most important thing. We did that more than once. I got to see theater pieces there. The prisoners of war organized parties, played theater, and some of them dressed up like women. And well done! Those were sometimes very nice shows. And we, the other deportees, we forced laborers, we would go, switch uniforms, and during this time the prisoners who wanted to go out could go out, but with our clothes.

[Foreign laborers] communicated in German and in gestures. The Russians didn't know much more German than we did, but that was the only international language that we could use. As far as the relations between the prisoners, above all between the Russians and the Poles, yes, there were tensions, sometimes that exploded. But between Poles and French and Belgians, that was okay. We understood each other well, there were no problems. And with the Russians we also got along very, very well. Except for later, in Buchenwald. That was a different story.

In March 1943, Kazimierz Tarnawski and a fellow prisoner, Josef, escaped from forced labor in Gelsenkirchen.

Kazimierz Tarnawski: It was a Sunday afternoon, we got bread and cigarettes from our colleagues. They all knew [about our plan]. They also wanted to escape, but they said that we should go first. Perhaps we would meet again. All of them were young, eighteen to twenty years old. In the afternoon we jumped over the fence with the barbed wire. Back then I could jump: Uh! It was already dark. We went to the cargo rail station. We rode with a military transport, and the German soldiers did not see us.

In Schneidemühl [today Pila, Poland] there was an air-raid siren. We knew nothing. Posen was being bombed. War is not good for me, and we were frightened because the soldiers ran out of the wagons, and then we ran out, too. There were these SS-Gestapo plain-clothesmen there. They had weapons. "Halt, come, documents," they yelled. We were already on the street. We wanted to go to another train station, to Schneidemühl-Pila, but the Gestapo had us. "You band of sows," they said to us. "How many of you are there?" "Two." "Are the others here too?" "I don't know." "Parachutists," they said to us. I said, "I am not a parachutist ... and I am not a soldier."

Then they arrested us and brought us to Moabit prison in Berlin. I said that I was from Cologne, not Gelsenkirchen, because many of my colleagues had worked at Ford in Cologne. This is why I did not tell the truth to the police in Berlin. They said: "Ah, from Cologne, good." We were only beaten a little bit, but ... Then we were transported by the police from Berlin to Erfurt, Weimar where Goethe was born, I saw the monument there. And then to Buchenwald, to the concentration camp.

Up against the wall, legs spread, hands on the back. There were a lot of prisoners there already, who had been arrested: Poles, Russians, French, all of them were positioned like us. I heard beautiful music then, a prisoner's orchestra was playing inside, and we were outside. There was a gate there with the sign "*Arbeit macht frei,*" but I didn't know where we were, whether or not it was Buchenwald. They told us nothing. Then I was struck many times, a lot by the SS, young SS men beat us, they beat us and kicked us. They took the handcuffs off, but they beat us for a long time. Then I had this kind of jogging suit I had to put on, then we had to go to the bathing room, and we got striped suits, a cap, underwear and a shirt. And then we had to go to the roll call, where we had to stand still. There our hair was shaved off and we got nothing to eat. Then we waited and heard this beautiful music, one never forgets that. Strauss. Red pants they had, and also these striped jackets. Germans were in this band, and a lot of Czechs, perhaps two hundred men in this orchestra, like in a military parade. And at the SS officers' mess hall they played. Thank God. I waited, still more people came who had tried to escape just like me, perhaps fifty men in all, new arrivals they were, French, Polish, Russians, all from one workplace.

After the roll call, ah roll call, there were perhaps twenty thousand men. Everyone had his block. Russians theirs, Poles, Germans, French. The orchestra played a march and we had to march, exactly like in the military. There we were struck over the whole body with a whip. On the face, head, it hurt. Young SS men did that. And they said: "Fast, to Block 17!" I didn't know what that was supposed to mean, Block 17. "Search and run fast, you sow Polish dog!" one of them said. Suddenly I was kicked in the small of the back, so that I fell to my knees and I was beaten. When an officer came the others had to salute, and I stood up and kept running. Wooden shoes we had on, oh God, they were so heavy. Then an older Frenchman, about forty years old, a Frenchman, but he could speak some Polish, said to me: "Come fast, or he will beat you until you break," and I ran fast to Block 17, that was the transport block. I knew nothing about that, and my companion didn't either.

Luckily I was not long in Buchenwald, perhaps three weeks, not quite a whole month. One night the SS men screamed: "Get up! Go! Get the packs down! But fast!" and again they hit us. "Line up at the square for roll call!" In the middle of the night and on foot, perhaps more than one thousand young men were raced to the train station and into the cars. There we got bread and soup. We ate like dogs, I was always hungry back then, as a boy you have to eat. Then we rode on the train to Cologne, to a cargo rail station. Everyone had to get off and run on foot to the Messe camp.

The older prisoners told us they had already been in Cologne. They had known we were going to Cologne. They told us it would be better than in Buchenwald. Some of them had even been in Auschwitz. They said that by comparison Buchenwald was a resort. Auschwitz was the worst concentration camp. In the Messe camp there was again barbed wire, I arrived there as a young man, and on the roll-call square the camp leader asked me something: "German? Whoever can understand German, go to the left. If not, then to the right side, and go, fast!" Since I could speak a bit of German I went to the left side. We had to run fast, then stand still and take the caps off.

A few hours before his interview in 1995, Kazimierz Tarnawski went into one of the cells in the basement of the former Gestapo headquarters, EL-DE Haus, now the location of the NS Documents Center (see photo: C12). During the interview he recalls that, on his first day in Cologne in spring 1943, he was suddenly taken aside and sent from Messe to EL-DE.

Kazimierz Tarnawski: I would like to get back to the EL-DE Haus. I said nothing [while we were] in the EL-DE Haus, because that was the worst for me. I don't know how I went through that at all. Those were tortures, you know, they treated us like dogs, it was terrible. One of them kicked me so that I fell down the stairs and smacked my head into the wall. When we first arrived with the transport, during the roll call my number was called: 465, and I didn't understand. No family, nothing, I only had the number. Prisoner number, ah I took many blows for that. "Step up!" Cap off and [I was sent] off to EL-DE.

That was as soon as you arrived in Cologne, on the first day?

Kazimierz Tarnawski: Yes, I forgot, excuse me. Imagine that this was supposed to be questioning, by an interrogator. He could speak Polish, but I didn't know that. He was very elegant, he smelled good, eau-de-Cologne, very nicely dressed, but always had the whip in his hand. At EL-DE Haus. That I don't forget. He hit me once, then again, and said to me like this: "You must tell the truth, you come from an intellectual family." I said: "*Herr Offizier*, that is all the truth, what I said."

What did he want to know?

Kazimierz Tarnawski: Whether I was a partisan or from the underground movement. I was so young then, seventeen and a partisan. He said to me in Polish, "You are a Polish Communist." I said: "I am no Communist, I am an officer's son, Polish officer." "You're lying!" What should I have done? Every day was like that, perhaps a week. Every day and the nights too.

Were you taken out of the cell or did he come to you?

Kazimierz Tarnawski: No, out of the cell and into the office. Upstairs and fast. And always the young SS men hit us. I always heard screams through the walls: "Help!" *Ratunku,* in Polish. Russian women screamed: *"Spasaties, Boga ne boitieses,"* ("Help, have you no fear of God, how do you want to answer for this?") Not always, but sometimes those ... in solitary confinement, or who were condemned to death and knew it, then they mostly also screamed, loudly, when they were taken away: "I'm going now to die, and we'll meet in heaven, we'll meet yet!"

I was afraid, believe me, I wanted to live, I was so young, why, I had nothing to do with politics. A Polish officer was with me in the cell. He was brought from Oflag (a POW camp for officers) because of an escape attempt. They had nabbed him at the Swiss border. But he was large, a typical career officer, that's how he looked, big. "You must live," he said to me. "Head high, we have the same nationality, you must be strong, you dare not cry. You are also a Polish soldier, you are a representative of Poland and you will survive." That encouraged me. I think he is dead, they shot him. I never saw him afterwards in the Messe camp. I don't know that. Perhaps he's still alive?

That was not quite a month. Perhaps three weeks, or 21 days or 18 days, I don't know exactly. But what I experienced there, it cannot be related.... That is why, when I was there now, to visit, I couldn't say a word. Frau Adamski [an organizer of the visitors' program] saw it, and the other people too. I take medication, my heart was like this ... and my head also like this ... when I recognized my cell again. I recognized the cell immediately. The smallest cell was closed, there in the museum, but when I was there, the smallest cells were only for those condemned to death. The cell where I had been was not a large cell. We were about fifteen, minimum ten men in there. We stood like this.... One of us sat for a little while, then another, and then again me, that's how we did it. EL-DE, Gestapo. After about three weeks I was sent back to Messe.

Did they let you go because they couldn't prove anything against you?

Kazimierz Tarnawski: Ah, they called me, there was an auto outside, and they brought perhaps ten men from EL-DE to Messe. We saw nothing from the auto, it had no window, nothing, darkness. The Russians called the auto *chorny voron,* the black raven. With the auto we were then transported to Messe. I was in my barracks room, there at our commando in the Messe hall. I got on my knees and prayed. My foreman asked me afterwards: "Have you gone crazy?" I said that I believe in God and I must thank my God that I am still alive. I went through a lot. The foreman was from

Gelsenkirchen, a German. He had refused to go to the war. He was our fore-man. He had an armband with a label on the striped shirt. It said that he was a foreman. He had a red triangle and the number. He got packages from his wife, cigarettes, and shared them with me.

Starting in summer 1943, Ostarbeiter were allowed out of the Ford camp on Sundays.

Nadia Shubrawa: They gave us a paper, listed us, gave it to the oldest one among us, said: "Go to the city." But they paid attention that we all came back on time. We go to the city, say me and you. And I am responsible for you, for all of you, that you all come back.

Anna Nesteruk: We had "OST" sewed on, at the gate they let us through—one of them standing there knows that the whole group is going into the city today. They said: "remain together," that we should all go together and come back together.

Nadia Shubrawa: I don't go for a walk when I don't want to eat something. We were looking for something to eat.

Anna Nesteruk: [In the city] you see a bakery, so you go there and stand in front of the shop. Germans go into the shop, and I stand at the door, my hand stretched out. I wait until they give me a bread coupon.

Nadia Shubrawa: We also bought things, we had money. We got some money, a few marks. We bought ourselves something. One time we found a baker in the city who sold us something.

Nadia Shubrawa: The boys would go and get a loaf from a German for five marks. They bring it into the camp and take fifteen from us. (Laughs).

Anna Nesteruk: Germans respected us, they gave us coupons. One approaches me from the front, he knows that I have nothing. He opens his wallet and takes a coupon out, and turns around again. He quickly hands over the coupon and then goes away. So it was. They had the coupon system. But you could sometimes stand around all day long and no one gave you anything. People from the barracks went to the vil-lage.… I went one time to beg, crawled under the barbed wire fence, and went to the village.

Anna Nesteruk: We walked and walked. "Why not? Let's go into this house." We went there, but there was a policeman there. And why he did-n't arrest us, I don't know. The woman was good. The German's wife was good, but the husband was a policeman. But we stood there and saw that the house was nice. The policeman comes out: *"Was hast du? Russki?"* I was frightened, but the woman came out, cursed him out, and gave us a loaf of bread. And he says: *"Kommt nie wieder, Kasematt!"* ["Don't ever come again, detention!"] And we went straight home to the barracks. Children, such a life we led!

Inna Kulagina: At first we could not leave, but then we became accustomed to the situation and learned to ask. The German foremen helped us, they brought us bread. And we became somewhat more confident, we were young. A few went to the French camp, but I did not. The police would let us through [the gate], one policeman loved Russian songs. We would sing him a Russian song and he would let us in. Then we even began to organize a few things ourselves. We would do popular arts on our own. We sang, we were all young, regardless of how terrible it was. Somehow we wanted to make life a little bit more fun. I think that's enough about the camp.

Mareno Mannucci was born in Scandicci, today a suburb of Florence, on 6 August 1924. In September 1943 the Badoglio government overthrew Mussolini and surrendered to the Allies. Rome and northern Italy were occupied by the Wehrmacht.

MARENO MANNUCCI: I come from a peasant family. We didn't feel much of the war, because we weren't hungry, since we were farmers. As a youth, I went to the Young Fascists and then to the first military service. That's how things were. Not that we liked the war, but we followed the propaganda. On 10 September 1943, twenty days after I was drafted, I was arrested in Pola, Italy, as a soldier of the 5th Artillery Regiment. At first we received promises that we could go home, but when we got to Venice, our ship was hardly in the harbor before it was surrounded by Germans. They stuck us in train cars, fifty to a car, and brought us to Germany. I saw people who cried like children in their anger. We rode four days and four nights to [Stalag] Stargard. One time they gave us a piece of bread and one time a vegetable soup. That was all we got for our thirst. Hunger you can forget about, but thirst is terrible.

After the deportation to Germany I was interned at Stargard Lager II D. On the day after our arrival we were crowded together in a small area. We were about 1,500 men, and together with a few Germans two Italian officers arrived in the uniform of the Fascist military. One of them said on the microphone that the cease-fire was a betrayal by the king and by Badoglio. He invited everyone to join the reconstituted Italian armed forces, now Republican, and described what we might expect in that case. But only a few went along, perhaps thirty, forty men. On the next day we were registered. I got the ID number II D 98644. The first work was at a plantation where we harvested potatoes. Three weeks later, when the harvest was done, we were brought back to Stargard, and from there I was sent to Meppen.

The five hundred Italian POWs at Meppen were transferred to Ford Werke in mid-November 1943, arriving first at the Nippes rail station to the south of Niehl.

Mareno Mannucci: We left Meppen, and it rained a great deal. They stuck forty in one car, not many. All of us were wet. We rode in the night, everything went very slowly. We saw this big river that we didn't know. They brought us to the train station in Nippes. They stopped us on a side track.

There was an alarm and everyone ran. Only we stayed in the car. Then they had us get out and we ran on foot to Ford. That took one hour and twenty minutes, one and a half hours. There they counted us. Every time they would take ten, fifteen of us and stick us in a barrack. Then it was ten in the evening. We got a vegetable soup in the French kitchen. Then they brought us back to the barrack. Suddenly the alarm went off, but I didn't hear it. I was so tired! For two hours there was an alarm, everyone else went into the shelters, but I slept. Whenever there was an alarm they turned off the power, the alarm ran via a different circuit. Then I woke up: "Where am I, where am I?"–"Help, help!" I screamed like a madman, running between these buildings. I yelled for help. I heard the sirens, the ones from the city of Cologne, the ones from Ford, and then the ones from Leverkusen. It was an incredible noise, and I didn't know where I was. I thought, if this is not over in an hour, then I am insane or dead. Because it's such a horrible thing, to scream like that, I screamed for my mother, screamed for help between these facilities, it was dark and there was no one there. If it's time to go insane, then you go insane. Then the lights came on. Everything was over. That was how I got to Ford.

In addition to the Germans there were a thousand Russian internees, 600 French prisoners, and a few hundred from other nations. Our work camp had the number 619 and was next to Camp VI G. It was next to the camp of the French and the Russians, only a few hundred meters from the factory. There were five or six soldiers from the Wehrmacht and a sergeant had the command. They were our guards. This sergeant was very nervous, even his soldiers admitted that. Any little thing would happen, he would bark: "Everyone out!" The next morning people from Ford put together index cards about all of us, to find out what kind of work we had done. The mechanics were sent to the mechanics, the carpenters to the carpenters. They gave us a work number right then, which was put on a little badge that we always had to carry on our breast. They gave out the numbers 15,001 to 15,500. I got number 15,450. They gave us a working uniform, gray and ugly, with the letters "IMI" on the back, for Italian Military Internee.

I was a farmer, so they stuck me in Department 33 II. It was a small department. It only prepared engines for shipment. Three hundred engines were produced every day, if there wasn't an alarm, and on average eighty trucks. I know that, because they all got numbers. I worked there with French, two Russians and a little German. It was a small department. Then there was the head of the department, and one office employee. They wrote the numbers on the engines that they sent off. We worked ten hours a day. The day began at five in the morning. Roll call was at 5:45 AM, everyone was counted and ready to work. Work started at 6:30 AM, and at 7:00 AM the second department would start. Late in the morning they would hold staggered 45-minute lunch breaks. At first we were always accompanied by an armed guard. We were led to the camp to eat, and then brought back to work. If you didn't get back on time, they would write down your number and send the report for the evening....

After dinner there would be a roll call at 8 PM, whatever the weather. We had to go out and line up in rows of five and be counted under a lamp. Lights out in the barracks was at 10 PM, and then it was rest time. But nearly every night there was an alarm, sometimes several times a night. As soon as you heard the warning you had to get up and go into the shelters, which were in a giant underground concrete tube. It was wet and cold there. In the beginning I was very depressed, I always had crises because I had been taken from home so suddenly. A crisis that was stronger than me. There were others who could deal with it better. There were people there with seven years' military service on their buckle, they were more used to this. And they gave me courage. They called me "ball," "*putto*," "child," because I was the youngest one there. There were twenty-four of us to a room and the barracks had six rooms each. We Italians were like a family. I have good memories of my friends from this time.

During the work you could try to talk to the others, but that was barely possible with all the factory noise. Talking was not forbidden, but we had trouble understanding each other. With the Russians you couldn't understand anything. With the Germans we communicated with body language. But the guard was standing at the oven.

At first we Italians were treated perhaps a bit worse than the others, because we were considered "traitors." But as time went by we got better treatment than the Russians. We were treated more or less like the French. At first the Germans cursed at us: "Badoglio, Badoglio!" But then many of them saw that the reality was sad. The reality that the war was lost. And besides, the people were much more worried about the bomb attacks. They were very afraid.

There was little to eat, a daily ration of two bowls of vegetable soup, 150 grams of bread and a little tap of margarine or a little piece of sausage. Dinner was soup with two pieces of bread. Saturdays and Sundays was better. There was no soup in the evening, but five pieces of bread, that was better than the soup. The distribution of bread in the evening was a real big event. The barracks officer would go get the bread. Then he would give it to the officer of the room. He would put a piece on the table and smear margarine on it. But bread wasn't distributed by the numerical sequence, because then someone would say: "But this piece is bigger than that one." So this is what we did. One man would turn his back to the bread, and the numbers would be called out at random: "This piece is for 450, this one for 327, this one 132."

The food was never enough. I thank my survival to an old man who always brought me corners of his bread. A few days after I started working in Department 33 II, a very old German man who was working there went missing for about twenty days, I guess for health reasons. I lost ten kilograms during this time, because I felt terrible, but also because of the lack of food. When the German came back, he saw this and talked about me with one of the French in the department. I couldn't understand what they were saying, but I figured out it was about the lack of food. After lunch, after I got back to work, the German took me aside. I thought it was about work. But he gave me a little package. I opened it and I saw that it was two slices of bread with butter and marmalade. I almost cried as I thanked him. I wrapped it up and put it in my pocket. But then I couldn't help myself, I hid behind a bunch of engines and ate. He hadn't eaten this himself, so that he could give it to me. Then I felt better. After that he gave me bread almost every day. I remember that he brought me a piece of cake for Christmas.

That is how it went for months, until finally I changed departments and didn't see him again. But I think about him and I will always remember him. He was a small man, but with a big heart. He was very old. Now he will have gone on to the next life. God rest his soul.

In the fall of 1943 Italian prisoners of war were also assigned to the brick plant in Antweiler, at which point Kamila Felinska and her husband were transferred to Ford. Because their documents were lost, they were assigned to the Russian camp.

Kamila Felinska: After a year at the brickworks the Italians came. They were prisoners of war. On 2 November 1943 I was sent to Ford. All those who had come with me to Antweiler, we were sent to Ford. Only the Italians stayed back there. We were driven on trucks, and then I was brought to a Russian camp, where I was for three months. [From there] we always went the short way to Ford under guard. After work a guard waited for us behind the hall. There was always a guard, and he always had a rifle. The barracks were fenced off, and at the four corners there were these high stations, and four guards stood there with dogs and rifles, watching the whole time.

In Antweiler they had lost our documents from Poland. We had no papers, and the Germans did not believe us when we said that we were not Russians. We were the only Poles among the Russians. We had not been made to wear a patch in Antweiler. Only once we got [to Cologne] did we have to wear an "OST." I did not agree with that. I did not want to wear "OST." I said I wanted a "P." I had to write home, and my parents sent us a certificate in German. I went straight to the camp leader, and they took us away from there right away. We had been in the Russian camp for more than three months.

In the new camp there were many French, Spanish, Italians and Dutch. There was no guard there, we got the "P," but the camp was not under guard, because the other nations were not supervised in the same way, and of the Polish there were very few. There were two Poles from Warsaw and someone else from Posen, altogether we were five or six people from Poland. Because there were only a few of us, there were no forms in the Polish language, but instead in French, which we filled out in French. Most of the guards therefore thought that we were French. I could not speak French, but there was one man, he originally came from Poland, but he was French. Of course he could speak both languages, and also very good German.

How was life in the Russian camp different from the French camp?

Kamila Felinska: That was like heaven and earth, that was a completely different life, we even got to dance in the evenings, there was coffee. It was a completely different life. It was that way because the French were getting Red Cross packages. The food was better there. That was served in the camp. At midday we would go from the factory to the barracks, and the food was there. We had one hour lunch break. That was also enough, because it was not far. You went past the guard and showed an ID. We all had to do that, the French too. There were many French women in the camp. They also worked in the factory. Everyone had her machine, for which she was responsible. Everyone had a standard they had to work up to, and when one did that then everything was okay, everything went well. Otherwise there were punishments, but I always did everything....

My fiancé and I, we had a room just for us, and beside the bed there was a cabinet, a table and two chairs, and that was very good.... In the French camp of course there was no freedom, but in comparison to the Russian it was a very big difference....

Today [visiting Ford Werke in 1995] I didn't find the machines again. I would have liked to see them again. I found those circles, but not gear-wheels like the ones I made back then. I didn't find any of those. Four holes would be drilled into the gearwheels, all in Department 8. I worked there with Germans. At that point I could already understand a great deal, and say things. Today I again know nothing. I could answer well back then. Perhaps I could remember again, if I were to stay here for a longer time.... I worked with a Belgian woman and a Russian woman. There were four Germans and an Italian, they called him Macaroni, the Germans too. We worked in shifts, and one week that was during the day from seven until seven at night, and the next week from nineteen at night until seven in the morning. Here at Ford the Sundays were free, but before, in Euskirchen, we had to work on Sundays too....

We played cards, with a Frenchman and a Belgian. Sometimes we had coffee, there was a Frenchman who could play accordion and then we went into the dining room and danced. On Sundays we went to church, we were allowed. We were even allowed to drink beer. I don't like beer, so I didn't go into the city, because I wasn't a beer drinker. As a Pole, actually, I was not allowed, but because our form was filled out in French everyone believed that we were French. No one paid any special attention to us, because we went together with the French.... We got fifty marks a month at Ford. [We bought] ice cream, lemonade, sweets. The company would provide twelve sanitary napkins per month to each woman. In the Russian camp we got nothing.

There were very many bombings, one trembled. I can still remember the first bombing I experienced, that was on the first day, when I arrived. The gates were open, I could finally run away, but out of fear we all crawled into a very large pipe, to hide there. Here at Ford there were bunkers. The entrance was on the square, right between the barracks and the factory. There were also bunkers that were right under the factory, but we did not dare to go in there, because it was always thought that the factory would be bombed, and then it would be all over....

On my ID [see photo: C9] I had the number 2472, we were very many. My room was at the end of the barracks. Next to that was an office, and then there were very many rooms, but I don't know how many altogether. There were a minimum of ten very long barracks, it was a very large camp. We tried hard to do the work. I was afraid that I would be hit, so I did the work. You also wanted to be liked for the work. The French would tell me that I was often praised by the Germans, and that I behaved well.

Fritz Theilen was not authorized to enter the Russian camp.

Fritz Theilen: With us you had a lot of Ukrainians, and a lot of young people among them. When we had *Osteinsatz* we were able to get acquainted with some of the women and the younger people. *Osteinsatz* was the Maultier action. That was the caterpillar truck we were building. We had to pack boxes full of spare parts for it. We weren't allowed to talk with the women and the Russians who were working with us, but that was where I got acquainted with them for the first time.

I never understood, until then. That was when the Nazi propaganda, that they were all subhuman, was exposed for me. When one of the women spoke to me in German, I was just overwhelmed. We tried to speak to the women, over the conveyor belt. She was from Rostov or Charkov, I don't remember that exactly. One woman was a German teacher, she had studied German literature. Her friend too. They spoke good German, you noticed the Russian accent, but they spoke German well. That was when I became conscious of it. I would have never thought that a teacher would be there on the line! I thought: they can speak German, but we can't speak any Russian.

I remember one thing that happened next to the hall, where a train-car was always brought up. They would load it up with shavings from the lathes, plane shavings, everything of that kind. A woman stood there who would shovel these shavings in with a spade. She was in a family way. Who the man who kicked her was, I don't know exactly, but it was a guard from company security. I saw it just as we were coming from the lockers, because we were passing by just then and there. He was yelling at the people around there, and the woman said something to him, and he kicked her in the belly. Right in the belly. What happened to her after that I don't know. There were some brutal supervisors, too, they would hit, smack. You could hit the Ostarbeiter, they were fair game. Them you could punch in the face, that was okay.

They were always hungry, constantly. How can I describe it? They were always hungry! I always took along a couple of rolls with butter, extra. And if it was only stale bread. We didn't have anything either, at the markets. We passed these to the Russians, especially whenever we'd have *Osteinsatz.* The women were always there then.

What exactly was *Osteinsatz*?

Fritz Theilen: As apprentices we would be commanded to go for *Osteinsatz*. Everything that wasn't needed directly in production had to be brought there. Replacement parts were packed into boxes, carburetors, engines, everything you can imagine, and sent to the Eastern Front. I committed serious sabotage with another colleague. The loaded boxes would be stacked at the Rhine, and we would go and take out, ignition coils, for example, and throw them into the Rhine, right at the quay wall. That was only possible in the dark. Inspectors would check the boxes, but afterwards they would be left in the open, nailed shut. We would pry them open in secret and take a part—we knew the parts, we knew what was important—out of the box! Then, when the box was nailed shut and opened up at the front: "What good is this? We got everything, just not the most important part!"

Mr. Tarnawski, who was sitting next to me during the gathering [in September 1995], could remember that there had been a big [police] action. They suspected that the Russian prisoners of war had been the saboteurs. That was a big action. We were the cause. They rounded up a whole bunch of [the Russian POWs] and after that we didn't see them again. I don't know what happened to them. They were brought to another camp or otherwise, but they weren't there anymore. Whether they were sabotaging too—we assumed they were also doing the same.

What would happen when sabotage was discovered? Who investigated?

Fritz Theilen: That would be the workers' representative, Brunckhorst. Like today, you have the head of the works council. Back then in the plant that was Brunckhorst. He had a bunch of lackeys with him who followed his every word, and the Gestapo accompanied them. What I didn't know back then was that Brunckhorst was also Gestapo. He was a Gestapo man. Later he interrogated me about another matter that had nothing to do with the plant. When saboteurs were caught, they would be taken to company security and interrogated. The head of security at that time was Schebem. He always wore the EK 1 ("Iron Cross, 1st Class") here on his side. He had a corset on, he'd been an officer in the First World War. He was one fierce dog. He didn't get back into Ford after the war. The Gestapo would come to the interrogations, and then usually the prisoners would be transported away. If there was the least bit of suspicion, they would be taken to Elisenstrasse (EL-DE Haus).

Fritz Theilen describes his first arrest.

Fritz Theilen: I'll never forget that, back then we nearly did it in our pants! But we weren't under suspicion. Not only because we were young. That we would actually dare to do such a thing, no one believed that. I should say that back then we were listening a lot to the English radio, "Radio Nippes" [codename for the BBC's German-language program]. They would have news pieces like this: "In Duisburg, there is a resistance group, they did this and that." That kind of story you wouldn't hear in the German news. You would only hear that from the English. Yes, and then we said: anything they can do, we can do too! That's where we got the inspiration. My colleague, who was with me, he was also an Edelweiss Pirate, he was an anti-Fascist. He was one or two years older than me. He was in his third or fourth year of apprenticeship. I had been there for two years. Rosenthal, he was called.

They suspected that we had damaged the caterpillars and tractors, that we had punctured the tires. We had broken off the heads of milk bottles, just regular milk bottles, and stuck those in the soil in front of the trucks. They were all parked in rows, one next to the other at the plant. When they were driven off, there was a "pssssht," and they were flat on the spot. We realized at the time that we couldn't do that for very long.... Those were just little needlepricks, recklessness. I think if we had been older we would have done other things. I was sixteen then. When the tires went flat on the trucks.... They made a big search. Then they announced extra special that no one was supposed to be at that lot.

One morning, it was still dark, we were there again ... and we were seen by two fellows who were really heavy Nazis. I said then: "Now we're not getting away from this." But Rosenthal said to me: "We have to put something on: I'll run after you, we pretend we had a fight, and so on." We were beaten soundly when they caught up to us. "What were you doing here?" "Yes, we were having a scrap." They only bought that story about halfway....

The two fellows who caught us were foremen, two old Nazis. One was S., a supervisor from the truck line. The other was W. After the war he ran Hall W. Both were from Berlin. W. punched me in the face. I fell flat on my ass, that day, when we were at the lot. I mean, we were lucky. They couldn't prove anything, we had no bottles in our pockets. There were bottles around the lot, but they couldn't prove anything. W. was in the NSKK, the "National Socialist Vehicle Driver Corps." That was the continuation of Motor-HJ ["Motorized Hitler Youth"]. If you did the four years of [Motor-HJ] training you would get into the S.A., and then you could go into the NSKK, a special formation. W. held an office, I don't know exactly what he was. And the other one, S., he always wore his party insignia, but he didn't have any other function....

The two of them caught us, and they took us to company security. There was a bunker under their place. They stuck us in there and kept us until the Gestapo came. The company security was [located] where today you have Halls F, K, and B. Those were barracks, but below them were bunkers. As apprentices we had our lockers there. The air raid service had their bunker in there too. They kept us locked up until the Gestapo came. Then we were interrogated.

Now it's obvious, I was known to the Gestapo, I was known in the plant, and the suspicion now, it was obvious. But they couldn't prove anything, right then. They believed us, but ... Rosenthal had to go be a soldier. He would have been taken as a soldier anyway, but not so fast. Instead he had to go straight to it. Within a few days he was gone, he was a soldier. I never heard from him again.

Because I was still too young, they stamped *wehrunwürdig* ["unworthy of service"] in my military ID. I had to give them my military ID and they stamped it.… I had been "Replacement Reserve II." I wouldn't have been recruited anyway. In '44, they would have conscripted me, but at that time, not yet. Then they said to me: "Here now, you can get rid of that stamp. You only need go volunteer for the Waffen SS." I wouldn't have had the stamp anymore. But I wasn't crazy enough to do that!

Yvon Thibaut: We were paid like Germans, like German workers who worked on the assembly line, those who were ranked as assistant workers. I don't know any more how much per hour, but we made good money. I never succeeded in sending any of it away from Ford. I asked everywhere, because in our camp at Ford there was an office for sending letters. And I asked more than one time, and they told me: "*Oh nein, ist verboten, verboten.*" That was always *verboten.* We could get and send letters, but there was a censor. When my parents got letters, they were all marked up in blue, oh, in all colors. The letter could still be read, but it was controlled and read, no doubt about that. With my father I had a secret code. When I wrote, say, that I had visited my old aunt, and that she was very sick, then this meant that there had been a bombing, or that a lot of trucks had been seen in the Cologne main station with German soldiers going to France. Everything had a meaning. Of course the censor who read that thought, "Well, maybe it is true. Maybe his old aunt is sick." We had all set up a secret code, so that my father knew exactly what happened. He often passed the information on to the right person in Charleroi, because we knew people who belonged to the resistance groups.

I myself never went to Charleroi on holiday, because there were others scheduled to go before us. They had to first come back before we would be allowed to go. The one that went for me was a father. He had four children. He was from the town of Huy, and I even said to him: "Listen, it's more important that you go back to your four children, than that I should go. You shouldn't come back, don't be worried about that." I never saw him again. I don't know what happened to him. He didn't give me his address, so I couldn't write to him after the war.

Inna Kulagina: The Russians and Ukrainians were nearly all children. Nearly all born in the same year, in '25. (Views photo: C6.) That is me. This one here, I know her very well. They were from educated families. And this one here, yes her. She is Armenian, she is not a Russian. Here is another Armenian. And that was Klara. And this one here, today she also lives in Belgium. That is Alla. This is Lenisa, but she lives today in Belgium. Ada now lives in France. She married a French man with whom she worked. (Views a map of the Ford grounds.) The Russian camp was the largest. And here were the French, Belgians and Dutch. The barbed wire fence was here, we were separated from them. They had it a bit easier, the Belgians and French, their Red Cross helped them somehow with the food. They had it better. There was excellent contact, the relations to the Russians were excellent. All were nice, the Belgians, Dutch, and French.... They always helped a little. They even shared their Red Cross packages with the Russians.... At work we were all together: here a Belgian was working, and here a Russian. In one department, only at different machines. Once the Italians came, when Mussolini was murdered, they were so helpless. We had by then already learned a lot, and we, the Russians, even helped the Italians a little bit, gave them leftover soup. They were completely helpless. I say this because it was that way: French, Dutch, Belgians and Italians were all men, but among us there were women. Women have a big heart, they share even their last piece of bread. Men are simply men by nature, but women have more sympathy. And we sympathized with them.

Mareno Mannucci: There was a rigid discipline in the factory. You didn't have to be missing for long or break much of a rule. Sometimes it was enough just if you didn't understand an order. A foreman would take your number down and send a report to the camp management. In the evening, after the roll call, you would get called to the camp office and the commander would sentence you to a punishment on the basis of the report. They had a rubber stick especially for this. You would lie down with your stomach over a stool and be hit as many times as the commander specified. Anyone who was hit would feel this for days. The strikes were delivered in a room next to the office of the camp sergeant. The hitting stopped when he was replaced by another commander. His method of punishment was making us stand still. He would have us stand erect for two hours near the fence.

During the winter of 1943–1944 many of the Italian POWs fell sick with tuberculosis and anemia.

Mareno Mannucci: One Sunday morning, towards the end of March (1944), without any kind of warning, a commission of the Red Cross came to the commanding sergeant of the camp. It was four men in civilian clothing together with an officer. The commander of Lager VI G, who was in charge of us, called us out to roll call at the small square. They went past the rows of us many times and observed us carefully, and one of them spoke to us as well as he could in Italian, asked some questions and took notes. We later learned the Red Cross was invited because a few of the managers were afraid of infection. But mainly they came because of the efforts of a Frau Müller, who worked in the personnel department and was acting on purely humanitarian grounds.

The next Sunday a big vehicle for radiological examinations came to the camp. Everyone was x-rayed. Many were found sick with tuberculosis. They were moved to the military clinic of Lager VI G in Bonn. After that there was always a "Monday exchange," that was when the sick were brought to Bonn every second Monday. New ones always arrived to replace them, so that there were always five hundred Italians in the camp. Those with fever went to a small sick station in the French camp. Those who were more serious were sent to VI G. The decision was made by the factory doctor.

The rest of us got a recovery cure. For thirty days straight we got two portions of whole grains every day, and these had a kind of thick and bitter marmalade, wrapped in wax paper, that was taken out of boxes from the Red Cross. The food improved. Those who lived in northern Italy, which was still occupied by the Germans, were allowed to write to their families, and a few got packages from home. I got four packages in three months.

I remember two Italians who escaped, out of desperation. They were from northern Italy. They wrote home but got no response. Those of us from northern or central Italy wrote a postcard every week, and it got there and our families wrote back. The two of them wrote to their families but got no answer. They were very desperate. One Sunday morning, I remember, they fled. That whole morning the guards had us standing on the square and interrogated us. From eight in the morning until midday. They even sent officers in from Bonn. I don't know if the two of them saved themselves or not. For us after that there were more rules. They locked us up. In the night they locked us in the barracks with the windows and doors locked, and we were dying of the heat. In the night we were dying of the heat. They did that until the commanding sergeant was changed.

The new camp commander, an enlisted officer, was also strict, but more understanding and humane.... It was spring now, and things generally got better. I was transferred from Department 33 II to Department 10, where the metal was tempered.... I liked the work, because no one was ordering you about. There was a good foreman there, he was a good person. He said to me: "Look how they do it." And I learned it very quickly. I was always tempering Material No. 7111. It was the pinion where the transmission shaft goes into the opening of the differential. You did your work and that was that. Not like in 33 II, where you were constantly being ordered around.

Anna Nesteruk: The policeman was such a cudgel: *"Aufstehen, Kinder! Butterbrot essen, arbeiten!"* ["Out of bed, children, eat your buttered bread, work!"] And we moved slowly, cried: "Oy, Mamotschka, oy, my God!"

Nadia Shubrawa: Little children, that's how it was.

Anna Nesteruk: He screamed: *"Warum weinen, Schweine Russki?"* ["Why cry, pig Russkies?"]

Nadia Shubrawa: Anton comes in, he had been taught Russian, and he says: "Fuck your mother, get up!" (*Laughs.*) He didn't know what this curse-word means, but he had been taught it, he came in and screamed.

Inna Kulagina: There were good foremen, who sometimes brought us butter rolls, and there were also very bad ones. I am telling how it really was.

It is not right to say that all of them were like animals. One foreman we had was called Franz, or Fritz. At night it was very difficult for us to work, in the night shift. And we often went away. When we were at Ford [today] I found this place again, where a kiln for machine parts once stood. And further up, up the stairs, there was a bathroom, it was warmed by this oven. A toilet and a shower. And the reason I showed it to you, I had a terrible experience there. I almost fell asleep on the nightshift. I was afraid that I would cut my finger off on the machine, and I felt already that I was falling asleep, so I ran up to the bathroom.

We wouldn't pull down our pants, we would sit there as though we were going to the toilet, and in reality we slept. The foreman saw that I was gone and he came upstairs. He opened the door, and I was sitting there, that was enough already. He hit me hard, on the solar plexus, and he dragged me down the stairs. I lost consciousness and was brought right away to the clinic. He was just such a lout. He had already hit many people. He also hit Elsa, many of us. I personally didn't get hit much, I was very obedient, I always tried hard. Only when I just couldn't anymore, only then. Otherwise I tried to work.

I was in bed for a short time in the sick ward, I was revived. By then it was already morning, and I went to the barracks. I was in the barracks until the next night. Everything was horrible but we were young, and that helped us survive. Because we hoped that everything would be over soon, that the war would end and that we could go back home.

Nadia Shubrawa: I once came from work, but the other girls didn't arrive. And I asked the policeman, he was a good one, good policeman. I say: "Let me through!" But there were also Anton and Matjas, they were very vicious, they didn't let one out for anything in the world. He was called Matjas (the "Hungarian" in Russian). I went out, he let me through: "Be here again by seven. Then there's a shift change, Anton comes, and you won't get home." And I didn't get back from the village so quickly, I wandered back and forth there, the evening came. I returned and got lost. I could no longer find the factory.

Nights, nights, there was no one there. I go and go and always come back to the same place. My head was spinning, and I didn't know anything anymore. And I went the whole night through the fields, until three in the morning. I saw something high above me with the letters "Ford."

And in the early morning Anton was on duty. I was afraid. I approached the camp carrying potatoes in a bucket, and a loaf of bread, that's what they had given me. And so I went through the whole night. And near our camp was a French camp, also fenced off. The doors were open there, I see someone walking with a flashlight in his hand. Anton, wearing a pistol here and a leather whip. He used it to strike the fence—tr-r-r-r! I was afraid to go any nearer.

Anton noticed that someone was there. And I opened the gate and slipped into the camp, to the French. An old man was working there, a

Frenchman, but you could see that he was Russian, that he was in France and ended up here. I had worked with him, he told me that he was Russian and was in France.... Just then Anton jumps up and says: "Who is there?" But [the French] say: "No one." And I go with this Frenchman to work in the factory. I couldn't go into the camp, the gate was locked. Among the French there were no women, they were prisoners of war. The French noticed that I had slipped in among them, but they said nothing. I got into the factory, and my girls said: "Oy!" They cried, they thought I had been lost.

Anna Nesteruk: I had potatoes, the foreman brought me a bag with pota-toes. But Misha, the (Russian) policeman, stood in the aisle. He was very vicious. And he says: "You stole potatoes." What should I have said? In our camp there was a detention bunker, and I was imprisoned there, in the detention cell. I was locked up in the cell. I thought: "What should I do? Should I scream now?" I sat there and cried. I was hungry. I spent the night there.

I lay there, the cell was small, plank bed. I fell asleep there. There was nothing there. They would keep people there sometimes for longer, for three days. I was there only one night. In the morning the foreman came and took me with him. The foreman said to the policeman: *"Bist verrückt?"* He asked why he had locked me up. I came out and started to cry. And the foreman says: "Why did you lock her up?" And the policeman says: "She stole potatoes." And the foreman says: "You are stupid, crazy." I cried, but the foreman was good and said: *"Nicht weinen, Mädchen."*

Nadia Shubrawa: He worked in the 25th department, no?

Anna Nesteruk: I got to the factory and he gave me something to eat.

Nadia Shubrawa: Once I had stolen beets. I brought them in and hid them in the mattress. And not the German, but the Russian policeman came and found them, and he locked me up in the detention bunker. We wanted to go to the toilet, but there wasn't one there, only a little window. So we took off the big wooden shoes, and in the shoes.... (laughs)

Anna Nesteruk: We got wooden shoes, such huge ones ...

Anna Nesteruk: Our people, the Ukrainians at the camp, all worked hon-estly. From my village there was a small boy. He worked near a German, and then he didn't do something quite right with the machine, and the Ger-man beat him. Apparently the boy had not understood something. Do you know him?

Nadia Shubrawa: Vasili, last name Lisovchuk.

So when you did any bad work there you were immediately punished?

Anna Nesteruk: Not I, the boy. It wasn't the foreman who hit him, but an older German who had worked next to him. He was taken away, the boy, and to this day no one knows what happened to him. A policeman came, took him away, and that was it.

Inna Kulagina: My acquaintance from Rostov, Nina, made friends with a Ukrainian … and they got a child. And they received … among us there was a family barracks, where there were small rooms where families lived. But there were only a few couples among us.… At that time I was not particularly interested in it. I still know that someone told me once: "This Ukrainian woman is not at all well, she carried out her own abortion." And then she was in the sick ward for a while, it was called *Sanitäter* [paramedic]. Who was there, which doctors were there, I don't know. I never saw doctors there.

Did anyone try to escape?

Elsa Iwanowa: Many of the Russian boys ran away. Later we heard that you should try to escape to the farmers. We met a few [who worked for the farmers] in the town: "Oh," one of them would say. "I work at a farmer. There is plenty to eat there." Then we would say to each other: "Oh, let us escape." We always escaped in pairs. This Tasia ran away, but the poor girl ended up in the KZ (cries). We were luckier. You might get lucky, you might not. [Tasia] ran away with Shura, they were very afraid.… After she escaped we looked for her. We found out she was in a penal camp. We went there … and called out, but the windows were all closed. They were sitting there, in the dark. And from this camp they were brought to a KZ. Tasia still lives in Rostov, but Shura died two years ago. She was Armenian. In Rostov every other person is Armenian.… She had curly hair, nearly all of them have curly hair. But the police grabbed hold of her and said: "Jewess! Jewess!" We all said: "No, she is an Armenian from the Caucasus." But of course they are not from the Caucasus. They have lived in Rostov for one hundred years.

Inna Kulagina: [Tasia] ran away because she was hungry. She wanted to go to the farmers. She ran away, she was caught and was brought to the KZ. The KZ was entirely horrible. We were in a labor camp, but that was a KZ. Today she lives in Rostov, she still has pictures of the KZ. They had striped uniforms and it was even worse. But it was all a matter of luck. A few ran away and nothing happened to them, as was the case with us. Others ran away and ended up in a KZ, and others were shot.

Stepan Saika: Some people from my village fled. They asked me to go with them. They fled, my neighbors from the village, and with them a young woman. They worked on a rail line, somewhere around here. They worked there at the railway loading and unloading boxes together with French prisoners of war. They were women from the village, they had not had much school. These French were officers, educated people. They said to them: "This car is going to Russia." My neighbor came to me and said: "Stefan, let us get away from here!" I was still young, and next to me there was an older man.... He told me: "Forget it, they will find you and kill all the men, and that will be that." I said: "I won't go."

They took some water along, a loaf of bread, hid between the boxes. Their French friends locked them up in the car. These cars were gathered from all the factories into a single train. This is what happened then, as my neighbor told it to me, when we came back home from Germany. Before they got to the Polish border, SS men went through the train with dogs, and the dogs were barking on the leash. All of the men were taken out of the cars and shot on the spot. The women were beaten. They were not sent back to the camp, they were sent to a farmer. One of them got pregnant with a Polish man and hanged herself. The other made it back home.

From 1943 to 1944 Kazimierz Tarnawski was assigned to a mobile KZ labor squad that defused unexploded bombs and helped in rescue actions.

Kazimierz Tarnawski: At that time there were heavy bombings. [Messe] was always being bombed, everywhere there was fire. The [Messe camp] leader spoke to us: "If you work well, you will one day be free. You should help the wounded." Only then did I begin to see how many people were wounded, even children. The streets around the train station were full of blood. I worked with other young men at the train station in a "bomb commando." We had to dig out bombs that hadn't exploded, the duds, and then wait until soldiers had defused the bombs....

Can you imagine, when a house burned, we had to go into the cellar. There were people there under the rubble. [The guards] would say: "Go, or you will die now." They would shoot [in the air] and we would run into the cellar. There was smoke, but still we went in. We had to open the doors and get the people out. We lay them out on the street and covered them with plastic tarpaulins. The military took the living to the hospital. The officer would say: "If you find something to eat, you can eat it. But if you find clothing and you don't give it to us, or if you keep it for an escape, then we will shoot you on the spot." From the city we got some soup, that was an additional allowance. We got a paper bowl, some soup, a piece of bread, two cigarettes at lunch. The rest we got in the camp, soup and bread, but not always.

All of Cologne burned, and one's heart wept at the sight. Every Sunday we had to work. When we marched to work, we had to sing. I couldn't sing back then. The German [prisoners] marched in front, the rest in back. We sang, together with the SS who accompanied us to work. The dead children we threw onto cars, trucks with shovels. Always there were more, and afterwards we had to bury them in the graveyard. One child after the next, in one grave. I always thought about my own family. Were they still alive? War is the worst thing in the world. I cannot relate everything that I went through in the war. Always hunger, beatings and fear.

There were six bomb commandos working in Cologne-Mülheim, Cologne Deutz. We were mostly in Cologne-Deutz and at the Cathedral. We dug out about fifteen bombs around the Cathedral. Six men dug for half an hour, then there was a break and the other six kept digging, et cetera. Our commando, we were eighty to one hundred men, all young, French, Polish, all mixed. There were even two Jews there, one of them was terribly afraid. German Jews, one was from Saarbrücken, on the French border. He spoke French and German.

[One time] we pulled the bomb out on a chain, put that on, prepared it until the soldiers came. The Pioneers always came in an auto. They defused the bombs. I had a break. We were just out of there for two minutes when one of our bombs exploded. All the SS men were killed. They were always in a higher position, so that they could see us better. Only my ears…. My comrades were all wounded. I found boots full of blood. Good shoes. I had wooden shoes. An SS man said: "Take that, you can put that on." I said: "No, I would rather have my wooden shoes." He was dead, the soldier. "Are you afraid?" [the SS man] asked.

Once I was in the sick ward. I was terrified that I would have to go back to Buchenwald. Thank God, after two, three, perhaps after just one week I was back with my commando. The doctors there were also prisoners: a Pole, a Jew who spoke Polish, a Czech, there were also French doctors. I was in the sick ward because I had eaten cakes in a bombed-out bakery, and afterwards got this horrible diarrhea. Same as the other prisoners too. One French man had to stay in the sick ward for three weeks. He said: "I never want cakes, never again in my life."

We were hungry, and that is why we ate the cakes in the bakery. The baker was wounded upstairs, we had carried him upstairs. He had cried and didn't want to let go of our hands. The SS men watched that and said something, but we had not understood what the baker was saying…. The SS man bent over him, and then the baker said quietly that he had a lot of cigarettes upstairs and these should be given to the prisoners, and the SS men did that.

Did they really do that?

Kazimierz Tarnawski: Yes, for everyone. For themselves nothing. You know, among the SS there were also good men. When we wanted to eat the leftovers from (their) breakfast, then some of them turned away and acted as though they didn't notice it.

There was a camp with Jewish women, we knew nothing about it. [One day] the whole commando was set marching … to these barracks, I don't know exactly, the camp was not far from the Rhine. It was not a large camp. They were Jewish women, not in Messe itself, but nearby, another camp. I don't know what they did. A hundred meters from this camp we couldn't get any closer, because there was a big fire there and everything was burning. The women were screaming, calling for help. The way the women screamed, your own heart stood still, because you could do nothing to help. The SS men: "Go, fast!" There was no pump, so we took the water out of the river with buckets. We made a kind of corridor. The women had open wounds, I took them on my back. I went in there at least three times and carried one away. They screamed from the pain. Five trucks came and the living women were taken in the auto, I don't know where. That was in Cologne-Deutz, but more north of Deutz. I don't know what that's called today.

Such was our work in Cologne. After the bombings were over, my commando was sent to Ford Werke. A few new people were added. The sick and wounded were gone or simply weak, starving. Only the healthy remained, I was also among the healthy. The sick went back to Buchenwald, and others were added. Together our commando, all boys, went to the Ford plant in military autos. There we had it better. The people from Ford were very good to us, the workers. The administration, too. We got a lot of soup there, bread too, but not so much. We had to work hard, however. That was dispatching and packing, outdoors. A few of our colleagues worked indoors, with the Russians in the hall on the welding machines, or painting the cabins of the trucks. [We were] outside, near the Rhine, with a crane or without, with large boxes. The boxes were labeled: Bucharest, Romania. Ford had a branch in Bucharest, we knew nothing about it.... I fell in the water once. We had a commando leader, that was Frau Schlesien.[2] She said: "You will live, don't be afraid." I dried myself then, inside in the Ford hall, and many young girls, Germans and Ukrainians, came to me, gave me cigarettes and food. A Russian woman, Tatiana was her name, very fine young woman, said to me: *"Takoj molodyj"* ("you are so young"). She gave me her bread and said in Russian: *"Dawaj kuschaj"* ("come, eat"). I got cigarettes from a German, her name was Christa, I have not forgotten the name, they were black [the cigarettes]. I thought she was a Frenchwoman, because she spoke French, a waitress. She had always said, whenever she saw me: "Come, come to me," and gave me a butter roll. I don't forget that. That was a young woman. She worked in an office at Ford. I asked if she was perhaps from a Polish family. "No, no, I am German. But I have faith and my mother does too, my mother always gives me extra food to take to work, and I share that."

[Going back] from the Ford plant, sometimes, no auto came, and we had to march, and sing while we marched. From Ford to the Messe hall. Over the old bridge, that's not there anymore, the SS blew that up, over the old bridge, always. The people watched, weren't afraid, women, still they threw cigarettes on the ground, bread. Sometimes the SS said: "Go, fast, don't take," but they didn't shoot, only screamed, they had their orders, and we got all of that.

As far as I know, I was in Cologne from April 1943 to about the end of June, beginning of July 1944. It was summer, beautiful weather, and we had to leave Cologne. At Ford Werke I worked until July 1944, but I was there as a prisoner. Then Gestapo came to Messe and *go, go*. We heard that Messe was being prepared for Italian prisoners of war, but we only heard that, I don't know how that was, and we were taken away. Some were sent to Buchenwald. We were loaded onto this ship, with such gangways, and we went to Bonn.

In June 1944 the U.S.-British expeditionary force established a beachhead in Normandy.

Inna Kulagina: When the second front was opened, the Americans and English took Belgium. Essen was bombed heavily and there were many Russian men working there in metal processing plants. After the bombing they couldn't keep working there, so they were brought to Ford. And we women, not all, but some, we were brought (away from Ford) to a different factory on the other side of the Rhine, where the work was easier. There we made military tents and gas masks. From pieces of this material we sewed ourselves a costume. One woman who we knew already from the Ford camp could sew, and we went to her. We thought up something, which turned out to be possible. We were young after all, and wanted to take off this uniform and put on a costume. They had plank beds and barracks over there, too. We were only there for a few days. I did not even see the entire camp. We escaped. When we had settled in there, we thought that we were not yet registered.

Elsa Iwanowa: We were sent there in a group with twenty to thirty people. We made gas masks there. Inna says there were tents too, but I can't remember that. We were not there for long. I think, about ten days. Inna and I wanted to flee, but we were afraid. "Come, we'll try!" I said: "Yes, it doesn't matter. I would rather die." I could no longer stand the hunger. We got away. In the new factory they had not registered our names yet. We could go out from the factory on to the street. Inna and I had a plan in mind: this, this, and this. We learned our roles like actors. We asked each other questions, to learn the same. One time we had met a couple of Russian women in Cologne who said to us: "We come from Berlin, everything there has been bombed. We worked in a restaurant kitchen and peeled potatoes."

Inna Kulagina: I said to Elsa: "Let's run away!" And we ran away, and I say: "Let's go straight to the Arbeitsamt!" That was on a Sunday, when they would let us out to walk around the factory. And so we ran away. We ran for the whole night. Cologne was being bombed and we were looking. We didn't know where the Arbeitsamt was, and we ran through all of Cologne. We asked and we were shown the way. When we got to the Arbeitsamt, we said that we had worked in Berlin in a restaurant, not at a factory, and that there had been bombing there, and so we had come to Cologne to look for our friends. We were threatened with the Gestapo: "The Gestapo is going to take you!" But Elsa and I had prepared well. We were asked: "What is the price of a ticket from Berlin to Cologne?" And everything was right.

How did you get away with this?

Inna Kulagina: We don't even know ourselves. Elsa was questioned by one lady, I was questioned by another. We used other names, not Kulagina and Iwanowa, otherwise we would have been sent back and then brought to the Gestapo. Looks like we were lucky. At the Arbeitsamt they threatened that if they caught us lying we would be brought to the Gestapo. And then two people came, Jungblut and Michel, and we were asked: "Who wants to go to whom?" And we said: "Doesn't matter who goes where." I was taken by Jungblut and Elsa went to Michel. Michel had a drug store. At our place, in the cellar, Jungblut managed a food store. At that time everything was on food ration cards, and he distributed the food.

How were they were able to get you as laborers?

Inna Kulagina: I don't know. I think it was Vitamin B, as the Russians say. Back then it was war, there were food ration cards. Jungblut had a food store and Michel a drug store. Apparently they asked the Arbeitsamt: "Help us find household help, and we will give you food for that." That's what I think. To this day I still don't know why. The Jungbluts, that was a married couple and the son was on the front. And they ran this store, they had two boys as workers and there was an accountant, an office. I was supposed to work in the house, cleaning.

Herr Jungblut was a member of the NSDAP, but he said that he needed this for his career. He himself was a good man. But the woman was very nasty. When the Americans bombed the city, she hit me and said: "Those are your friends, the Americans. Our Germans are dying while you live and still eat my bread." She was terribly nasty, but the man was good. He was more thoughtful. When he picked me up and we drove in the car–I was very thin after the camp and so emaciated–he said: "Fräulein, are you sick?" And later I recovered, despite everything I ate well there and slept in a clean bed. For me that was everything, oy, like paradise after the time in the camp. I recovered, but she was annoyed that I had become a human being again. She didn't hit me often, just on occasion. I answered her questions in Russian a couple of times, and she didn't understand me. I cursed her out. She hits me and I say: "Oh, you …!" And she: "Again!" and hits me, but not as hard. Of course, I cursed her in Russian. If I had said it in German, maybe she would have hit me even more.

I did housework. Cleaning the floors, cooking the food, washing the laundry. I ran the whole house. As a girl back home of course I had never done that, but here I did everything, cleaned and tidied up, I took care of the whole house. Elsa and I visited each other. It was not far away, between Aachener Strasse and Dürener Strasse. Elsa often visited me, because Herr and Frau Jungblut would drive to Troisdorf, where they had two rooms and a veranda. Whenever Cologne was bombed they would drive there.

Mareno Mannucci: After many months, on 1 September 1944, the status of military internees was changed to civilian internees. There were various changes. We got a new work number. I got No. 2,537. In the camp we were guarded by the Werkschutz and not by soldiers. You could go to work on your own, without being controlled. We got an ID with a photo, which showed that we belonged to Ford and we were allowed to leave the camp. But all this did not last long. The Anglo-Americans were coming closer, and the western Rhine area was declared into a war zone, and all foreigners there were guarded and controlled by the soldiers and also the SS. So for us

Italians this limited freedom only lasted for a few weeks. On 14 October, a Saturday, around midday, a flying fortress dropped several hundred bombs on the zone, but nearly all missed their target. They were perhaps meant for the Bayer plant, on the other side of the Rhine. Four of them fell outside our camp. We were already in the shelter, and everyone was okay. But the barracks were damaged by the shockwave. There were no more windows and everywhere the wind came through, and everywhere the rain leaked in. There were dead among the French and two barracks were in flames. There was chaos for a few days. No power, no water, nothing to eat. But divine foresight helped us. Not far from the fence there was a field with potatoes and sugarbeets that had not yet been harvested. Several bombs fell on this field. The sugarbeets and potatoes flew through the air and landed again. We only had to gather them. For a few days that was the only food for us, for the Russians and the French.

Mareno Mannucci describes in detail the five-step process by which the Italian internees made molasses out of the sugarbeets.

Mareno Mannucci: But the human spirit wants more. With the molasses we made grappa!

Men on the nightshift secretly used the factory repair station to build a home-made distillery. This blew up, but the police who investigated were in good spirits, and made no arrests, although they confiscated the Italians' oven.

Mareno Mannucci: But back to the bombing raid. A single bomb fell on the factory. It fell on the vehicle department, totally paralyzing production. Many vehicles were immediately taken out of the factory. It was said they were brought to a tunnel and that production was continued there. The assembly line had not been damaged. After a few days production was continued with replacement parts from the various warehouses. But production was only possible for a few days a week. The ovens were turned off, and I was sent to do work like unloading coal in the Glanzstoff textile factory nearby. This factory had not suffered damage and had its own generator. It was providing Ford with power.

For about a year, Yvon Thibaut had attended secret meetings of Belgian and French Catholic activists in the city. He was arrested by the Gestapo at the Ford camp in summer 1944, and brought to Gestapo headquarters in EL-DE Haus. There he saw an estimated sixty of his fellow activists had also been rounded up. For weeks he and the others were beaten, interrogated and tortured by the Gestapo, kept in small dark cells packed with prisoners. He was moved to a prison in Brauweiler.

Yvon Thibaut: I often saw other prisoners there, mostly Germans in civilian clothing. Among them there was a priest with a Roman collar. I think I can still see him before my eyes. I was happy, because I thought he had seen me. I gave him a sign like, "come, take my confession." I think he understood me. When he ended his walk in the courtyard, he made the sign of the cross towards me with his hand. And I said to myself: "I have been forgiven, that is the absolution." Soon after that, a sort of scaffold was built. And I think, it was four or five, I can't remember, their heads were chopped off with the axe. They were beheaded. I saw that, and then I couldn't sleep for three days and nights, because I was so upset. I said to myself: "My God, how is that possible?" Then I said to myself: "That's it, that is our fate too," because in the interrogations we were threatened with the most horrible and unimaginable deaths, to get us to confess.

One day we were taken away, we were brought to IVA [Messe].[3] From there we were taken on 16 September 1944 in cattle cars to Buchenwald. The journey was incredibly difficult, because it took three days. We had only eaten before, and during the three days we had nothing to drink. Hunger and thirst! I know that besides our own people we had Russians and Poles in our train-car. We had our shirts off, it was so hot. The car was closed, there was no air coming in and we were thirsty. I still remember exactly how we suffered. Of course many died on the journey. When we got to Buchenwald, we first unloaded the dead out of our car. And what scared me the most was the SS with their machine pistols, their little machine pistols. And then the dogs, there were dogs there, how were they? Wild, nasty. Then we had to march in rows, to get out of the train station. I don't know how long it took from the station to the camp. But I can still remember the big gate. There was a sign with the words: *"Jedem das Seine"* ["To each his own"]. And I said to myself, "Okay, let's see."

We had a good impression when we went in. We saw the door that opened up, and there were pretty flower beds and fountains. And you think: "My God, it's chic here, that's good." Yes, but, that was the facade. And then they had us march, I remember, we marched to the left, and then we saw big, massive barracks of concrete. In front there were some of concrete, behind those there were barracks, and far to the back, towards the end of the camp, there were tents. That was the quarantine camp, that was where you had to wait, to avoid spreading contagion to the others, because supposedly we brought diseases in with us. We went to a large hall, where we had to undress, all naked, we were forced. Then barbers came in with electric shavers, they shaved us everywhere, the hair, all smooth. Then we went to the rear corner of the hall, in a corridor, that was like a store, if you will, like a long corridor and on the side there was a counter and a bit behind that there were shelves full of clothes, there were hats, caps, shirts, no underwear, we didn't get underwear, but shirts, all civilian clothing. The jackets and the pants had a triangle or a square with a different color from the suit, for example a brown suit with a red sign or a green or a yellow one, depending, but these signs had different colors from the suit, so that it would stand out.

But before that, I forgot to say, we got numbers. We had a sign with a card, they hung that around our necks, when we were all naked, and that was your entry number as a prisoner in Buchenwald. I had number 481756.

You had to be able to read that in German and remember it, because constantly, when you were in the camp, later, you might be called for any reason, they called us by number, never by name: "Number one hundred seven...." Whenever I heard my number, I had to go to the tower! To ask for my orders, to know where I was supposed to go. Or sometimes they called for whole rooms or pavilions, like this: "All of Pavilion 9, or 11 or 14, assemble at the square!" At this big square we had to sometimes stand at attention for hours. In the evening it was deadly, because it could take three hours, four hours, five hours, sometimes seven hours. And then with the dead, and these dead, we carried them, the comrades carried them voluntarily, to bring them to the barracks. The SS counted the people and that was the number of rations that we had, but when someone was dead, he could no longer eat, then his rations would be shared, at least those who had carried him would get something. I saw that, it is true.

We were first kept under quarantine, and then to the "big camp," as it was called. I was in block—unfortunately I don't remember the number anymore—but we went to the block. The roll call started, we got up around four, four-thirty in the morning. When we were all gathered, which took at least half an hour, there were 55,000 prisoners, and what a group to get in line, especially since they had to run hundreds of meters to get there, and always running. Then there was SS, prison guards who counted us, but sometimes one of them would make a mistake, and he would have to start over again. In the morning this went very quickly, because they didn't really want to count people but assign work.

In Buchenwald I did only one thing: I went to the quarry. It was five kilometers away. Then we had to take a rock, but not one that was too big and not one too small, because, when they took one that was too small, they would get another one piled on top of that, to crush them, so you always had to search carefully. And sometimes we had disputes, we would have fights sometimes to get exactly the rock that we had decided on, or perhaps others, two or three others. Then we took these on our shoulders, we changed shoulders sometimes, depending, and we went the five kilometers back to the camp. At the camp entrance we put the rocks in a pile, so that, when there were thousands of us, an enormous pile was built. There they let us take a break, they gave us soup, I think. That was water with a couple of things in it, it was nothing big. And then we went back to the quarry, brought more stones back and we went back to the camp, without a rock. And then, we had done twenty kilometers in a day, ten kilometers back and forth, and a second time ten kilometers back and forth, so twenty, on foot. It was about that, perhaps it was a little bit more or less, but according to what my comrades said and I could estimate, it was about that.

Because we were dirty, we were taken to a large hall, a kind of movie theater, but it was no movie for us, it was the theater for the bosses and even the SS.[4] They had nice films, well, yes, because sometimes we saw the previews. But we never, we never had that. It was there, where we went to change. We would undress completely and we had to give up our clothes, so that they could be disinfected, and we waited an hour, two hours, or if things went well a half-hour, but that was seldom. Often it was two, three hours, four hours and when it wasn't finished, when they could no longer get all the clothes clean, they would give us a cover and in that case, I think the SS was informed in advance, the SS would set up in two rows and we had to go through the middle and then there were pigs from the SS, who pulled you on the ... you know what I mean, or who slapped you on the butt or tried to pull you to them, there were scenes there, it was horrible! I was in this several times and it wasn't just me, a whole bunch of others, that was really disgusting. We went with the cover back to the camp, until the next day. Before we had to go work, a long time before the roll call, we were called out in rows again, we went to the service and they gave us our clothes again.

We only got the striped prisoner clothing and the triangle with B for Belgian, D for German and so on when we were assigned to an Aussenkommando. [At the camp itself we only] had our numbers. These had to be on the jacket and also on the pants on both sides, so that our prisoner numbers could be seen. Later I was supposed to be assigned to Dachau with a few other comrades. I never found out for what reason. I only know that my number was called for Dachau. When I was first registered for Buchenwald, I myself had specified the reason [that I was later assigned to Dachau]. It was this: "Are you Catholic?" *Est-ce que vous êtes catholique?* "Yes." Pater Léon Leloir, who had also been in Buchenwald, once heard that we had said that. "Oh," said Pater Leloir, "that's it, you signed your sentence, you will be sent to the hardest and most terrible camp." Yes, but we didn't know it then, and there is a certain pride in saying it. I am a Christian and period.

Stepan Saika: I was working the nightshift [at Ford], but during the day I didn't sleep. I watched if anything was being supplied to the canteen, hoping to steal beets or a few potatoes when the supplies were unloaded. Then, when I went to the nightshift and fell asleep there, this Fritz would come near my ear and say very loud: "Ste-fan!" And laugh. He was a good man. In my village there is still another man, whom this Fritz also took to his house. Fritz took me to his house and said: "I'll go to the camp and say that I need wood, that you should help me with chopping wood." But there was nothing to chop there.

Another time it was Sunday [at the camp], and the police came to me: "Four eight and fifty! Come to the guard house!" I went there and I saw it was Fritz. We took the train, long time, and then there was an alarm. Into the bunker. After we were out of the bunker we kept riding, a long time, and finally got there, I no longer remember the street.... We sat down, his wife seemed to be Belgian, and there was a daughter, a girl. And as we sat at the table, the window was open, and that was when Hitler was sending the boys of fourteen and fifteen to the front. You know about that here too. And these boys marched by, with their carbines around their necks. They went over the street and sang some kind of marching song. But Fritz's wife looked through the window, took her head in her hands and said: "*Ai, ai, ai!* God forbid, how much young cannon fodder that is!" And she cried.

Mareno Mannucci: Around the middle of November [1944] five Italians and two Germans were sent every day to Weilerswist, where Ford had a big warehouse. There we would get spare parts, soldiers and civilians. It was a dangerous adventure, every day 100 kilometers with a truck that was run on a wood burner, through snow and ice. It got to minus twenty degrees centigrade. There was a constant danger from the air raids. In mid-January [1945] they were altogether out of materiel. We were no longer sent to Weilerswist. The production of trucks was broken off due to material shortages. Many Italians had already been transferred [away from Ford]. For a few days I was assigned with others to fill the bomb craters at the train station grounds of Cologne-Nippes. Then I was in a group of sixty people who were transferred to Organisation Todt. When we left Ford the police took our camp ID. Each of us got 50 reichsmarks. That was the only pay we ever received for fourteen months' work at Ford.

Then everything got much worse. Four S.A. men had us under guard. They took us in rows of five, as we had earlier been escorted by the soldiers, to the south of the city, where the front was only a few kilometers away. They brought us to a barrack, which was next to a small camp. The strangest thing about that camp was that the people who were fenced in spoke German, and the SS, who were guarding them, spoke Russian and Polish. We were brought there to dig a trench against trucks, from a small lake to the railway grounds. Three civilians from Organisation Todt gave us orders, while the four old S.A. men guarded us. They were so nasty, we feared them as much as we feared the Germans from Organisation Todt. The work was very hard, digging earth from morning to evening. The good part was the food. It was almost enough. Cologne was hit with more heavy bombing raids in those days. We were told to break off digging the trench, and brought to the city to search for people in the ruins of the houses. Our task was to go into basements, move away walls where it was thought there might be people caved in. We had the right equipment, hammers, pickaxes, but it was all pointless. The snow was melting and the Rhine flooded over, the sewage system had been damaged too. The basements were flooded so that we couldn't get in. After four days we were brought back to digging the trench. Two days later it was March. The Allied offensive was getting heavier, and when they got closer, we were quickly evacuated across the Rhine and ordered to take actions that would delay the crossing, closing tunnels and breaking up roads.

Supposedly as a stop on the way to Dachau, Yvon Thibaut was transferred in late 1944 or early 1945 to a camp at Dessau,[5] which he describes as "paradise compared to Buchenwald." After a period of heavy manual labor for the Reichsbahn, he was assigned to a factory, drilling holes in metal parts.

Yvon Thibaut: There was no sabotage, the factory was too small. We were observed the whole time.... Although there were Germans there in Dessau, although we were enemies–we carried the sign of the political prisoner, a "P" in a red corner, and they knew it–there were still some who gave me bread, who now and then gave me something to eat. I admire that because it takes courage, especially in a small factory, where one is seen by everyone else. That was a rivalry among the Germans. Someone was afraid he would be betrayed by someone else, and the other one was just as afraid, it was always like that. Ah, at Ford I had seen guys complain against the regime. The next morning you wouldn't see them anymore. I said afterwards: "What about the one who was there?" "Oh, I don't know." Nobody dared say a thing. They were taken away too, even the Germans, that's how it was.

In late 1944 Kazimierz Tarnawski's air raid commando was sent through Dortmund, Essen, and other locations, all of which were bombed repeatedly. Finally, in early 1945, he was with a group of KZ laborers under SS command, digging tank trenches on the Dutch border. There he met his friend Josef, the man with whom he had attempted his first escape attempt.

Kazimierz Tarnawski: We knew already that the American troops were in Holland. France was already liberated, after the invasion, and I attempted my last escape, with seven men. I had a lot of lice, everywhere I touched myself there were lice. We were in makeshift barracks that were always bombed by the Americans. There was little food and always work, always fast-moving, always work. One night, it was already cold. American soldiers seized us and lined us up against the wall in a hall. We had civilian clothes on we'd found at a farm, those were working pants, shirts and clean underwear. We had civilian clothes but no hair and a lot of lice. That's when the American soldiers seized us. The Americans thought we were German soldiers who were running away. That was at the farmer's in a village, broken windows and a lot of tanks, shooting. Everyone had chewing gum, the Americans were young like us. "*Deutsche Soldaten*, German soldiers, go!" The officer had spoken German. I don't want to imagine I am a hero, but I was the first to speak. I said: "We are not Germans, we are from the concentration camp, we are not German soldiers." "KZ, KZ." I said a few words in English. One of us was bleeding, because he had been wounded, but we had not known that, and he fell over. They took him to the military hospital and we waited. We were all Polish, young men. He said something in English and a soldier went away at a run and got another officer who spoke Polish. He said to us in Polish: "How did you survive that? This place changed hands six times!" He said to us: "Do not fear, you're going to a camp."

That was a quarantine for us, they had orders from above. They put us through a disinfecting. It was a military auto, there was a bathing room there, we had to undress, give up all our things, we only kept the documents, the things were burned. We bathed, got soap, everything American. That was behind the front, perhaps three kilometers. We got a new guard, pajamas and military suits, these field suits. We also had to do things there. I was the youngest, I got coffee. I worked as "ordnance" for the American major, who also spoke German and had his own office in an auto, where there were many pistols, many clocks, cards. He gave me gloves and a clock and a small pistol too. That's how I became a soldier. I also got chewing gum. I was just like the Americans. One time the major came with Willis: "Kasimir, how are you?" "Very well, Major." "I got you some medals." He gave me a Polish eagle and a field cap, many candies and milk, like for a child. He said: "That's all for you." Chocolate, a whole packet, Jesus Maria. I got sick from that.

In Cologne the Jungblut house, where Inna Kulagina was working, was destroyed by bombs. Later the Michel house, where Elsa Iwanowa was working, was also hit.

Inna Kulagina: Everything was being bombed. I didn't know where to run. Herr Jungblut put me in the car and we drove to Troisdorf. Everything was burning, fire. I could not at all imagine where to go and how, it was night. And in Troisdorf he brought me to an office.

It was the office of Herr Jungblut, he sent me there to get papers. They lived on a hill, it was a spa area. I went there and the planes flew up. The Americans bombed as follows: a lot of airplanes fly up and they call that carpet bombing. All airplanes let go of their bombs simultaneously and that was like this: bombs, bombs, and then another wave of bombs. And everything collapsed, and I was buried under there. The priests of this town organized a special brigade to shovel out the cellars and get the people out. At first I heard something and then I yelled, but then I lost consciousness and I no longer remember how I was taken out. Then I was brought to a hospital. I could no longer walk. I was buried, like after an earthquake, and the blood no longer circulated in my legs. The legs are fine now, but I couldn't walk, because my muscles were paralyzed. I lay there. There were nuns there, I even learned to pray. They gave us rosaries. Wounded Germans lay there and I lay there. And then the Americans came around.

Kamila Felinska: After the [Ford] machines were transferred to the other side of the Rhine we went to dig trenches. There we were put under the supervision of the SS, and so it was until the end of the war. I no longer went back to Ford. There things went very poorly for us. We got hardly anything to eat, and I was very thin, like a stick. We were liberated on 9 April. There was a bombing, we all sat in the bunker and we were very afraid. All at once soldiers came in with rifles, pointed them at us. I thought then that we would be killed, because I thought they were Germans. Then I considered that there were also Germans among us, from the nearby settlement. When the Americans came to our bunker, you could not directly recognize that they were Americans, because the Germans looked just like the Americans and were similarly dressed. They spoke German to us, and then they said to us that we should all go up above. The German women who were with us in the bunker were also very afraid that they would die. I thought then: if we die now, then all together.

We were divided according to nationality, all we Poles stood together. The soldier took his mask off, so that we could recognize his face, and he said: "I am an American, and we have come to free you." There was yelling and celebration and I was very happy. We got chocolate and cookies, everyone got that, the Germans too. That was very justly distributed, everyone got something. Only the Germans were allowed to eat that, not us, because that was too dangerous. We were so starved that if we ate too much all at once that could have gotten very serious. The Germans stayed there, and the other nationalities were then driven in a truck to Bonn.

In late March 1945, Mareno Mannucci's group was digging trenches at a village about fifty kilometers northeast of Cologne, on the eastern side of the Rhine.

Mareno Mannucci: We found leaflets dropped by planes. These said that the Americans had crossed the Rhine. One of our guards was very nice, he read the leaflet and told us exactly what was on it. "The Americans have already crossed the Rhine and they are getting nearer." We were all happy. We dreamed of tanks with a white star. We would hear tanks going by and ask: "With a white star?" "No, with a cross."–Damn! Because when you're twenty, then despite bad conditions you're still a bit playful. We always dreamed of tanks with the white star.… That evening everything was confused, we slept in a theater. All the windows and doors had been barricaded, except one door to the street. Soldiers would take turns guarding. The evening came, before we fell asleep. We slept in our clothes, full of lice, on the floor. The German cursed: "Sleep!" He cursed: "Quiet!" Because we were talking. In the night someone said: "Listen, tanks!"–"Listen!" A big grenade, shot by the Americans, a big grenade. Wham! Damned mess! The roof came off from the shockwave and fell around us. I put on my wooden shoes to get out, but the German didn't let us go: "No one gets out!" Two or three shots missed and I felt a big heatwave, but not the explosion. And then everything fell on us. Then he let us go and I ran together with three or four others. We got to a square and we sat down there. After a while we lay down on top of each other and that's how we went to sleep.

When I woke up, it was just getting light. At first I was confused: "Where am I, where am I?" The others were leaning on my shoulders, sleeping. And I heard church bells from afar. I remember that it was Easter morning [1 April 1945]. I remember that my feelings overwhelmed me and I cried. And as the day broke, we went back into the village and I was sorry for the residents, because all the houses were destroyed. Before nothing had been hit. The whole village had still been intact. The poor people, they were carrying furniture and clothes out of their houses. I was upset, all the old people, children, there were no men, everyone was in despair. And then it was terrible, to go back to the theater. We saw horrible things. Everything was full of blood from those who had stayed there. Of the sixty a few others got away. How many died, I do not know. There were only twenty left from the sixty. We were all white, all full of the dust from the explosion, so we washed a bit, and then an officer said to us: "Carry them away, carry them away!" Two units came to clear the streets and bury the dead. And outside we found a fountain, we took off our clothes and washed, but our hair stayed all sticky, until the liberation we all ran around with this mud and mire. It rained, and how! They put us onto trains that were partly destroyed. They brought us food, a lot of food. We ate in silence, thinking of our comrades who had stayed under there. Yes. We saw the church tower of a town from the train, we saw this church tower and thought of the men and the last days. A sorrowful day, terrible! We spent the night in this car and the next day they put us together with Russians. Then everything dissolved, there was no longer any organization.

After a week they brought us to Lüdenscheid. We got out, and in this city all the guards left. When air raids came, the guards blew whistles: "Alarm!" We lined up and went into the forest, we hid there. When they saw there was no more danger, they called out: "It's over! Everyone out." But once we waited for an hour, two hours, and they didn't whistle any more. It was dark and we went to look. They were gone. We dispersed into the woods. And then we saw tanks with the white star coming. I still remember an older man. He was born in 1899, [he was with the Italian] finance police. He was my roommate at Ford. He saw the tanks and it was like a great shock. He fell back and forth and cried. We were liberated not far from Meinerzhagen by the Americans on 13 April 1945. For me it was to this day the most beautiful day in my life.

After helping move Ford machines to a dispersal location, Anna Nesteruk and Nadia Shubrawa were evacuated by the retreating German forces to regions east of the Rhine.

Anna Nesteruk: We were evacuated, but I don't know to where. We were brought over the Rhine to the other side. We were brought to dig trenches.

Nadia Shubrawa: To Oberhausen. We were forced to go to the other side of the Rhine, and then the Americans occupied the area eighty kilometers around us, to the Rhine, here. And then—we were so hungry, there was nothing to eat, at that point no one was giving us anything anymore. We were driven back and forth: "Go there, go here!" We carried the doors over, our machines were transported a hundred kilometers away. When the front came nearer, there was no bombing, but shelling. We carried the machines and the rest. But they were not set up there, it was obvious that the front was coming nearer. And then we got to this stream. And after that we went to the trenches. We all dug trenches in the forest. We dug trenches, where we hid ourselves. Shovels and picks. Our prisoners of war were there, they said: "Girls, don't go to work. The American is there." Still we went to work, and then we see—all at once a shell exploded, then another. And the [German] troops pulled back. We were no longer entertaining any hope. We hid in the trenches. And an older German comes to us, and we run to the bunker. In the bunker there were a lot of people, and we went there, and sat for a while. And then the Americans came in.

Nadia Shubrawa: And then the Americans came into the bunker. They looked around: "Russian, Russian." They asked if any German soldiers were there. We took a white bedsheet, put it on a stick and hung it up outside. "We give up!" Then, as the front came over, we all ran to the shops. There was a butcher's, sausages were hanging, smoked hams. We took something to eat.

Anna Nesteruk: Everything was allowed.

Nadia Shubrawa: There were no more guards, nothing. We took a lot of lard and ate till we were full. We were hungry, and then we got diarrhea. And many died. The war ended, and many died of the dysentery. A slaughterhouse, where the livestock was. There was sausage there. We went there and ate until we were full. We got diarrhea, the people began to die. And there were such fascists there. They had a canteen, there was steamed cabbage, meat, potatoes and sauce. They sprinkled poison in it, and a lot of people were poisoned because they had especially sprinkled it in.

Kazimierz Tarnawski: In May or at the end of April 1945, still before the capitulation, I was in [American-occupied] Cologne with my colleagues, of whom two had been together with me in the concentration camp, and a Polish Jew, a Polish soldier and an officer. We were in the cathedral, the Cologne Dom, one tower was heavily damaged, but inside a priest held a mass. At the Messe camp everything was destroyed. Many people, foreigners: Dutch, Gypsies, Jews. They were all in the Messe camp. Not everything was destroyed there. They slept there, ate. There were also many criminals there.

The death march out of Dessau started around 11 April 1945, and joined up with other death marches.

Yvon Thibaut: The Americans, the English got closer and the Russians came in from the other side towards Dessau. The SS were afraid. The camp commander said: "Okay, I'm sending the column to Czechoslovakia." He wanted to surrender us to the International Red Cross, who had their headquarters in Prague. They set that up extra for the evacuation of all those suffering who came from the area of Berlin or of Buchenwald. They had us march 400 kilometers! Four hundred kilometers on foot in six days! Because we had to take detours. It was reported that enemy troops were in the area. Then we had to go back, we took detours. Still we made it to the Elbe. I don't know anymore where exactly. There we were put on to tractors. We stopped often to work. We were 3,500 men on the tractors, and the living were forced to clear ruins out of the road wherever the tractors were forced to stop. Or we built barricades against tanks at crossings. We made trenches, put up tree trunks. All this without getting food. I think we got something like three slices of bread in Schandau, but three slices that weren't too thick. Three slices for twenty, no, we went twenty-five days without food. For two days we got three slices, no more, and then twenty-five days without food. We drank out of the Elbe. And all these corpses.

In the beginning we couldn't, but then we piled the corpses in the middle of the tractor. We had to, to make space. In the beginning we didn't have much space, we were 120 on a platform and that was about the size of a cattle truck, where you can fit eight horses or forty people. There were 120 of us in there, of course it was very tough in the beginning. Later we had space, unfortunately, because we threw out all the corpses. The first three, four days we didn't want to throw them out, but it stank. After two days a corpse stinks, that stinks terribly, especially under such conditions. Fourteen days we were allowed to throw the corpses in the water, then along the whole river on the way to Czechoslovakia. When you could count, when you could, because it's impossible, all the corpses, that were there, to count … it's unbelievable. The corpses were treated like objects, those were objects that disappeared, like one had got rid of a burden. I had friends among them, whom I had met, and I know exactly, that they were thrown overboard. Although I can no longer remember their names today.

We were liberated in Czechoslovakia, and that was on 8 May 1945, at around four in the afternoon. That means, they left us on an island. That was a small island on the Elbe, a small island, you could see from one end to the next. They left us there. I no longer know how many. We were about 800. They used whatever ammunition they had left to shoot at the men, and hardly two hundred survived. All of the rest were shot by the SS. Once the SS had shot their magazines off, they got onto a tractor and drove back to Germany. And they left us there. On the other side of the island you could get across because there was a small dike, which was flooded. We waddled through the water. And from then on we were free. We started being free.

At the displaced persons camp in Bonn, summer 1945:

Kamila Felinska: There was a doctor there in the barracks, after the examination they gave us food rations, so that we didn't eat too much all at once. That took about a month, then we got more and more, and then we all felt much better. A military chaplain in Bonn married us. He spoke Polish, but I am not sure whether he was a Pole. When we got back to Poland it was not recognized. I said, how many times do I have to marry? Then we had to ask the bishop for permission, because we were related. I was annoyed. Why should I marry the same man twice? I then got married again in the Bydgoszcz region, no longer as solemn as the first time, and not on a Sunday but on a Tuesday afternoon, not with a veil, but with a hat. I had been in Bonn until November, then already on 5 November I was in Stettin, in Poland. First I found the family of my mother in the district (*Woiwodschaft*) of Posen, then the family of my father in the district of Allenstein. My father was so hard-working that he had worked gladly in Prussia for Germans. I wrote to my father that he should come back. Otherwise we will go back to Germany. So my parents came back. My sisters and brothers were in the meantime in the Posen region, but at that time I didn't know it yet. Then the family gathered together, when the parents came back, and we all went to Szprotawa. After 1947 we lived in Szprotawa, until I moved, not far from Posen. I only want to say the truth. At the beginning it was terrible for me, but in the last months in Germany it was better for me. The worst days were digging the trenches. And that is the whole truth. Thank you.

Nadia Shubrawa: And so we were occupied by the Americans, and then we came to a transit camp. There were 20,000 of us in this camp. We were with the Americans for about three months, they fed us.

Anna Nesteruk: The Americans fed us well.

Nadia Shubrawa: Yes, then things were better, people there began to marry and to celebrate. (Laughs.) We got alcohol–there was a factory there with wood spirit, which was used for paint. But the Russian is a pig after all. He went there and took it. "Piggery!"

Anna Nesteruk: Yes, we will tell all! (All laugh.)

Nadia Shubrawa: They drank that and they all died. Yes, they got drunk on schnapps. With you here it's so nice, you put something on the table, pour a little bit for yourself, you sit. Ours get a hold of something, they get totally drunk and then drop their head into the soup. Oy, that was a grief, we survived a hard time.

Anna Nesteruk: We were brought home and the Russians also gave us a "good welcoming." They called us traitors: "You sold yourselves to the Germans, you worked for them."

Nadia Shubrawa: They said to us: "You are trophies." Now, like the machines. They said that Stalin didn't need us. You had Hitler, we had Stalin. Russian soldiers said to us, when we arrived: "Why are you coming? Stalin doesn't need you."

Anna Nesteruk: I got back to my house on 30 October. When the Germans retreated they had burned the house down. The whole village was evacuated. Mother was alive, she did not die. But the house was gone, it was burned down.

Nadia Shubrawa: There were [some of us] here in Germany who had been sent home [earlier, by the Germans]. They were sick. They were sent to the Ukraine. Sick. They drank salty coffee and stood in the pond until their legs began to swell. The Germans thought they were sick, and they were sent away. But they had nothing, only their legs were swollen. They were sent home, and then the Germans started falling back [on the Eastern Front]. They were sent home in '43. Then, when the Germans retreated, someone cut the wires, the telephone lines were cut. And they were taken as hostages. They were such beautiful people. Among us there was a prisoner of war, they were such young men. They had to line up in a row. Ten people were shot because of this telephone line. These lines were cut, but the Germans were so vicious, that with their retreat they took them hostage–"You cut the connection"–and they were shot. They were also buried there.

Nadia Shubrawa: In another village all of the people, 436 people were killed. They had to line up, they were marched to a deep ravine. The Germans chased children out there, everyone they ran into, and they shot them all with machine guns. Two survived. When they were shot, one grandson was back to back with his grandfather. They shot from the machine guns, and he fell with the rest. Two boys survived. Everyone was shot. They are still alive today. On 24 January it was fifty years since they were killed. They have a memorial. The two men were children, and today they are old. They come here, and it's been fifty years since they were killed. One of them can talk about it. The other one can't. When he says anything, he starts crying right away. He can't talk about it. What a grief that was, the blood mixed with the earth. Worobjewka village, Wolonski district, Chmelnizky region. They were covered with soil. Today they have fixed it up well, built a gate, hung up a bell, surrounded the grave with trees. A monument was set up. Were you there, Ania?

Anna Nesteruk: Yes.

Nadia Shubrawa: A beautiful monument was placed on the grave. The people go there on 24 January, and also on the day of victory. On 9 May, they celebrate the victory. The school children go to the sepulcher, music is played, people hold speeches. I go there. That was where my cousin was killed and three little children. Yes, the war was over, and we saw: many people have died.

Nadia Shubrawa: We did not see each other so often after that. We got married afterwards, but now and then we talked to each other.

Nadia Shubrawa: We were together for nearly three and a half years. We are something like sisters. We were not related, but we lived together.

The Jungbluts did not visit Inna Kulagina while she was in the hospital in the summer of 1945.

Inna Kulagina: You know, I'd like to say the following to you: Madame Jungblut treated me so poorly, she was afraid that when the Americans came I would tell it to them and she would be punished for it. She didn't come to me, no one did. Then, when I started getting around a bit on crutches, the Americans came through Troisdorf and then went on. The hospital was taken by the Americans, and American doctors treated me alongside the Germans.

Three or three and a half months, I lay in bed for a very long time. During this time all the Russians were split up. A few went to Belgium. Because in April the war was still going on. When the war ended, there began a division into zones, into the English zone, the American zone. I was in the

English zone. Everyone was gone and I was looking, alone, as a Russian. I was trying to find out which camp I should go to. I didn't know where I should go, where the Russians were being collected and sent home. I was in the English zone. Oy, the English also treated the Russians poorly. There was a camp there, I don't remember in which city, where the Russians were collected. Then we were transferred to the American zone after the zones were divided. I was in the camp and waited until we were brought home. I was brought from the American zone to Brandenburg, that was the camp, in the last days of September. No, in the first days of September. I was in this camp for a whole month, waiting for the transport to Russia. And again a camp, and again a lot of people and bad food. A Russian camp, where the Russians waited for the return home. I was transported from Brandenburg back to Rostov in cattle cars, again like livestock, and arrived home. I had gone away on 6 October '42. I came back on 6 October '45. Some coincidence in the time.

Then the KGB interrogated us. There was an interrogation and everything that I said was recorded, where I had been, what I did. For a long time we weren't allowed to study. That was the rule for those who had been in Germany. The Germans had abducted us, and now our own people believed that we were enemies of the people. Now it began again. I was forced to lie again. I reached a decision. The KGB knew everything about me. I started saying that I hadn't been in Germany, so that I could find a good job. I didn't want to go to the factory. I could no longer even see a factory. I started a correspondence course, this manner of studying was possible. I graduated from a college of library sciences, and began working in the Geology Department as the head librarian of the geological and technical library. I worked there for thirty-five years, in one and the same place. I was very respected there. I collected a long career experience. And that is my whole life. When I was buried under the rubble, something in me was damaged and I couldn't have children anymore. I had a husband, he died, and now I live alone.

Like many other forced laborers in Cologne, Stepan Saika was brought to the eastern bank of the Rhine at the beginning of 1945, where he was forced to dig trenches. After liberation he spent a few months at a Displaced Persons Camp in Cologne-Wahn. Upon returning to the Soviet Union he was directly assigned to work in the Donbass coal-mining region. He first returned to his home village in 1949.

Kazimierz Tarnawski took up with a Polish exile unit under the command of the U.S. Army. For months they were shuttled through many cities and military bases around western Europe. He fell sick and was sent to an Allied military sanitarium.

Kazimierz Tarnawski: I was slightly wounded on the hand. I had my arm in a cast. The doctor sent me to the hospital in Marmeron, not far from Paris, and from Marmeron I was sent to a spa in Palermo. That was a military sanitarium, a lot of military there, also captured German soldiers. When

I came to myself again, I no longer thought about marrying, only strolling, only dancing with girls. They were beautiful girls. The nurses in the hospital, when I lay there, they were beautiful girls there. They only wanted Germans. My bed was like this, and here was a German soldier. It doesn't matter. They all helped us. We had good food there. There was theater there. Every day an orchestra played and you could dance on the dance floor with the nurses.

Many Americans left for America, and we kept serving here in Europe, in France and Italy. We Polish soldiers. We were afraid of the Russians. Poland was under Russian occupation and we were afraid. I had an offer to go to the Foreign Legion, when the Polish army was dissolved, to Suez, where the Jews were fighting with the Arabs, cholera! They told us: if you want to serve in the American army, then you have to learn English. After three years we would have had to sign a contract with the Americans. After three years service in the American army you directly get American citizenship. But there were very many Polish officers there … in the American army.

These were Polish squads, everything was Polish, but under American command. The food was American, money, everything. I was an American soldier, only with a white-and-red Polish flag, nothing more. We guarded an SS internment camp. A lot of them there spoke Polish. I stood with a rifle and guarded over the Germans, and then they sometimes came to me and begged for cigarettes. I often gave them cigarettes. Why not? Before the Germans had also given me some. They were also very young people. They were sixty thousand German soldiers, Heilbronn-on-the-Neckar, nice region there. We were also allowed to shoot, just like the Germans had, but we didn't do that. The Germans in Heilbronn, they could tell you that, if that interests you. They could say what the Poles did, they know it. Surely some of them are still alive, who could confirm it.

That was the situation. We could not go to Poland, go home. All the same I had a great yearning for Poland. I only wanted to go to Poland. I didn't want any American chocolate, cigarettes. I'd had enough. They sent us to every dangerous hole, some they had sent to Madagascar, some to Suez, the Americans and the English. That's how the work was. Everywhere it is best to put out the fire with a stranger's hands, not true? That is why … Some of our officers said: "Your place is in Poland, you are a Pole. You must train and work for your home." I listened to that. I went back....

Warsaw looked just like Cologne, totally destroyed. Like after the uprising, still no people on the street. But this was 1947! There were quarters of the city where there were no people, only candles burning at points where someone fell. Many people lived in cellars. I was in uniform. At many corners there were signs informing that a hundred or fifty people were shot there, at these I had to stand and salute. I met an older woman and she said to me: "My son, why have you come? Tomorrow you go to Siberia."

I went to Stettin, to work. I registered at the railroad technical institute. I wanted to train and work. I got an assignment and at that time I didn't know that my two sisters were already living in Stettin. I had a bit of money, dollars and marks, chocolate, cigarettes, and leather to sell. But the young are often reckless, and do not know what is coming. We were so reckless that we began to drink, with my friend. We were in fights a couple of times with the Russian soldiers stationed there. That is why I was arrested. There was an incident, a high-ranking Russian man was shot. Nobody knew who shot him, but it was obvious it had to be Poles. We were under suspicion because we wore the English uniforms and came from the West. It was July 1947. I had returned to Poland in May. I was arrested.

After an hour they struck me on the head with a pistol, dragged me into an auto in Stettin. Blood all over the place, and in that state they brought me to Potsdam. They had a central court there, NKVD. Thirteen people they arrested back then, all Polish soldiers from the Anders army, and they sent them all to Siberia. I was sentenced to death. Then I was taken from Potsdam. In June I was arrested and in October 1947 I was sentenced to death, but they commuted that to twenty-five years imprisonment.

It was already 1948, spring, Easter Sunday just then. We were taken on a train through Poland. We only moved at night, during the day we stood on the connecting tracks, and so people could approach us. There were many Germans with us, and Russian soldiers who had fought against Germans. They were all taken with us to Siberia. If a Russian soldier had vodka or beer with an American and he didn't get back to the barracks before curfew time, he got Siberia. Twenty-five years.

At the Polish-Soviet border, not far from Brest-Litovsk, a Russian officer tried to convince me to run out of the car.... The others tried to escape. They overwhelmed the soldiers guarding us, took their weapons. They were shot at, and they shot back. There was a very bad shoot-out. Many were killed. I lay on the floor. A dead man fell on me and that was my luck, that I wasn't shot. After that everyone got handcuffs. We were put in other cars and sent to Moscow. Lubjanka was the name of this prison....

With the transport I was sent from Moscow to Sverdlovsk (Urals). Perhaps I was there for a couple of months. That was already the end of 1948. I was then sent from Sverdlovsk back to Moscow. In Moscow I was in another prison, not Lubjanka this time, but Butynki. From Butynki-Moscow to Kirov, to Gorky on the Volga, from Gorky to the forest, to work. That was a Russian concentration camp. I got my number there, on the back and pants, cap. C428 was my number in the Soviet camp. In the fall of 1949 I went through Novosibirsk, Krasnoyarsk, to Taishent. Taishent is a city, a camp, which runs along about 200 kilometers, from Taishent to Brack. That is a line along which there were only camps and more camps, in every camp about 2,000 people. This kind of camp is called SPECLAGER, so-called OZERLAG, NWD, in Russian: *polititscheskij zakrytyj*. Then from Taishent to Brack on the Angara. I did everything. I worked in the brick factory. I built a railroad line along the Lena, the place and the river were called Lena. Everywhere was taiga.

So it went, until 1956. After Stalin died, in March 1953, something was already up. From then on everything got better. There were shops in the camp. We could grow our hair, no more shaved heads. We could buy ciga-rettes in the shop. Money we got too, a part of the money. A part was saved up for when someone was found innocent, or had his sentence up, so that we would get this money when we left. In July I went to the office of the camp commandant, three men and I. One of them still lives in Warsaw. We got an amnesty. I had twenty-five years and in 1956 I had worked for nearly ten. Every day you worked well was counted as two, as though you had worked there for two days. And so, although I had not yet been there for ten years, it meant that I already had sixteen years of labor. I was released before my time was up....

The Second World War ended for me on 19 December 1956. Polish sol-diers. I was brought to Biala Podlaska. There we got clothes, a thousand zlo-tys per person and a free train ticket that was good for a week. They announced our names on the radio, said that we had arrived, that were look-ing for our families. In Biala Podlaska there was a camp for those who had no contact to their families. My sister was in Stettin and she heard my name. She called my father, who lived at the time between Allenstein and Marien-burg. She said to my father: "Daddy, Kasimir is alive and he is back from the Soviet Union!"...

The meeting, finally, cannot be described. There was a feast, my sisters came from Stettin. One with the children, a girl. One daughter is married today, an engineer, she lives in the U.S., Lucyna, my niece. At that time they all came. My brother was a marine officer, he came from Danzig. We all met again. Then I told my father everything. Sometimes I had sent a card home from Germany while I was hiding. I spoke with my father then. For some-thing like three days we did not sleep, only vodka. We went to sleep, we were in bed, but after five minutes my father would come to me again and say: "Tell me please, how was that? That is not possible." He could hardly believe the story I told, so I had to repeat it, over and over. My father was married for the seventh time. His wife said: "Dear men, go to sleep already!"

After the war Ford Werke at first refused to re-hire Fritz Theilen.

Fritz Theilen: I got a letter from the commandant of the city, Colonel White, saying that they had to let me in. In August 1945 I was back and I went straight to Ford. I went to Ford and they didn't want to hire me, although they were hiring others. When I realized what was going on I went to the "Political Welfare Office," on Hansaring at that time. They sent me to Genter Strasse, where the English had their offices. The commandant of the city, he had his office at Allianz. I went there and they gave me a letter that Ford had to rehire me. But that was like running the gauntlet, back then. All the old Nazis were still [at Ford]. They had rehired a lot of our old trainers. We had twelve or fourteen trainers, apprentice trainers. They were all more or less old Nazis. There was hardly one there of whom I could definitely say he wasn't one! I had been beaten by them. The first time I came out of Gestapo arrest I was fair game, as far as they were concerned. Everyone wanted to show what a powerful man, what a great Nazi he was. They beat me but right. Then they had the cheek to come to me in 1947, when the de-Nazification began, to come to my house and ask me if I would vouch for their *Persilschein* ["certificate of blamelessness."] My mother threw them right out the door. After all that, to give them a signature!

I knew about their past. Sometimes I would show how fat D. had marched through the shop with his dagger, and everyone would crack up laughing. I knew it all! No one talked about that, they were too scared to do that, but I would talk about it. I called the child by its name. Always after that, when there was some argument with somebody, I would say: "Yeah, what do you still want, you old Nazi?" I would always let them know it. And they would do it the other way against me.

What would they say to you? Did they call you a Communist or what?

Fritz Theilen: No, no. "Traitor to the fatherland," that was always the kind of thing they said. I had been against the Nazis and I had been locked up for that reason, so to them I was a "traitor to the fatherland." And they always had their problems with that. As long as I was at Ford. Then I went away from Ford for nearly ten years. Only after all the Nazis were gone, around the end of the fifties, some people from Ford who knew me called me back in. My father was there again, and they said: "Come, the Nazis are gone, we can get him back again." And then I was there again, from 1960 on. It was different then. Although a few [Nazis] were still there, they kept themselves restrained. Said nothing more. Some were still hall managers, high executives, but you can't just abuse them without consequences. It wasn't easy, back then.

Was the Nazi era ever discussed at Ford?

Fritz Theilen: No, there was never a discussion about that. Never. That was a taboo. All the managers at that time at Ford, they were all Nazis. All of them. And they were known persons, like Z., W. of whom I spoke, S. who had been in the party, and—What was his name again? We called him "the friendly sir." Mr. Z. They were all Nazis. I know them still. When anything wrong was going on I would be there. When they harassed people I would say: "The old Nazis, just like back then!" Then it was too late.

The old barracks from the labor camp were still used for a long time. Germans lived in there. A colleague of mine had lived in there, a former Ford apprentice. He had been a prisoner of war of the Russians, and he was alone when he came back. I asked him: "Where do you live?" He said: "In the barracks." I said, "What, in the barracks?" "Yes, in the Russian camp." I said: "That can't be true!"

Did you ever get any kind of compensation?

Inna Kulagina: Yes, '92. Only after there was perestroika, Yeltsin.... I went to Belgium in '86. I visited Elsa there, it was not easy. The KGB interrogated and observed me because I was going abroad, but they let me travel. And there I found out that Elsa's Belgian husband gets a pension. I returned to Russia and wrote to the embassy of the Federal Republic of Germany. I asked: "Why aren't we getting paid?" They wrote back: "Your government relinquished compensations in 1953." I thought, "*Ai yai*. Oh well, that's it then." Then came perestroika, and Yeltsin and the government submitted new demands. I was apparently not the only one writing letters. They reached an agreement that those who had been minors [during the time of forced labor] would receive a certain sum for having worked in Germany. Kohl had come up with an amount for compensation: 400,000 marks or 400 million marks, I don't know anymore. For the Ukraine, Belarus and Russia. Then they divided it, and divided it. For all the time that I worked there, I was supposed to get 1,300 marks. This sum goes only to minors. I have still not received any money to this day [September 1995]. Our rulers have apparently put the money in the bank to earn interest on it. The people are thus betrayed, and I have gotten nothing. When Yeltsin came to power, we received this ID. It reads: "The holder of this ID has the right to benefits and privileges accruing to those formerly imprisoned in fascist camps as minors and so on...." That was '94. Before I had a different ID, but with nothing on it about minor-age prisoners. Later I was put in that group. You can ride the train and the street car for free. And fifty per cent off the rent. And what else? I may get some money. When exactly, nobody knows.

When it was made known that we had been, so to speak, pardoned, I went to the KGB. In '92. I got a certificate then. When I went to them, I told them everything. Everything had been kept by them. They compared to see if my statement today matched the one I made back then. Then they gave me a certificate stating that I had been in Germany from then to then, and that I had taken no actions against our country, against Russia. And then they gave me this ID.

In the last months a lot of people have started writing letters. For example in the Ukraine no one has gotten anything yet. I asked them. A few people there have got something. A lot of people get invited in groups and then get paid. They are probably waiting that we all die soon and that some money is left over. (Laughs). I suffered under Russian bombings, there was bombing there, Rostov was bombed. Under the Germans I suffered, America bombed me out and I ended up in the hospital. When I returned to Russia I suffered again. No one wanted to take me, I had to lie. *Das ist meine Geschichte.* No, no, my fate.

What effect did your time as a forced laborer have on the rest of your life?

Inna Kulagina: Of course it made a mess of my life in many ways, because it was believed that I had, so to speak, worked for the Germans. Although I was taken away by force. And for a long time, until perestroika, I never told anyone about it. I would not have been allowed to work at the Geology Department. Raw materials—oil and gas—were considered secret matters. I concealed and lied. And only through my work did I prove that I am a true patriot, that I am not an enemy, as was thought of us at first. I was very respected at work, I did a lot of charitable work. At work things were good for me, but by our standards I still hardly earned anything. And the charitable work allowed me to go on spa holidays, we had these leisure resorts.

I mostly arranged events by lay artists' groups at geological organizations. Then we organized these festivals and chose which groups performed best. I had no children and therefore I was burdened constantly with charitable activities.... One day I read in the newspaper *Pravda* that a woman had come here to Cologne. But there was no exact address given. I sent this notice to Elsa and said: "Can you perhaps find out whether more people are going to be invited?" Elsa wrote here, five years no answer. This year finally she called me up: "Inna, I was invited!" And I said: "And me?" Then she wrote me a letter, I wrote a letter to the Bürgermeister and then got an invitation. I wanted to see Elsa again and I thought: "What luck!"

You know, it's already fifty years past. The memories are no longer so intense. I only couldn't stand it anymore [today] when I saw those stairs, where the foreman had hit me. Over at Ford nothing remains from that time, only very little. Only this hall is still there, or this department. I don't want to gloss over anything, but I also want to say the truth, what happened to us there, that we were hit in this way there, that we nearly died. It was very hard. Now you tell about it, and it is hard to express with words what you went through. It helped that we were young. Then you can go through something like that more easily.

Nadia Shubrawa: Three years, what should anyone say? And so my youth went by, like the nightingale leaves in winter, my hair became gray, oh how sorry I am for my youth (laughs). In our life there was something to remember. We had such times in our lives. Hunger ruled in '33, hunger also ruled from '45 to '47, after the war ... I brought twins into the world. My husband fell sick, he went to his brother in Vilnius, in Lithuania to take a treatment for three months. He left me alone with four children: one born '47, the daughter, the boy born '49, and the twins born in '51. They said he had tuberculosis in the bones, there would be no cure. He went to his brother, he was examined there. They said that he had tuberculosis of the bones, the "lubrication" had dried up, but they gave him paraffin and everything was okay again, he even worked. I was alone with four children, there was nothing to cook. I bore a lot of grief, a lot. It was hard, after the war there were no diapers, no clothes, nothing. And they got big, and now one has been called out to Chernobyl. Do you know Chernobyl?

Yvan Thibaut: I became a priest. First I will tell you how I recognized the calling. I already thought about it as a child of six, seven. Afterwards I forgot about it and my parents thought it was just a childish thing. Then, when I was in Buchenwald ... One day, we were at roll call and it took so long. We were there for hours and it snowed, and I complained about the Germans. Abbé Cléton said to me: "But why are you complaining?" And Roger Pannier said to me: "Why don't you make the sacrifice?" Then I accepted that as my sacrifice, and in that moment I experienced a fantastic joy and a presence, really nearly a physical presence of our Lord, of Jesus. That was as though, as though he came inside me and gave me power and courage. So much so that I was ready for everything, for everything. You would have to say to me in the end: "Hey, hey, don't exaggerate." Everything, everything there was, I would have given up my bread, I gave everything. I don't know, I was happy, I was content. Such a joy I have never again experienced, except on the day of my ordination, that is the truth. Otherwise I never again experienced such a joy. That cannot be explained, that is an inner peace, but so deep, and it must glow, it must be sung everywhere, I could have sung: "The Lord is good, the Lord is beautiful," really. Now I am no longer like that, not at all like that. That was at any rate the moment, in which I was convinced I would become a priest, whatever the difficulties....

Returning to Cologne today, that did not especially scare me. What did disturb me a bit, was, I said to myself that I would see the places again where I had met many comrades of my age, who are no longer there now. That was hard for me, because they should have been here with me. But I am also very happy to be in Cologne again. What saddens me is that I also won't meet the Germans again who helped me during my time of deportation in Cologne. Especially my foreman at the lathe shop at Ford in Niehl. I have a very good, really outstanding memory of him, because I taught him French and he taught me German. He invited me to his house, which was a chance every time to get better food than in the camp.

Anna Nesteruk: [May God protect my children and grandchildren from the horror of the last war. Neither I nor my people have the right to blame the German people. In every nation there are good and bad people.

[We also had moments of happiness. A German supervisor would give us a piece of bread or his buttered roll. Those were moments of boundless joy and gratitude. But there were other moments, as when we were humiliated and called "Russian pigs," or when we were struck with truncheons.

[Today I am retired, my pension is rather low although I worked for more than forty years in the collective. The money is just enough for bread, I don't even want to mention clothing. My husband is dead, I live alone, my health is failing, my legs hurt, many maladies besides that, but I am not laying down my hands. From morning until night I look after the house alone and take care of the garden. That is my whole life. I am grateful to you that you have remembered us.... If you do provide humanitarian help through your center, then please send it to an old person!]

Under the statement validating the authenticity of her interview, Inna Kulagina wrote:

I am in agreement with the interview. After fifty years everything is smoothed out, and hunger, beatings and injuries are forgotten, but it will always remain in memory that I was not Kulagina Inna, but <u>No. 987</u> with the "OST" insignia on my chest.

CHAPTER 6

MEMORY AND LIABILITY

For few groups did 1945 pose more of a new beginning, and a challenge, than for the foreign forced laborers and concentration camp prisoners who were liberated by the arrival of Allied troops in Germany.[1] So many of them had lost their families or friends, or suffered personal injury. Most of them had nothing. As displaced persons, they were returned in the first months after the war to their home countries, where long years of fighting and occupation had wreaked devastation. Those who went back to what became known as Western Europe had little to hide. They were accepted, their stories were believed by their fellow citizens, they could re-enter society. For the majority of forced laborers returning to Soviet-dominated Eastern Europe, going home was not as easy. In the Stalinist world-view, they were seen as having collaborated with the enemy, whatever the coercion. Prisoners of war and male civilians were especially subject to police measures. Many thousands were sent to the gulags after returning, like Kazimierz Tarnawski. The largest number of former forced laborers therefore fell silent. To avoid discrimination, they tried to hide their experience, like Inna Kulagina. As for compensation, or even payment of just wages, as we shall see only a small number of Reichseinsatz laborers from Eastern Europe ever received payments of any kind.

As the Allies moved towards total victory over the Reich, the United States, Britain, and the Soviet Union in 1944 and 1945 debated the price Germany should pay for its actions as the aggressor. All sides agreed that the main perpetrators of Nazi crime would be put to trial before an International Military Tribunal (IMT), located in Nuremberg starting in 1945; that German property abroad would be confiscated; and that Germany would be made to pay the high costs of the military occupation. The Soviets, and for a time the French, favored state-to-state war reparations in kind, to be taken out of current German production, or by dismantling industrial plant and moving it to countries Germany had attacked. The United States, as a territory nearly undamaged in the war, preferred financial reparations. This entailed keeping Germany economically self-sufficient and hence solvent. The Americans were especially keen on expropriating the patents for Germany's technological marvels, such as rockets and television.

At the Potsdam Conference of July and August 1945, the U.S., Britain and the USSR agreed to divide Germany into zones of occupation. Each victor nation would be free to draw reparations in kind from its own zone. The Soviets would receive 25 percent of the industrial plant dismantled in the Western zones. Reparations for Poland would fall under Soviet authority. Most importantly, the Western allies recognized the new borders of Poland and Germany, as already redrawn by the Soviets in a fait accompli.[2]

The Potsdam agreement was the first formal step towards the official division of Europe. The Soviet Union began to plunder the eastern German industrial base. U.S. policy makers gradually adopted the idea of rebuilding western Germany as a major industrial power, even if this meant abandoning the Roosevelt Administration's plans for reforming the highly cartelized German corporate structure. For a few months, the Western Allies shipped plant from western Germany—including a production line from Opel Russelsheim—to the Soviets. But in March 1946, the U.S. occupation control council suspended all industrial dismantling measures in the American zone and stopped delivering machinery to the east.

The subsequent confrontation between the Soviet and Western camps ended negotiations on further reparations from western Germany to the Soviet Union and its satellites. The Federal Republic of Germany, founded in 1949, for many years did not maintain diplomatic relations with Eastern bloc countries, and first established relations with the Soviet Union in 1955. The German Democratic Republic was founded in 1949 as an officially anti-fascist state. By its own definition, it later declared itself not liable for further reparations or compensations for Nazi crime. In fact, by 1953 East German citizens had put up the highest reparations sum per capita of any Axis territory, albeit mostly to the Soviet Union, and according to the Stalinist state's schemes. Once the two Germanys, each based on competing ideological visions, became the main theater for the Cold War, Soviet policy towards the GDR changed. The Soviet Union and the Moscow-directed government in Poland in 1953 *as states* agreed to forego all further reparations claims against Germany. However, this implicitly left out the issue of restitutions to individuals.

The Federal Republic had met its initial reparation payments by incurring debt. Payments on that were regulated in the London Debt Accords of February 1953, to which Eastern European countries were not party. Two clauses in the accords implicitly suspended restitution payments, for forced labor or other Nazi crimes, to individuals in countries with which West Germany did not have diplomatic relations, until such time as a final peace treaty for the Second World War was achieved. The former "Ostarbeiter" and Polish forced laborers, representing the majority of potential forced-labor restitution claimants, were thus barred from compensation.

The Federal Republic as the legal successor to the Third Reich negotiated additional state-to-state "global" reparation and restitution agreements with Israel (in 1952) and various countries in Western Europe (in 1959 to 1964). These governments in turn were free to use the funds to provide aid or compensation for wartime injuries and damages to individuals among their nationals.

In the years after the London Debt Accords, West Germany was able to rapidly pay off its state-to-state reparation obligations and take off in an "economic miracle." The Transition Treaty (Überleitungsvertrag) between West Germany and the Western allies, which took effect in 1955, obligated the FRG to make further arrangements for individual restitutions to the victims of Nazi persecution.[3] These obligations were covered under the West German federal compensations law of 1956, known in German as the Bundesentschädigungsgesetz (BEG). BEG broadly defined as claimants those individuals who had sustained damages "on the basis of race, religion and world-view, or due to political imprisonment."[4] Further determination of who actually qualified was left to West German courts and agencies. Among the groups subject to persecution under the Reich who were excluded as BEG claimants over the next decades by court rulings or official interpretation were gypsies, homosexuals, objectors to military service, and supporters of a totalitarian regime, i.e. communists. The Romany and Sinti were later recognized.

The largest group excluded from compensation claims under BEG was that of forced laborers from Eastern Europe. Adopting the logic established in the London Debt Accords, a "diplomatic clause" in BEG excluded residents of countries with which the FRG did not maintain relations.[5]

The final deadline for filing claims under BEG expired in 1969. At any rate, the continuing payments to non-Eastern European claimants under BEG became the single largest category of restitution payments from the Federal Republic to the victims of Nazi crime. Of course, suffering and injury cannot be measured or made good in money, but the payments drawn from West German taxpayers were by no means insignificant, as Table 4 shows.

These figures must be treated with care. The German finance ministry keeps a running total, mixing deutschemarks at the far higher 1953 values with payments made in the 1990s. Aside from that, the differences among the various types of payments have been extreme, and work out to wildly different totals actually paid to individuals. These might range from absurdly low pocket change to one-time payments of several thousand DM, or modest but steady pensions. (No restitution payments were made to the Czech Republic during the round of payments to Eastern European countries in the early 1990s after the wall fell, because of German counterclaims on properties confiscated from ethnic Germans expelled from the Czech Sudetenland after the war.) The different treatment of different groups, claimants, and countries has been related more to international and West German political circumstances than to the real degree of damage suffered by individuals. In other words, restitutions for the victims of Nazi

TABLE 4: German Restitution and Reparation Payments after 1945

A. Combined state-to-state reparation payments, 1945–1953 not including costs of military occupation in 1938 dollars

	Total	Per Capita
Western German zones, FRG	$4.8 billion	$103.10
Eastern German zone, GDR	$11.4 billion	$621.40

Source: Fisch (1992), 319.

B. Post-1953 West German restitution payments, nominal DM Running totals: no adjustment for inflation!

Estimated total as of 1 January 1998	102 billion DM

Includes (among other items):

Global compensation payment to Israel, including arms shipments, under 1952 treaty:	3 billion DM
1952 payment to Jewish Claims Council (JCC) to aid displaced European Jews settling outside Israel:	450 million DM
Payments to individual claimants found valid under BEG, 1956–1997 (continuing, future payments estimated at 24 billion DM):	78.4 billion DM
Other domestic payments to individuals under the General Consequences of War Act or the Social Insurance Compensations Law (WGSVG):	est. 12 billion DM
Payments to 12 Western European states under treaties reached in 1959 to 1964:	1 billion DM
Payments to Poland in the 1970s for victims of medical experiments, and to help defray previous Polish government pension payments to Nazi victims:	1.3 billion DM
Payments to funds in Poland and CIS states for compensations to victims of Nazi persecution (not specifically forced labor) in agreements since 1991:	1.8 billion DM
Further charitable payments to the Baltic states in the 1990s:	6 million DM
Payments to Albania, Bulgaria, Romania, and Slovakia, combined, in 1997 and 1998:	80 million DM

Sources: FRG Ministry of Finance; *Die Welt,* 4 October 1998; *Entschädigung für NS-Zwangsarbeit,* 49–50.

Comparison:

Estimated total of payments to injured German civilians and soldiers under the West German War Victims' Welfare Act (KOV), 1949 to 1996	395 billion DM

Source: FRG Ministry of Finance; *Entschädigung für NS-Zwangsarbeit* (1998), 49.

crimes have often been the chip in a game of international poker among countries, parties, and bureaucracies, often to the detriment of the real claimants–as we will now demonstrate using the case of compensations for forced labor.

After the treaties of 1952 to 1955, the potential forced-labor compensation claimants, especially those from Eastern Europe, faced a complicated and contradictory political and legal situation. However, the West German judicial history with regard to compensations up to the 1990s is easy to summarize. Only a tiny minority of forced labor claimants not recognized (for other reasons) under BEG succeeded in getting any form of even symbolic compensation, either from the West German government, or from a former employer of forced laborers. On six occasions, companies that lost forced-labor compensations cases at the local level, or that came under public pressure, negotiated agreements out of court with the Jewish Claims Council (JCC). Companies that pursued the appeals process invariably got favorable rulings from higher courts, at the latest from the German Supreme Court (BGH).

West German governments, backed by BGH rulings, for many years held that claims from Eastern Europe were too early, as allowable legal action on these had been suspended by the London Debt Accords. At the same time, forced labor claims filed by West German nationals were turned back for having missed the FRG's three-year statute of limitations in civil cases, which would have run out in 1952, three years after the country was founded. In short, a forced labor compensations claim could be too early, or it could be too late, but it was never at the right time.[6]

The first well-known compensation case against an employer of wartime forced labor was filed by the former KZ laborer Norbert Wollheim in 1952 against I.G. Farbenindustrie in Liquidation, the legal leftover of the IG Farben combine in receivership.

IG Farben's leading role in the economy of the Third Reich, and in slave labor and genocide at Auschwitz, was explored in a 1947 IMT trial of the chemical empire's leading executives. They were indicted for planning, preparing and leading a war of aggression, robbery and plunder, imposition of slave labor, and the killing of civilians, prisoners of war, and KZ prisoners.[7] Nine Farben executives were found guilty of plunder and spoliation of property in occupied territory; four of them additionally of imposing slave labor and inhumane treatment on civilians and prisoners of war. Among the latter was Carl Krauch, who chaired the IG Farben directorate, and who after 1940 also served as deputy to Heinrich Albert on the Ford Werke directorate.[8] The evidence against him included documents proving that he had lobbied insistently with Reich authorities to get more KZ laborers for Farben's operations at Auschwitz.[9]

In their defense before the international tribunal, the IG Farben war crimes defendants forwarded two claims[10] that IG Farben in liquidation later also employed during the 1953 Wollheim compensations case. The defense argued, first, that responsibility for decisions to use KZ labor lay with the SS, the Nazi Party, and the German Reich. Compensation claims could therefore only be made valid against the "legal successor of the Third Reich," i.e. the West German government. Second, the defendants in both cases claimed that the situation of the KZ prisoners was actually improved through their removal from a main KZ camp and use as forced laborers at industrial workplaces:

> I do not accept the claim that an unusual number of KZ camp prisoners who were employed by industry therefore died. On the contrary, the people were happy when they got out into industrial companies, because they received reasonable care and a chance to survive, which was not granted to them in the KZ extermination camps, as is well known.[11]

This argument was not accepted in the IG Farben war crimes trial. In 1952, Wollheim was also able to refute it by presenting witnesses who testified that IG Farben's forced laborers worked under a constant fear that they would succumb to mistreatment and undernourishment. Wollheim won his case. However, a simultaneous suit against IG Farben filed by Polish forced laborers was rejected on the grounds that IG Farben had acted only as an instrument of the Third Reich.[12]

IG Farben in liquidation appealed the Wollheim ruling. The appeals court decided to wait out the results of negotiations with the newly founded JCC. After years of negotiations, the Farben successor in December 1957 agreed to pay 30 million DM in compensations to former KZ laborers, of which 27 million DM was to be distributed through the JCC. This became the pattern in the six cases, up to 1998, in which a company agreed to pay compensations for KZ labor—almost always through the JCC—to cover claims from former KZ laborers found valid.

The total specified in Table 5 represents less than one-half percent of the restitution and reparation payments to wartime victims financed by German taxpayers in the same period. None of the six companies recognized a legal liability. The payments were presented as voluntary humanitarian acts. No payments were made to the majority of civilian forced laborers who had not been deployed through KZ camps. No other companies came forward with voluntary restitutions for forced labor before 1998, with the exception of Daimler-Benz in 1988.[13]

Well into the 1980s, the legal and political situation allowed the vast majority of companies who had employed forced laborers during the war to simply ignore the history, to keep silent, or, if forced by circumstances, to deny, to stonewall. Even in the early 1980s, speakers of the affected companies still felt secure presenting defenses such as the following:[14]

> There is no profit in working someone to death. Perhaps this was an attempt to save these people, so that they could be kept working longer.

> *Peter-Jürgens Lüders, Siemens, 1984*

TABLE 5: Company Restitution and Other Payments, 1945–1997

Company[1]	Total Payment through JCC in million DM	Per Claimant
I.G. Farbenindustrie (December 1957)	27.8	2500 DM for six months slave labor; 5000 DM for more than six months; 6500 claimants total
Krupp	10.0	3300 DM per person
AEG	4.0	1800 DM per person
Siemens	7.0	3500 DM per person
Rheinmetall (May 1966)[2]	2.5	1700 DM per person
Feldmühle Nobel (January 1986)	5.0	2000 DM per person
Total	**56.3**	

[1]Does not include the Daimler-Benz payment of 1988.
[2]A military contractor, Rheinmetall entered into negotiations with JCC after the Pentagon threatened to cancel a $50 million artillery order.

Source: JCC, as in *Entschädigung für NS-Zwangsarbeit,* 46.

In a giant operation–I think Krupp employed a half-million people–it can't be avoided, especially given language difficulties and the stress of war, and the aerial attacks, that a supervisor or a foreman may sometimes resort to blows.

> *Otto Kranzbühler, lawyer for Krupp, 1984*

I think the time for feelings of guilt and pangs of conscience, it's time to forget all that, now finally.

> *Helmut Eppe, Mauser-Werke, 1982*

Forced Labor in the Third Reich: Volkswagen intends to do justice to a historic obligation through public education work and charitable projects. No legal possibility for individual compensation: The legal successor to the Third Reich is the Federal Republic of Germany.... Volkswagen orients its actions to justice and the law. Under the interpretation of the law applicable until now, [compensation] claims can only be posed against the state.

> *Volkswagen press release*

The last statement actually dates from June 1998, just weeks before Volkswagen's historic reversal of its position.[15]

Time meanwhile took care of a majority of potential claimants through the "biological solution." But the legal, political, and cultural edifice that blocked compensations claims for so many years did finally crumble in the 1990s, in part because of developments in historical scholarship, but primarily because of the transformation in Eastern Europe.

LOOKING BACK on postwar German historiography, the historian Bernd Faulenbach in 1987 wrote: "It may be very roughly stated that [German historians'] perspective on the Nazi era was at first nearly exclusively centered on Hitler." During the postwar period the focus of research moved gradually from leaders and policy makers to political and social structures and processes. "In recent years the local and everyday history has drawn the primary interest."[16]

This shift in scholarly interest reflected the larger development in West German society, away from a culture of leader worship and denial; and the gradual passing from power of a generation of politicians who had fought in the war, or who had been among the Nazi regime's supporters and perpetrators. In Germany, the global protest movements of the late 1960s were played out specifically in a confrontation by the generation of the "sons and daughters" against that of "the fathers," who were still considered culpable for the Nazi past.

Starting in the late 1970s and early 1980s, parallel to the emergence of Holocaust Studies in the United States, German historians turned away from the mainly academic debates that had dominated the 1970s. These were largely extensions of Cold War ideologies, and often posed misleading or simplistic questions.[17] A return to the depth of documentary detail of the old Allied investigations and trials was encouraged by the release, starting in the late 1960s, of thousands of documents previously kept confidential by Allied authorities.

The new ideal was hands-on, bottom-up, and location-oriented. It gave greater emphasis to town studies, to the sites of Nazi crimes, to oral accounts, and to social phenomena in addition to the movements of armies and statesmen.[18] Scholars "rediscovered" groups of victims who had been forgotten, such as the Romany and Sinti, the mentally handicapped, and homosexuals. The breakthrough with regard to forced labor was achieved starting in the mid-1980s with the work of Ulrich Herbert. A long series of studies, beginning at that time, focused on the Nazi-era histories of specific companies.

One of the first new company histories to gather attention was *Das Daimler-Benz Buch*. Planning to commemorate the 100th year of its existence during 1986 and 1987, Daimler-Benz AG began gearing up the celebrations well in advance. As the milestone approached, however, the company's publicity was disrupted by recurrent press about Daimler's wartime use of forced labor. Daimler therefore commissioned the business research center Gesellschaft für Unternehmensgeschichte (GUG) to write a history of the company under the Third Reich.[19] A left-leaning foundation in Hamburg, the Stiftung für Sozialgeschichte des 20. Jahrhunderts, thereupon set out to refute what they claimed was GUG's sanitized version of history in *Das Daimler Benz-Buch*[20] and a sister volume of primary documents. GUG itself was ultimately moved to issue a revised account of Daimler-Benz's history.[21] The bad press about Daimler's wartime involvements did not let up.

Finally, in 1988, the company moved to improve its damaged public relations image through a voluntary payment. This focused as narrowly as possible on Jewish KZ labor, the worst of all Nazi forced-labor crimes, without considering the majority of civilian non-KZ forced laborers in Reichseinsatz. Daimler made available to the JCC a sum of 20 million DM, with stipulations that this did not constitute a recognition of legal liability. The funds were earmarked exclusively for the support of old-age and nursing homes in regions where large numbers of former forced laborers resided.[22]

This case demonstrated that the findings of scholarship, combined with the press, could affect a company's policy towards forced labor restitution claims.[23] Following Daimler's payment, a number of companies, including Volkswagen and Deutsche Bank, began to sponsor research into their histories, even to fund their own historical institutes.

Meanwhile, the world was turning on its head. Repression failed to tame the uprising of Polish civil society against Communist rule. Gorbachev came to power in Moscow with a program of glasnost and perestroika. The former forced laborers of Eastern Europe could finally come out into the open. In the late 1980s they established large associations to pursue their interests. The Polish association of victims of Nazi crimes, founded in 1987, numbered 700,000 members by 1996. It claimed that 2,460,000 Polish citizens had been used as forced laborers under Reichseinsatz, of whom 137,000 had died during the war.[24] The later Ukrainian association of former forced laborers took in 650,000 claims applications, and by 1996 had narrowed these down to 540,000 well-documented cases.[25]

An important cycle of anniversaries dating from the Second World War, commemorating the passing of fifty years, began quietly in September 1989. It coincided with the end of what had been called the postwar world. In the two years that followed, the bipolar international order that had emerged after 1945 underwent a radical transformation. Six European countries overthrew Soviet control. Under the 2+4 Treaty of 1990, reached between the FRG, the GDR, and the four occupation powers, East Germany was allowed to join a sovereign Federal Republic. In December 1991, the Soviet Union was dissolved into its fifteen constituent republics. That month, the countries of the European Union signed the Maastricht Treaty, embarking upon an ambitious course of integration, currency union, and expansion. There followed much discussion of a worldwide economic process usually called globalization, and of a corresponding new international order.

The wartime Allied powers ceremoniously withdrew their remaining token occupation forces from Germany in the summer of 1994. There followed a final wave of fifty-year anniversary ceremonies, held through the summer of 1995 in capitals and at sites of war events around the globe. That year, anyone who was twenty at the end of the war entered their seventies. The political end of the postwar era seemed to foreshadow the passing of the Second World War from living memory. As we know now, the combination of perseverance on the part of former forced laborers who never gave up their claims, the opening in Eastern Europe, the end of the Cold

War, and the new historical research instead led to a series of international confrontations over restitutions for the living victims of Nazi-era crimes.

ONE DAY IN SEPTEMBER 1995, six women and two men, all in their seventies and eighties, arrived at the gates of the Ford Werke car plant in Cologne. They were former forced laborers. Fifty years after the war, the mayor of Cologne had invited them to return for a visit at the city's expense. The program, put together by city and private organizations, was supposed to include a look at the visitors' erstwhile workplace. At first, however, they were barred from entering the Ford Werke grounds in the accompaniment of journalists. They refused to be turned away. A city representative negotiated with company executives. Finally, the gates to factory Hall A were opened for the entire group. Factory tour guides were called upon to escort the guests around the shop floor, just as they would any other group of visitors (seven of the visitors are among the interview partners in Chapter 5; see Photo Set C).

The men and women moved within the rattle and din of workers and machines, searching for remnants of anything they remembered. Deeply moved, they were escorted by Ford Werke executives to a conference room. There, they were presented with sales-video tributes to the latest Ford models, cars with powerful engines and comfortable features. Elsa Iwanowa-de Meyer, who had settled in Belgium after the war, later described her feelings to a BBC film crew: "They didn't want to speak with us at all. They gave us nothing, nothing other than this pin." In the film, she holds up a badge with the Ford logo.[26]

Amid the motions of nations and sweep of abstractions, history begins with stubborn details. The badge, most likely the innocent gesture of a tour guide doing her job, was one of those details. Elsa Iwanowa perceived it as a final indignity.

The next year brought a surprising reversal in the German legal situation. The losing plaintiffs in two KZ labor claims cases, originally filed in 1990 and 1992, had followed the appeals process up to the German Supreme Court, the BGH, in 1993. BGH deliberated for an incredible three years before returning both cases to the Bonn regional court and asking for a new ruling. The Bonn court ruled in May 1996 that the 2+4 Treaty fulfilled the functions of a peace treaty for the Second World War, and thus obviated the clause in the London Debt Accords that had prevented individual restitutions for forced labor since 1953.[27] With restitution issues in mind, the German side in the 2+4 negotiations had in 1990 insisted that the treaty not be called a "peace treaty." Legal experts interpreted all this as meaning that the statute of limitations for civil cases first became active with the May 1996 ruling. Assuming that, a three-year window of opportunity for filing new group and individual claims to take advantage of the incipient new situation was open until May 1999.

Enter the Swiss security guard. One night in January 1997, at the offices of the Swiss UBS bank, the watchman Christoph Meili discovered and rescued a large number of wartime documents that had been set up for shredding. For releasing these stubborn details to the press, he was fired. In Switzerland, he and his family were subjected to anonymous hounding, so that they later felt compelled to move to the United States.

The documents saved by Meili showed that after the war, UBS had kept the abandoned accounts of Jewish victims of the Nazi genocide without searching for or informing the possible heirs. There followed many months of negotiations between the major Swiss banks and Holocaust claims groups. The two sides could not agree on a global sum to compensate account holders and their heirs.

In the United States, the Swiss banks were slapped with class actions represented by the high-powered lawyers Ed Fagan and Michael Hausfeld. Threats of a boycott were raised. The State of New York threatened to impose sanctions. Senator Alfonse D'Amato, Republican of New York, was especially insistent in public statements favoring a high settlement. Finally, in August 1998, the Swiss banks more than doubled their previous "final offer" of compensations. A settlement of $1.25 billion was reached.[28]

The Swiss episode roused great international attention and became the prelude to subsequent controversies involving the mostly German-owned former employers of KZ labor and forced laborers under Reichseinsatz.

Several months before the Swiss banks gave in, on 3 March 1998, Elsa Iwanowa was listed as the first plaintiff in a class action filed with the U.S. federal district court in New Jersey. The lawsuit, backed by the well known Milberg Weiss firm in New York, accused Ford Motor Company of complicity with the Nazi regime, and of willing participation in the German Reich's forced labor program. The main argument was based on "unjust enrichment." Assuming the case cleared the technical hurdles of jurisdiction and statutes of limitation, then the plaintiff needed only to show that Ford derived financial benefit from the use of forced labor and never returned that benefit. Then the company would be required to pay compensation. That would be the case even if Ford could prove it had no influence over wartime decisions at its Cologne subsidiary.

In their first two motions to dismiss, the Ford lawyers did not contest the accusations. They instead argued that the court had no jurisdiction over what was rightfully a matter for international treaties and negotiations among sovereign states. Whatever happened in Germany during the war, it was not for a judge in New Jersey to decide fifty-three years later.[29]

Iwanowa vs. Ford was followed in the spring and summer of 1998 by a series of class action claims in U.S. courts against the avatars of German business: Daimler-Benz (now DaimlerChrysler), BMW, Siemens, Bosch, Bayer, Volkswagen, Hochtief, Degussa, and many dozens more, even the Hugo Boss clothing firm, where forced laborers once sewed uniforms for the SS.[30] The U.S. lawyers in these cases, among them leading civil trial attorneys such as Hausfeld, Fagan, and Melvyn Weiss, cooperated openly with German counterparts who pursued the new wave of compensations claims in Germany set off by the May 1996 Bonn court ruling, among them

Michael Witti and the perhaps aptly named Klaus von Münchhausen, who had organized group claims against Volkswagen.

As many as sixteen leading German companies by September 1998 entered into informal talks aimed at forging a common strategy with regard to the claims. As reported by the German press, these were organized informally under the umbrella of the main German industrial association, known as BDI.[31] Two fronts formed among the companies. Some were open to the idea of establishing a joint fund to transact individual compensations, assuming this could be bound to guarantees of freedom from further legal liabilities in the United States. According to the reports, these companies were led by the Volkswagen AG; as "mass producers," they felt vulnerable to potential boycotts on the American consumer market. Other companies, said to be led by the major German steel producers, insisted on taking a hard line against all claims. The reports characterized this group as business-to-business suppliers who were relatively immune to boycott.

The same reports revealed that Ford and General Motors were sitting in on the talks as observers.

A few weeks after the Swiss banks settlement, in early September 1998, the directorate of Volkswagen AG convened in Wolfsburg to approve a plan, in the works since June 1998, to set up a humanitarian aid fund for the Nazi Volkswagenwerk's former forced laborers. The funding of 20 million DM was intended to provide 10,000 DM to each valid claimant. Volkswagen emphasized that its announcement of the fund did not imply or entail a legal obligation. BMW and Siemens soon followed suit and set up similar single-company fund schemes.

Volkswagen's move carried unusual political weight, because 20 percent of Volkswagen AG shares are owned by the German state of Lower Saxony. The state premier therefore sits on the company's supervisory board. In 1998, the governor of Lower Saxony (since 1990) was none other than Gerhard Schröder of the Social Democratic Party (SPD), the man heavily favored as candidate for chancellor in the German national elections of 27 September. Schröder was reported to be on exceptionally good terms with the VW chief executive, Ferdinand Piëch. It was even said that the company's public relations director, Klaus Kocks, had come up with Schröder's campaign slogan: "The Power of the New."

Already in June 1998, Schröder had expressed in general terms his support for a company-financed global compensations fund. His presence in the background of the Volkswagen fund decision was interpreted as a campaign promise to finally settle the restitutions question. By contrast, the incumbent chancellor, Helmut Kohl of the Christian Democratic Union (CDU), was repeatedly quoted that he would "not open the restitutions cash-box again." In the election, Schröder's SPD won a plurality of the seats in the Bundestag, and formed a majority together with Alliance 90/The Greens as junior partner. In the past, the Green party had often called for a federally financed forced labor compensations fund.

The chancellor-elect held his first formal meeting with German industrial leaders on 21 October 1999, to discuss the issue of forced labor restitutions with the chief executives of twelve large corporations facing U.S. class actions. As a moral gesture, not a legal obligation, the men agreed in principle to establish a joint federal and company fund. Other companies remained aloof. Although no agreement had been reached with the claimant side, a number of headlines promptly put the settlement in the present tense: "Firms Compensate Forced Laborers."

The Schröder government initially offered to coordinate the fund without providing state payments. The companies at first refused to specify an amount they were willing to put up, and instead called upon the plaintiffs' lawyers to drop their cases in advance, and demanded U.S. guarantees that German companies would not face further legal claims after a settlement. An idea circulated among the companies that claimants from Eastern Europe were entitled to about three-quarters less than those from the U.S. and Israel, because the buying power of the deutschemark is much stronger in Eastern Europe. Poland and the Ukraine protested, and this particular form of differential compensation was later dropped.

A coalition of a dozen companies in late 1998 and early 1999 set up the legal prerequisites of a humanitarian aid fund to compensate former forced laborers. These companies and the German government, at first represented by Schröder's chief of staff, Bodo Hombach, entered into negotiations with eleven countries, including Poland, the Ukraine, Russia, Belarus, the Czech Republic, the United States and Israel, and with the various Eastern European forced-labor claims associations and the Jewish Claims Conference. The U.S. negotiator was Stuart Eizenstat, an undersecretary of state also charged with trade matters. The fund negotiations at times ran parallel to other talks between Eizenstat and Hombach on general trade issues, inadvertently making Nazi-era forced labor look like a bargaining chip on a much longer agenda.

Politicians in the U.S. once again joined in as public combatants. The comptroller of New York City, Alan Hevesi, raised the specter of sanctions on German banks. In March 1999, Governor Gray Davis of California joined a lawsuit against Ford, General Motors, and several German companies, invoking a state law allowing interested private citizens to act as co-plaintiffs in class actions. The case was represented by Michael Hausfeld, one of the U.S. lawyers sitting at the international talks.

The plaintiff lawyers in the U.S. and German cases (whose formal inclusion in the talks the companies at first resisted) struck a hard line, raising demands as high as $30 billion for the prospective compensations fund. The first German news reports of a sum the companies were willing to provide had it hovering at around 3 billion DM. (At the time, in the spring of 1999, the dollar was going for about 1.80 DM.) Often depending on political preference, media reports emphasized either the high nominal total of the fund, or the low total that would ultimately accrue to the average claimant. In addition, the companies and the claimant side disagreed on the likely number of claimants, the prerequisites for a claim, and the difference in amounts to be paid to "slave laborers" (former KZ inmates) as opposed to "forced laborers" (civilians in Reichseinsatz).

The various sides at first entered five different plans for a comprehensive solution. Each was declared untenable by one side or another. The talks expanded to include other claims relating to the Nazi "Aryanization" of Jewish properties and to Holocaust victims' abandoned bank accounts and insurance policies (for example, with Deutsche Bank, Allianz and, later, the Italian insurer Generali). A long series of high level conferences in Germany and Washington and informal meetings came and went. The U.S. and German plaintiff lawyers accused the companies of playing for a "biological solution." The companies accused the lawyers of greed in delaying a settlement, and of ignoring the sufferings of their elderly plaintiffs, many of whom are in bad financial straits.

Starting in July 1999, the German government offered to also pay into the forced labor fund. In August 1999, Hombach was appointed to oversee the Western countries' economic program for Kosovo after the war in Yugoslavia. He was replaced as the German delegate to the forced labor talks by Otto Graf Lambsdorff of the Free Democratic Party (FDP), also known as the Liberals. Count Lambsdorff, who heads the European branch of the Trilateral Commission, has been a mainstay of West German politics for nearly thirty years. He is an outspoken champion of business, but also known as a thoughtful man who gets results.

Now things began to move. More companies joined the fund, raising the total of declared participants to twenty by November 1999. Many more companies were said to be lying in wait, ready to join as soon as agreement on a global sum was reached. The company fund spokesperson, Walter Gibowski, on the one side always maintaining a stony attitude towards the lawyers, nevertheless joined public calls to get hold-out companies into the fund. The German offer was raised to 6 billion DM, 2 billion from the state. In reality, that was closer to 4 billion from the state, as Chancellor Schröder stressed that the companies' contributions would be tax-deductible.

A majority of the German media and press reports throughout this time were clearly sympathetic to the cause of the former forced laborers. Many reports brought new information to light about specific companies' Nazi-era involvements. Reporters routinely contrasted current profit statements against the relatively low cost of participation in the fund. Polls of the public revealed strong and steady public support for compensations; however with a majority finding that the German offer of 6 billion DM was already sufficient.[32] The head of the Deutsche Bank's historical institute, Manfred Pohl, in October 1999 rather disingenuously warned that further delays in reaching a settlement could produce a dramatic anti-Semitic backlash among the German public.[33] In reality, there were no signs of this.

In September 1999, the U.S. federal district court in New Jersey ruled that several of the U.S. class actions, including *Iwanowa vs. Ford*, were outside the jurisdiction of U.S. courts. The plaintiffs went into appeal, and a group in the United States launched a series of negative advertisements in major American papers criticizing Ford, which had not yet joined the proposed fund, and Volkswagen and Daimler-Benz, which had.

A few German labor court decisions went in favor of the claimants, granting awards averaging around 10,000 DM per individual, but with the defendants going into appeal. A case of five former forced laborers against Porsche was thrown out by a Stuttgart regional court in November 1999 for having missed the three-year statute of limitations. The court defined the statute of limitations as beginning in 1990, with the 2+4 Treaty, and not, as the German plaintiff lawyers had argued, with the later Bonn court ruling in 1996 that 2+4 constituted a peace treaty for the Second World War. A new loophole had been discovered. Immediately after its victory, however, Porsche announced its own voluntary fund, offering to pay claimants 10,000 DM in humanitarian aid.

Faced with these legal setbacks, the plaintiff lawyers involved in the global compensations talks lowered their demands to figures between 10 billion and 14 billion DM. Still, a full conference round of all participants in mid-November 1999 failed to produce an agreement. The German government thereupon raised its offer by a billion to 3 billion DM. The companies involved in the talks, after a week's hesitation, raised their promised share to 5 billion DM. On 8 December 1999, amid widespread reports that no agreement would be reached before the year 2000, Chancellor Schröder declared that the German total offer of 8 billion DM was final. The lawyers countered with 11 billion, 1 billion of which would come from foreign-owned companies. A week later, the German state popped another 2 billion into the pot. A settlement of 10 billion DM was announced to great fanfare in the media. The next day the German president, Johannes Rau, delivered a speech apologizing for the wartime practice of forced labor. Everyone went home for the holidays.

The celebrations were premature. A new round of disputes followed, this time centering on the division of the money among claimant groups, the purposes for which the money is to actually be used, and the German government's draft of a bill to regulate the fund. These issues proved nearly as delicate as the matter of reaching a global sum in the first place.

The first versions of the German legislation set extremely difficult standards for validating a claim, and defined the fund as the closure for all claims related to the Second World War, for all time. Although hundreds of German companies joined the fund during the first months of 2000, the company till as late as mid-February was reported as being more than half empty, at a mere 2 billion of the 5 billion DM required. (As of late May 2000, media reports claimed that the companies had raised no more than 3 billion DM, although there are now said to be 1,600 companies participating in the fund. The company fund spokesperson is threatening to name and publicly excoriate companies who are refusing to participate.)

In February 2000, the plaintiff lawyers filed a U.S. suit to demand that the German side immediately pay the entire 10 billion into an escrow fund and let the claimants work out the rest. The Eastern European countries demanded that 9 billion DM of the fund be earmarked for compensations to individual former laborers. Several lawyers insisted on a billion or more for Aryanization and property issues. The German side remained committed to the idea of a billion for a "Memory" foundation to fund historical research, education, and charity work.

The World Jewish Council in February 2000 accused the German government of encouraging an unseemly struggle among the claimants, which Lambsdorff vehemently denied. Eizenstat in March sent a brief shockwave through Germany by raising the surprising claim that questions of state-to-state wartime reparations were not yet settled, as Germans had long imagined. Figures as high as 100 billion DM in further payments were cited.

Finally, in Berlin on 22 and 23 March 2000, the various sides agreed to a division of the sums. Equal amounts of almost 2 billion DM each would be reserved for Jewish KZ laborers and Polish civilian forced laborers, effectively amounting to average individual compensations of more than 10,000 DM for "extermination through work" and of about 5,000 DM for "Reichseinsatz." Altogether, more than 8 billion DM are to be paid to the various country funds and claims groups for forced and slave laborers. About 700 million DM are earmarked for covering property and monetary claims, and a similar amount will go toward financing the German educational and charitable fund.

Barring an unlikely reversal, at least the material question of compensations for wartime forced labor was thus settled, after much political crossfire, six weeks short of fifty-five years after the end of the war. Under the agreement, the U.S. class actions are to be dismissed, although many cases are still pending as of May 2000. The fund is supposed to be set in German law in July 2000, and to start paying validated claims in the summer and fall of the year 2000. According to prevailing estimates, as many as 240,000 slave laborers from the Nazi camps survive, and will qualify for a payment. Forced laborers under Reichseinsatz are subject to a stricter qualifications rule. It is expected that as many as one million former forced laborers who are still alive today will qualify for a payment of some kind.

BECAUSE IT INVOLVES American-owned companies and thus crosses the conventional borders of national interest, the history of Ford and General Motors in Germany has been a flashpoint in the greater dispute. During the events of 1998 and 1999, it was reported that Ford dispatched a "research army" to comb through the National Archives in Washington, the German state and historical archives, and the company's own war-period files in Dearborn and Germany.[34] An international round of negative stories on Ford and General Motors was set off by a November 1999 *Washington Post* report on the two companies' wartime histories. At that time, General Motors's spokesperson issued a "categorical denial" of GM involvement in Opel after September 1939, claiming the company was seized by the German authorities right at the start of the war.[35]

Opel in December 1999 announced its intention to participate in the German forced-labor aid fund. Ford Werke held out, but relented after it was included in a list, released that month by the American Jewish Committee (AJC), of 630 companies with apparent forced-labor involvements who had not yet joined the German company fund. Whether Ford Motor Company and General Motors will thus escape further legal complications is unclear. The U.S. case lawyers and other participants on the claimant side are still planning to set up the separate compensations fund of 1 billion DM to be financed by non-German companies, as was assented to in principle by the United States in the December 1999 global-sum agreement with Germany. (In May 2000, U.S. and German press reports claim that up to sixty U.S. companies that own former German employers of wartime forced labor have tentatively agreed to set up a further compensations fund, amounting to $100 million. As prominent participants, the reports name Ford, General Motors and Kodak.)

> An international business, operating throughout the world, should conduct its operations in strictly business terms, without regard to the political beliefs of its management, or the political beliefs of the country in which it is operating.
>
> *Alfred Sloan, General Motors President, 1938*[36]

IS THE OLD STATEMENT TRUE that what is good for General Motors is good for America? The great questions of the laws and forces that presumably govern the affairs of men cannot be answered here. We can compare and criticize different business practices and economic systems around the world. We can create competing theories about fascism and totalitarianism, how they arise, what the true causes are. Whatever the results of such examinations, Ford Motor and General Motors can not be blamed for Nazi ideology, or for the rise and development of the Third Reich.[37] The histories in this book reveal differences between the conditions the two companies faced and the policies they adopted in Nazi Germany, and show how both plan and accident played important roles. There is, however, an undeniable bottom line: both of the two U.S. auto giants were prepared to aggressively pursue a growing business with the Wehrmacht in the pre-war and early war years, and to provide advanced technology to a regime of terror bent on conquest. The complexity of motivations and other causes cannot make light of the companies' substantial material contribution to the Blitzkrieg, or conceal that this contribution began well before the war, under the direction of executives dispatched to Cologne and Russelsheim by Dearborn and Detroit.

After the war, Ford Motor and General Motors paid no penalty for their help in arming the Nazi regime, or for the use of forced labor at their subsidiaries. They were allowed to resume full control of expanded European assets. More than a few of the German executives who had managed wartime operations were returned to top positions. Most of the machinery at both companies survived the war, in part thanks to the Reich's 1944 emergency program, powered by forced labor, to disperse production plants to hidden locations. Ford Werke escaped the Allied bombing raids nearly undamaged–to the astonishment, as Reinhold Billstein writes in chapter 2 of this book, of the U.S. soldiers who discovered it intact amid the ruins of a leveled city. The two U.S. brands proceeded to assume co-leadership, with Volkswagen, of the European automotive market, a predominance which has lasted to the present day. In contrast to Ford, GM, and Daimler-Benz, the less active and less successful private companies within Albert Speer's arrangement of the wartime vehicle industry are now history.

The practices that allowed Ford and General Motors to act in this fashion, under which big businesses based in the United States receive government support or (as in this case) are permitted to pursue profits and interests abroad by the means they see fit, regardless of the costs to foreign peoples, have not been reformed. As a reading of chapters 1 and 2 makes clear, a few of the General Motors managers who shaped their company's policies in pre-war Germany were rewarded with appointments to influential positions within the postwar occupation government, and within the U.S. policy-making apparatus for Germany.

The same antitrust elements within the Roosevelt Administration who once hoped in vain to reform the preponderance of big business at home failed to curb the excesses of American big businesses abroad. Nor did they realize, beyond the dismantling of I.G. Farbenindustrie, their postwar vision of breaking the dominance in Germany of the big German corporations and banks.

In the immediate postwar years and ever since, the motto instead remained: "What is good for General Motors," and other powerful American businesses, "is good for America." This may be nothing inherent in either business as such or the capitalist mode of economy, but it has applied far more often than not in the real historical confluence of specific interests and U.S. government policies. Only in exceptional cases has a big U.S. business operating outside the United States in a nation too corrupt, weak, or dependent to put up effective resistance been brought to task by the U.S. or any other government for making use of unjust labor practices, supporting undemocratic or repressive rule, or poisoning the local environment. More often than not, business transactions with dictatorships still receive the U.S. government's implicit blessing. The price is sometimes paid, as it was most dramatically in the case of Nazi Germany, in the rise with support from American companies–in more recent decades, even with support from the U.S. military and intelligence complex–of enemies who later pose threats to our own country.

In the service of historical honesty, we are overdue in finally establishing as a given the relations of Ford and General Motors to the Nazi regime, without resorting to apologetics. First, because most of the forced laborers who were used to keep production running and balances rising at the German subsidiaries during the war were never until now compensated for their suffering or for their work, but simply ignored. The few who survive as elderly people should finally see a modicum of justice, although in the end any payment can only be symbolic.

Finally, we must recover this history because the story of Ford, General Motors, and Nazi Germany was not an isolated case, merely an extreme one.[38] The "business as usual" logic behind it still has a decisive impact upon the way many American corporations do business in the world—and in the way the U.S. and other governments regulate or promote the foreign activities of companies based in their countries.

— Nicholas Levis

ACKNOWLEDGMENTS

Reinhold Billstein, Karola Fings, and Anita Kugler patiently introduced me to their years of research, guided my editing and translation of their studies, provided advice and photos, gave me access to their primary sources, and carefully proofed the English versions of their chapters. They are authorities in the subjects they cover, and I am grateful for all that I have learned while working with them. It was, furthermore, a pleasure.

Professor Horst Matzerath, the director of the NS-Dokumentationszentrum der Stadt Köln, and Elisabeth Adamski, who oversees the documents center's contacts to former forced laborers, both found precious hours to give advice and to search out papers and photos. Ursula Reuter has for many years participated in the Cologne visitors' program for former forced laborers as a researcher and interviewer. She read and corrected my rendering of the transcripts in Chapter 5. Eberhard Illner of the Stadtarchiv Köln and Herby Sachs of the photo agency "version" in Cologne each located and reproduced photos for this book.

Professor Hans Mommsen read earlier versions of several chapters. His counsel resulted in important changes and improvements. Professor Henry Turner of Yale University graciously provided a copy of the unpublished James Mooney memoirs and the Mooney-Lochner correspondence. For parts of the Chapter 6 retrospective on the history of postwar German restitutions for forced labor, I am indebted to Karl Brozik and to the political scientist Günter Saathoff, both specialists in the field.

Johannes Raschka of the Hannah Arendt Institute in Dresden read the manuscript, and many of his corrections and excellent suggestions are reflected in the final version. The editors Ginger Diekmann and Sabine Reul helped me sharpen my style, although they should not be blamed for barbarisms that snuck in anyway. Marion Berghahn was always patient and supportive, going beyond the normal duties of a publisher. Beatrice McGeoch took on the copy-editing, including the daunting task of getting the notes to behave. Shawn Kendrick was active, creative, and patient in giving the book its typeset form. The historian Annette Weinke served the project from beginning to end as a consultant on methodology and German history. She knows well how much I owe her besides. My heart is hers. Only the mistakes are entirely my own. Thanks to all—and thanks to Bessie and Van.

– *Nicholas Levis*

NOTES

Books and articles listed in the select bibliography are cited here by author and year, edited volumes by title and year. Secondary research and commentary by the present editor in brackets.

Introduction
By Nicholas Levis, Berlin

1. A few facts on the significance of Ford Motor Company and General Motors at three points in the twentieth century: 1907, 1929, and 1999. In 1907, several hundred pioneer enterprises built 44,000 automobiles in the United States, making it the leading car-producing nation in the world. Cars ran on mostly dirt roads. The rapid development during the next twenty years of production technology, infrastructure, vehicles and markets caused a revolutionary transformation of Western and especially North American society. In 1929, the United States boasted roughly twenty-seven million cars, rolling on nearly one million miles of paved roads. The innovations in standardization and production process that made this possible were associated above all with the name of Henry Ford, whose company after 1908 introduced the first mechanized assembly lines and the first fully standardized mass production car, the Model T. Henry Ford was celebrated around the world as the most famous man of his age. In Germany, for example, mass production was reverently called *Fordismus*. However, his autocratically run, family-owned firm was to be far surpassed by the acquisitive conglomeration of various carmakers known as General Motors. Under Alfred P. Sloan, GM pioneered modern corporate structure and management. By 1929, car production was highly capital intensive. Market maturation, saturation and competition had resulted in a consolidation of producers into a few giant companies. The "Big Three," General Motors, Ford, and Chrysler, accounted for 80 percent of U.S. auto sales, with the U.S. market representing most of the world market. Most European producers had no chance of keeping up. General Motors purchased Adam Opel AG in April of that year. The history presented in this book picks up from there. In 1999, the Big Three are the three largest multinational corporations by revenue, and still hold a similar share of the present-day U.S. automotive market. According to its 1998 financial report, General Motors last year produced 8.1 million motor vehicles, amassed $161 billion in revenues, and employed 594,000 personnel at its factories, development centers, offices and distribution points in dozens of countries around the world. Ford Motor Company in 1998 employed 345,000 people, producing 6.8 million vehicles for $144 billion in sales revenue. The second largest corporation by revenue in 1998 was DaimlerChrysler, Stuttgart, created that year in a friendly merger of the German Daimler-Benz AG, Stuttgart, and the Chrysler Corporation, Detroit. DaimlerChrysler boasted 1998 revenues of $154 billion, with 441,000 employees producing 4.4 million vehicles and a multitude of aerospace and other high-tech products. These figures do not reflect the millions of people employed by the Big Three's component and service suppliers and far-flung sales and maintenance networks.

2. Verena Lueken in *Frankfurter Allgemeine Zeitung* (FAZ), 22 Dec. 1998. Amid the many reports on restitutions for forced labor since March 1998, a few covering Ford or General

Motors in greater detail include, in English: Martin Wilson, "Newsnight," BBC London TV, 23 Feb. 1998; Michael Dobbs, "Ford and GM Scrutinized for Alleged Nazi Collaboration," *Washington Post*, 30 Nov. 1998; Doron Levin, "Ford, GM Need to Account for Past," *Detroit Free Press*, 3 Dec. 1998; Roger Franklin, "Ford and the Fuehrer," *The Age* (Melbourne), 5 Dec. 1998; Michael Hirsh, "Dirty Business," *Newsweek*, 22 Dec. 1998; Barry Meier, "Holocaust Lawsuits Spark Demand for Historians," *New York Times* (NYT), 18 Feb. 1999. Contact Ford (spokesperson: John Rintamaki) and General Motors (John Mueller) for their press statements. See also the advertisement by a group supporting the plaintiffs against Ford in NYT, 6 Oct. 1999. On Internet, ABCNEWS.com featured broad coverage by Terence Nelan and Erin Arvedlund. For longer German reports on Ford/GM see: FAZ, 12 Mar. 1998; Ingrid Müller-Münch, *Frankfurter Rundschau*, 27 Mar. 1998; Christiane Schlötzer-Scotland, *Süddeutsche Zeitung* (SZ), 6–7 June 1998; *Kölnische Rundschau*, 23 July 1998; Elke Biesel, *Kölner Stadt-Anzeiger* (KSA), 10 Sept. 1998; Uwe Knüpfer, KSA, 16 Sept. 1998; Hans-Jürgen Deglow, KSA, 2 Dec. 1998; Holger Schmale, *Berliner Morgenpost*, 2 Dec. 1998; *Der Spiegel*, No. 50, 1998; Philip Gassert, *Die Zeit*, 14 Jan. 1999; Jens Gleisberg, "Lokalzeit Köln," WDR TV Cologne, 24 Mar. 1999; Andreas Mink, *Aufbau* (New York), 14 Sept. 1999; Andreas Förster, *Berliner Zeitung*, 8 October 1999; Hans Leyendecker, SZ, 29 Oct. 1999. On Internet in German, see: hagalil.com. In French: *Liberation*, 4 Dec. 1998; Patrick Sabatier, *Liberation*, 11 March 1999. Japan: Takaaki Takai, Program Director NHK News, July 1999 (TV report).

3. *Iwanowa et al. vs. Ford Motor Company and Ford-Werke AG*, Civil Case No. 98-959 (JAG), Hon. Joseph A. Greenaway, U.S. District Court, District of New Jersey, 4 Mar. 1998.

4. On Reichseinsatz generally, see Herbert (1985), available in English as Herbert (1997).

5. Cf. Herbert (1998), 17–32 and tables by Herbert in *Entschädigung für NS-Zwangsarbeit* (1998), 337–40. Polish association figures in Gawlowski (1998), 159f.

6. For the definitive history of the Wehrmacht and its Soviet prisoners of war see Streit (1977/1997), here 9f., 128f. He notes (301f.) that there are serious disagreements about the number of German prisoners of war who died in Soviet captivity after 1945. A commission of German historians in the 1950s estimated more than 1 million dead out of 3.15 million German POWs. Soviet historians' estimates range at around 300,000 out of 3 million, which Streit seems to favor.

7. One of the most important of the many books on the SS and KZ system is by the historian and Buchenwald survivor Eugen Kogon (1999/1974), available in English as Kogon (1998). The original manuscript was written immediately after the war, on behalf of the Allied prosecutors. See also Ferencz (1982).

8. Brozik (1998), 33–34. Transcript of a speech in Dr. Brozik's present-day capacity as a representative of the Jewish Claims Conference in Germany.

9. Primo Levi, *Gespräche und Interviews* (Munich/Vienna, 1999), 89. Brozik (1998), 35.

10. Spoerer (1998:2), 2.

11. Ibid.

12. Tables (by Herbert) in *Entschädigung für NS-Zwangsarbeit* (1998), 338. Figures on Hungary from Herbert (1998), 31.

13. Spoerer (1998:2), 1.

14. Spoerer (1998:2) points out at least two factors that might skew the results. First, a company that resisted KZ assignments, or one that was coerced to take a squad, would be more likely to keep the documentation and to report openly about it than a company that took the initiative in arranging a KZ deployment. The management of the latter would have been more likely to cover up or destroy evidence at the end of the war. Assuming that, it would seem that the one case of coercion by the authorities was truly exceptional, whereas the sixteen cases wherein a company took the initiative stand for many more that were covered up. However, Spoerer also argues that historians who choose to study this question are more likely to be critical of capitalism in the first place. They might prefer to document cases in which the company's guilt is evident, or even extend criticism of a company beyond what the evidence warrants. This rings true, and much of the research is written by obviously reform-minded and liberal people. Spoerer does not ask whether

the opposite is also possible: i.e., when a corporate think-tank or a company itself sponsors the research. Until proven otherwise let us hope, and presume, that every serious scholar is committed to high standards of research, interpretation, and logic. Given the lack of a sufficient mass of literature to reach a conclusive answer to his original question, Spoerer's rigorously logical article ends by calling on future researchers to focus more closely on the problem of responsibility, and on the degree to which a given firm's management had a chance to get its way against the will of the Reich authorities.

15. See also Theilen (1984), and *Gegen den braunen Strom* (1991), 172–181.

16. General works on Nazi Germany and on the literature about it used as guides and references in editing this book, and recommended by the editor as introductions to the subject, include Shirer (1993/1950); Wistrich (1982); *National Socialist Extermination Policies*, ed. Herbert and Aly (2000); *Das III. Reich 1933–1945*, ed. Overesch and Saal (1991); Kershaw (1989); *Faschismus*, ed. Ruckhaberle and Ziesecke (1976); Neumann (1942); Arendt (1951); and Rosenbaum (1998). These books represent and discuss a number of different approaches to the problem, all of which are valuable. In my view the most useful treatment of the literature (which fills many libraries) is Kershaw (1989), who is very good at unraveling semantics and irrelevant debates. Like Herbert and Aly (2000), Kershaw prefers to first draw out "what actually happened," and then ask what terms we should apply to events after the fact. Shirer (1993/1950), who saw Nazi Germany and Hitler firsthand as a reporter in the years 1933 to 1941, and who spent years going through the documents available after 1945, presents an excellent, comprehensive chronological treatment of the political events of the era, despite occasional analytic simplifications.

17. Since the mid-1980s there have been many studies of companies during the Nazi era. For the literature on Ford, see the "Historiography in Brief" in Ch. 4 (and Ch. 4 notes 12 to 16 and 47, below) and Ch. 2 notes 2 and 3. For the previous works on Opel and Ford by the authors of this book, see the first notes to chs. 1, 2, and 4, below. Spoerer (1998:2) provides a comprehensive bibliography of the literature on forced labor up to 1998. Three recent books deal with the automotive industry, and are particularly relevant here. On the history of the Volkswagen project and its German and foreign laborers, see Mommsen with Grieger (1996). On forced labor in Munich, concentrating especially on BMW, that city's largest company, see Heusler (1996). In English, Gregor (1998) presents Daimler-Benz as a case study in the evolution of the Nazi economy. He treats in detail the relations between Daimler and Opel, covered here in Ch. 1, and his introduction summarizes the historiography of industry under the Nazi regime. See also: *Das Daimler-Benz Buch,* ed. Ebbinghaus (1987). On IG Farbenindustrie, Peter Hayes, *Industry and Ideology: IG Farben in the Nazi Era* (Cambridge, 1987) is considered the standard work. For a general study of the treatment of foreign-owned companies in Nazi Germany, see Lindner (1991).

18. Flink (1998), 129.

19. Ibid.,131.

20. Fisch (1992), 321.

21. Ibid., 318.

22. Gregor (1998), 36.

Prologue
By Nicholas Levis, Berlin

1. Kugler (1987:2), "Von der Werkstatt zum Fliessband," in: *Sozialgeschichte*, ed. Rürup, 303–39, here 338. The sections here on Opel draw heavily on discussions with Anita Kugler and her work in general. Dates in the general chronology rely on *Faschismus* (1976), 134–167, and *Das III. Reich* (1991).

2. GM executive C.R. Osborn to General Motors Corporation Executive Committee, 18 March 1960, Appendix C ("History of Opel Operation"), Adam Opel Archive, 2. Copy from Anita Kugler.

3. Cf. Neugebauer (1997), 169–94, here the prewar history starting on 171.

4. Kugler (1987:2), 338.

5. Osborn, "History of Opel Operation," 1.
6. Ibid., 2.
7. Recalling Rosenbaum's (1998) point that those who set out to "explain Hitler," our era's image and embodiment of ultimate evil, may be doing so for their own psychological reasons, the following outline of the Nazis' rise to power presents nothing new, but may be interesting anyway: Economic circumstances do not provide a blanket explanation for the acts of individuals. The presumed injustice of the Versailles Treaty tells us nothing about why the Nazis would take up a conspiracy theory in which Jews were the source of all evil, or why this would convince so many people. Their ideology was an expression of personal pathologies rooted in German particularisms, drawing upon and exploiting the broader Jew-hating (a term Rosenbaum forwards as an alternative to "anti-Semitic") currents of European history. It was sold successfully as a salvation religion in hard times. Therefore, only in the confluence of irrational mass and individual psychopathology with economic factors can we find the beginnings of an "explanation." By his account in *Mein Kampf*, Hitler's first contact with the minute Bavarian "German Workers' Party," as Member No. 7, was as an informant for military intelligence. The Nazis moved among militarist elements who never accepted the Republic, who upheld the myth that Germany might have won the World War if not for betrayal from within. From the time Hitler took over the party and renamed it, they employed shocktroops and terror against political opponents, acting always with ruthlessness and with the sole goal of taking power over the state. In the years after the failure of Hitler's and Ludendorff's 1923 laughable beer-hall putsch in Munich, the leadership adopted a more cunning approach, striving to win favor among military elites and especially big business. While Nazism cannot be blamed on the inevitable workings of an abstract capitalism, there were more and more individual German businessmen, starting in the middle and late 1920s, who supported and financed the Nazis' rise. (Was Henry Ford among the material supporters? See Ch. 2.) Of course, Nazi rhetoric appealed most to insecure and aggressive males, of which there was no shortage in all classes of people. The shocktroop regiments of the S.A. grew to over 2 million by 1933, waging campaigns of intimidation and murder, poisoning the polity. At the same time Hitler and most Nazi leaders belied their "socialist" pronouncements and pledged unconditional acceptance of private property and its traditional prerogatives to their wealthy backers. Hitler delivered his most obvious statement in this regard in his famous speech to the Dusseldorf industrialists' club in January 1932. During the world economic crisis the established parties lost credibility and the workers' movement was split in factional feuds. Thanks to the extreme concentration of German industrial and financial power in a few men, it did not take many of them to tip the balance to Hitler: "Sitting on the management boards of six large banks and seventy huge industrial combines and holding companies, fewer than one hundred men controlled over two thirds of Germany's industrial system," writes J. S. Martin (1950), 18.
8. The letter is reproduced in *Faschismus* (1976), 11.
9. Mommsen with Grieger (1996), 54ff. The discussion in the next sections of the Volkswagen also draws on Flink (1998), especially 261f.
10. Flink (1998), 262.
11. Author's interview with Reinhold Billstein on the military significance of the Autobahn, 14 May 1999.
12. Flink (1998), 262.
13. See the discussion in Mommsen with Grieger (1996), 54f., esp. 66–67 and 111f.
14. Figures from Flink (1998), 261, 263.
15. Gregor (1998), 36.
16. Osborn, "History of Opel Operation," 2, 3.
17. Roth (1987), 111; Flink (1998), 261. The discussion of Daimler-Benz here relies on Roth's study and on Gregor (1998).
18. Gregor (1998), 103f.,115f.
19. Ibid., 36f.
20. *Faschismus* (1976), 13.

21. Lindner (1991), 122.
22. Osborn, 6.
23. Ibid., 2.
24. Mommsen with Grieger (1996), 66–67.
25. *Faschismus* (1976), 13.
26. Ibid., 147.
27. Gregor (1998), 13.
28. Ibid., 14.
29. *Gefolgschaft*, lit. "the following," among Germanic tribes denoted a voluntary association of young freemen called *Gefolgsmänner* (follower-men) around a leader (*Führer* or *Gefolgsherr*, usually a king or prince), normally formed for the purpose of a war or tour of plunder (*dtv-Wörterbuch*, 1990, 6: 232). A Nazi-era dictionary defined the term as "a community that follows the will of a leader," (*Der neue Brockhaus*, Leipzig 1936–38 and 1941–42). Although it was also used to refer to company employees before the Nazi period, after 1933 *Gefolgschaft* replaced the more common term *Belegschaft* (personnel) in labor law and company pronouncements. It was also used as the term for divisions in Hitler Youth (Duden, 1989). Company executives were called *Betriebsführer* or *Werksführer*. Given the Nazi compulsion to work as a sacred national duty, the brutal suppression of independent labor or workplace groups, and the strict organization of German personnel under the DAF, the message was clear: "One Management, One Following" was meant as the workplace corollary to "Ein Führer, Ein Volk." Therefore I propose the use in English of "the Following" as an accurate translation. Cf. *NS-Deutsch. "Selbstverständliche" Begriffe und Schlagwörter aus der Zeit des Nationalsozialismus*, ed. Karl-Heinz Brackmann, Renate Birkenhauer (Strälener Manuskripte Verlag, 1988 = Europäisches Übersetzer-Kollegium Strälen, Glossar Nr. 4).
30. Mommsen with Grieger (1996), 148.
31. Ibid., 161f.
32. Ibid., 227f.
33. Ibid., 191–195.
34. *Faschismus* (1976),156.
35. Mommsen with Grieger (1996), 196f.
36. Flink (1998), 256.

Chapter 1 Airplanes for the Führer

By Anita Kugler, Berlin (all primary research, most secondary research, original versions) with Nicholas Levis, Berlin (secondary research, new sections). Combines new findings with two earlier studies of Opel during the Second World War in Kugler (1997: 1 and 2).

1. Snell, "American Ground Transport" (1974), A-22, A-17.
2. Ibid., A-16, A-17.
3. [Operations at German stock corporations (*Aktiengesellschaft* = AG) are run by a management board (*Vorstand*) headed by a "speaker" or chairman, who in the old days was usually called the *Generaldirektor*. Management board members oversaw traditional corporate departments such as finance, development, production, purchasing, marketing and sales. A directorate (*Aufsichtsrat*), normally including representatives of major shareholders and creditors, met several times a year to pass verdict on the managers' performance, but rarely made operative decisions. Ultimate authority rested (and rests) with the owners and their general assembly, unless the state or the law determine otherwise. Nowadays a key difference is that labor representatives hold nearly half the seats on German directorates, something inconceivable until well after the war. –Ed.]
4. Snell (1974), A-85, specifically claimed that the U.S. nationals Sloan, Mooney, Howard and John T. Smith, all Opel directorate members starting in 1929, remained on the directorate and influenced business at Opel "throughout the war." According to the German legal record, Sloan, Mooney and Howard retained their (by then nominal) directorate posts until 30 Mar. 1942. Smith had resigned in 1938, and Elias ("Pete") Hoglund and

Cyrus Osborn joined in 1939 (Adam Opel AG annual reports and regional Handelsregister, 1929–1941).

5. [Unfortunately we were unable to locate a copy of Howard's 1940 book. The economic historian James Stewart Martin (1950), hired by the U.S. government during the war as an expert on German industry, writes (p. 24) of arriving in England in February 1945, "into a fog-covered beehive called Bushy Park, headquarters for the future military government of Germany." To his astonishment, he discovered that the U.S. Colonel Graeme Howard was Director of the Economics Division. "Colonel Howard was only the first of many who turned up, riding into Germany with the future military government, helping to deflect the policy back into old grooves. Colonel Howard, it is true, was straightway relieved of his duties before we left Bushy Park for the Continent; in fact, just after General Wickersham," the commanding officer of USGCC, "received a copy of his book from the Intelligence Division." –Ed.]

6. Snell (1974), A-22, A-85.

7. General Motors, "The Truth About 'American Ground Transport'" (1974), A-107-09, quotes on A-108-09.

8. Snell published only a brief version of his findings, "General Motors and the Nazis," in *Ramparts*, vol. 12, no. 11 (June 1974), 14–16. His planned history of General Motors and the automotive industry, twenty-five years in the making, is scheduled for publication in the near future. Snell's theses were taken up in the United States by Higham (1983) and in Germany by B. Martin (1976).

9. Alfred P. Sloan, *My Years with General Motors* (New York, 1963); *Räder für die Welt*, ed. Automobile Quarterly and Princeton Institute for Historic Research (Stuttgart, 1975); Hans-Jürgen Schneider, *125 Jahre Opel, Autos und Technik* (Cologne, 1987), 212, 214. [Cf. the similar account in Flink (1998), 268f. –Ed.]

10. Budrass (1998), 557f.

11. *Faschismus* (1976), 147.

12. Bundesarchiv-Militärarchiv (BA-MA), FRG Military Archives, Freiburg im Breisgau. BA-MA RL 3/63, fol. 7432.

13. cf. Budrass,594f.

14. BA-MA RL 3/2199.

15. James Mooney, unpublished memoirs, manuscript 1946 (quote here, 1), in "Papers of Louis P. Lochner," Box 7, folder #39, State Historical Society of Wisconsin, Madison, WI. Includes the Lochner/Mooney memo of 19 October 1939 and Lochner's correspondence, in 1940 to 1955, concerning Mooney, the fate of Heinrich Richter, and plans to publish the memoirs. Lochner first revealed parts of Mooney's memoir in his *Stets das Unerwartete, Erinnerungen aus Deutschland 1921–1953* (Darmstadt, 1955). On Mooney's 1939–1940 mission, cf. Higham (1983), 166f. and B. Martin (1976).

16. Mooney memoirs, 22. Ford was induced into a similar rubber barter arrangement, see Ch. 2.

17. Mooney memoirs, 21–33, cf. ch. 9 in Higham (1983).

18. Budrass (1998), 585–91f.

19. Ibid.

20. Mooney memoirs, 33.

21. Richter to the president of the Landgericht, 3 Dec. 1941, in Bundesarchiv (BA), FRG Archives, Koblenz and Berlin: BA R 87/6338, fol. 4, 251ff.

22. Ibid., 34–35.

23. In the wake of recent legal cases General Motors has allowed selected independent researchers access to its Detroit and Russelsheim archives for studies into the company's wartime history. The present study was completed in advance of the publication in 2000 of a German-language book on Opel by the historian Günter Neliba.

24. cf. Budrass (1998), 594–95.

25. Ibid.

26. Ibid., 596–97, cf. Mommsen with Grieger (1996), ch. 5.4ff.

27. Wehrwirtschaftsinspektion XII, the military inspectorate of the Wiesbaden district, Kriegstagebuch (war journals), no. 1, 24 Aug. to 21 Dec. 1939, 24, in BA RW 20-12. Also

Rüstungsinspektion XII (RüInsp), the armaments inspectorate of Wiesbaden, Lage-berichte (situation reports), 21 Sept. 1939 to 2 Feb. 1940, in BA RW 20-12/17.

28. In the German publication of the present study (Kugler 1997: 1 and 2) I placed Mooney in meetings with Hitler and Göring at the same time, on 19 and 20 September 1939. This was due to errors in my notes. Confirmation was difficult because I was in the past denied access to the Mooney memoirs, for example a written request on behalf of the Archiv und Museum der Stadt Rüsselsheim to the State Archives of Wisconsin, 11 Feb. 1986, was answered on 1 Mar. 1986 that the memoirs were no longer in the State Archives' posses-sion. On the two days in September 1939, Mooney according to his account was in Wies-baden, not necessarily at Inspectorate XII. He met Göring on 19 October 1939, and Hitler on 4 March 1940. Discovering this error naturally caused me to again carefully review the materials presented here. I apologize if this has been cited as a fact by other researchers. —Anita Kugler.

29. Osborn to General Motors Corporation Executive Committee, "History of Opel Opera-tion," 18 March 1960, Appendix C, Adam Opel Archive, 6.

30. "Discussion on Integrating the Adam Opel Company in the JU-88 Program," Wehrwirtschaftsinspektion XII, Wiesbaden, Kriegstagebuch, BA-MA RW 20-12, 1, 24.

31. BA R 87/6335/1, 27.

32. Shirer (1993/1950), 838f, 851f.

33. Mooney memoirs, 42, on which he also relates meeting Göring once before, in June 1936, at a dinner where Göring "decorated Mr. Lindbergh."

34. Lochner papers, "Mr. James D. Mooney's Memorandum of Conversation with Field Mar-shal Hermann Goering, Berlin, October 19, 1939," 2–3.

35. Lochner, "Mr. James D. Mooney's Memorandum," 4–5.

36. Mooney, 45.

37. Mooney, 41, cf. 51, and subsequent passage on 50. [How seriously can we take Mooney's assessment of Wohlthat's and Göring's intentions? During the "Phony War," there "formed in Germany an opposition front of the military, organized in the ministerial bureaucracy, the diplomatic corps and business, with the declared goal of getting rid of Hitler before the attack in the West, which was considered suicidal, and replacing him with Göring." Some of the delays in Hitler's demanded offensive are attributable to this group, although they entirely lacked the courage and resolve of a Stauffenberg, who put a bomb under Hitler's conference table in July 1944. These machinations were also seen as a hope by some in England, but "the heterogeneity of the German opposition front and Göring's always loyal behavior to his Führer in a crisis allowed Hitler to put through his program." Quotes from B. Martin (1976), 66f., here: 80; also cf. Higham (1983), ch. 9, and Shirer (1993/1950), ch. 19. It is possible that Wohlthat subtly communicated to Mooney an honest desire to over-throw Hitler, but seems very unlikely that Göring did so, unless it was a ruse for the pur-pose of gathering intelligence about English war aims—the task with which Göring explicitly charged Mooney. Göring's loyalty to Hitler is hard to doubt, although it may have fluctuated. Even in late April 1945, when Hitler retreated to the bunker and left no one in charge, Göring still saw fit to write his Führer for permission to take over the Reich, as the long-standing heir apparent. Hitler had him arrested and stripped of all posts. (A few days later Hitler shot Eva Braun and himself; Göring was sentenced to death at the Nurem-berg trials and hanged himself just before his execution.) By comparison, Himmler in late April 1945 simply declared himself the new Führer, although no one noticed. (He was caught trying to sneak into Denmark, and swallowed a poison capsule.) —Ed.]

38. Handelsregister, 20 Dec. 1939. In his function as an industrialist and honorary "Geheim-rat" (Privy Councilor of State) Wilhelm von Opel had occasion to release statements through the press, such as the following on 24 March 1936, on the upcoming yes-no "elec-tions" to the Reichstag: "Germans, on 29 March give the Führer your vote to show your gratitude, to prove your loyalty, to support his will! The Führer united us, the Führer ful-filled our hopes, the Führer fights for our honor and freedom. To him our labor, to him our heart, to him our vote!" *Das III. Reich 1933–1945* (1991), 271. That Sunday, 29 March 1936, "Yes" beat "No" by 99 to 1.

39. Wilhelm von Opel and Osborn to Wagner, 7 Feb. 1940, in appendix to Richter, letter to Johannes Krohn, 12 Dec. 1942, BA R 87/6336/2, 173.
40. Kugler (1985) and Kugler (1987:2).
41. Mooney memoirs, 85, cf. ch. 9 in Higham (1983).
42. B. Martin (1976), 86, cf. Higham's (1983) interpretation of Roosevelt's motivations with regard to Mooney.
43. Shirer (1993/1950), 852f.
44. Reich Foreign Ministry notes in preparation for Mooney's May 1934 meeting with Hitler, 13 Apr. 1934, BA R 43 II/1465, fol. 1, 88–92, here 92. Cf. "Hitler, Westrick und – General Motors," *Deutsche Volkszeitung*, 20 June 1974. On the ambivalence of many American industrialists with regard to the Third Reich, see Wilkins (1974), 188f.
45. Mooney memoirs, 127.
46. Shirer (1993/1950), 905n.: "A quite unofficial American peacemaker [in addition to Sumner Welles] was also in Berlin at this time, a vice-president of General Motors. He had been in Berlin, as I recall, shortly before or after the outbreak of the war, trying … to save the peace. The day after Welles left Berlin, on March 4, 1940, Hitler received Mooney, who told him, according to a captured German record of the meeting, that President Roosevelt was 'more friendly and sympathetic' to Germany 'than was generally believed in Berlin' … Hitler merely repeated what he had told Welles two days before. On March 11 [Hans] Thomsen [the German chargé d'affaires in Washington] sent to Berlin a confidential memorandum prepared for him by an unnamed American informant declaring that Mooney 'was more or less pro-German.' Thomsen's memorandum states that Mooney had informed Roosevelt on the basis of an earlier talk with Hitler [!? presumably Göring] that the Fuehrer 'was desirous of peace and wished to prevent the bloodshed of a spring campaign.' Hans Dieckhoff, the recalled German ambassador to the United States, who was whiling away his time in Berlin, saw Mooney immediately after the latter's interview with Hitler and reported to the [Reich] Foreign Office that the American businessman was 'rather verbose' and that 'I cannot believe that the Mooney initiative has any great importance.'"
47. Mooney memoirs, 20. Günther Pistorius, executive engineer at the Russelsheim factory from 1940 to 1945, recalled (interview with Kugler, 8 Aug. 1985) being sent to Berlin as an adviser to Mooney in reserve on matters of production conversion in early Sept. 1939. He did not meet Mooney until spring 1940, when he remembers accompanying Mooney on a tour of the Russelsheim plant with Ludger Westrick, a member of Göring's "Industrial Council of the Luftwaffe." This was later reported in the *New York Herald Tribune* of 1 Aug. 1940.
48. Wachtler to Mooney, Lochner papers (note 15), 12 Sept. 1947.
49. BA R 87 921-100/1, 114; Krohn notes, 11 Apr. 1942, BA R 87/6335/1, 119.
50. Hoglund to Reichsbank Director Wilhelm, 1 Feb. 1941, copy attached to Krohn, notes after discussion with Konsul Belitz on 25 Mar. 1942, in BA R 87/233. On Deutsche Bank's plans to buy Opel see Roth (1987), 268.
51. "Comments of Former American Directors of the Opel Werke, Germany," in USSBS, "ADAM OPEL RUSSELSHEIM": "In January, 1942, Messers. R.K. Evans, E.S. Hoglund, and C. Osborne, all executives of the General Motors Corporation, were asked to give their views … with specific reference … to Adam Opel A.G. … these men were among the last Americans to leave Germany and their comments may prove interesting."
52. BA-MA RW 19/171.
53. Von Opel and Richter wrote to Krohn on 7 Jan. 1942 that: "After getting through the confusion of the first weeks of transition, the conversion to war production of the plants in Russelsheim and Brandenburg was completed by November 1939. Adam Opel AG has since then worked *exclusively* for German armaments production. Since the termination of [domestic] passenger car production the main plant in Russelsheim has worked for the Luftwaffe, the Army, and the Navy" (BA R 87/233). In January 1940, two months before Opel's export car production was also terminated, Russelsheim Plant 1 sent out 298 train cars and 280 trucks full of aircraft parts, according to Lüer, writing to Gritzbach, 22 Jan. 1942, BA R 87/233. On production at Opel, see Rüstungsinspektion XII, Lageberichte,

BA-MA RW, 20-12, vol. 18. Opel produced 50,000 shell casings for the German Navy in March and April 1940 (BA-MA RW 20-12, vol. 2, 37). By September 1940, Opel had supplied the Luftwaffe with 585 cockpits, 431 suspensions, 412 exhaust systems, and 3,000 radiators and hydraulic systems. (*Opel in der Ju 88 Fertigung, Ein Kurzbericht in Wort, Bild und Zahl*, Deutsches Museum, Munich / ASD LDR 02622).

54. Opel financial reports in BA R 87/6341/7. See Wiskott to Lüer, 9 Dec. 1941, Bodo Fischer Archive, Adam Opel AG; Lüer to Gritzbach, 21 Jan. 1941, BA R 87/233.

55. Ibid. Bartels, "Opel im Kriege," in *Waffen-Arsenal* (no year), 47. "Opel Military Cars," in *Wheels and Trucks*, vol. 10, 1979, 31ff. Here see Table 3 for the surprisingly modest wartime German truck production figures.

56. On the military draft and "combing actions" as described in the following paragraphs, see BA-MA RW 20-12, vol. 1/5 and Rüstungsinspektion XII Lageberichte, BA-MA RW 17-20.

57. BA-MA RW 20-12/4, 24.

58. See Ch. 3. Shop-floor resistance at Opel and underground activities against the Nazis in the Gross-Gerau region are covered chronologically and at length in Ulrich (1997). The graffito incident is reported in Wehrwirtschaftsinspektion XII, War Journals, BA-MA RW 20-12, vol. 3, 63.

59. On Avieny see *OMGUS: Ermittlungen gegen die Dresdner Bank,* ed. Hans-Magnus Enzensberger (Nördlingen, 1986), 216ff.

60. "Comments of Former American Directors of the Opel Werke, Germany" (note 51), 4.

61. Museum der Stadt Russelsheim, Collection Rau.

62. Herbert (1985), 97.

63. Bangert to A.E. Till of Opel Berlin, 19 September 1941, in response to Claus Litten and A.E. Till to Bangert, 4 September 1941, Museum der Stadt Rüsselsheim, Opel collection.

64. Rüstungskommando Potsdam, Service Journals, BA-MA RW 21-50, vol. 1 and 2.

65. Rüstungsinspektion XII Lageberichte, BA-MA RW 20-12/21.

66. BA-MA RW 20-12/18, 91.

67. "Ordinance on the Treatment of Enemy Property," 15 Jan. 1940 in the *Reichsgesetzblatt* (Reich Legal Register). For a complete contemporary legal reading of the regulatory situation before and after the decree, see Helmut Strebel, "Die Behandlung des feindlichen Vermögens," in *Zeitschrift für ausländisches öffentliches Recht und Völkerrecht* 10, No. 1–2 (Oct. 1940), 887–919.

68. This ground is well-covered in Lindner (1991).

69. The court could reject the Reichskommissar's personal nomination, but could not reject a trusteeship as such.

70. A custodian required the Reichskommissar's explicit approval for making major changes in operations, such as large-scale conversions of plant, new construction, or new partnerships.

71. Files of the Reichskommissar at the Bundesarchiv Koblenz, BA R 87. Krohn's own extensive notes and documents can be found in BA NL 141.

72. *Wehrwirtschaftsführer:* See Ch. 2, note 184, below.

73. Biographical information thanks to Professor Dr. Ernst Schraepler of Berlin. See also Lindner (1991).

74. Lüer on "The development of the custodial question at Adam Opel AG," undated, likely Dec. 1941, in BA R 87/233. Krohn, notes after discussion with Wagner, 8 Apr. 1942, BA R 87/233.

75. Lüer, speech to a roll call of the "Following" (*Gefolgschaftsappell*), 21 June 1941, unsigned, Museum der Stadt Russelsheim.

76. Lüer, "The development …" (note 74).

77. Krohn, notes after discussion with Wilhelm von Opel, 9 Mar. 1942, BA R 87/233.

78. *Der Opel Kamerad,* Yr. 12 (1941), no. 4, 165.

79. E. Stockhorst, *Wer war was im 3. Reich* (Wiesbaden, no year), 279.

80. Lüer on "The relation of Mr. Eduard Winter, Berlin, to Adam Opel AG," undated, likely Dec. 1941, in BA R 87/233. Krohn, notes after discussion with Colonel Thönissen on 10 Jan. 1942. On Winter see Speer (1981), 164f.

81. Richter to Krohn, 7 Jan. 1942, BA R 87 6335/1, 93.

82. BA R 87/6335, vol. 1, 97.
83. BA-MA RW 20-12, vol. 8, 66 and vol. 9, 5. As of April 1942 Opel was making use of 1,735 French prisoners of war as laborers (BA R 87/6335, vol. 1, 137).
84. Herbert (1985), 138.
85. BA-MA RW 20-12/19, 26.
86. Streit (1977), cf. Shirer (1993/1950), 1240f.
87. The Opel engineer G. Pistorius described the camp at length in the 1985 interview with Kugler.
88. W. Hildebrandt, testimony on behalf of Arthur Liebermann, 20 Sept. 1949, Museum der Stadt Russelsheim, B. Rau collection.
89. Sworn testimony by Anna Leitschuh, 26 Aug. 1949, in Arthur Liebermann's denazification appeal procedure.
90. Dr. Schäcker, a former Opel personnel executive, "Historische Rückblick auf die Entwicklung der Personalabteilung der Adam Opel AG," company report on the history of its Personnel Department, March 1961, Bodo Fischer Archive.
91. BA-MA RW 20-12/12, 49.
92. BA-MA RW 20-12/12, 164.
93. Lüer and Nordhoff at Krohn, minutes, 8 Dec. 1941, BA R 87/233, Rk 41/41.
94. Richter to Krohn, "Memorandum on the situation at Opel," 7 Jan. 1941, BA R 87/233, 90–95, quotes 93; cf. Richter to Lüer, 10 Jan. 1942, BA R 87/233.
95. Winter at Krohn, minutes, 10 Jan. 1942, BA R 87/233, Rk 12/42.
96. Krohn, notes after phone call with Lüer on 14 Jan. 1942; notes after phone call with Schell on 15 Jan. 1942; notes after discussion with Richter, 20 Mar. 1942; in BA R 87/233.
97. Krohn, notes after discussion with Nordhoff and Richter on 19 Jan. 1942; notes after phone call with Richter on 13 Jan. 1942; in BA R 87/233.
98. Krohn, notes after discussion with Konsul Belitz on 25 Mar. 1942, in BA R 87/233.
99. Krohn, notes after discussion with Nordhoff and Richter on 19 Jan. 1942, BA R 87/233. Cf. Krohn, notes after discussion with Goetz (Deutsche Bank) on 23 Mar. 1942; notes after discussion with Gritzbach on 27 Mar. 1942; in BA R 87/233.
100. Krohn, notes after discussion with Richter on 20 Mar. 1942; notes after discussion with Belitz on 25 Mar. 1942; notes after discussion with Wagner on 8 Apr. 1942; in BA R 87/233.
101. Richter to Opel executives, 1 Apr. 1941, BA R 87/6335/1, 117–21; Krohn notes, 1 Apr. 1942, in BA R 87/233.
102. *Selbstverantwortung* = "self-responsibility."
103. Krohn, notes after discussion with Winter and Nordhoff, undated, some time around 24 Mar. 1942, BA R 87/233.
104. Dietrich Eichholtz, *Geschichte der Deutschen Kriegswirtschaft*, vol. II (Berlin, 1985), 43ff.
105. Roth (1987), 302ff. *Die Daimler-Benz AG 1916–1948,* ed. Roth and Schmid (1987), doc. 53a-53l. Pohl et al. (1986), 31ff. and doc. 3–9 and 20. B. Bellon, *The Workers of Daimler-Untertürkheim 1903–1945. A Study in History of German Labor*, Ph.D. diss., Columbia University (1988), 498ff. Cf. Gregor (1998), 92f. On Kissel see note 119 below.
106. Werlin to Göring, copy, 22 Apr. 1942, BA R 87/233.
107. Opel AG statement on the "liquidity problem," 7 July 1943, BA R 87/6338, vol. 4, 96ff. Lüer to Kellermann, copy, 3 July 1943, BA R 87/6338, 122. List of rejected investment plans, ibid., 128. See *Neue Zürcher Zeitung*, 4 Aug. 1942, No. 241.
108. Krohn, notes after discussion with Richter, 29 June 1942; Richter, memorandum, 29 June 1942, BA R 87/233.
109. Pohl et al. (1986), *Die Daimler-Benz AG*, 94; Roth (1987), 284.
110. Lüer, notes, copy, 13 May 1942; Lüer to Wilhelm von Opel, copy, 15 May 1942; in BA R 87/233.
111. Ibid.
112. Discussion at Führer Headquarters on 13 May 1942. Institut für Zeitgeschichte (henceforth IfZ), BA-MA 217 RK 264/42. Hitler also approved the idea of "Opel assisting in the expansion of 3.7 cm flak manufacture, to guarantee rapid production through its experience at such operations." See *Deutschlands Rüstung*, ed. Boelcke (1969), 114.

113. Richter memorandum on expansion in Brandenburg, 25 June 1942, BA R 87/233.
114. Krohn, notes after phone call with Gritzbach, 18 May 1942, BA R 87/233. Of Lüer, Göring supposedly said: "He is a very big man in the Party, but he understands nothing of these matters."
115. Krohn, notes after discussion with Richter, 22 May 1942, BA R 87/233. On the SS plans see Speer (1981), 37ff.
116. No evidence that Opel employed or requested SS prisoners is found in the reports and war journals of RüKo and RüInsp III or XII, or in the minutes of the Opel advisory council meetings of 1942–1944.
117. Adam Opel AG Personnel Department, "Aufriss unserer Gefolgschaft," March 1939, Library of the Museum der Stadt Russelsheim, as well as various statements in the RüKo XII war journals. On the shop-floor resistance at Opel Russelsheim, see Ulrich (1997), 93–157.
118. Roth (1987), 285. Roth is exaggerating. Daimler-Benz's procrastination and raw materials shortages largely crippled licensed Blitz production during the war. The agreement remained in force after the war, however. In fact, Daimler was the only company to produce the three-ton Opel Blitz (as the Mercedes L 701) after the war, and did so until 1949.
119. Roth, 284, and Krug and Lingnau (1986), 152. Kissel's animosity to Opel was deep-seated. Complaining about Himmler's 1938 recommendation that the SS purchase Opel vehicles, Kissel in a letter at that time to Werlin (Daimler-Benz-Archiv, XIV 10) asserted that General Motors was "an exceptionally Jewish company." [Gregor (1998), 140f., attributes Kissel's death in July 1942 to suicide, brought on by the death of his son in the war and his loss of control at Daimler. The latter was signaled by the Daimler management's decision to build the Opel Blitz on license at Mannheim, instead of a new version of Daimler's three-ton truck, the design of which Kissel had been especially proud. –Ed.]
120. Historians have at times downplayed or misunderstood the negotiations leading to the licensing agreement. Pohl et al. (1986) write (94) that Opel promised a rise in production in a mid-May memorandum, that Jakob Werlin submitted the proposal to Hitler and recommended the establishment of a "production circle," and that Speer approved the plans on 13 May 1942. Only then did Paulus supposedly evaluate the idea and judge it feasible for Daimler (also cf. Roth (1987), 284). Daimler-Benz AG claimed to have no records of this. According to my findings, this version is insupportable. The debate on 13 May 1942 was between the Lüer concept, i.e., an expansion of the Brandenburg plant, and the Speer concept, i.e., a new plant in the occupied "East." Talk of a "production circle" came only after the Riga location was rejected, during the planning for the next meeting of the Main Vehicles Committee. Jakob Werlin picked up the licensed production idea after the "Führer Decision" of 4 June. That day, one week after the Main Vehicles Committee meeting and one day before the Daimler-Benz management board convened, a decision was met at Führer Headquarters to "immediately tackle" conversion of Daimler Mannheim to Opel Blitz production, with the provision merely that Werlin be contacted before "commencement." See: Point 19 of Speer's *Führerprotokoll* of 4 June 1942 in *Deutschlands Rüstung* (1969), 133.
121. Speer in ibid.
122. Contract in *Die Daimler-Benz AG 1916–1948* (1987), doc. 99a.
123. Monthly production figures of the Main Vehicles Committee in U.S. National Archives (NA), NA R 3/3177.
124. Production statistics for Opel Blitz, Bodo Fischer Archive, Adam Opel AG. Bartels (no year), p. 47. See *B.I.O.S. Overall Report No. 21: The German Motor Car Industry During the Period 1939–1945* (London, 1947), 10ff.
125. Sprenger to Göring, copy, 15 May 1942, BA R 87/233.
126. See the "concluding report" of the Reichskommissar, 14 July 1945, in BA B 129/76, and the revision of September 1948, BA B 129/62/63.
127. Göring to Sprenger, copy, 30 June 1942, in BA 87/233. Harsher drafts of this letter may be found in IfZ, MA 144/5 P. 3669–774.
128. Göring to Wagner and Lüer, copy, 30 June 1942, BA R 87/233.

129. Krohn, notes after phone call with Richter, 7 July 1942, BA R 87/233. [In his doctoral study of Krohn's agency, Lindner (1991) presents a summary (122–24) of the conflicts among functionaries and executives leading up to the appointment of a custodian for Opel. His depiction differs from the one here on only one point: Richter's sudden July 1942 shift in support to Lüer. Kugler follows Richter's formal line of argument, interpreting the reversal as a defense on principle against Göring's extralegal interference in Opel's internal affairs. Lindner instead argues that Richter was surely angered by Wagner's unauthorized negotiations with Daimler, and that the Main Vehicles Committee under Speer coerced Opel into the Blitz licensing agreement. Gregor (1998) writes (133) that the Daimler-Benz plant in Mannheim "ended up producing the lorries of another company–Opel–under a state-sanctioned licence agreement forced on both parties in the context of Speer's rationalization drive." Given the lack of definitive documentary evidence, for example of orders or complaints from GM in Detroit to Richter, the question of Richter's motivations remains open. To me it seems he pursued a strategy of stubbornly playing one side against the other so as to maintain the status quo. –Ed.]

130. Richter to Krohn, 10 Aug. 1942, BA R 87/233.

131. Ibid.

132. Krohn, notes after discussion with Richter, 9 July 1942, BA R 87/233. Lüer asserted the exact opposite, as in Sprenger to Göring, 15 May 1942, BA R 87/233.

133. Wilhelm von Opel to Wagner, copy, 8 July 1942, BA R 87/233.

134. Krohn, notes after talk with Lüer, 26 Aug. 1942 (Lüer's report on the talk between Lüer and Göring, 21 July 1942), BA R 87/233.

135. Grönert and Göring to Richter, telegrams dated 23 and 24 July 1942, copies, BA R 87/233.

136. Grönert to Warncke, carbon, 14 Aug. 1942, BA R 87/233.

137. Lüer's certificate of appointment as Custodian, OLG Darmstadt, copy, 25 Nov. 1942, in BA R 87/6338. F.4 P.27. Published in the legal gazette, *Deutschen Reichsanzeiger und Preussischen Staatsanzeiger Berlin,* no. 295 (16 Dec. 1942).

138. Göring, in Ifz MA 144/4 P. 7309/10 and MA 613 P. 7268/69: "In the interest of achieving the greatest possible rise in production I designated the technical director of Adam Opel AG, Wagner, to assume the position of Chairman of the Management Board by order of 30 June 1942. In keeping with the requirements concerning the treatment of enemy property, I further command:

    1) … Lüer to be appointed as the Custodian of the Adam Opel AG.
    2) [as quoted in text.]
    3) The wishes of the Adam Opel AG Management Board are to be given serious consideration insofar as questions arising from the establishment of a trusteeship need be coordinated with the Management Board."

139. Lüer's certificate of appointment.

140. BA-MA RW 20-12/12 P. 83 and Appendix No. 9, 138–39.

141. BA R 87/6337/3.

142. BA-MA RW 20-12/14, 60.

143. Lüer on behalf of Opel AG, secret report to Krohn, 6 Feb. 1943, BA R, 87/6337/3, 95. See also Minutes of the Adam Opel AG Advisory Council and Management Board Joint Meeting, 25 May 1943, BA R, 87/6335/1, S. 48. Lüer seems to have been uncertain about his own figures. In a letter to the Advisory Council of 13 May 1943 (BA R 87/6335/3, 284) he cites a total active personnel of 24,541, of whom 4,419 were civilian foreigners and 1,630 French prisoners of war.

144. Nordhoff, memo on "Developments at Opel Brandenburg Since the Beginning of the War," 7 May 1943, BA R 87/6335/3, S. 133.

145. BA-MA RW 46/47 App. 1, 25c.

146. BA-MA RW 46/460 App. 4, 13.

147. BA-MA RW 20-12/14, 95.

148. Stadtarchiv Russelsheim VIII/55/16.

149. "Guidelines of the Finance Department," 12 Apr. 1943, signed by the deputy finance director, O.W. Jensen. Museum der Stadt Russelsheim, Library, No. 62/2 P. 1–13.
150. Lüer to Krohn, 25 May 1943, BA R 87/63337/3, 329: "Since the start of the Russia war and the hostilities in North Africa we have witnessed a true test of the German Wehrmacht's vehicle stocks. The Opel Blitz three-ton trucks, more and more of which are equipped with four-wheel drive, have proven as effective in the northern reaches [of Russia] as in the African desert. The Opel Blitz three-ton truck is today the true carrier of army mobilization, in every sense of that word."
151. Lüer to Krohn, 12 Aug. 1943, BA R 87/6337/3, 147.
152. I viewed this photo album at the Opel company archives in the spring of 1987, but I was not allowed to copy it. A later request to view it was denied. I was told instead that there were no pictures of K-Werk Pleskau.
153. Lüer to Krohn, 1 Mar. 1944, BA R 87/6338/4, 300.
154. *Morgen kommst du nach Amerika*, ed. Schirmbeck (1988), 232.
155. As of 31 December 1943, the Warsaw K-Werk employed twenty-nine "Reich" Germans, five ethnic German Soviets, and 311 Poles. Lüer to Krohn, 1 Mar. 1944, BA R 87/6338/4, 301. Dr. Schäcker, "Historische Rückblick" (note 90), 12, states Opel also maintained a K-Werk in Neprepetrosk to serve Army Group South, although no such location is mentioned in the files of the Reichskommissar.
156. F.E.W. Kohl, finance office in Vienna, to K. Mees, Rüsselsheim, 9 December 1942. Stadtarchiv Rüsselsheim, Rau Archive.
157. According to an Opel finance report of 16 June 1943, in BA R 87/6338/4, 126ff. Liquid assets exceeded 150 million RM in 1943, almost double the company's share equity. Of that sum, 81 million RM were kept as securities and Reich treasury papers in a blocked account with the Reichsbank. (Opel 1943 balance sheets in BA R 87/6339/5, 56ff.)
158. Osborn to General Motors Corporation Executive Committee, "History of Opel Operation" (note 29), 4.
159. Memorandum of the discussion between Lüer, Richter, and Dr. Saager of RWM in Berlin, 30 January 1943, in BA 87/6337/3 P. 74ff.
160. Discussion between Ribbentrop and Hitler, 30 Jan. 1943, in memo by Richter, ibid., 73.
161. BA 87/6337/3, 283.
162. Lüer to Krohn, 4 Jan. 1943.
163. BA 87/6337/3, 270. According to Pistorius, interview with Kugler (note 47), GM was kept informed via Switzerland of Opel's innovations in electronics and new lubricants for high-performance engines. GM did not reply to my inquiries into this subject.
164. Osborn, "History of Opel Operation," (note 29), 4, further quote on 5. General Motors' conditions before it would "again resume control of Adam Opel" included "no further advancement of capital by General Motors, complete freedom of action in selection and control of personnel, numbers of employees, their type, efficiency, etc., products to be produced and prices...." The U.S. government's largesse continued through 1967, by which time "GM had collected more than $33 million in reparations and Federal tax benefits for damages to its warplane and motor vehicle properties in formerly Axis territories," according to Snell (1974), A-22.
165. BA-MA RW 21-64/2 App. 2, 37.
166. BA R 87/6339/5, 5.
167. *Morgen kommst du nach Amerika* (1988), 232.
168. BA R 87/6337/3, 301 and 302.
169. Lüer to Krohn, 12 Aug. 1943, BA R 87/6338, 147.
170. BA R 87/6338/4, 213 and 214. By mid-September 1943, as detailed by Lüer to Krohn (BA R 87/6337/3, 302), the "reduction in the number of male Followers" and increased employment of German women had continued apace and Opel counted 9,535 German men and 1,851 German women in production. But the number of "other foreigners" rose dramatically starting in summer 1943, until there were 3,525 at the end of that year (1,331 "Ostarbeiter") as opposed to 11,884 remaining in the "German Following." "However,

based on all of our experiences until now the prospects of getting new labor in 1944 are considered dim."

171. Krohn, notes, 2 July 1943, BA R 87/6337/3, 736.
172. BA R 87/6338/4, 90.
173. Lüer to Krohn, 13 Aug. 1943, BA R 87/6337/4, 149 and Lüer to Krohn, 1 March 1944, BA R 87/6337/4, 304.
174. Minutes of the Adam Opel advisory council of 26 November 1944, BA R 87/6337/4 P. 1.
175. Richter to Kellermann, 17 Nov. 1944, BA R 87/6337/4 P. 52.
176. Pierre Cuillier, French POW with Kommando 1737/B, diary of 1 April 1944 to 25 March 1945, in Stadtarchiv Russelsheim.
177. BA R 87/6339/5, 168.
178. "Industrial Targets in Western and Central Germany, USAF, Op. 484, Air 40/688, 14/2663 (Attached: RAF GN-3156, 10 Sept. 1944)," in USSBS, "Adam Opel AG – Russelsheim."
179. War damages as of 1 Oct. 1944 are described in BA R 6340/5, 23ff.; see also Richter to Consul Belitz, 8 Aug. 1944, in BA R 87/6339/5 P. 175 and Richter to Kellermann, 11 Jan. 1945, in BA R 6340/6,72. As for the Brandenburg factory in the Soviet zone after the war, in its official rebuttal to Snell (1974) before the Senate, General Motors (1974) wrote: "As the war drew to a close, the Russian army occupied what remained of the Opel facility at Brandenburg.... The Russians dismantled the plant and shipped all machinery and equipment by rail to Kutau in the Russian Caucasus. The dismantling even included removal of portions of the buildings. (It should be noted that the Potsdam Agreement of 1945 specifically provided that the Soviets could satisfy their claims against Germany by removing property from the Soviet Zone.)" This was one basis for General Motors's postwar collection of U.S. federal funds in compensation for its wartime losses.
180. RAF, as in note 178.
181. Cuillier diary, as in note 176. The German reports were of 115 dead: R/6339/5, 218.
182. Thomas Frickel, "Vor vierzig Jahren: Die Amerikaner sind da: Hasserfüllte Bürger erschlagen wehrlose US-Soldaten. Bombenangriff auf Rüsselsheim treibt die Menschen zu brutaler Lynchjustiz," *Rüsselsheimer Echo* (28 June 1985), 8–9.
183. USSBS, as in 178.
184. Lüer to Krohn, BA R 87/6340/6,76f.
185. BA R 87/6340/6, 81.
186. Cf. Neugebauer (1997), 169. Andrea Neugebauer is currently overseeing a project to gather oral testimonies of the war in Russelsheim, including from former forced laborers.
187. Richter to Kellermann, BA R 87/8975, 1.
188. Ulrich (1997), 125.
189. Richter to Kellermann, BA R 87/8975, 1.

Chapter 2 1945. How the Americans Took Over Cologne
By Reinhold Billstein, Hamburg. Researched and written for the present volume. Sections are based on Billstein and Illner (1995).

1. Michael Hirsh in *Newsweek*, December 14, 1998: "Recently declassified U.S. documents show that at least 300 American companies continued doing business in Germany alone during the war, says Marc Masurovski, a former Justice Department historian.... While the U.S. Trading With the Enemy Act prevented direct dealings, a loophole permitted third-party transactions—usually through neutral nations. Two of the Big Three automakers, Ford and General Motors, have also faced allegations that their German subsidiaries used slave labor during the war; both companies have denied all or most responsibility for such actions during wartime."
2. Nevins and Hill (1963), Wilkins and Hill (1964).
3. Higham (1983). Reiling (1997), the most recent study to examine Ford Motor's activities in Germany during the Nazi era, also fails to deal with forced labor, see 365–415. Nevins and Hill (1963) presented a line of argument, when in doubt favoring the Ford Motor Company, that was later picked up by Reich (1990). In his Chapter 4, "The Wing and a

Prayer: Ford on the German Periphery," Reich takes a political economy approach in pre-senting the company's German involvements starting in the mid-1920s, relying mainly on sources from the company's archive that were previously accessible to Nevins and Hill (1963) and Wilkins and Hill (1964). As Reich's title implies, he argues that Ford-Werke AG played only a peripheral role in Germany in the years 1933 to 1945. He claims that Ford was especially disadvantaged by the Nazi regime in comparison to General Motors and the German companies, and therefore achieved only marginal business success. "The company returned profits between 1934 and 1939, but its development was stymied" (119). "Early years of solvency were ruined by catastrophic subsequent years" (124). The question of why the company continued doing business with the regime, even after the beginning of the war and despite the political and economic restrictions, is answered in a value-neutral fashion. At worst it is seen as indicating a problem in the capitalist value sys-tem: "Although the long-term goal of the company remained maximizing profits, its more immediate concern was simple survival as a corporate entity. Ford was willing to adhere to state policy if that was the price of economic survival, thereby revealing much about corporate priorities in a capitalist system" (118f.). Reich was the first U.S. author to devote several pages to the use of forced labor at Ford in Cologne, but he refrains from a critical evaluation of the matter.

4. The section title was a headline in the *New York Times* (NYT), 7 Mar. 1945.
5. "The Lesson of Aachen," NYT, 14 Oct. 1944. "Aachen: A Test of Nazi Fanaticism," NYT, 15 Oct. 1944.
6. The RAF dispatched 5,087 bombers on sorties to Cologne from January 1942 to Sep-tember 1944, dropping a cumulative 13,199 tons. The U.S. first assumed a significant role in the attacks in fall 1944. Public Record Office (PRO), Kew by London, AIR 14/36822 2269: Cologne, Raid Data; National Archives, Washington DC, Record Group 243, Box 401: "Cologne-R.A.F. (Bomber Command) Attacks" (dated 28 Mar. 1945, lists all British air attacks on Cologne in the years 1942 to 1945), and "Cologne-U.S.A. 8th A.F. Attacks" (dated 30 Mar. 1945, lists all U.S. raids on Cologne).
7. Until October 1944, strategically deployed repair teams, many of them employing forced laborers, usually succeeded in restoring infrastructure and plant to functioning order.
8. "U.S. Tanks Cross Erft 7 Miles from Cologne," NYT, 1 Mar. 1945.
9. Howard Katzender, in YANK, *The Army Weekly*, 20 April 1945.
10. Associated Press (AP), 3 Mar. 1945.
11. In early April 1945, E1H2 registered 42,000 persons in Cologne west of the Rhine. The municipal authorities later estimated that only twelve to fourteen thousand people wit-nessed the arrival of the American troops in early March 1945.
12. "Total Destruction," *Chicago Times*, 19 Mar. 1945.
13. Margaret Bourke-White, *Deutschland, April 1945* (Munich, 1979), Plate 22.
14. NYT, 9 Mar. 1945. The *Washington Post* of 8 Mar. 1945 drew a less friendly picture: "The citizens here are the most obnoxious we have yet met in Germany," AP reporter Hal Boyle quoted an infantry major. "We've had difficulty with many of those living in the bet-ter districts of Cologne who don't yet seem to realize they have been conquered. The more you see of these people, the more you see there still is a good deal of resistance left in Germany.... One of the first things they ask is whether there will be more air raids now that the Americans are in the city."
15. NA, RG 243, Box 118: SHAEF, Psychological Warfare Division (PWD), Intelligence Sec-tion: Weekly Intelligence Summary for Psychological Warfare, #25, 21 Mar. 1945, 3.
16. Ibid.
17. NYT, 8 Mar. 1945, followed up by a story on the survivors, "Camden Yank Finds Family in Cologne," NYT, 9 Mar. 1945. The figures here do not account for the number, still unknown today, of Jews from Cologne who saved themselves at least temporarily by emi-grating to other countries. *Widerstand* (1974) on 149 estimates that 11,000 Cologne Jews "were sent to the extermination camps." Emigration or flight to neighboring countries only meant safety until those countries were occupied by German forces. Becker-Jákli (1993) writes (352): "Persecution, incarceration and deportation was thus also the fate of

Cologne Jews who sought refuge in the neighboring western countries of Belgium, the Netherlands, and France.… Only a few survived, and only a few came back to Cologne."

18. Katzender, as in note 9.

19. E1H2, Daily Report, 9 Mar. 1945. Rusinek (1989) devotes a chapter (441ff.) to Gestapo terror in the last days and weeks before the occupation of Cologne.

20. "Political Prisoners," *Washington Post*, 17 Mar. 1945. "Gestapo Prisoners," *Washington Post*, 18 Mar. 1945.

21. On 29 Oct. 1945 the *Kölnischer Kurier*, the newspaper of the (by then British) occupation force, cited a figure of "well over 2,000" Gestapo executions of political prisoners in Cologne, most of the victims having been Soviet or Polish forced laborers.

22. For a complete treatment of E1H2's structure and personnel, see Billstein and Illner (1995), 77–113.

23. Ibid., 123–33.

24. "Creating Order Out of Cologne Chaos," *The Observer*, 25 Mar. 1945.

25. The following excerpt (E1H2, 9 Mar. 1945) documents some of the unit's activities on the day E1H2 officially took over Cologne: "The superintendent of Distribution and Maintenance of the Water System was interviewed and plans of the system were obtained with all known information on ruptures in the lines. The Hochkirchen pumping plant can be put into the line in two days if provision is made for transportation of coal. The manager of the plant departed several days ago. A conference was held with the Maintenance Superintendent of Transmission and Transformation of Power within Cologne proper. Coal will be the key to the water problem. With a 150 KW set, water can be put into about one half of the city. This set is needed to activate the pumping plant and a 13,000 KW generator.… During the day, 36 Displaced Persons were listed. These people were French, Belgian, Dutch and Polish. They are to be evacuated and some are having difficulty obtaining food because they do not have ration tickets. Food distribution points are being instituted so that these discriminatory practices will cease. Displaced Persons and Jews will be issued cards when the ration system is reestablished. The MGO of the 104th Inf Div was contacted relative to procedure to be followed on all DP uncovered in their area. They agreed to handle it. It was reported that several hundred French workers are in the immediate area.… The Detachment Public Health Officer and Capt Burns, Medical Inspector of the 104th Inf Div went to the Health Office, 15 Neumarkt and found the records on typhus for the past 25 years, including considerable information regarding the present epidemic and possibly a large number of localities of cases. The Health Office is destroyed. Considerable quantities of German typhus vaccine were located and turned over to the 104th Inf Div pending release of civilian medical supplies to Military Government. A conference was held with Colonel Barr, Surgeon, VII Corps, wherein it was arranged for two ambulances to be assigned to this detachment for two weeks to transport typhus cases."

26. For a complete standard treatment of foreign and forced labor in the Third Reich see Herbert (1985), here 332, and *Europa und der Reichseinsatz,* ed. Herbert (1991). In the introduction to this later collection, Herbert estimates that the total number of foreign workers brought to Germany for Reichseinsatz during the whole of the war would have numbered about 9.5 million. About 400,000 KZ prisoners were also deployed as forced laborers within Reich territory during the war. That meant that 33 percent of the overall labor force at the high point in the use of "foreign labor" in September 1944 would have been "foreign civilians," "prisoners of war," or "KZ prisoners." They represented 46 percent of the workers in agriculture, 36 percent in mining, and "up to 80 percent at given workplaces with a high proportion of unskilled labor."

27. George Orwell, "Allies Facing Food Crisis in Germany: Problem of Freed Workers," *The Observer*, 15 April 1945.

28. SHAEF, PWD, Weekly Intelligence Summary for Psychological Warfare, No. 13, 27 Dec. 1944. Polish workers were first subjected to a 15 percent surcharge on their wages, described as a "social equalization charge," in 1940. Businesses using laborers from the Soviet Union paid an "Ostarbeiter" surcharge, which they would extract from the workers'

nominal wages. Wages for "Ostarbeiter" and Poles were officially equalized in summer 1944, but this was by no means uniformly enforced. The system of social discrimination subjected upon foreign and forced laborers is described extensively in Herbert (1985).

29. SHAEF, PWD, Weekly Intelligence Summary for Psychological Warfare, No. 13, 27 Dec. 1944.

30. The list was compiled in January 1949 and based on a survey commissioned by the municipality and carried out by police precincts. HAStK, Acc. 606, No. 2.

31. Herbert (1985), 447. The number of "Ostarbeiter" at this time was given as 11,652, meaning 41.1 percent of foreigners in Cologne. For a more complete treatment of the use of foreign laborers and prisoners of war in Cologne's industry see Rüther (1990), 342–52.

32. See Rolf Wagenführ, *Die deutsche Industrie im Krieg 1939–1945* (Berlin 1963), 148–57.

33. The Ford Werke A.G. advisory council had been appointed in May 1942 under the Reich enemy property decrees to replace the supervisory board (directorate) of the company. Its members were simply the German members of the former supervisory board. The minutes of the meetings are available at the Bundesarchiv Berlin (BA), in the files of the Reichskommissar for the Treatment of Enemy Property, Johannes Krohn: "Protokoll über die Beiratssitzung der Ford-Werke A.G." (minutes of the Ford Werke advisory council), BA R 87, No. 6205.

34. Ibid., 13 Jan. 1943.

35. Ibid., 1 July 1943.

36. "Factory Brief on Ford Werke A.G., Cologne," prepared by the USSBS Motor Vehicles–Tanks–Armored Vehicles Section, 31 Oct. 1944 (henceforth: USSBS "Factory Brief"), in NA RG 243, USSBS, Box 690. The actual living conditions were obviously different. Rosellen (1986) writes (178f.) that the forced laborers "cost Ford Werke only a fraction of the hourly wage of a regular laborer. The foreigners were under the supervision of the German authorities, who were also provided them with food. Feeding the foreign laborers at Ford was a particular problem. This is exemplified in the leaflets distributed among the permanent personnel: 'The begging for bread among the Ostarbeiter has taken on such dimensions that now everyone must help in doing away with this begging,' one of these read. According to the leaflet, the foreigners did not beg because they were hungry, but 'entirely in order to enrich themselves. The loaves acquired through begging are resold at fantasy prices of up to 30 RM.'" Rosellen devotes all of a paragraph to forced labor. As his source he cites "interviews with leading employees of Ford Werke Cologne from then and now," without naming anyone. His account reduces the number of foreign laborers and prisoners of war by two-thirds and dates the advent of compulsory labor by foreigners at Ford to 1943 (instead of 1940). Nevertheless, he did not hesitate to draw the conclusion that "unlike many other companies, Ford took care of its foreign laborers. The relationship is supposed to have been so good that Russian prisoners of war once ran for help, showing great consternation, when the factory employee in charge of them (*Werks-Betreuer*) had an accident. Thanks to the good relations, there was never any looting after the end of the war."

37. Unfortunately, the U.S. embassy's original report on Schmidt's visit to Lisbon has yet to be found.

38. See also Ford Werke's long in-house memo by C. Paul, "Bericht über Reise nach Spanien und Portugal vom 22. Juni 1943." Paul's memo devotes only nine barren lines to the "very short" visit to Portugal. It is Exhibit 219B in the "Report on Ford Werke Aktiengesellschaft," 5 Sept. 1945, in NA, RG 407, The Adjutant General's Office, Box 1032: External Assets Investigations Branch (henceforth: "Report on Ford Werke").

39. "Foreign laborers in Germany averaged between twenty and twenty-four years of age, but many children of thirteen and fourteen were also registered as 'employed'. One-third of all foreign civilian workers and fifty percent of the Soviet and Polish civilian laborers were women, most of them not yet twenty." *Europa und der Reichseinsatz* (1991), 7.

40. NYT, 12 May 1944.

41. "Handbook of Military Government," 1 Sept. 1944, Para. 483–511.

42. "Displaced Persons and Refugees in Germany," SHAEF Memorandum, No. 39, 18 Nov. 1944, and revised version of 16 April 1945.

43. Jacobmeyer (1985), 31.
44. NYT, 14 Mar. 1945.
45. E1H2, Daily Report, 7 April 1945.
46. E1H2, 17 April 1945.
47. E1H2, 19 and 21 April 1945.
48. E1H2, 17 April 1945. The Knaepper bread factory was commissioned, at the City of Cologne's expense, to bake exclusively for the DP camps.
49. Administration was assigned to a former POW "Russian captain," who had run a similar camp near Aachen. The new center was opened the next day.
50. By then the U.S. 12th Army Publicity and Psychological Warfare detachment had already established a German newspaper, the *Kölnischer Kurier*. According to the edition of 5 May 1945, "The Allies have taken 50,000 to 60,000 foreign deportees in the Cologne region into their care since the beginning of the occupation.... Tens of thousands have found shelter in three large camps, where they are being cared for until they can begin their journey home." There were 10,000 Russians in Ossendorf and 5,000 Poles in southeastern Cologne, the paper reported.
51. Jacobmeyer (1985), 41f. and 59f., especially the statistical overview on 60; Ziemke (1975), 284; Henke (1995), 420f.
52. In detail: Billstein and Illner (1995), 77–113.
53. *The New York Sun*, 8 Mar. 1945, quotes MG Officer Lt. Col. Patterson and his executive Major Ross at their first press conference in Cologne on 7 Mar. 1945: "We [had gotten] together forms of all descriptions for reports on public utilities, industries and the case records of people. We worked out instructions to banks, police officials, fire chiefs and various other people. All of whom have ceased to live here." In "Bringing Cologne to Life," *Time*, 26 Mar. 1945, 20: "They had moved into this wasteland of 'wrecked masonry surrounded by city limits' on the hot wheels of the doughboys. They had been preparing for the job since last Sept. They knew from aerial maps what damage the city had taken."
54. E1H2, 9 Mar. 1945.
55. E1H2, 10 Mar. 1945.
56. "Directive for Military Government of Germany Prior to Defeat or Surrender," 9 Nov. 1944, Section III, Trade and Industry, 9a, allowed production only of: "(i) Food products; (ii) Medical supplies; (iii) Sanitation supplies; (iv) Soap; (v) Liquid fuels; (v) Solid fuels; (vii) Fertilizers; (viii) Raw materials, semi-finished goods, repair parts and equipment required for production of the above items, and for current maintenance of the plants and mines." NA RG 165, War Department, Civil Affairs Division (WD, CAD), Box 23.
57. A complete list of the companies assessed is found in Billstein and Illner (1995), 219.
58. "Ruined Germany," *Washington Post*, 21 Mar., 1945. "Ruined Cologne," *Washington Post*, 20 Mar. 1945, also in *Chicago Times*, 19 Mar. 1945: "You cannot conceive the meaning of complete destruction until you see this ruin." Childs cited a figure of 125,000 civilian casualties. The City of Cologne later determined that 20,000 people had died in the air war. Forty percent of all structures in the city were destroyed, including 90 percent of the city center.
59. See also Schwarz (1980), 92ff.
60. John McCloy Diaries, Amherst College Archives, 5, 6, 8 April 1945.
61. NYT, 27 April 1945.
62. "At Nordhausen there were reported to have been found 3,000 bodies apparently died of starvation. 2,000 survivors remained, including prisoners of war, forced laborers, and political prisoners, all suffering from various diseases, neglected severe malnutrition. At Iserlohn there were reported 23,000 Allied prisoners of war and displaced persons, mostly Russians. Approximately 9,000 are ill, 900 with tuberculosis."– SHAEF, G-5, Military Government–Civil Affairs Weekly Field Report, No. 46 (28 April 1945), 10f. (NA RG 243, Box 50).
63. Novick (1999), 7, cites William Casey, who in 1945 headed secret intelligence in the European theater for the Office of Strategic Services (the OSS, predecessor to the CIA) and who became director CIA in the 1980s.
64. "Civil Affairs Weekly Field Report," No. 45, 21 April 1945, 6.

65. Ibid., no. 50 (26 May 1945), 3.
66. Drew Middleton, "'Hard' Policy Fixed for Ruling Reich. Elimination of Germany's War Making Capacity Set as First Goal by SHAEF Deputy," NYT, 17 May 1945.
67. Ibid.
68. NYT, 27 May 1945.
69. Anonymous paper, "undated, filed 7 July '45," presumably written by a high official in the Finance Division USGCC. NA RG 46, Senate National Defense Committee, Box 995.
70. *American National Biography*, vol. 6 (New York, 1999), 798 (Ellis W. Hawley on Lewis William Douglas); NA RG 46, Senate NDC, MG in Germany, Box 995, Military Government Personnel (on Graeme Howard). Howard had gone on record with his politics, not far removed from those of Henry Ford, in his 1940 book, *America and a New World Order*. On his role at Ford Motor Company in 1947 and 1948 see Wilkins and Hill (1963), 366ff.
71. John McCloy's important role in shaping U.S. policy towards Germany as assistant secretary of war in 1945 is trenchantly described in Bird (1992), 228–39. General Draper, a Wall Street banker and a vice president at Dillon & Read, was also a career officer in the U.S. military administration. In Germany he was a "realist" from the start and played a key role in Clay's military government. He rose to undersecretary of war in 1947, gaining even greater influence over developments in Germany.
72. USGCC, Political Division, J. W. Tutthill to Robert H. Murphy, 2 Mar. 1945: "At the present time the Finance Division, US Group CC, is expanding its staff with Justice and Treasury Department officials interested in cartel investigations.… It is my view that all of the cartel investigations … should be kept under *operational* control by the Political Division." Murphy to Despres, 4 April 1945: "I talked yesterday with Colonel Bernstein … and he tells me that he has now a total of forty people on his staff including a certain number of Treasury and Justice officials interested in Cartel investigations and the Safehaven project. Naturally I feel that cartel investigations should be kept under the general wing of the Political Division. The Treasury Department of course does have a legitimate interest in the Safehaven operation to the extent of foreign exchange questions and the like." BA (Koblenz), OMGUS, RG 260, POLAD/737/26–28.
73. Moses Abramovitz to Dr. Lubin, report, Trip Through Western Germany (14 May 1945), 10: "The most generally expressed sentiment, met at every level of the organization from Generals Clay and McSherry down to local MG detachments, was that German economic activity must be restored. This is put forward in a general way and without specifications of the kinds of activity to be permitted or their proportions." NA RG 165, WD CAD, Box 26.
74. Ibid., 5.
75. E1H2 Daily Report, 11 Mar. 1945. In addition a "survey was made of Glanzstoff-Courtaulds, manufacturers of artificial silk and wool; ownership 50% British capital. The plant was only 5% damaged but its product would not be of any use to the Army."
76. E1H2, 11 Mar. 1945.
77. Total personnel numbered at least 5,742 in early 1944 and well above 5,200 in the third quarter of that year, according to Reichskommissar Krohn's "Final report on Ford-Werke AG," which he delivered to the Allied military on 1 Aug. 1945 (BA R 87, 6206).
78. E1H2, 11 Mar. 1945.
79. E1H2, 14 Mar. 1945.
80. EOU Aiming Point Report No. IE-2, May 29, 1943, Ford Motor CO., Cologne. The documents on Ford collected by USSBS also included the Justice Department report on German Ford from 10 May 1943. NA RG 243 (USSBS), Box 690.
81. "Production was hindered by lack of transportation from industrial centres that had been bombed. Ford, Cologne was supposed to get radiators from plants in France, Belgium and Holland but due to sabotage the production of these three countries did not cover the needs of the plant." USSBS "Factory Brief" (note 36).
82. Report No. 67, UK Field Information Agency, Technical (FIAT), 13 Dec. 1945, on "Causes of the Decline in German Industrial Production in Autumn, 1944." Among the exhibits is a statement by Wilhelm Schaaf, "Director of BMW and Head of the powerful 'Main Committee for Motor Vehicles' in the Speer Ministry." According to Schaaf: "The

precision bombing of factories had a far greater effect than the attacks on towns and the blast of fire damage which individual factories suffered on these occasions. An example of this is the difference between the effects of the successful bombing of the STEYR motor car factory at Steyr and the OPEL factory at Brandenburg [6 Aug. 1944], and the effects of the regular attacks on, for example, Mannheim and Cologne with regard to the output of DAIMLER BENZ and FORD.... The production program in the above mentioned factories did not decline more than 20% through the bombing of towns." "The complete decline of production was only achieved by the systematic destruction of the means of transport." NA RG 260, Industry Branch, Box 1.

83. USSBS "Factory Brief" (note 36): "2 Oct. 1944, Area [attack], 111 [planes]; 15 Oct. 1944, Precision, 17 [planes]; 18 Oct. 1944: Precision, 68 [planes] ..." U.S.A. 8th A.F. [all] Attacks [on Cologne], Listing from 30th Mar. 1945 (NA RG 243, USSBS, Box 401).–Five hundred and twenty tons of explosives fell next to the plant and on the other side of the Rhine. See also Rosellen (1988), 11.

84. Interpretation Reports ("Attack on Cologne") nos. S.A. 2840 (15 Oct. 44), 2841 (16 Oct. 44), and 2847 (19 Oct. 44). NA RG 243, USSBS, Box 36.

85. Interpretation Report K. 3362, "Locality: Cologne, 14th Nov 1944," in NA RG 243, USSBS, Box 401. Also "Report on Ford Werke" (note 38), exh. 204: R. H. Schmidt to Lord Perry of Stock Harvard, 28 May 1945.

86. Ibid.

87. Minutes of Ford-Werke AG advisory council, 13 Jan. 1943.

88. Ibid., also "Report on Ford Werke," exh. 204, Schmidt to Lord Perry, 28 May 1945.

89. Minutes of Ford-Werke AG advisory council, 20. Between August 1944 and the end of the war approximately 4,500 three-ton Ford trucks were produced in Cologne and a total of 3,500 Opel trucks at Daimler-Benz. On the Mannheim plant see Gregor (1998), 148f.

90. German Economic Department, Control Office for Germany and Austria (COGA), London: "German Industrial Complexes: Ford Werke A.G., February 1946" (henceforth: COGA, "German Industrial Complexes"), 4. NA RG 260, OMGUS, Econ. Div., Box 312. Also: Boyer (1985), 35. Boyer cites company employees who stated that replacement parts production was continued with forced laborers at the Ford dispersal locations behind the German lines until the beginning of March 1945.

91. "Report on Ford Werke," exh. 205, Schmidt to Lord Perry, 28 May 1945, 7: The "plant was occupied by combat units.... A few hours before the occupation and caused by American shelling our emergency offices in which we had worked ever since October, burned down entirely and with them many papers, prints, invoices, etc." On 15 June 1945 Marion Dogerloh, secretary to managing director Schmidt, made the following statement: "One day before the occupation of Cologne ... I took the records (concerning Maschinenfabrik Walter Arendt GmbH) to our emergency offices in the barracks.... I had to leave the barracks because of very heavy shell fire in the course of which the barracks burnt down entirely." "Report on Ford Werke," exh. 165.

92. Ibid. See also Interpretation Report K 300(R), 18 July 1945, based on aerial reconnaissance of 2 June 1945. NA RG 243, USSBS, Box 687.

93. "Report on Ford Werke," exh. 205, Schmidt to Lord Perry, 28 May 1945, 7: "In August 1944 we received an order to evacuate all machines from Cologne into six different places on the other side of the river.... However, no progress was made until Nov 16th, when, threatened by drastic measures on the part of the German Government, and until the last day before the occupation we evacuated about 80% of our machinery. This machinery was set up in six [pencil: 5] various localities and with the exception of one place is ready to operate. Two [pencil: 3] places are operating at present."

94. J. Gilbert Jones and Walter K. Schwinn ("Civilian,") "Target Inspection Report," 20 Mar. 1945, G-2 Economic Section SHAEF, in NA RG 243, USSBS, Box 690.

95. Colonel Bernstein to General Wickersham (Acting Deputy, USGCC), 5 April 1945: "Report on Project to Investigate German International Assets," 5 Apr. 1945 (henceforth: Bernstein, "Report on Project," 5 Apr. 1945), 5. NA RG 260, IG Farben CO, Box 2.

96. Quoted in J.S. Martin (1950), 16.

97. Bernstein, "Report on Project," 5 April 1945, 2.
98. "Germany: General Objectives of United States Economic Policy with Respect to Germany," approved 4 Aug. 1944, final report 15 Mar. 1945, in "Policy Decisions of the Executive Committee on Economic Foreign Policy (ECEFP)" NA RG 59, Notter Files, Box 32. More detailed papers were prepared by the Special Committee on Private Monopolies and Cartels (SCPC), also coordinated by the State Department, e.g., Cartel Memo 137, dated 15 May 1945 and titled "U.S. Policy Towards German Domestic Cartels and Cartel-Like Organizations," NA RG 165, War Dept. CAD, Box 26. Therein the "general objectives" of U.S. policy were formulated as follows: "(a) a limitation of the power of the larger industrial aggregations in Germany, many of which were linked with the Nazis in their program of military and economic aggression; (b) depriving Germany of the economic means of resuming hostilities and making impossible the repetition of the long series of acts by which Germany was converted into a war economy and placed in a position to launch and sustain a total war of aggression; (c) the promotion, as far as possible, of conditions of unrestricted trade both in Germany's domestic market and in Europe generally."
99. See Henke (1995), 986f., "Der Primat des Pragmatismus."
100. Robert Murphy to General Wickersham, General McSherry (Deputy Assistant Chief of Staff, Civil Affairs) and Colonel Bernstein, 11 April 1945–NA RG 260, USGCC, Box 1.
101. Headquarters US Group CC, Committee on German Cartels: "Preliminary Report" (4 May) and reports for May (31 May) and June (30 June). NA RG 260, USGCC. Box 1. The new tasks resulted from the sudden intensification of the action against IG Farben. See OMGUS, *Control of I.G. Farben: Special Report of Military Governor U.S. Zone*, 1 Oct. 1945: "The objectives of the seizure of I.G. Farbenindustrie–the largest corporation in Germany and the largest chemical corporation in the world–were to forever destroy its monopolistic control over German industry and to eliminate the war potential which it represented. Specific objectives of the seizure included making its plants available for reparations, destroying certain plants utilized for strictly war purposes, decentralizing the management and dispersing the ownership of individual units, terminating interests in cartels and cartel-like arrangements and preventing research for war purposes." NA RG 260, USGCC, Box 1.
102. *Roosevelt and Morgenthau*, ed. John Morton Blum (Boston, 1970), 630.
103. Bernstein, "Report on Project," 5 Apr. 1945, 2. See also J.S. Martin (1950), 18, for an account of how the group was formed, and Greiner (1995), 103–108, 217. Although the British emphasized an effective policy of control and were skeptical of structural intervention, their Control Commission supported Bernstein's investigation program and assigned men to the detail in July. "The importance of uncovering Germany's Foreign Assets has been recognized by the British and American Governments." Therefore "Joint US/BR Financial Teams will investigate the main German industrial combines and companies and are already at work on I.G. Farben, Krupps, Vereinigte Stahlwerke, and other large concerns. Their work includes the examination of financial records and balance sheets, foreign correspondence files, directors' personal files, patent files, etc., and the interrogation of vital personnel." NA RG 260, IG Farben CO, Box 11: Chief Finance Division of the British Control Commission for Germany, "Financial Investigations into German External Assets," circular, 2 July 1945.
104. Bernstein, "Report on Project," Annex 1: "List of Initial Objectives (by Cities and Companies)," 5 Apr. 1945.
105. D. Lewis, *The Public Image of Henry Ford* (Detroit, 1976), 241–250, and Nevins and Hill (1964), first chapter. Harry J. Carman et al., *A History of the American People*, vol. II (2nd ed., revised), New York 1964, 617. Carman et al. write that a 1930s Congressional investigation found "unparalleled force, brutality, and deception had been used to combat unionism." But "among the great American corporations using such tactics, Ford's antiunion work was most shocking. Instead of hired outside detectives, the Ford Service men, a group of about 800 thugs, intimidated and beat up workers suspected of union activity. The Ford empire had police-state tendencies; crimes ranged from talking on the job to joining a union."

106. Wilkins and Hill (1964), 308: "As noted earlier, Ford liked the German people: their cleanliness, thrift, technical aptitude, and discipline. He seems even to have admired certain traits of Adolf Hitler: his capacity for leadership, his successful war against unemployment, his urge to build an automobile industry in the Reich, and perhaps [!] his anti-Semitism, although Ford had no sympathy whatever with the Fuehrer's ruthlessness, violence, or plans for conquest."
107. Ibid., 282.
108. Ibid., 317.
109. "Report on Ford Werke," exh. 171A: Albert to General Zuckertort, 26 June 1940.
110. J. John Lawler, Office of the General Counsel, Treasury Department, "Report of Investigation of Ford, Societé Anonyme Francaise; Machinery Suppliers, Inc., Matford S.A., Fordair S.A.," May 1943 (henceforth: Lawler, "Report of Investigation of Ford," May 1943), in Charles Higham Collection, University of Southern California, Archives of Performing Arts, Cinema/Television Library, Los Angeles, Box 1.
111. Ibid. and Randolph Paul, Treasury Department, "Statement for Henry Morgenthau, Jr.," 25 May 1943.
112. Lawler, "Report of Investigation of Ford," May 1943, 1–5.
113. Ibid., and Randolph Paul, "Statement," 25 May 1943.
114. Lawler, "Report of Investigation of Ford," May 1943, 26 f.
115. Ibid., 34, 40f.
116. Ibid., 63 ff.
117. Ibid., 68: "Under these circumstances, there would seem to be at least a tacit acceptance by Mr. Edsel Ford of the reliance by Mr. Dollfus on the known neutrality of the Ford family as a basis of receipt of favors from the German Reich."
118. Ford Archives, Henry Ford Museum and Greenfield Village in Dearborn, Michigan, Acc. 713, Box 3, "Cologne: Memorandum," 26 July 1945 (henceforth: "Cologne: Memorandum," Ford Archives): "The Treasury Department and Department of Justice have checked all of the records and correspondence relative to the German company as well as other Ford companies in France, etc., and these transactions are therefore all a matter of record with the proper government departments. No criticism has ever been made by any government department with reference to transactions with our French and German companies." Johannes Reiling kindly provided me with a copy of this document.
119. Higham (1983),XVI.
120. "There are probably as many as one hundred German industrial and financial organizations, including such as the Vereinigte Stahlwerke, Siemens, Osram, AEG, and the principal banks whose records should be examined in any comprehensive inquiry of this sort. To date the investigation has been largely concerned with a single company, I.G. Farben." Norman Bursler to Orvis A. Schmidt, 13 June 1945, NA RG 260, IG Farben CO, Box 29. Bursler (from Justice) and Orvis Schmidt (Treasury) were among Bernstein's closest associates in the spring of 1945.
121. In larger cases "the key documents and personnel will ... be brought to Frankfurt and held there for the use of the team in developing the case." Finance Division, "Procedure for Financial Investigations," 20 June 1945, NA RG 260, IG Farben CO, Box 2. See also Wilkins and Hill (1964), 345. Schmidt wrote fifty-two of the fifty-seven interrogation statements used in the "Report on Ford Werke."
122. Henry Schneider submitted the "Report on Ford Werke" to Lt. Albert I. Edelman, Chief, External Assets Investigations Branch (EAI) under US Forces European Theater (USFET), Financial Branch.
123. Lindner (1991), 161. Reichskommissar Krohn surrendered himself and his files to the Americans on 17 April 1945 in Bavaria, but at that time it seems nobody informed the intelligence people charged with corporate investigations of Krohn's files on Ford and other companies. The Krohn archives are now stored in Berlin at BA R 87.
124. "Report on Ford Werke," 1, 4, 6, 7.
125. Ibid., exh. 1, "Memo concerning Ford-Werke A.G., as to whether a complete Germanization would be necessary or advisable," 25 Nov 1941, translation of the German original

(exh. 1A). Hoping to get the appointment as enemy property custodian of Ford Werke, Albert again belabored Ford's services to the Reich in a letter to the Reichskommissar on 12 Dec. 1941, the day after Germany went to war against the United States. He took a shot at the competition: "General Motors repatriated profits to the U.S. directly and indirectly until very recently. Ford-Werke A.G. has always kept all dividends due to the American parent company as loans or new share capital." BA, R87/6205, Berlin.

126. "Statement of Orvis A. Schmidt, Director of Foreign Funds Control, before the Kilgore Committee," 2 July 1945, NA RG 260, IG Farben CO, Box 2.

127. Ibid., 3.

128. "The Washington Merry-Go-Round," *Washington Post*, 17 July 1945.

129. On Albert see Reiling (1997), esp. 365–415, and Wilkins and Hill (1964), 270–285.

130. "Cologne: Memorandum," 26 July 1945, Ford Archives, Dearborn, states that such agreements applied "to all foreign owned German companies": "An objectionable feature of the transaction was that instead of using all the raw material imported into Germany as a result of this arrangement [Ford Werke was] obliged to deliver 100% of the rubber according to the instructions of the German authorities. Only 70 per cent was allocated to our German company, but, of course, they were paid for the total quantity supplied in local currency."

131. See Reiling (1997), 365–415, and Wilkins and Hill (1964), 270–276.

132. Kümmel (1995), 123, had access to all documents relating to Ford-Werke A.G. held at the Ford Archives in Dearborn.

133. Wilkins and Hill (1964), 278 f. and Boyer (1985), 26.

134. Kümmel (1985), 131.

135. Ibid., Albert to Sorensen, 20 Sept. 1937 (Ford Archives, Dearborn, Acc. 38, Box 40).

136. Reiling (1997), 378.

137. Ibid., 385, Sorensen to Albert, 17 Jan. 1938 (Ford Archives, Dearborn, Acc. 38, Box 40).

138. Wilkins and Hill (1964), 282.

139. "Report on Ford Werke," 6.

140. Ibid., exh. 4, "German manufacturers collecting information from American sources," 22 June 1945, and exh. 5, "German manufacturers collecting information from American sources–supplement," 6 July 1945.

141. COGA, "German Industrial Complexes," 2. Wilkins and Hill (1964) write (283f.): "In 1934 the company had sold 10,008 vehicles; in 1938, 36,748. It stood in forth place in the sale of passenger vehicles, with 23,969 units, with Opel (114,020), DKW (50,340) and Mercedes (25,330) ahead of it and held second in trucks, its 12,613 being surpassed only by Opel's 22,430.... For the first time in its history Ford AG paid a dividend in 1938. Its exports were soaring to a new high."

142. "Report on Ford Werke," 4.

143. Kümmel (1995), 134f., relies on documents written by the company's top executives: "In April 1939 the Cologne management expressed concerns similar to Dearborn's. The issue then was a further order to Dearborn for 1,500 to 3,000 trucks, which were intended for the Sudetenland." In such cases, according to Kümmel, the company's "desire for an increase in sales and profits was instrumentalized by the German government.... The armaments program was developed further even as German resources were preserved through the company's use of internal shipments from the U.S."

144. Wilkins and Hill (1964), 308.

145. Kümmel (1995), 137: "Dearborn supplied materiel such as metal mills well into the years 1940–41 and put in orders with American manufacturers that were intended for Cologne."

146. "Report on Ford Werke," exh. 190: Albert to Edsel Ford, 18.11.1940.

147. Ford-Werke A.G. (Schmidt and Krauch) to Reichskommissar Krohn, 18 June 1941. BA, R87/6205.

148. Ibid.

149. NSDAP Gauleitung Köln-Aachen, Gauwirtschaftsberater (Kurt von Schröder) to Kanzlei des Führers der NSDAP, 7 Feb. 1942, copy, BA R87/6205. See also Trepp (1993), 25f.

150. Kanzlei des Führers to Reichskommissar Krohn, 13 Feb. 1942, BA R87/6205.

151. COGA, "German Industrial Complexes," 5.
152. "Report on Ford Werke," 4. Three statements by Schmidt: exh. 89, "Ford trucks with army," 26 June 1945; exh. 90, "Capacity of Ford plants," 20 Aug. 1945, and exh. 91, "Halftracks," 10 July 1945. According to Rosellen (1986), 174, Ford produced about 14,000 half-tracks, Opel 4,000, Magirus about 2,500 and Mercedes-Benz 1,500. In late 1942 the Armaments Ministry delegated coordination of the Maultier program to the Ford Werke manager Alfons Streit. (Minutes of Ford-Werke AG advisory council, 13 Jan. 1943, BA R87/6205).
153. "Report on Ford Werke," exh. 161–70 (Schmidt's statements on Arendt GmbH).
154. Ibid., exh. 171A: Albert to General Zuckertort, 26 June 1940.
155. Ibid., 7.
156. Ibid., exh. 205, Schmidt to Lord Perry, 28 May 1945. Here Schmidt reduces the problem of foreign and forced laborers to three short references concerning employment of 200 French in 1941, 800 Russians in 1942, und 200 Italians in 1943.
157. Ibid., 7f.
158. Ibid., exh. 186: Albert to Edsel Ford and Sorensen, 11 July 1940; exh. 187: Schmidt to Ford and Sorensen, 19 Sept. 1940. Exhibit 206 of the "Report on Ford Werke" is an internal memorandum of 10 Mar. 1943, from Schmidt to A. von Gusmann of the company's Berlin office, concerning tactics for dealing with European Ford companies and with the Reich Economics Ministry (RWM): "Please pay a visit to Geheimrat Albert and with him write up a new statement [to RWM] which will do justice to our interests. Be guided by the tendency that even if we have no legal influence over the various companies, still they are greatly dependent upon us. At the same time you must not go too far with that, so as not to bind our hands if at some point we need RWM's help for a possible endeavor on our part to lay our hands tighter on these companies, such as through acquisition of a majority or the like. The latter is very unlikely, but it must always be considered as possible. We also need to keep in mind that we don't want our position to be nailed down in case the war should end favorably."
159. Ibid., exh. 208: Edsel Ford to Albert, 10 Oct. 1940.
160. Ibid., exh. 188: Edsel Ford to Schmidt, 31 Oct. 1940.
161. Ibid., exh. 191: Albert to Schmidt, 30 Dec. 1941, trans. as in the report.
162. Reichskommissar Krohn, "Final report on Ford-Werke A.G.," 1 Aug. 1945, BA R87/6206.
163. "Report on Ford Werke," exh. 205, Schmidt to Lord Perry, 28 May 1945.
164. Minutes of Ford Werke AG advisory council, 13 Jan. and 1 July 1943, BA R87/6205.
165. "Report on Ford Werke," 41, n.110.
166. E1H2, 18 April 1945.
167. E1H2, 28 April 1945.
168. E1H2, 3 May 1945.
169. Wilkins and Hill (1964), 344f.
170. E1H2, 8 May, 5 June 1945: "Mr. Neil Sullivan, Pathé News, completed the Military Government film on which he has been working for the past five weeks here in Cologne." The *New York Times* on 13 May covered the story as follows:

    Reich Ford Plant Open
    COLOGNE, Germany, May 12 (AP)– The explosives-scarred Ford plant here has started the assembly of motor trucks for occupation forces under an American-organized industrial revival. Renewal of operations was authorized by Supreme Headquarters May 4, the first truck was ready May 8 and the output now is approaching ten a day. Lieut. Col. Maurice Driscoll of Winthrop, Mass., who started the project, said there was sufficient stock on hand for 100 trucks of two and one-half-ton size immediately, and that 90 per cent of the necessary equipment was available to turn out 3,000 vehicles. The plant formerly employed 1,000 foreign workers. Its laborers now are Germans screened by military intelligence officers. The Ford works was bombed once by Allied planes, but it suffered more damage from the artillery of the retreating Germans in March.

171. Boyer (1985), 36.
172. Wilkins and Hill (1964), 345.
173. Figure from E1H2, 4 June 1945.
174. *Kriegsende und Neuanfang am Rhein,* ed. Küsters and Mensing (1986), 123.
175. Hilgermann (1961), 35, 48.
176. Ibid., 35.
177. Henke (1995), 244, quoting the "Historical Report of the 6th Army Group," April 1945 (back translation).
178. "Instructions from the Military Government of Cologne to the director of the German municipal authority," 26 Mar. 1945, Historical Archives of the City of Cologne (HaStK), Acc. 901, No. 20. Also E1H2 Daily Report, 2 May and 7 June 1945. According to NYT, "Americans Evolve Occupation Policy. Cologne Administration Drops Expediency, Barring Posts to Any Former Nazis," 26 Mar. 1945: "The aim of Col. John K. Patterson of California ... is to establish a city administration untainted by any former Nazis. But it is not easy, and the attempt to carry it out to the letter has resulted in considerable delay in getting the wheels turning again. Nazism, through terror and favoritism, got such a grip on the life of the community that finding a man or woman who had no connection with the party is an extremely difficult task. But many joined the party or its affiliated organizations with tongue in cheek and rendered only lip services. The trouble is that every Rhinelander, whether ardent Nazi or passive member of the party, insists that he joined merely because he had to do so to live and eat. It is not an easy job to determine who is lying."
179. Hilgermann (1961), 18.
180. Schneider and his team asked Schmidt to write an autobiographical note, exhibit 12 in the "Report on Ford Werke." Schmidt therein claimed that an E1H2 property control officer named Skinner, just before leaving Cologne in mid-June, informed him that he and Vitger were on "prewar status again," but also that the Military Government would not allow the executives Alfons Streit and Hans Löckmann to work at Ford or hold "any job influential on company matters." The MG men obviously knew that Streit and Löckmann were members of the NSDAP, but they were unaware of Schmidt's possible membership. Throughout his long de-Nazification procedure, Schmidt insisted he was not a member. He was believed. The more recently discovered letter from Kurt von Schröder to the Kanzlei des Führers (note 149) is still the only evidence that Schmidt was lying.
181. Rosellen (1988), 224.
182. Wilkins and Hill (1964), 334f.
183. Ibid., 285.
184. The Nazi daily *Völkischer Beobachter,* which was used for official statements, on 16 Dec. 1937 published an article on the "tasks and purposes of the Wehrwirtschaftsführer Corps": "The Reich War Minister and the Wehrmacht High Command can bestow the title of Wehrwirtschaftsführer on those German citizens who have performed or are performing exemplary duties towards the material strengthening of the Wehrmacht. This title expresses the voluntary commitment of business to in every way support the country's defense, as motivated by an attendant conviction and by every individual's duty to serve the Wehrmacht. Those who receive the title Wehrwirtschaftsführer are in turn especially obligated to uphold their loyalty to the State and to the Wehrmacht." See also *Sachwörterbuch der Geschichte Deutschlands und der deutschen Arbeiterbewegung,* vol. 2 (Berlin, 1970), 790f.
185. The Trading with the Enemy Act as amended prior to 1 May 1943 is reproduced in Martin Domke, *Trading With the Enemy in World War II* (New York, 1943), 385ff.
186. Bernstein to Clay, 9 Sept. 1945 (NA RG 407, Box 1032).
187. Dearborn memo of 26 July 1945, Ford Archives (note 118).
188. *The New York World Telegram,* 19 Sept. 1945. See also *Eleanor Roosevelt's My Day: Her Acclaimed Columns,* vol. 2: 1945–1952, ed. David Emblidge (New York, 1990). During the forties Eleonor Roosevelt's syndicated column "My Day" appeared six days a week in more than one hundred papers throughout the country.

189. The figures are from the Ford-Werke AG General Assembly Report, 1 July 1999 (www.Ford.de).
190. *Economist,* 7 Aug. 1999, 56.

Chapter 3 Walter Rietig and the Effort of Remembrance

By Bernd Heyl, Russelsheim. Originally appeared as Heyl (1997: 2). Brief sections have been adapted from other works in that volume (see notes 5 and 11–13).

1. *Als die Synagogen brannten* (1993), 4, 34f., 63–64.
2. Fogel (no year), 128.
3. After the First World War, the middle class and conservative parties were of only secondary significance in Russelsheim. The conservative Deutsche Volkspartei gathered just 770 votes in the Reichstag elections of 1928. That fell to 375 votes in the Reichstag election of November 1932, with a corresponding rise for the NSDAP. SPD, KPD, and the Catholic Center party were able to hold their ground in Russelsheim, suggesting that it was voters of the DNVP and other conservative parties who switched to the Nazis. See *Vom Beginn,* ed. Schirmbeck et al. (1988), 97.
4. This strategy was well-documented in the museum exhibition "Die neue Zeit und ihre Folgen – Alltag-Politik-Personen, Gross-Gerau 1869–1956." In 1932 the KPD organized a strike against cuts in support to unemployed people forced to perform "duty work." They posed their demands to the SPD Deputy Nold—who had no choice but to act as a municipal representative—with the express intent of "exposing" him. *Die Neue Zeit,* exh. cat. (1992), 46f.
5. The 1929–1930 events at Opel, as covered in the next two paragraphs, are treated in detail in Heyl (1997: 1), 15–34.
6. Christine Wittrock, *Egelsbach in politisch bewegter Zeit 1914–1950* (Frankfurt, 1991), 96–97:

> When the Friends of Nature chapter in Langen attempt to join the Free Sport and Singing Society, a group mostly of Social Democrats, a rough exchange follows between the Social Democrat and Communist members.… The Communist youth argue that the Langen chapter belongs to the Federation of Proletarian Friends of Nature, and consider it intolerable that it should be subordinated to, or be dissolved within, a bourgeois association. A vote is held. The Communists lose. They are now faced with expulsion from the group. This was a routine occurrence. Sometimes entire state associations were expelled.
>
> A compromise is finally reached within the regional youth organization. The Friends of Nature in the neighboring town of Egelsbach accept the more communist-thinking members from Langen. The Langen chapter will maintain a Social Democrat orientation. That way, at least, everyone remains in the organization.

7. *Hessische Gewerkschafter,* ed. Ulrich (1984), 159.
8. Busch (1988), 43f.
9. *Die Neue Zeit* (1992), 51f. A key figure in the Communist resistance was Herbert Wehner. "As the 'Lead Adviser of the Southwest,' meaning as the highest-ranking coordinator of the illegal KPD groups in southwestern Germany, Wehner tried … in the course of his travels to get KPD members to cooperate with Social Democrats." Wehner later fell out with the KPD, during a series of purges steered behind the scenes by Moscow. After the war he joined the West German SPD and served as its Bundestag floor leader until the 1970s.
10. Ibid.
11. A complete overview of known resistance activities at Opel and in Russelsheim during the Nazi era is given in: Ulrich (1997), 93–157. He appends documents (138–41) on the Friends of Nature by Fritz Grünewald and Albert Lehmann.
12. *Hessische Gewerkschafter* (1984), 60.
13. Ulrich (1997), esp. 93–98. [Aside from problems with documentary and oral sources on Nazi-era resistance, Ulrich maintains that the most serious distortion of history in this regard is ideological. In postwar West Germany an official mythology was built around

the military conspiracy that attempted to assassinate Hitler on 20 July 1944. Commentators still tend to style the disloyal Prussian generals who led the failed coup into the spiritual fathers of the Federal Republic. In a fiftieth-anniversary speech, on 20 July 1994, Chancellor Helmut Kohl said of the conspirators that: "They were not many, but they were the best." But most of "the relatively small group of conservative military men and bourgeois opposition figures associated with the 20th of July" (as Ulrich puts it) were originally loyal to the Nazis. They took action only late, when it was obvious that the "Third Reich" was doomed, and mainly in the hope of delivering a nationalist Germany from total destruction. Some among them entertained illusions of continuing the war against the Soviets with Western support after the coup. During the Cold War many West Germans were loath to admit instead that the "main part in the resistance," such as it was, had been "played by the suppressed workers' movement," with Communists in the forefront, starting in 1933. Of course, while focusing on resistance is important, it begs the question of why a majority of Germans supported the regime, or at least assented to it, to the bitter end. As Ulrich concludes, neither the shattered post-1933 workers movement nor the idealized "Men of 20 July" were able to topple the Nazis or stop the war. That took millions of Allied soldiers. −Ed.]

14. On Zängerle's role immediately after the war, see Neugebauer (1997) and Ulrich (1997).
15. Quoted in Herbert Bauch, "'Vergesst mich nicht …' − Vor fünzig Jahren starb Walter Rietig durch das Fallbeil," manuscript, City Archive of Russelsheim.
16. Fogel (no year), 132.
17. Ibid., 132f. In her dissertation Fogel favors the documents over the oral testimony. She views Walter Rietig's death as a case of arbitrary Nazi injustice, and questions whether he should be considered a resistance fighter: "It is not at all proven that Walter Rietig upheld contacts to the Communist resistance, for this claim is based on the testimony of a single Opel worker, and is in no way confirmed by the documentary sources …" (Fogel, 205). Our main source is indeed the testimony of a single witness. The story that Fritz Zängerle told many years after the war was, however, identical to his written account of 1946. Therein he wrote: "During this time, my intermediary to the foreigners (Walter Rietig from Langen) fell victim because of his anti-Fascist activities, and was executed for high treason in Berlin on 23 December 1942. (See the notes taken by Traiser from Gross-Gerau after his arrest by Massoth, apparently the source of the information about our activities.)" Fritz Zängerle, "Report on My Activities in the Illegal Factory Group," 3 January 1946, private collection. Even if Walter Rietig did not directly participate in one of the resistance groups, he was in close contact with them, and never renounced the beliefs he had formed while in the workers' movement. He was ready to participate in resistance activities. His death sentence, and the fact that he betrayed no one in the face of death, must be judged accordingly.
18. *Meldungen aus dem Reich,* ed. Boberach (1984), vol. 12, 4599.
19. Quoted in Bauch, "Vergesst mich nicht …" (note 15).
20. For a review of the various cases see Ulrich (1997).
21. Fogel (no year), 136.

Chapter 4 Forced Labor at Ford Werke in Cologne
By Karola Fings, Cologne. Researched and written for the present volume and completed in May 1999. The section on the Buchenwald satellite squad is adapted from Fings (1996). Brief passages are adapted from Fings's introduction and articles in *Zwangsarbeit bei Ford* (1996).

1. Cologne Standesamt (Office of the Registry), October 1949, statement on investigations into the whereabouts of foreigners missing from the Nazi period, in Hauptstaatsarchiv Dusseldorf (henceforth: HStAD), Gerichte Rep. 118/1179.
2. Fritz Theilen, at a public gathering during a visit by former forced laborers and the exhibition "Forced Labor at Ford" in Cologne, Sept. 1995.
3. Stepan Ivanovich Saika, letter to the NS-Dokumentationszentrum der Stadt Köln (henceforth: NS-Dok), 13 Feb. 1995.

4. Appeared in English as Herbert (1997). In his introduction Herbert writes of an earlier work by Homze (1967), which went almost unnoticed in the Federal Republic. Forced labor was the subject of studies in East Germany, for example Seeber (1964). Many studies dealt specifically with forced labor at the IG Farben combine. The different attitude in the GDR meant that far more material was secured in East German archives and is available for research today. For one overview of documents, see *Zwangsarbeit in der Provinz Brandenburg 1939–1945: Spezialinventar der Quellen im Brandenburgischen Landeshauptarchiv* (Frankfurt am Main, 1998).

5. For an extensive bibliography of company studies see Spoerer (1998:2).

6. *Das Daimler-Benz Buch* (1987); *Die Daimler-Benz AG* (1987).

7. See *Unternehmen im Nationalsozialismus*, ed. Gall and Pohl (1998).

8. For additional research on Daimler, see Hopmann et al. (1994) and Gregor (1998). On Volkswagen, see Siegfried (1988) and Mommsen with Grieger (1996).

9. Two extensive bibliographies are in Mommsen with Grieger (1996) and Mark Spoerer (1998:1), "Die Automobilindustrie," in *Unternehmen*, 61–68, carmakers specifically on 67. A preview of possible upcoming studies on Ford and General Motors is given in "Holocaust Lawsuits Spark Demand for Historians," NYT, 18 Feb. 1999.

10. For an overview of the history of restitutions for Nazi-era forced labor, see *Entschädigung für NS-Zwangsarbeit* (1998).

11. The Cologne visitors program and similar initiatives are described in Fings (1998), a brochure published by the Hans Böckler Foundation.

12. *Zwangsarbeit bei Ford* (1996).

13. Heidrun Edelmann, *Vom Luxusgut zum Gebrauchsgegenstand. Die Geschichte der Verbreitung von Personenkraftwagen in Deutschland* (Frankfurt am Main, 1989); Karl Heinz Roth, "Nazismus gleich Fordismus? Die deutsche Autoindustrie in den dreissiger Jahren," in *1999. Zeitschrift für Sozialgeschichte des 20. und 21. Jahrhunderts*, vol. 5 (1990), no. 4, 82–91; Barbara Schmucki, "Automobilisierung. Neuere Forschungen zur Motorisierung," in *Archiv für Sozialgeschichte*, 35 (1995), 582–97; Hans Christoph Graf von Seherr-Thoss, *Die deutsche Automobilindustrie. Eine Dokumentation von 1886 bis 1971* (Stuttgart, 1979); Johannes A. Stölzle, *Staat und Automobilindustrie in Deutschland*, Ph.D., diss. (Freiburg, 1959).

14. Higham (1983); Nevins and Hill (1963); Reich (1990); Wilkins and Hill (1964). Government reports have played an important role in keeping up the interest, for example: Maurice Olley, "The motor car industry in Germany during the period 1939–1945," BIOS Overall Report no. 21 (London, 1949); and Snell (1974).

15. See Rosellen (1986). Rosellen's affirmative popular treatment is usually reliable with regard to company policy but almost entirely fails to cite sources. He devotes a few lines (179) to the topic of forced labor, giving mistakenly low numbers and claiming, without evidence, that in contrast to other companies Ford took care of "its foreign laborers."

16. Lessmann (1993); Lindner (1991); Reiling (1997).

17. The interviews used as sources in this essay, henceforth to be cited by name, include: Z 10.569, Iwan Fedosowitsch Ananitsch (1992); Z 10.568, Nadjeschda Fedosowna Ananitsch (1992); Z 10.613, Kamila Felinska (1995); Z 10.584, Marian Gazinski (1993); Z 10.620, Elsa Iwanowa-de Meyer (1995); Z 10.617, Inna Kulagina (1995); Z 10.662, Mareno Mannucci (1998); Z 10.616, Anna Nesteruk (1995); Z 10.633, Tamara Jefimowna Nosik (1996); Z 10.623, Anna Awtonomowna Obuchowskaja (1996); Z 10.618, Klawdija Nikiforowna Podobed (1995); Z 10.661, Josif Iwanowitsch Radjuk (1998); Z 10.615, Stepan Iwanowitsch Saika (1995); Z 10.616, Nadija Machtejewna Schubrawa (1995); Z 10.605, Marta Asrentewna Sankowitsch (1994); Z 10.639, Lidija Solotarjewskaja (1996); Z 10.614, Kazimierz Tarnawski (1995); Z 10.663, Yvan Thibaut (1993); Z 10.559, Franciszek Wojcikowski (1990).

18. Fings (1996), 152–54.

19. See Everhard Kleinertz, "Hausgemachte Probleme? – Die städtischen Behörden in Köln und die Aktenüberlieferung der NS-Zeit," in *Versteckte Vergangenheit*, ed. Matzerath et al. (1994), 277–306.

20. See Chapter 2. A group of U.S. military men entered the nearly intact factory in Cologne, blew open a safe, and confiscated company documents in March 1945. In the

Forties, various U.S. investigators had access to documents that later became unavailable. Many of these have been released as a result of the legal investigations since 1998. In his "Report on Ford Werke Aktiengesellschaft," Schneider cites letters to the Gestapo from Ford's "counter-intelligence representative" (*Abwehrbeauftragte*).

21. See Mommsen with Grieger (1996), 51ff.
22. BA-MA RW 19/1576, 108. To compete for Wehrmacht contracts, Ford needed certification as a "German Product" (*Prädikat "Deutsches Erzeugnis"*), granted only if 95 percent of the parts were made in the German Reich. See the extensive correspondance in BA-MA RW 19/1576. Reiling (1997) cites ample evidence that Dearborn was well-informed about Ford Werke's Wehrmacht orders, 365ff.
23. The new name was approved at the shareholders assembly of 21 July 1939, see *Kölnische Zeitung*, 28 Jan. 1942.
24. A letter from the Ford-Werke AG management and supervisory boards to the Reichskommissar for the Treatment of Enemy Property, 18 June 1941, states that IG Farbenindustrie AG held 1.75 million RM of 32 million RM in company shares (about 5 percent), see BA R 87/6205, 8–11. In the very thorough audit by the high-ranking tax inspector Hiller, dated 26 Sept. 1943, IG Farben's share is given as 42 percent (13.36 million RM), see BA R 87/67, 103b. In reality, Ford and IG Farben had worked together closely since the 1920s. Edsel Ford was on the board of directors of Farben's U.S. unit, American I.G. Chemical Company, dating back to 1929, see Borkin (1979), 162. Cf. the verdict in the IG Farben trial, *Das Urteil im IG-Farben Prozess* (Offenbach, 1948): "Charge 3: imposing slave labor and killing of civilians, prisoners of war, and concentration camp inmates," 107–40.
25. Ford-Werke AG Cologne to Reichskommissar Krohn, 18 June 1941, in BA R 87/6205, 8–11.
26. Heinrich F. Albert (1874–1960) started out as a lawyer with the Imperial Interior Ministry in 1901 and served as its economic agent in New York from 1914 to 1917. Returning to Germany at the outbreak of war with the U.S. in 1917, Albert was appointed "Trustee for Enemy Property," an imperial position comparable to the later Reichskommissar. After the First World War, he became a state secretary at the Chancellery and a minister in the Cuno cabinet in 1922 and 1923, then administered the Ministry for Reconstruction starting in April 1923. He opened a law practice in Berlin in 1921. See Reiling (1997).
27. Reiling (1997), 394.
28. See Lindner (1991), esp. 48–59.
29. BA R 87/6205, 8–11.
30. Ibid.
31. Ford-Werke AG, 1940 annual report, 9.
32. See Lindner (1991), 161ff.
33. See Chapter 2. The Cologne banker Kurt Freiherr von Schröder was an early sponsor of the NSDAP and a member in 1932 of the party's economic advisory circle, the "Keppler Kreis." He arranged a 4 January 1933 agreement between Adolf Hitler and ex-Chancellor Franz von Papen that smoothed Hitler's appointment as Chancellor, an event later called the "hour of the Third Reich's birth." Papen and Hitler met at Schröder's villa in Cologne. Schröder also organized the "Friends of Himmler," a group of industrialists who financed and did business with the SS, many themselves SS officers. From 1933 to 1945, Schröder was the President of the Chamber of Commerce IHK Cologne and a city councilman, and held a high SS title. See Asendorf (1987) and Soénius (1997), here: 175ff. According to Higham (1983), 2ff., Schröder was also a director of the Swiss-based Bank for International Settlements, which was chaired by an American and figured in the Nazi's international gold and money intrigues.
34. BA R 87/6205, 38–41. The letter from Schröder, dated 7 Feb. 1942 (38) is the only surviving evidence that Schmidt was a member of the Nazi Party. No evidence of membership was presented at Schmidt's de-Nazification procedure, see HStAD NW 1049/76.620.
35. BA R 87/6205,67. This was Albert's idea. Krauch was an expert on wood and coal generators, a vital military subject given the Reich's raw materials shortages. Bötzkes was responsible for finance. Hünemeyer was the contact man to the NSDAP. Albert had

hoped to be custodian but was forced to make do with the chair of the advisory council and a custodian's post at Ford S.A.F. in Paris, see Lessmann (1993), 224.

36. BA R 87/6205 and 6206.
37. BA R 87/6205, 117, 146, 215.
38. BA-MA RW 21-35/1, 25.
39. See BA-MA RW 21-35/1 and BA-MA RW 19/56, 5, 34, also the long description of Ford's military production in NA RG 407, E 368, Box 1032.
40. See the production plans as described in Lessmann (1993), 223, which does not provide the actual production figures. The use of Ford vehicles on all of the German Reich's fronts is confirmed impressively in Frank (1990), an issue of *Waffen-Arsenal,* a picture book series for military buffs and Wehrmacht veterans. The magazine is filled with technical data and wartime photographs of Ford models in action, taken on all fronts and apparently collected over many years by the author (see Photo Set B for some samples).
41. BA R 87/6205, 115 und NA RG 407, E 368, Box 1032, 7.
42. Ford Werke advisory council minutes of 17 Aug. 1942, in BA R 87/6205, 115.
43. Ford Werke advisory council minutes of 13 Jan. 1943, in BA R 87/6205, 148.
44. See Herbert (1985), 11.
45. Ibid., 270f.
46. The various decrees against specific groups are described in Pfahlmann (1964). On the development of this particular body of law see Herbert (1985), 74–79, 154–57. On concentration camp prisoners see *"Deutsche Wirtschaft"* (1991) and *Konzentrationslager,* ed. Kaienburg (1996). On company leeway in choosing the type and number of forced laborers, see Spoerer (1998:2), 14ff., which examines this with regard to KZ prisoners.
47. Reich (1990), 121, dates the presence of French POWs at Ford starting in 1941. Ford is reported to have held eighty to ninety French POWs from 1942 to 1945 in a list of wartime labor camps, dated 18 Apr. 1949 and compiled by the Cologne Police 17th Precinct in response to a survey by the Red Cross International Tracing Service for persons missing from the war, in Historisches Archiv der Stadt Köln (henceforth: HAStK) Acc 606/2. Many of the numbers in that list are dubious. The most reliable source is the U.S. government "Report on Ford Werke Aktiengesellschaft," 5 Sept. 1945, which cites contemporary documents and investigations held immediately after the war. It states that Ford used foreign laborers starting in 1940. Ford's balance sheets for 1941 specify 24,000 RM for building a prison barrack. Detailed business figures for 1940 are unavailable. See accounts auditor Dipl. Kf. Knipprath, "Ford balance sheets as of 31. Dec. 1941," in BA R 87/6209, 13.
48. BA-MA, RW 21-35/4, 20ff. BA-MA RW 21-35/5, 3ff. BA-MA RW 20-6/1, 65, 83.
49. See Hopmann et al. (1994), 286ff.
50. The relevant archival store, BA-MA RH 49 ("Prisoners of War, Labor und Construction Units") at the Freiburg Military Archive (BA-MA) unfortunately contains no files from the Stalag in Bonn.
51. Mareno Mannucci.
52. Herbert (1985), 96–98, estimates 1.2 million French POWs were used for labor in the Reich. On their treatment and on conditions generally see Mommsen with Grieger (1996), 713–20.
53. "Report of the Belgian Ministry for Reconstruction, General Directorate for Personal Claims, Final Report," no. 79, "Complex Cologne," 11 April 1952, 23, in Ministère des Affaires Sociales, de la Santé Publique et de l'Environnement, Service des Victimes de la Guerre, Brussels.
54. Robert H. Schmidt, writing as the custodian of Ford Motor Company in Antwerp, letter to the military administration of Belgium and northern France, 8 Feb. 1944, in the archives of Institut für Zeitgeschichte (IfZ), MA 677/5, 700–702.
55. See Herbert (1985), 98–100.
56. Mareno Mannucci.
57. Pietro Badoglio (1871–1956) headed the Italian government from Mussolini's fall until 1944 and negotiated with the Allies the cease-fire of 3 Sept. 1943.

58. See Schreiber (1990); Luigi Cajani, "Die italienischen Militärinternierten im nationalsozialistischen Deutschland," in *Europa und der Reichseinsatz* (1991), 295–316; and Lang (1996).

59. Wierschheim, "camp leader" in the "Russian camp" from 1942 to 1945, stated in his testimony of 26 Dec. 1945 that Soviet civilians were first assigned to Ford in April 1942, see HStAD NW 1048-34/272.

60. Herbert (1985), 154–57.

61. Ibid., 76–79, on the "Poland Decrees."

62. Anna Wasiljewna Nesteruk, letter, 27 Sept. 1994, in NS-Dok.

63. Almost certainly this was the intermediary camp run by the Arbeitsamt in the Wuppertal district of Sonnborn; see the express letter from "Reichsführer-SS und Chef der Deutschen Polizei," Heinrich Himmler, to the "plenipotentiary for the labor deployment" GBA Fritz Sauckel, 16 Aug. 1944, in BA R 41/463, 31f.

64. Advisory council minutes, 17 Aug. 1942 in BA R 87/6205, 115. A Gestapo investigation plan of 21 Jan. 1943 names a figure of 685 "Ostarbeiter" at the Ford camp, see HStAD RW 34/12.

65. BA-MA RW 21-35/13, 2ff., 20ff.

66. Ford Werke advisory council minutes, 1 Jul. 1943 in BA R 87/6205, 212.

67. Ibid., 225. On the other camps in Cologne, see the catalogue of forced labor, prisoner of war and KZ camps in Cologne from 1939 to 1945 compiled by Ursula Reuter in NS-Dok. Still being updated, the list now numbers about 250 forced labor camps and locations.

68. See "10 Jahre Kölner Fordwerk," in *Ford Werkszeitung*, Yr. 4, July 1941, 12, which mentions 10,000 employees working for Ford indirectly at about 350 suppliers.

69. See the map of Ford Werke drawn up by U.S. forces in October 1945, in NA, RA II, RG 243, Box 687, Folder 77a 20, 1 of 2. The first "Ostarbeiter" were put up in garages near the Glanzstoff factory in Niehl and "commuted" to Ford, where they built their later camp, see Stepan Saika.

70. See listing of wartime "foreign camps" by the Cologne Police 17th Precinct, 18 June 1949, HAStK, Acc 606/2, 69. The figures given therein for inmates are far too low.

71. Report of 26 Dec. 1945 in HStAD NW 1048-34/272.

72. Written report by Stepan Saika in NS-Dok.

73. According to Wilhelm Knipprath, Dipl. Kfm., audit of Ford Werke year-end balance as of 31 Dec. 1942, 7–10, in BA R 84/393.

74. Written report by Stepan Saika in NS-Dok.

75. Bulletin of the Cologne detective division (Kripo), 23 June 1941 in HStAD, "Polizeibehörden vor 1945," No. 38.

76. Kamila Felinska. Because there were no entry forms in Polish, Mrs. Felinska and her husband were registered in French. As a result the guards mistook them for French and gave them far better treatment.

77. Stepan Saika, Tamara Nosik. More Germans employed by Ford in the camp are named in HStAD NW 1048-34/272.

78. Written report by Stepan Saika in NS-Dok.

79. Ibid.

80. See the account by a former Ford employee in *Kölner StadtRevue*, 11 (1986), No. 11, 38.

81. Ibid.

82. See HStAD RW 23/121, 11–12.

83. Anna Nesteruk, letter of 27 Sept. 1994 in NS-Dok.

84. BA-MA, RW 21-35/12, 33.

85. Rosellen (1986), 179.

86. Former Ford worker in *Kölner StadtRevue*, 38.

87. HAStK, Acc. 1231/1, list of Russian civilians buried at Westfriedhof (the "Ausländerfriedhof") in Cologne-Bocklemünd. One file lists two Polish babies (one was one year old, the other six months) as having died in the district of "Niehl," i.e., possibly from the Ford camp.

88. HAStK, Acc. 1231/1 und Acc. 606/17. These figures include only those who were definitely working at Ford. Some of the dead were listed as being from "Niehl" and may have

also come from the Ford camp. A few of the laborers buried at Westfriedhof are unidentified. The unidentified woman whose date of death is given as 3 Jan. 1945 was likely the Ford laborer killed by a fire bomb mentioned in the report of the Cologne 17th Police Precinct, 3 Jan. 1945, in HStAD BR 1131/125.

89. Ford Werke advisory council minutes, 1 July 1943 in BA R 87/6205, 212f.
90. Josef Lorenz, letter, 1 Nov. 47, in HStAD, NW 1048-34/272.
91. Wenzel, letter, 1 Nov. 1947, as cited in ibid.
92. Herbert (1985), 247f. The treatment of pregnant women changed over time but always depended on whether the father was considered foreign or "Aryan." See Bock (1986), esp. 440–451.
93. Statement of 26 Sept. 1947 in HStAD NW 1048-34/272.
94. Minutes of 14 Sept. 1947 and notes of 7 Oct. 1947 in HStAD NW 1048-34/272.
95. Statement by the Cologne Medical Association (*Ärztekammer*), 8 Nov. 1947, in ibid.
96. See Drobisch (1965). To date no scholar has devoted a longer study specifically to company security or its role in the system of repression.
97. Herbert (1985), 156.
98. Drobisch (1965), 220. Cf. Rainer Fröbe, "Der Arbeitseinsatz von KZ-Häftlingen und die Perspektive der Industrie 1943–1945," in *"Deutsche Wirtschaft"* (1991), 62, n.96.
99. See order of Reichsführer-SS Heinrich Himmler, 25 Sept. 1944, "concerning the assurance of discipline and productivity among foreign workers," in BA R 13 VIII/156.
100. Mentioned as a third "Abwehrbeauftragter" is a man called Schebem, who disappeared in spring 1945. Buchwald was arrested in March 1945 by the U.S. Counter Intelligence Corps (CIC), see 12th Army Group Main, Intelligence Report No. EW-Ko 13, 18 March 1945, in NA RG 243, U.S. Bombing Survey, 243/190/62, Box 687, SB 33838. The reports by Buchwald, mentioned in NA RG 407, E 368, Box 1032, 36f. were unavailable during my research.
101. BA-MA RW 21-35/16, undated note.
102. "S.D.," a 17 year-old Russian, on 24 Nov. 1942 for "misappropriation," see HAStK, Acc 606/8, 115; "A. W.," a 19 year-old Russian, on 13 June 1944, on suspicion of bike theft, see HAStK, Acc 606/8, 111R.
103. HStAD, BR 2034 VH I/1327. Cf. Gabi Lotfi, *Die Arbeitserziehungslager im Zwangssystem des Dritten Reiches*, Ph.D., diss., Ruhr-Universität Bochum, 1999 (publication forthcoming, Stuttgart, 2000).
104. HStAD BR 2034 VH I/1295 and 1296.
105. See Huiskes (1983).
106. Ibid., inscriptions nos. 850, 861, and 844.
107. The following is according to HStAD NW 174/267 I-IV. Originally set up to try and condemn the Nazis' political opponents, the *Sondergerichte* over the course of the war developed into "summary homefront courts." With the air war raging, even minor thefts were given the death sentence, as a deterrent. By the end of the war, Sondergerichte had delivered 11,000 death sentences across the Reich. See *Strafjustiz*, ed. Wrobel (1991–1994).
108. HStAD RW 34/8, 48: Ref. IV 2a, Weekly Report, 19–26 Nov. 1944.
109. Ibid., 48R.
110. Advisory council minutes, 1 Jul. 1943, in BA R 87/6205, 213.
111. Robert H. Schmidt, writing as custodian for the Ford Motor Company in Antwerp, to the commander of the military administration of Belgium and northern France, 8 Feb. 1944, in IfZ, MA 677/5,700–702; here: 701.
112. Ibid.
113. Ibid., 700 and BA R 87/6205, 230ff. It is unknown whether and how many unfree workers were involved in this operation. Antwerp assembled 3,400 trucks in 1943 and sold 110 million Belgian Francs in parts.
114. *Ford-Werkszeitung*, Yr. 4, July 1941, 13.
115. Staatsarchiv Nuremberg, NI-4181.
116. See Herbert (1985), 97.
117. BA-MA RW 20-6/5, 36f.

118. NA RG 407, E 368, Box 1032, 36.
119. BA R 87/6205, 224.
120. BA R 87/6206, 42.
121. Ibid., 45.
122. Lindner (1991), 124–134.
123. Report by the tax inspector Hiller, 26 Sept. 1943, examining "profits at enemy property," in BA R 2/30.027, 23–48. As additional factors, Hiller mentioned the unavailability of new capital goods for purchase, warehouse clearance-sales of goods out-of-production, liquidation of accruals through valuation of undervalued inventory, rationalization and savings measures, good management, minimal debt, good prices and reliable debtors (the Reich) and a rise in gross margin at rising revenues due to unchanged fixed accounts.
124. Lindner (1991), especially 160ff.
125. See BA R 87/6205, 32f, 110.
126. The background on the decision to use KZ labor in truck production is taken from *Deutschlands Rüstung* (1969), 396. On the following see the chapter on KZ Buchenwald Aussenkommando Köln-Ford in Fings (1996), 152–154. The list of prisoners transported from KZ Buchenwald to Ford on 12 Aug. 1944 is available in HStAD, Gerichte Rep. 118/1179.
127. NS-Dok, Collection Projektgruppe Messelager, Interview with Michel van Ausloos. Ausloos relates being transported from Messe to Ford, where he and other prisoners were forced to build trenches. Wladimir Lebedev from Messe also worked at Ford, unloading carts as part of the "Carrier Commando." See HStAD, Gerichte Rep. 118/1179, Z 10.530, interview with Wladimir Lebedev.
128. Mareno Mannucci.
129. Fings (1996), 145–158.
130. [The case of KZ labor at several Daimler locations, among the worst in this regard, is well-documented in *Das Daimler-Benz Buch* (1987) and Gregor (1998). Heussler (1996) writes on BMW as the center of the war economy in Munich. Thousands of prisoners from nearby KZ Dachau were forced to work at the main BMW plant in Allach-bei-München. To cut travel times a large satellite camp was set up next to the factory in 1943. It lodged "thousands of KZ prisoners under wretched conditions, of whom many died as a result of uncontrolled brutalities by the guards and the catastrophic food situation." Heussler's conclusion (31): "Management and directorate reacted to the conditions with apathy." Volkswagenwerk did not employ as many KZ laborers as BMW or Daimler, but this was not for a lack of trying. Far from being forced to employ KZ labor, VW was among the companies that demanded more KZ labor than the authorities could provide. That case is worth a closer look, as it demonstrates the often arbitrary workings of decision-making with regard to forced laborers. According to the definitive study on VW, Mommsen with Grieger (1996, ch. 8.3): Starting in summer 1943, Volkswagenwerk planned a new labor camp near its main factory, possibly for use after the war. Eight hundred KZ prisoners arrived for construction at the planned "Laagberg" location in May 1944. The project was managed by VW, the prisoners controlled by the SS and kept under horrible conditions. Survivors from the original contingent worked as slaves on the uncompleted project until a few weeks before liberation. Later, "Volkswagenwerk entered the industrial plant-dispersal program in autumn 1943. It was clear that the necessary labor could only be gathered from the reservoir of KZ prisoners" (859). Ferdinand Porsche "intervened" with Himmler to demand more KZ prisoners for VW. A VW engineer went to Auschwitz in early 1944 to select workers, picking out a group of 300 for the VW main plant and 500 for the VW underground dispersal location at Tiercelet. The first group were greatly relieved to depart Auschwitz and arrive at the VW main plant. Soon thereafter, however, they were transferred to the KZ satellite Thil, joining the 500 others from Auschwitz to work at the Tiercelet location. That was a nightmare. Meanwhile the VW management hoped to "raise personnel to 10,000, with plans focusing mainly on Hungarian KZ inmates." After various negotiations and setbacks: "With help from the Nancy Armaments Commando personnel in August [1944] was raised by about 2,000 laborers, about 800 of them KZ prisoners, but the hoped-for group from Auschwitz did not arrive" (868).

SS, Volkswagenwerk, and the Reich construction department, the *Sonderbauabteilung,* began deliberating plans for an additional commando, "Volkswagen Dernau," to employ 750 KZ women. The first transports, arriving in August 1944, were actually of 168 men, later another 299 men, all from KZ Amersfort. Through September four more transports arrived from Buchenwald, numbering 30, 33, 179, and 200 men. During the final waves of bombings, these contingents were shifted around locations in efforts to dig underground factories to shelter VW and other war producers. Finally they were liberated, or put on death marches away from their "main" KZ camps (Mommsen with Grieger [1996], chs. 9.3ff.). In the dubious matter of getting KZ slave-laborers, Volkswagen had an advantage over many other companies, although Ferdinand Porsche's wish of getting 10,000 KZ prisoners was never fulfilled. –Ed.]

131. Survey of prisoner camps and deployments at the German State Justice Departments, Coordinating Bureau for Nazi Crimes (Zentrale Stelle der Landesjustizverwaltungen in Ludwigsburg, henceforth: ZStLJ), IV 406 AR 85/67, 18. Three of the Ford KZ squad were designated prisoner-overseers (kapos) or foremen. Listed by trade, the others included six carpenters, four bricklayers, one heating engineer, two plumbers, one welder, two electricians, one paramedic, one barber, one shoemaker, twelve tailors, and a secretary. See HStAD, Gerichte Rep. 118/1179.

132. Thüringisches Hauptstaatsarchiv Weimar (henceforth ThHStAW), NS 4 Buchenwald No. 136a, 139, 144.

133. Ibid., 117–146 und NS 4 Buchenwald No. 136b, 2–42.

134. ThHStAW, NS 4 Buchenwald No. 136b, 42. Three prisoners were kept at Ford. One of them escaped on 6 March 1945, the other two were assigned to the Buchenwald "Kommando Westwaggon," see ibid., 45 and Marian Gazinski.

135. See Chapter 2. An official report later said that the target area had been mislabeled. See also NS-Dok interview with Franciszek Wójcikowski.

136. See "Plan of Factory Ford-Werke AG," 19. Oct. 1945.

137. Dispersal of Ford Werke was first raised as an issue when Cologne was subjected to heavy bombardment in the summer of 1942, but the high costs always caused hesitation. Planning for a "shadow factory" began in mid-1943, see BA R 87/6205, 116, 214. Schmidt received orders to evacuate in August 1944. A reluctant withdrawal began in mid-September 1944, see NA RG 243, US Bombing Survey 243/190/62, Box 687, SB 33835.

138. See Tamara Nosik, Kamila Felinska, Mareno Mannucci. According to a memorandum of the Cologne Armaments Commando (RüKo), 4 Dec. 1944, operations east of the Rhine were completely unprepared for the "sudden appearance of thousands of foreign laborers from the areas near the Front." Accommodations and conditions were accordingly terrible, as described vividly by the interviewees.

139. NSDAP Cologne District Authority, order to evacuate the city, in HStAD RW 23/14.

140. *Das nationalsozialistische Lagersystem,* ed. Weinmann (1990), 407.

141. NA RG 243, US Bombing Survey 243/190/62, Box 687, SB 33835.

142. BA R 87/6206, 23–28.

143. Billstein and Illner (1995), 186.

144. According to the U.S. "Report on Ford Werke Aktiengesellschaft," 5 Sept. 1945.

145. Rosellen (1988), 17f.

146. Ibid., 15f., 25.

147. See HStAD NW 1049/24.776, NW 1049/27.566, NW 1049/401; NW 1048/11. In their directive of 12 October 1946, the Allied authorities defined five categories of former National Socialist Party members, each subject to different sanctions. Group I consisted of primary perpetrators, II of committed accomplices (activists, militarists, beneficiaries), III of lesser accomplices, IV of faithful supporters, and V of exonerated or incidental members. See *Entnazifizierung,* ed. Vollnhals (1991).

148. The following is according to HStAD, NW 1048-34/272.

149. The following is according to HStAD, NW 1049/76.620 und NW 1037-A/Reg. 4566.

150. See the tables in Rosellen (1988), 413f. Hans Grandi, at Ford since 1931, chief engineer, directed the Cologne plant during the war. Ernst Sagebiel, at Ford since 1930, ran the

purchasing department. Hans Schmidt, assistant to the General Director, acted as on-site manager and representative for Robert H. Schmidt in Antwerp. Max Ueber, at Ford since 1929 and export director in Cologne starting in 1936, served as assistant to the General Director starting in 1942.

151. Rosellen (1986), 179.

Chapter 5 *"And they took the 38 of us to Ford"*

Interviews by NS-Dokumentationszentrum der Stadt Köln. The Cologne visitors' program and similar initiatives are described from a how-to perspective in Fings (1998). Subjects were interviewed in their mother tongues by researchers and interpreters of the NS-Dokumentationszentrum der Stadt Köln. The interviews, tapes, German transcripts and donated materials are available to the public and to researchers from the NS-Dokumentationszentrum der Stadt Köln, EL-DE Haus, Appelhofplatz 23–25 (Elisenstr. 11), D-50667 Cologne, Germany. Contact: Elisabeth Adamski. Several of the German transcripts were published previously in *Zwangsarbeit bei Ford* (1996).

1. No research to date has found that Jews from Poland had been deported into Germany as of 1942. At the time, the use of Jews from the occupied countries as forced laborers in Germany was still prohibited by the Nazi authorities on racial grounds. In fact, Polish Jews had been deported away from the areas of western Poland annexed to the German Reich. It is possible that the Jewish workers in Antweiler recalled by Kamila Felinska were German or stateless Jews of Polish background, or else Polish Jews whom the authorities mistook for German Jews.

2. Presumably the contact person to the commando from Ford Werke, as a woman could not have been Mr. Tarnawski's "commando leader."

3. From 1942 to 1944 the Cologne Messe camp included a Gestapo prison, from which there were also deportations to KZ camps. On the Messe tower the letters I.V.A. stood for the "International Transport Show," which had been planned for 1940, but was canceled due to the war. Many former prisoners therefore describe the Messelager complex as the "IVA Lager," see Fings (1996).

4. The use of the movie theater at Buchenwald as a torture center is described in Kogon (1999/1974), 216.

5. The Dessau camp is listed by the Red Cross International Tracing Service as having existed from November 1944 until 11 April 1945, with an inmate population of about 340, cf. *Das nationalsozialistische Lagersystem*, 566.

German interview transcripts © NS-Dokumentationszentrum der Stadt Köln:

Kamila FELINSKA, 12 September 1995, NS-Dok Z 10.584. Interview: Ursula Reuter. Language: Polish. Interpreter: Anna Bartoszek. German translation: Jerzy Adamski.

Elsa IWANOWA-DE MEYER, 16 September 1995, NS-Dok Z 10.617. Interview: Monika Braasch. Language: Russian. Interpreter, German trans.: Hildegard Günteberg.

Inna Jefimovna KULAGINA, 16 September 1995, NS-Dok Z 10.662. Interview: Monika Braasch. Language: Russian. Interpreter, German trans.: Hildegard Günteberg.

Mareno MANNUCCI, "Report on My Detention in Germany, 1943–1945," and interview, 8 September 1998, NS-Dok Z 10.616. Interview and editing of combined version: Karola Fings. Language: Italian. Interpreter, German trans.: Sylvia Klemen. A newspaper journalist, and a historian assigned by Ford, were also present at the interview.

Anna NESTERUK, 12 September 1995, NS-Dok Z 10.633 and Nadia SCHUBRAWA, 12 September 1995, NS-Dok Z 10.605. Interview: Karola Fings. Language: Ukr. Russian. Interpreter, Ger. trans.: Hildegard Günteberg.

Anna NESTERUK, letter to NS-Dok, 27 Sept. 1994. Language: Russian.

Stepan Iwanowitsch SAIKA, 12 September 1995; NS-Dok Z 10.616. Interview: Christian Welke. Language: Russian. Interpreter: Alexander Vladykin. Ger. trans.: Hildegard Günteberg.

Kazimierz TARNAWSKI, 13 September 1995, NS-Dok Z 10.663. Interview: Ursula Reuter. Language: Polish. Interpreter, Ger. trans.: Anna Bartoszek.

Yvon THIBAUT, 28 Aug. 1993; NS-Dok Z 10.559. Interview and translation: Manfred Etscheid. Language: French. Edited version: Karola Fings.

German interview transcript © Fritz Theilen:

Fritz THEILEN, May 1996. Interviewer: Karola Fings. Language: German. Transcript: Martina Domke.

Chapter 6 Memory and Liability
By Nicholas Levis, Berlin

1. This essay assumes knowledge of the other chapters.
2. This and the following two paragraphs draw upon Fisch (1992), 69f., 307f., 318f.
3. Kranz (1998), 111–34, here 121f.
4. Saathoff (1998), 50f.
5. Ibid., 51–53, Kranz (1998), 121f.
6. Saathoff (1998), 54.
7. On IG Farben, Bernd Wagner, *IG Auschwitz*, Ph.D. Diss. (Bochum, 1998) and OMGUS (1986).
8. Presumably Krauch's operative activities as a Ford Werke director at least partly related to his status as an expert in coal and wood generators. Ford Werke produced wood-powered vehicles. As Billstein and Fings relate here, he often lobbied Reich authorities on Ford Werke's behalf. A Reich tax audit of 26 September 1943 revealed that IG Farben at that time owned 42 percent of Ford Werke shares (Ford Motor owned 52 percent, and Ford of England owned the rest, according to Oberinspektor Hiller, BA R 2/30027). Beyond that the story of the Ford-Farben cooperation in Germany, the knowledge either company may have had of the other's activities, and the connections between Farben and Ford in the U.S. remain questions for further research.
9. Krauch to Himmler, quoted in Brozik (1998), 37.
10. Cf. Bernd Boll, "Der IG-Farben-Prozess," in *Der Nationalsozialismus vor Gericht* (1999). IG Farben properties were confiscated by USGCC in summer 1945, and ordered liquidated in November 1945. Farben was broken up into new corporations, the larger ones still familiar today as Agfa, BASF, Hoechst and Bayer, as well as the legal successor "in liquidation." The men convicted in the 1947 Farben war crimes trial were already free by the time the Allied High Commissioner for Germany, John McCloy, released many other German industrialists from their war crime sentences in January 1951. One of the convicted Farben executives, Fritz ter Meer, later became the chief executive of Bayer. Another, Friedrich Jähne, that of Hoechst.
11. Otto Kranzbühler, defense attorney in the 1947 IG Farben war crimes case, later explaining his position in: "Vernichtung durch Arbeit," documentary by Lea Rosh, SFB-TV, 4 Nov. 1984, quoted in Brozik (1998), 36.
12. Brozik (1998), 40, 41.
13. Brozik (1998), 38–41. Altogether only a tiny percentage of the forced labor compensation cases before 1996 were decided in favor of the claimants. A few rulings resulted in laughable compensation sums: In 1957 the former KZ laborer Adolf Diamant was awarded 177.80 DM from his wartime employer, the Büssing engineering firm. Diamant's "outstanding wages" were calculated at 1 RM per hour for an estimated 1,778 hours of slave labor, divided by an exchange rate of 10 RM to 1 DM as based on the currency conversion of 1948. No account was taken of further damages Diamant may have suffered by the fact of his slavery. In a case against the Heinkel firm, the former KZ laborer Edmund Bartl won a series of appeals in 1962 to 1965. This prompted the FRG Ministry of Finance to intervene on the company's behalf. The government provided legal counsel and a court brief favoring Heinkel's position. Finally, in June 1967, the supreme court rejected Bartl's case, citing the statute of limitations. Saddled with the court costs, Edmund Bartl went into bankruptcy.

14. Taped statements in "Panorama," ARD-TV, 19 November 1998.
15. Volkswagen AG press release, 15 June 1998. Volkswagen AG was among the few companies that could credibly claim the defense of not being a "legal successor," as it was in fact a Nazi-inspired project first set up as a legal entity in 1937. It was owned by the Nazi DAF, until its later rechartering as a private stock corporation by decision of the British occupation authority.
16. Faulenbach (1987), 29.
17. For example, on whether there was a "primacy of politics" over economy in the Nazi state, whether "fascism" was an inevitable consequence of "capitalism," whether the Third Reich was more "fascist" or "totalitarian." This is by no means meant to dismiss all such debates, or to discredit the fine scholarly work undertaken in the 1970s, but rather to describe the general atmosphere in 1970s German-language writing on the Nazi past.
18. Not that a golden age therefore began. The new scholarship has often been overshadowed by the self-perpetuating media circuses of "coming to terms with the past." These date back to the fortieth anniversary of the war's end, the visit of U.S. President Ronald Reagan and German Chancellor Helmut Kohl to the German military cemetery at Bitburg in 1985, and the speech by President von Weizsäcker that year, in which he stated Germany itself was also liberated by the Nazi defeat. In 1986 there followed the "historian's battle," (*Historikerstreit*) sparked by the historian Ernst Nolte and his argument, published in 1986 in the *Frankfurter Allgemeine Zeitung,* that the Nazi movement and its crimes must be understood as a defensive adoption of existing Bolshevik practices. The philosopher Jürgen Habermas promptly fired a countering broadside through the liberal *Die Zeit,* maintaining that Nazi Germany was without parallel in its horror and arose independently of developments in other countries. The German press was promptly filled with protestations pro and con, enough to fill the later volume of reprints, *Historikerstreit* (1987). This manner of newsprint battle has returned at ever shorter intervals, for example in the exchanges over "totalitarianisms" left and right after German unification. In its crassest form, that discussion put the "two German dictatorships" on the same level. Then again, during the resurgence of xenophobic violence in 1991 to 1993, the question arose of whether the skinhead attacks on foreigners and non-German citizens of the FRG were primarily "political" (i.e., deriving from the older history of nationalism) or "socioeconomic" (a product of youthful disaffection due to unemployment). In 1996, Daniel Goldhagen's revival of the vision of an extreme and exclusively German anti-Semitism in *Hitler's Willing Executioners* (New York, 1995) produced wild reactions among many writers. From the latter episode, Ulrich Herbert concluded that whatever the possible shortcomings of his work, Goldhagen had posed the right questions: "For all the criticism against the book by Goldhagen it is certainly positive ... when the discussion of National Socialism and 'Holocaust' now finally returns to the real events, concentrates on the mass murder itself, on the motives of the perpetrators and the suffering of the victims. By contrast, questions like whether or not the murder of the Jews should be seen as a phenomenon of Modernity, or if it was a form of putative defense against the presumed desire of the Bolsheviks to murder the European bourgeoisie, and other questions that defined public debate in recent years, receded into the background." (Herbert in German introduction to *National Socialist Extermination Policies* (2000), 7). Perhaps this was premature: the constant spectacular stretching of theses on all sides, in the search for new publicity and sensations, has tended to legitimate in public the new-old forms of abstractionist diversion long left behind by the best scholarship. A form of nationalist revisionism has in recent years gained unprecedented respectability in the Federal Republic. The most recent chapter in the *Historikerstreit* saw the German political elites—who have taken to conjuring something undefined called the "Berlin Republic"—applaud an October 1998 speech to the Frankfurt Book Fair by novelist Martin Walser, who decried the supposed "use of Auschwitz as a moral cudgel" against all Germans.
19. Pohl et al. (1986).
20. *Das Daimler-Benz Buch* (1987).
21. Hopmann et al. (1994).

22. Brozik (1998), 46.
23. Here I shall cite one further exemplar of the new historical approach: The NS Documentationszentrum der Stadt Köln, which played a peripheral but catalytic role in the background to the 1998 Ford case. Its director, Professor Horst Matzerath, locates the institute "on the borderlines between scholarship, education, and politics." (Interview with Horst Matzerath, 10 Mar. 1999.) In doing so, he shows a clear sense that it is doubly important that the scholarship itself be accurate, sound, and fair. The Documents Center, like the Cologne visitors' program with which it is associated, was born of a political struggle in the late 1970s and early 1980s. A citizens group lobbied the city for years before EL-DE Haus, the former Gestapo headquarters and prison in Cologne, was saved from a restoration that would have destroyed the inscriptions scrawled during the war by prisoners on the walls of their cells. The building was instead given over to the new Documents Center, its research institute and museum.
24. Gawlowski (1998), 161.
25. Luchnikov (1998), 184–85, is the head of the Ukrainian group "Understanding and Reconciliation" in Kiev.
26. Iwanowa in Martin Wilson, "Newsnight," BBC London TV, 23 Feb. 1998. The story here of the 1995 visit by eight former forced laborers to Ford Werke is taken from several press and media accounts, as confirmed to me by two witnesses. See Photo C16.
27. Küpper (1998), 250.
28. As covered in the press, and in a day-by-day chronology from 1995 to 1999 by the Swiss legal scholar Bruno Giussani, www.giussani.com/holocaust-assets.
29. Iwanowa vs. Ford, New Jersey Civil No. 98-959 (JAG). Ford briefs in support of motions to dismiss, 30 Mar. 1998 and 1 June 1998.
30. Report on Hugo Boss, including an interview with a historian hired by the company and later barred by contract from presenting her findings, NDR-TV on ARD-TV, 30 Nov. 1999.
31. The rest of this section is based on numerous press reports dating back to the spring of 1998, especially in the following newspapers: *Frankfurter Rundschau, Süddeutsche Zeitung, Berliner Zeitung, Frankfurter Allgemeine Zeitung (FAZ), Die Welt, International Herald Tribune, tageszeitung,* and *Handelsblatt.*
32. FAZ, 30 October 1999. The poll however did not ask for opinions on the appropriate amount of compensation per individual.
33. Pohl, interview in FAZ, 17 Nov. 1999.
34. In Cologne, Ford Werke's administrative building was destroyed by fire in 1945, just before the Americans moved in. A further (well-timed?) office fire broke out in February 1946. Everything else of interest was probably confiscated by the occupation forces, and ended up as exhibits in the September 1945 U.S. government "Report on Ford Werke Aktiengesellschaft." It is reasonable to think Henry Ford, the Ford family and Ford Motor would have been very sensitive about hiding incriminating documents. It is my opinion that Ford Motor can today allow researchers to go through these archives, knowing it unlikely that anything interesting would still be waiting for a researcher to discover fifty-five years later.
35. GM spokesman John Mueller, press release, 2 December 1999.
36. Quoted in Lindner (1991), 166.
37. Whatever the personal inspiration Hitler and other Nazis may have drawn from Henry Ford, or his possible private financial support for Hitler.
38. See R.C. Longworth, "Democracies Paying the Price. Globalization Survey Reveals U.S. Corporations Prefer Dictatorships," *International Herald Tribune,* 19 November 1999:

> Democratic countries in the developing sector, as Poland and South Africa, are losing out in the race for American export markets and American foreign investment. Dictatorships such as China or semidictatorships such as Indonesia are winning. And the trend is growing. As more of the world's countries adopt democracy, more American businesses appear to prefer dictatorships. If trade and investment strengthen developing countries, then U.S. businesses may be weakening the very countries they say they most want to help. These are the conclusions of a report recently released by the New

Economy Information Service (NEIS), a think tank set up to gauge the effects of globalization. "The democratic countries in the developing world are losing ground to more authoritarian countries when it comes to competing for U.S. trade and investment dollars," NEIS said. "This finding," it said, "raises the question of whether foreign purchasing and investment decisions by U.S. corporations may be inadvertently undermining the chances for survival of fragile democracies." NEIS compiled the report using U.S. government and World Bank figures on trade and investment. It borrowed political ratings compiled by Freedom House, a human rights organization that ranks countries as "free," "partly free" or "not free" based on the level of their political rights and civil liberties. In 1989, when the Cold War ended, democratic countries accounted for more than half–53.4 percent–of all U.S. imports from Third World countries, not counting oil. Today, with more democracies to choose from, the democratic countries supply barely one-third–34.9 percent–of U.S. imports from the Third World, it said. After the same decade, democracies got 28 percent of American manufacturing investment in developing countries, up from 26.2 percent when the Cold War ended. This slight improvement–1.8 percentage points–paled beside the 5.7 percentage-point growth in U.S. investment reported by dictatorships, especially China.

APPENDIX

CONCEPT 1: Organization of the Forced Labor System at War Operations

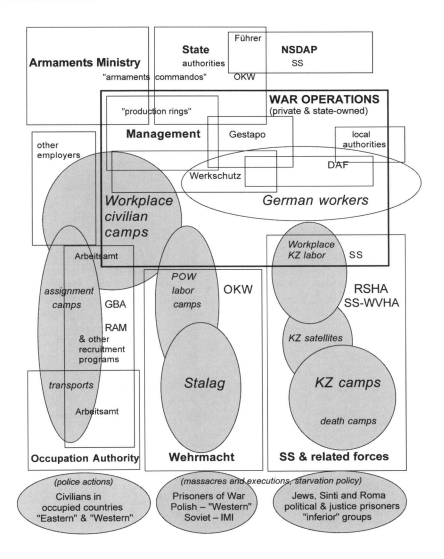

Maps are simplifications. This one sketches how foreign and forced laborers were placed in camps (shaded areas) in the Reich war industry, within an extremely complex structure of overlapping forces and institutions (rectangles).

Roughly, the bottom section is located in the occupied countries, the top in Germany. The roles played by various authorities are made clear in this book's studies; see especially chapters 1, 2, and 4. The sketch says nothing about who made a given decision, but shows areas

(continued)

of influence. Not every possibility is depicted–rather, the common paths experienced by forced laborers within a changing apparatus, during the period of its full development from 1942 to 1944.

As an example, starting from the bottom left and moving up through shaded areas, a typical "Ostarbeiter" was arrested or summoned by an occupation authority and transported to an assignment camp in the Reich. There, he or she was either chosen (in effect bought) by a company agent, or assigned to a civilian workplace camp by an Arbeitsamt. The typical KZ laborer (from the bottom right) may have been sent to a KZ by SS, police, Gestapo, an occupation authority, a court sentence, or another non-KZ camp, but once there prisoners remained under the control of the SS and KZ authorities, even after assignment to a satellite labor squad.

The overlap between POW and civilian camps reflects that many non-Soviet prisoners of war were reclassified as civilian workers. Among the omissions is the wartime system of agriculture–within which about 40 percent of foreign and forced laborers were employed. (NL)

GLOSSARY

Arbeitsamt One of a network of regional labor agencies subordinated to RAM (Reich Labor Ministry) in Berlin; extended to the occupied territories during the war as recruitment offices for foreign laborers

Aufsichtsrat Directorate (a.k.a. supervisory board or board of directors) of a German stock corporation (AG)

Ausländereinsatz Foreigner deployment, i.e., as laborers in the German war economy

Aussenkommando "Outside commando," a satellite labor squad from a KZ camp

Autobahn The world's first system of modern highways, built in Germany starting in 1934

Betriebsrat Works council of representatives elected by the employees of an enterprise

DAF German Labor Front, founded 1933, by 1939 the largest mass organization of the NSDAP, headed by Robert Ley

Fremdarbeiter Foreign workers

gau Administrative district in the Nazi Reich, run by a governor or *Gauleiter* appointed by the Party

KdF Strength through Joy, the DAF slogan; also the name of the DAF department charged with organizing leisure activities for workers. Used in reference to the *Volkswagen*, which was known officially as the KdF Car

KZ *Konzentrationslager*, denotes the hundreds of concentration and extermination camps within the system administered by the SS (also called KL)

Luftwaffe Reich Air Forces under Reichsmarshal Hermann Göring

Organisation Todt Special labor army of the Armaments Ministry (RMfBuM/RMfBuK)

Ostarbeiter "Eastern workers," i.e. civilian forced laborers from the German-occupied territories of the Soviet Union after 1941

Ostländer	Civilian workers from Ostland, the territorial unit set up by the Nazis in 1941 to administrate the German-occupied Baltic countries
Reichseinsatz	General term for the practice, during the war, of deploying foreigners as laborers within the territory of the German Reich
Reichskommissar	Reich Commissioner for the Treatment of Enemy Property. Starting in October 1941: Johannes Krohn
S.A.	Sturmabteilung, the political stormtrooper corps of the NSDAP, instrumental in the seizure of power, lost influence after the Nazi internal purge of 1934
SS	Schutzstaffel (Protective Echelon), the elite military corps of the NSDAP which after 1934 achieved a dominant position within the state, headed by the "Reichsführer-SS and Chief of German Police," Heinrich Himmler
Vorstand	Management board of an AG company
Wehrmacht	Armed Forces of the German Reich, known until 1935 as the Reichswehr
Wehrwirtschafts-führer	Defense Economy Leader, the Nazi honorific for about 400 top industrialists in the war economy
Werkschutz	Armed company security forces recruited from personnel, under the joint control of management, Gestapo, and military counter-intelligence
Westarbeiter	Western workers, i.e. civilian laborers and forced laborers from German-occupied France, the Low Countries, Denmark and Norway

SELECT BIBLIOGRAPHY

Als die Synagogen brannten, war es zu spät. Ed. Volkshochschule der Stadt Rüsselsheim. Russelsheim, 1993.

Arendt, Hannah. *The Origins of Totalitarianism.* San Diego, 1951.

Asendorf, Manfred. "Hamburger Nationalklub, Keppler-Kreis, Arbeitsstelle Schacht und der Aufstieg Hitlers." *1999. Zeitschrift für Sozialgeschichte des 20. und 21. Jahrhunderts,* no. 3/2 (1987): 106–50.

Bartels, Eckhart. "Opel im Kriege." *Waffen-Arsenal,* no. 82. Friedberg, Vienna, no year.

Becker-Jákli, Barbara. *Ich habe Köln doch so geliebt. Lebensgeschichten jüdischer Kölnerinnen und Kölner.* Cologne, 1993.

Billstein, Reinhold, and Eberhard Illner. *"You are now in Cologne. Compliments." Köln 1945 in den Augen der Sieger. Hundert Tage unter amerikanischer Kontrolle.* Cologne, 1995.

Bird, Kai. *The Chairman: John J. McCloy. The Making of the American Establishment.* New York, 1992.

Bock, Gisela. *Zwangssterilisation im Nationalsozialismus. Studien zur Rassenpolitik und Frauenpolitik.* Opladen, 1986.

Borkin, Joseph. *Die unheilige Allianz der I.G. Farben.* Frankfurt am Main and New York, 1979.

Boyer, Erich. *Ford-Werksgeschichte, 1924–1957.* Manuscript, 16 Dec. 1985.

Brozik, Karl. "Die Entschädigung von nationalsozialistischer Zwangsarbeit durch deutsche Firmen." *Entschädigung für NS-Zwangsarbeit* (1998): 32–49.

Budrass, Lutz. *Flugzeugindustrie und Luftrüstung in Deutschland 1918–1945.* Schriften des Bundesarchivs, no. 50. Dusseldorf, 1998.

Busch, Arnold. *Widerstand im Kreis Gross-Gerau 1933–1945.* Gross-Gerau, 1988.

Das III. Reich 1933–1945 und 1939–1945. Eine Tageschronik der Politik – Wirtschaft – Kultur. 2 vols. Ed. Overesch and Saal. Dusseldorf, 1991.

Das Daimler-Benz Buch. Ein Rüstungskonzern im "Tausendjährigen Reich." Ed. Angelika Ebbinghaus, Hamburger Stiftung für Sozialgeschichte des 20. Jahrhunderts. Nördlingen, 1987.

Das nationalsozialistische Lagersystem. Ed. Martin Weinmann. With research by Anne Kaiser and Ursula Krause-Schmidt. Frankfurt am Main, 1990.

Der Nationalsozialismus vor Gericht. Die alliierten Prozesse gegen Kriegsverbrecher und Soldaten 1943–1952. Ed. Gerd Ueberschär. Frankfurt, 1999.

"Deutsche Wirtschaft." Zwangsarbeit von KZ-Häftlingen für Industrie und Behörden. Ed. Hamburger Stiftung zur Förderung von Wissenschaft und Kultur. Hamburg, 1991.

Deutschlands Rüstung im Zweiten Weltkrieg. Hitlers Konferenzen mit Albert Speer 1942–1945. Ed. Willi A. Boelcke. Frankfurt am Main, 1969.

Die Daimler-Benz AG 1916–1948. Schlüsseldokumente zur Konzerngeschichte. Ed. Karl Heinz Roth and Michael Schmid. Nördlingen, 1987.

Die Neue Zeit und ihre Folgen. Exh. cat. Ed. Magistrat der Stadt Gross-Gerau. Gross-Gerau, 1992.

Drobisch, Klaus. "Der Werkschutz – betriebliches Terrororgan im faschistischen Deutschland." *Jahrbuch für Wirtschaftsgeschichte*, no. 6 (1965): 215–47.

Entnazifizierung. Politische Säuberung und Rehabilitierung in den vier Besatzungszonen 1945–1949. Ed. Clemens Vollnhals. Munich, 1991.

Entschädigung für NS-Zwangsarbeit. Rechtliche, historische und politische Aspekte. Ed. Klaus Barwig, Günter Saathoff and Nicole Weyde. Baden-Baden, 1998.

Europa und der "Reichseinsatz." Ausländische Zivilarbeiter, Kriegsgefangene und KZ-Häftlinge in Deutschland 1938–1945. Ed. Ulrich Herbert. Essen, 1991.

Faschismus. Exh. cat. Neue Gesellschaft für Bildende Kunst in Berlin. Ed. Dieter Ruckhaberle, Christiane Zieseke. Berlin, 1976.

Faulenbach, Bernd. "NS-Interpretationen und Zeitklima. Zum Wandel der Aufarbeitung in der jüngsten Vergangenheit." *Aus Politik und Zeitgeschichte. Beilage zur Wochenzeitung Das Parlament*, no. 3 (1987): 19–30.

Ferencz, Benjamin. *Lohn des Grauens. Die Entschädigung jüdischer Zwangsarbeiter – ein offenes Kapitel deutscher Nachkriegsgeschichte.* Frankfurt am Main, 1982.

Fings, Karola. *Messelager Köln. Ein KZ-Aussenlager im Zentrum der Stadt.* Schriften des NS-Dokumentationszentrums der Stadt Köln, vol. 3. Cologne, 1996.

———. *Begegnungen am Tatort. Besuchsprogramme mit ehemaligen ZwangsarbeiterInnen, Kriegsgefangenen und KZ-Häftlingen. Ein Leitfaden.* Dusseldorf, 1998.

Fisch, Jörg. *Reparationen nach dem Zweiten Weltkrieg.* Munich, 1992.

Flink, James. *The Automobile Age.* Cambridge MA, 1998.

Fogel, Heidi. *Eine Stadt zwischen Demokratie und Diktatur – Dokumentation zur Geschichte Langens von 1918–1945.* Langen, no year.

Frank, Reinhard. *Ford im Kriege. LKW – Maultier – PKW. Waffen-Arsenal*, no. 123. Friedberg, Vienna, 1990.

Gawlowski, Karol. "Die Sklavenarbeit der polnischen Bürger im Dritten Reich." *Entschädigung für NS-Zwangsarbeit* (1998): 158–69.

Gegen den braunen Strom. Kölner WiderstandskämpferInnen heute in Portraits der Arbeiterfotografie Köln. Ed. NS-Dokumentationszentrum der Stadt Köln. Cologne, 1991.

General Motors. "The Truth About 'American Ground Transport.' A Reply by General Motors." Presented to the Committee on the Judiciary, Hearings before the Subcommittee on Antitrust and Monopoly, Industrial Reorganization Act. United States Senate, 93rd Congress, 2nd Session. Washington DC, 1974.

Gregor, Neil. *Daimler-Benz in the Third Reich.* New Haven, 1998.

Greiner, Bernd. *Die Morgenthau-Legende. Zur Geschichte eines umstrittenen Plans.* Hamburg, 1995.

Henke, Klaus-Dietmar. *Die amerikanische Besetzung Deutschlands.* Munich, 1995.

Herbert, Ulrich. *Fremdarbeiter. Politik und Praxis des "Ausländer-Einsatzes" in der Kriegswirtschaft des Dritten Reiches.* Berlin, 1985.

———. *Hitler's Foreign Workers: Enforced Foreign Labor in Germany Under the Third Reich.* Trans. William Templer. Cambridge, UK, 1997.

———. "Zwangsarbeiter im Dritten Reich – Ein Überblick." *Entschädigung für NS-Zwangsarbeit* (1998): 3–18.

Hessische Gewerkschafter im Widerstand 1933–1945. Ed. Axel Ulrich. Series: DGB-Bildungswerk Hessen und Studienkreis zur Erforschung und Vermittlung der Geschichte des deutschen Widerstandes 1933–1945. Giessen, 1984.

Heusler, Andreas. *Ausländereinsatz. Zwangsarbeit für die Münchner Kriegswirtschaft 1939–1945.* Munich, 1996.

Heyl, Bernd. (1): "Der 'Opel-Putsch.' Ein 'wilder Streik' im Februar 1930." *"... ohne Rücksicht auf die Verhältnisse"* (1997): 15–34.

———. (2): "'Vergesst mich nicht ...' Zur Erinnerung an Walter Rietig." *"... ohne Rücksicht auf die Verhältnisse"* (1997): 157–68.

Higham, Charles. *Trading With The Enemy. An Exposé on The Nazi-American Money Plot 1933–1949.* London, 1983.

Hilgermann, Bernard. *Der große Wandel. Erinnerungen aus den ersten Nachkriegs-jahren. Kölns Wirtschaft unter der amerikanischen und britischen Militärregierung.* Cologne, 1961.

Historikerstreit. Die Dokumentation der Kontroverse um die Einzigartigkeit der national-sozialistischen Judenvernichtung, 2nd ed. Munich and Zurich 1987.

Homze, Edward L. *Foreign Labor in Nazi Germany.* Princeton, 1967.

Hopmann, Barbara, Mark Spoerer, Birgit Weitz, Beate Brüninghaus. *Zwangsarbeit bei Daimler-Benz. Zeitschrift für Unternehmensgeschichte,* suppl. no. 78. Stuttgart, 1994.

Huiskes, Manfred. *Die Wandinschriften des Kölner Gestapo-Gefängnisses im EL-DE-Haus 1943–1945.* Cologne and Vienna, 1983.

Jacobmeyer, Wolfgang. *Vom Zwangsarbeiter zum Heimatlosen Ausländer. Die Displaced Persons in Westdeutschland 1945–1951.* Göttingen, 1985.

Kershaw, Ian. *The Nazi Dictatorship: Problems and Perspectives of Interpretation.* London, 1989.

Kogon, Eugen. *The Theory and Practice of Hell: The German Concentration Camps and the System Behind Them.* Berkley, 1998.

———. *Der SS-Staat. Das System der deutschen Konzentrationslager.* Munich, 1999 (1974).

Konzentrationslager und deutsche Wirtschaft 1939–1945. Ed. Hermann Kaienburg. Opladen, 1996.

Kranz, Jerzy. "Zwangsarbeit – 50 Jahre danach: Bemerkungen aus polnischer Sicht." *Entschädigung für NS-Zwangsarbeit* (1998): 111–134.

Kriegsende und Neuanfang am Rhein. Konrad Adenauer in den Berichten des Schweizer Generalkonsuls Franz-Rudolph von Weiss 1944–1945. Ed. Hanns Jürgen Küsters and Hans Peter Mensing. Munich, 1986.

Krug, M., and G. Lingnau. *100 Jahre Daimler-Benz. Das Unternehmen.* Mainz, 1986.

Kugler, Anita. "Arbeitsorganisation und Produktionstechnologie der Adam Opel-Werke von 1900–1929." Internationales Institut für vergleichende Gesellschafts-forschung. Berlin, 1985.

———. "Amerikanisierung der Produktion. Die Opel-Werke in den 30er Jahren." *Schriftenreihe der Akademie der Wissenschaften.* Lecture trans. no. 202. Berlin, 1985.

———. "Arbeit und Arbeiten am Automobil." *Auto, Auto über Alles.* Ed. Jobst Krais. Freiburg, 1987(1).

———. "Von der Werkstatt zum Fliessband. Etappen der frühen Automobilproduk-tion in Deutschland." *Sozialgeschichte der Technik.* Ed. Reinhard Rürup. *Geschichte und Gesellschaft,* no. 3 (1987:2): 303–39.

———. (1): "Das Opel-Management während des Zweiten Weltkrieges. Die Behand-lung 'feindlichen Vermögens' und die 'Selbstverantwortung' der Rüstungsindus-trie" *"... ohne Rücksicht auf die Verhältnisse"* (1997:1): 35–68.

———. (2): "Flugzeuge für den Führer. Deutsche Gefolgschaftsmitglieder und aus-ländische Zwangsarbeiter im Opelwerk in Rüsselsheim 1940 bis 1945." *"... ohne Rücksicht auf die Verhältnisse"* (1997:2): 69–92.

Kümmel, Gerhard. *Transnationale Wirtschaftskooperation und der Nationalstaat. Deutsch-amerikanische Unternehmensbeziehungen in den 30er Jahren.* Stuttgart, 1995.

Küpper, Herbert. "Die neuere Rechtsprechung in Sachen NS-Zwangsarbeit." *Kritische Justiz,* no. 31 (1998): 246–54.

Lang, Ralf. *Italienische "Fremdarbeiter" im nationalsozialistischen Deutschland 1937–1945.* Frankfurt am Main, 1996.

Lessmann, Peter. "Ford Paris im Zugriff von Ford Köln 1943. Das Scheitern des Projekts eines europäischen Automobil-Konzerns unter deutscher Leitung." *Zeitschrift für Unternehmensgeschichte,* no. 4 (1993): 217–233.

Lindner, Stephan. *Das Reichskommissariat für die Behandlung feindlichen Vermögens im Zweiten Weltkrieg. Eine Studie zur Verwaltungs-, Rechts- und Wirtschaftsgeschichte des nationalsozialistischen Deutschlands. Zeitschrift für Unternehmensgeschichte,* suppl. no. 67. Stuttgart, 1991.

Luchnikov, Igor. "Ansprüche aus Zwangsarbeit seitens der Geschädigten – Ukraine. Die Tätigkeit der ukrainischen nationalen Stiftung 'Verständigung und Versöhnung.'" *Entschädigung für NS-Zwangsarbeit* (1998): 179–185.

Martin, Bernd. "Friedensplanungen der multinationalen Grossindustrie als politische Strategie." *Geschichte und Gesellschaft,* no. 2 (1976): 85–120.

Martin, James Stewart. *All Honorable Men.* Boston, 1950.

Meldungen aus dem Reich. Die geheimen Lageberichte des Sicherheitsdienstes der SS 1938–1945. Ed. Heinz Boberach. Frankfurt am Main, 1984.

Mommsen, Hans, with Manfred Grieger. *Das Volkswagenwerk und seine Arbeiter im Dritten Reich.* Dusseldorf, 1996.

Morgen kommst du nach Amerika. Ed. Peter Schirmbeck. Bonn, 1988.

National Socialist Extermination Policies: Contemporary German Perspectives and Controversies. Ed. Ulrich Herbert and Götz Aly. *Studies on War and Genocide,* vol. 2. New York, 2000.

Neugebauer, Andrea. "'… die Räder wieder ins Rollen bringen!' Die Opelwerke nach 1945." *"… ohne Rücksicht auf die Verhältnisse"* (1997): 169–94.

Neumann, Franz. *Behemoth.* New York, 1942.

Nevins, Allan, and Frank Ernest Hill. *Ford. Decline and Rebirth 1933–1962.* New York, 1963.

Novick, Peter. *The Holocaust in American Life.* New York, 1999.

"… ohne Rücksicht auf die Verhältnisse." Opel zwischen Weltwirtschaftskrise und Wiederaufbau. Ed. Bernd Heyl and Andrea Neugebauer. Frankfurt am Main, 1997.

OMGUS. *Ermittlungen gegen die I.G. Farbenindustrie.* Ed. Hans Magnus Enzensberger. Trans. Dokumentationsstelle zur NS-Politik, Hamburg. Nördlingen, 1986.

Pfahlmann, Hans. *Fremdarbeiter und Kriegsgefangene in der deutschen Kriegswirtschaft 1939–1945.* Ph.D. diss. Wurzburg, 1964.

Pohl, Hans, Stephanie Habeth, and Beate Brüninghaus. *Die Daimler-Benz AG in den Jahren 1933 bis 1945.* Stuttgart, 1986.

Reiling, Johannes. *Deutschland: Safe for Democracy? Deutsch-amerikanische Beziehungen aus dem Tätigkeitsbereich Heinrich F. Alberts, kaiserlicher Geheimrat in Amerika, erster Staatssekretär der Reichskanzlei der Weimarer Republik, Reichsminister, Betreuer der Ford-Gesellschaften im Herrschaftsgebiet des Dritten Reiches – 1914 bis 1945.* Stuttgart, 1997.

Reich, Simon. *The Fruits of Fascism. Postwar Prosperity in Historical Perspective.* Ithaca and London, 1990.

Rosellen, Hanns-Peter. *"… und trotzdem vorwärts." Die dramatische Entwicklung von Ford in Deutschland 1903 bis 1945.* Frankfurt, 1986.

———. *Ford-Schritte. Der Wiederaufstieg der Ford-Werke Köln von 1945 bis 1970.* Frankfurt am Main, 1988.

Rosenbaum, Ron. *Explaining Hitler. The Search for the Origins of His Evil.* New York, 1998.

Roth, Karl Heinz. "Der Weg zum guten Stern des 'Dritten Reichs': Schlaglichter auf die Geschichte der Daimler-Benz AG und ihrer Vorläufer 1890–1945." *Das Daimler-Benz Buch. Ein Rüstungskonzern im "Tausendjährigen Reich."* Ed. Angelika Ebbinghaus, Hamburger Stiftung für Sozialgeschichte des 20. Jahrhunderts. Nördlingen, 1987: 15–336.

Rusinek, Bernd-A. *Gesellschaft in der Katastrophe. Terror, Illegalität, Widerstand – Köln 1944/45.* Essen, 1989.

Rüther, Martin. *Arbeiterschaft in Köln 1928–1945.* Cologne, 1990.

Saathoff, Günter. "Die politischen Auseinandersetzungen über die Entschädigung von NS-Zwangsarbeit im Deutschen Bundestag." *Entschädigung für NS-Zwangsarbeit* (1998): 49–63.

Schreiber, Gerhard. *Die italienischen Militärinternierten im deutschen Machtbereich: 1943 bis 1945. Verraten – verachtet – vergessen.* Munich and Vienna, 1990.

Schwarz, Hans-Peter. *Vom Reich zur Bundesrepublik. Deutschland im Widerstreit der außenpolitischen Konzeptionen in den Jahren der Besatzungsherrschaft 1945–1949.* Stuttgart, 1980.

Seeber, Eva. *Zwangsarbeiter in der faschistischen Kriegswirtschaft. Die Deportation und Ausbeutung polnischer Bürger unter besonderer Berücksichtigung der Lage der Arbeiter aus dem sogenannten Generalgouvernement 1939–1945.* Berlin, 1964.

Shirer, William. *The Rise and Fall of the Third Reich.* New York, 1993 (1950).

Siegfried, Klaus-Jörg. *Das Leben der Zwangsarbeiter im Volkswagenwerk 1939–1945.* Frankfurt am Main and New York, 1988.

Snell, Bradford C. "American Ground Transport. A proposal for Restructuring the Automobile, Truck, Bus and Rail Industries." Presented to the Committee on the Judiciary, Hearings before the Subcommittee on Antitrust and Monopoly, Industrial Reorganization Act. United States Senate, 93rd Congress, 2nd Session, 26 Feb. 1974. Washington DC, 1974.

Soénius, Ulrich S. "Die Zeit des Nationalsozialismus." *Die Geschichte der Unternehmerischen Selbstverwaltung in Köln 1914–1997.* Ed. Industrie- und Handelskammer zu Köln. Cologne, 1997: 120–225.

Speer, Albert. *Der Sklavenstaat.* Stuttgart, 1981.

Spoerer, Mark. "Die Automobilindustrie im Dritten Reich: Wachstum um jeden Preis?" *Unternehmen im Nationalsozialismus.* Ed. Lothar Gall and Manfred Pohl. *Schriftenreihe zur Zeitschrift für Unternehmensgeschichte,* vol. 1 (1998). Munich, 1998 (1).

———. *Profitierten Unternehmen von KZ-Arbeit? Eine kritische Analyse der Literatur. Diskussionsbeiträge aus dem Institut für Volkswirtschaftslehre Universität Hohenheim,* no. 161. Hohenheim, 1998 (2).

Strafjustiz im totalen Krieg. Aus den Akten des Sondergerichts Bremen 1940 bis 1945. 3 vols. Ed. Hans Wrobel. Bremen, 1991–1994.

Streit, Christian. *Keine Kameraden. Die Wehrmacht und die sowjetischen Kriegsgefangenen 1941–1945.* Bonn, 1997 (1977).

Theilen, Fritz. *Edelweisspiraten.* Including documentation by Matthias von Hellfeld. Frankfurt am Main, 1984.

Trepp, Gian. *Bankgeschäfte mit dem Feind. Die Bank für Internationalen Zahlungsausgleich im Zweiten Weltkrieg.* Zürich, 1993.

Ulrich, Axel. "Betrieblicher Widerstand gegen die NS-Gewaltherrschaft am Beispiel der Opelwerke in Rüsselsheim." *"... ohne Rücksicht auf die Verhältnisse"* (1997): 93–157.

Unternehmen im Nationalsozialismus. Ed. Lothar Gall and Manfred Pohl. *Schriftenreihe zur Zeitschrift für Unternehmensgeschichte*, vol. 1. Munich, 1998.

Versteckte Vergangenheit. Über den Umgang mit der NS-Zeit in Köln. Ed. Horst Matzerath, Harald Buhlan and Barbara Becker-Jákli. Schriften des NS-Dokumentationszentrums der Stadt Köln, vol. 1. Cologne, 1994.

Vom Beginn der Industrialisierung bis 1945. Exh. cat. Museum der Stadt Rüsselsheim. Ed. Peter Schirmbeck et al. Russelsheim, 1988.

Widerstand und Verfolgung in Köln 1933–1945. Ed. Historischen Archiv der Stadt Köln. Cologne, 1974.

Wilkins, Mira. *The Maturing of Multinational Enterprise. American Business Abroad from 1914–1970.* Cambridge MA, 1974.

Wilkins, Mira, and Frank Ernest Hill. *American Business Abroad. Ford on Six Continents.* Detroit, 1964.

Wistrich, Robert. *Who's Who in Nazi Germany.* London, 1982.

Ziemke, Earl F. *The U.S. Army in the Occupation of Germany 1944–1946.* Washington DC, 1975.

Zwangsarbeit bei Ford. Ed. Projektgruppe Messelager. Cologne, 1996.

ILLUSTRATION SOURCES

Photo Set A: Homefront Opel

A1   *Der Opel Kamerad,* Jan. 1941 (Anita Kugler)
A2   Adam Opel AG
A3   Adam Opel AG
A4   *Der Opel Kamerad,* Dec. 1941 (Anita Kugler)
A5   *Der Opel Kamerad,* Jan. 1936 (Museum der Stadt Rüsselsheim, Bibliothek)
A6   *Der Opel Kamerad,* Dec. 1940 (Museum der Stadt Rüsselsheim, Bibliothek)
A7   *Der Opel Kamerad,* Jan. 1941 (Anita Kugler)
A8   *Der Opel Kamerad,* July 1941 (Anita Kugler)
A9   *Der Opel Kamerad,* July 1941 (Anita Kugler)
A10   *Der Opel Kamerad,* June 1942 (Anita Kugler)
A11   *Der Opel Kamerad,* May 1941 (Museum der Stadt Rüsselsheim, Bibliothek)
A12   Adam Opel AG
A13   Adam Opel AG
A14   Adam Opel AG
A15   Adam Opel AG
A16   Presse Illustration Hoffmann, Berlin
A17   Stadtarchiv Rüsselsheim, Fotosammlung

Photo Set B: Discoveries

B1   U.S. National Archives and Records Administration (NARA), Washington, DC
B2   NARA, U.S. Army Photograph SC 203633
B3   NARA U.S. Army Photograph SC 206174
B4   NARA U.S. Army Photograph SC 201767-S
B5   NARA U.S. Army Photograph SC 333100
B6   Cover to German edition of *The International Jew,* Leipzig, 1921
B7   Projektgruppe Messelager, Cologne
B8   *Ford-Werkszeitung,* Oct. 1939 (NARA RG 407)
B9   *Das Waffen-Arsenal,* Podzun-Pallas-Verlag, Vienna
B10   *Das Waffen-Arsenal,* Podzun-Pallas-Verlag, Vienna
B11   *Das Waffen-Arsenal,* Podzun-Pallas-Verlag, Vienna
B12   NARA, U.S. Army Photograph SC 262214
B13   NARA, U.S. Army Photograph SC 262213

B14   NARA, U.S. Army Photograph SC 203860
B15   Fotoarchiv Horst Adamitz, Langen, Germany
B16   VVN Offenbach, Germany

Photo Set C: Returning to Cologne

C1   NS-Dokumentationszentrum der Stadt Köln (NS-Dok, Cologne)
C2   NS-Dok, Cologne
C3   NS-Dok, Cologne
C4   Fritz Theilen
C5   NS-Dok, Cologne
C6   NS-Dok, Cologne
C7   NS-Dok, Cologne
C8   Herby Sachs, version, Cologne
C9   NS-Dok, Cologne
C10   NS-Dok, Cologne
C11   Herby Sachs, version, Cologne
C12   Manfred Wegener, *Stadt Revue* (NS-Dok)
C13   Hacky Hagemeyer, transparent, Cologne (NS-Dok)
C14   Herby Sachs, version, Cologne
C15   Herby Sachs, version, Cologne
C16   Herby Sachs, version, Cologne

THE AUTHORS

REINHOLD BILLSTEIN studied history, the social sciences, and geography, and holds a doctorate from the University of Cologne. During his many years at research institutes and universities in Germany and the United States, he has specialized in the founding of West German society under the Allied occupation, and the history of Cologne dating back to the early nineteenth century. He co-authored *"You are now in Cologne. Compliments." Köln 1945 in den Augen der Sieger. Hundert Tage unter amerikanischer Kontrolle* (Cologne, 1995), a best-selling account of the city during the one hundred days of American occupation in March to July 1945. His contribution to the present volume is based on research under the auspices of the German Historical Institute in Washington DC, into the influence of the U.S. occupation on German industry. Billstein heads the International Office at the University of Applied Sciences in Hamburg. He is writing a study on the wartime training, at American elite universities, of prospective U.S. Military Government officers for Germany.

KAROLA FINGS is a historian who lives in Cologne and has worked together with former forced laborers for more than ten years. She has specialized in the study of the Nazi-era concentration camp system and the problems faced by emigrants returning to Germany after the war. She authored a comprehensive documentary book on the "Messelager" labor camp in Cologne, a satellite of the Buchenwald concentration camp: *Messelager Köln. Ein KZ-Aussenlager im Zentrum der Stadt* (Cologne, 1996). Available in English translation is her study, "Romanies and Sinti in the Concentration Camps," in *From "Race Science" to the Camps* (Hertfordshire, 1997), part of a series overseen by the Gypsy Research Center in Paris. Fings's ongoing doctoral work, at Heinrich Heine University in Dusseldorf, concerns mobile labor squads from the Buchenwald, Neuengamme and Sachsenhausen concentration camps, the so-called "SS construction brigades."

BERND HEYL teaches History at the comprehensive school in Russelsheim, plays an organizing role in various regional research projects, and supervises the "We All Make History" series at the Adult Education Center of Russelsheim.

After training in the book trades, **ANITA KUGLER** studied history, transport and labor in Detroit, Geneva, Göttingen and Berlin (M.A. and Dipl. Pol.), and undertook research work at the International Metalworkers Federation in Geneva. She specialized in the history of labor and production at Adam Opel AG during the early and mid-twentieth century, publishing six in-depth studies and collecting a private archive of Opel-related documents. She then worked for ten years as a journalist and editor at the daily newspaper *die tageszeitung* in Berlin, covering Nazi-era forced labor and the continuing tangle of Germany's "coming to terms with the past." Her forthcoming history, to be published by Kiepenhauer and Witsch, reveals the story of an SS officer who adopted a false identity after the war and played a key role within the West German agencies supervising restitutions to the Jewish victims of the Nazis, until he was exposed and put to trial.

NICHOLAS LEVIS, B.A. in Political Science from Williams College, is a writer and editor from New York City. He has lived the last ten years in Cologne and Berlin, working as a translator and researching the automotive industry and corporate politics. He edited and co-authored *Global Circus: Narratives of Globalization, International Journal of Political Economy* (New York, 1996), translated and edited Ulrike Klausmann and Marion Meinzerin, *Women Pirates and the Politics of the Jolly Roger* (Montreal, 1997) and co-translated Sandro Bocola, *The Art of Modernism: Art, Culture and Society from Goya to the Present Day* (Munich, 1999).

NS-DOKUMENTATIONSZENTRUM DER STADT KÖLN is an educational museum and research center of Nazi-era history. It is located in EL-DE Haus, the former headquarters of the Gestapo in Cologne. The NS Documents Center is a leader within a new historical current that in the last twenty years has extended knowledge of Nazi crimes and given voice to the victims through oral history projects, regional studies, detailed documentation of the sites of terror, visitors' programs, and educational events.

INDEX